The Botanical City

jovis

The Botanical City

Matthew Gandy and Sandra Jasper [eds.]

jovis

Contents

The city as a botanical field

Matthew Gandy and Sandra Jasper

> The one tree in Francie's yard was neither a pine nor a hemlock. It had pointed leaves which grew along green switches which radiated from the bough and made a tree which looked like a lot of opened green umbrellas. Some people called it the Tree of Heaven. No matter where its seed fell, it made a tree which struggled to reach the sky. It grew in boarded-up lots and out of neglected rubbish-heaps and it was the only tree that grew out of cement. It grew lushly, but only in the tenement districts.
>
> Betty Smith, *A tree grows in Brooklyn*[1]

In Betty Smith's description of the tree of heaven (*Ailanthus altissima*), also known as the "ghetto palm," the tree is contrasted with the memory of a school poem that evoked the "forest primeval" with its "murmuring pines and hemlocks." For Smith, writing in the early 1940s, the presence of this tree was a marker, or even harbinger, of neighbourhood decline. The tree of heaven serves as a symbol of an American modernity gone awry. In this essay collection, by contrast, we are interested in disentangling some of these aesthetic and ideological strands that suffuse the idea of "weeds" or "alien plants" in the urban landscape. We explore a series of intersections between cultural and scientific readings of urban space in which the presence of spontaneous plant life serves as a portal into alternative interpretations of urban nature.

What does it mean to regard the city as a botanical field? The history of botany and the history of urbanization are deeply entwined. We know that many early cities had elaborate gardens and other complex reconstructions of an idealized nature: plants from distant places were often chosen to symbolize the geographical reach of imperial power. Plants were selected on account of specific properties, such as their aesthetic characteristics or shade-providing foliage. There is also evidence for the widespread cultivation of plants in cities for culinary and medical use, with some of the earliest treatises on urban botany devoted to useful species growing within and around the city.[2]

However, the historical record contains less information about those traces of vegetation that simply developed spontaneously in association with human settlements or emerged in the wake of previous waves of human activity. The emergence of "urban botany" as a distinctive field of scientific curiosity can be traced to unexpected profusions or distinctive combinations of plants. The ecological effects of disturbance, for example, were observed in London after the fire of 1666, while a growing fascination with the flora growing on walls and ruins is exemplified by Richard Deakin's study of Rome's Colosseum, published in 1855, where he found some 420 different species, including several highly unusual plants found nowhere else in Europe.[3] During the nineteenth century, some of the first "urban floras" were published based on intricate investigations of modern cities, often taking advantage of new railway lines to explore fragments of nature on the urban fringe. In the twentieth century, new spaces of urban botanical discovery emerged in the wake of wartime destruction, especially from the creation of "rubble landscapes" or "bomb sites," along with the establishment of security zones engendered by geopolitical tensions. From the early 1970s onwards, urban ecologies were further transformed through the impact of economic dislocation and demographic decline, which produced a variety of post-industrial "wastelands" and other types of anomalous spaces. Comparative studies of urban vegetation have drawn attention to the high levels of species diversity to be found in cities, comprising not just the persistence of previously existing plants but also a range of new arrivals. This leads to a distinctive pattern of elevated levels of overall biodiversity, combined with increasing degrees of homogeneity at larger spatial scales, marked by the global success of more well-established synanthropic species.[4]

Ecologies of neglect or abandonment have produced a variety of unusual biotopes that have been a focus of both cultural and scientific fascination. For many decades, urban botanists have been challenging existing conceptions of "plant sociology," along with a variety of vegetation taxonomies derived from "natural" ecological systems that have an uncertain relationship with landscapes modified by human activity. In a parallel development, "urban ecology" has gradually become a more significant element within the broader science of ecology, even to the extent that "anthropogenic biomes" are framed as the new analytical focus under the Anthropocene, with one study suggesting that just 11 percent of terrestrial ecosystems can be regarded as "wildlands."[5] From the perspective of urban botany, however, it is very much the innate "wildness" or spontaneity within urban ecosystems that remains the focus of attention.

Ruins, wastelands, and other types of interstitial spaces serve as heterotopic spaces of discovery and collective memory. When we encounter plants in cities it is helpful to differentiate between "remnant," "constructed," and "adaptive" kinds of ecological assemblages. Remnant vegetation encompasses the kind of plant communities that predated intensive human modification of the regional landscape: in terms of contemporary urban landscapes, these "remnant ecologies" might include areas of woodland that have become incorporated into park systems or pockets of lacustrine vegetation alongside lakes or rivers. Constructed forms of nature, by contrast, emphasize the range of plants that have been specifically selected for gardens, parks, streets and other intricately modified spaces. Adaptive plants are different again, and include the many species that have simply arrived, and in some cases flourished, within urban environments.[6] In practice, however, this threefold distinction can become decidedly blurry: there are several examples of plants that were chosen on ornamental grounds and then simply abandoned as fashions changed, yet which now persist within the interstices of the city merely as "weeds" or have in some cases been recast as invasive species such as Japanese knotweed (*Reyneutia japonica*) and giant hogweed (*Heracleum mantegazzianum*).[7] During the twentieth century, urban botany became a distinctive branch of urban ecology, as early pioneers such as the French botanist Paul Jovet began to apply a range of scientific methods to the study of spontaneous urban plants. Jovet's studies of Paris, for example, paid attention to specific effects of human activity such as trampling on the characteristics of urban vegetation.[8] Specific questions began to emerge from the study of urban vegetation, such as the effects of the "urban heat island," the distinctively cosmopolitan character of species assemblages, and the diversity of micro-biotopes associated with the chance dynamics of seed dispersal. More recently, studies have explored the adaptability and evolutionary dynamism of urban plants so that cities are framed as ecological laboratories for the tracking of future natures.

In evolutionary terms, future ecologies are already unfolding, with evidence that some plants have embarked on an accelerated evolutionary pathway in response to the specific selection pressures of urban environments. Examples include the advantages of reduced seed dispersal so that less offspring are lost to concrete surfaces or other inhospitable substrates.[9] Extreme forms of habitat fragmentation and the diverse environmental challenges created by urbanization are also acting as a spur for accelerated rates of evolutionary change. Yet the implications of elevated levels of genetic drift among small or isolated populations, together with the precise dynamics of "gene flow" within urban environments, remain only partially understood.[10]

Just as we might connect literary or theoretical tropes with specific cities, we can also discern distinctive geographies of urban botany. The diverse ecological characteristics of urban space can be mapped onto an intellectual geography of the field. The development of urban botany in London, for example, is especially associated with the study of "bomb sites" and the observations of spontaneous vegetation by figures such as Edward Salisbury and Richard Fitter.[11] Similarly, a distinctive school of urban botany developed in post-war Berlin around Herbert Sukopp, Hildemar Scholz, and a team of researchers from the 1950s onwards who had become fascinated by various types of *Brachen* (urban wastelands) produced by wartime destruction, but also by geopolitical divisions.[12] This highly influential school has found international resonance through the exchange of methodological expertise with botanists in Bangalore, Tokyo, and many other cities.[13] More recently, Berlin has emerged as an intellectual focal point for experimental ecologies at the interface of art and science, thanks to the work of Maria Thereza Alves,

Ulrike Mohr, Alex Toland, and other artists: these innovative works mark an aesthetic counterpoint to the earlier waves of scientific investigation.[14] In the city of Sheffield, by contrast, the interest in unusual urban flora emerged in relation to post-industrial spaces but also linked with wider cultural and political interest in the "urban commons" as articulated by the lichenologist Oliver Gilbert.[15] In Paris, the emphasis has recently been on the intricate interactions between human activity and the richness of urban flora, extending the earlier work of Jovet by adding more recent investigations by Audrey Muratet, Nathalie Machon, and others that connect botany with public cultures of natural history to produce a series of innovative urban field guides.[16] The latest guides to the urban flora of Paris, Birmingham, Hamburg, and other cities combine many years of grassroots labour by botanical societies with new advances in cartography, digital photography, and the sharing of scientific expertise.[17] In the case of Hamburg, the new guide to botanical walks in the city draws from over 125 years of research and brings together insights from 30 active botanical societies.[18] The state-of-the-art flora of Birmingham (which also includes fungi, lichens, and bryophytes) was initiated in the mid-1990s and finally completed in 2012.[19]

In Brussels, we find an emphasis on the "urban laboratorium" and the relationship between plants, climate, and urban topography as developed in the work of the influential ecologist Paul Duvigneaud, who devoted the earlier part of his career to the study of tropical rainforests.[20] In North America, the pioneering work of Peter Del Tredici, with his popular field guide to over two hundred species of plants occurring in the urban North East, covering the flora of Boston, Detroit, Montréal, and other cities, marks a striking synthesis between botanical science and critical approaches to landscape design.[21] Tredici's close engagement with design questions has brought a more nuanced emphasis to the appreciation of plants that can withstand human environments, including interest in species that might flourish under the climatic conditions of future cities.[22]

Although the field of urban botany has now become more global in scope, significant ecological lacunae remain. There are many major cities for which no comprehensive botanical survey has yet been undertaken: a recent study found that no comprehensive botanical knowledge exists for 27 of the 50 most populous global cities, including Ankara, Bangkok, Caracas, Hyderabad, Sao Paulo, Seoul, and Tokyo.[23] In the case of East Asian cities, there has been an emerging interest in botany as part of a wider set of environmental management discourses: the botanical characteristics of Beijing, Chengdu, and other Chinese cities have been related to themes such as invasive ecologies, the protective role of vegetation against flood risk, and the wider significance of "urban green space" in spatial planning.[24] Elsewhere in South Asia we find novel perspectives emerging at the interface between urban botany and post-colonial interpretations of urban landscapes: the historian Bhavani Raman's itinerary through Chennai brings plants, remnant wetland ecologies, and other fragments of nature into a nuanced urban environmental history.[25]

Botanical interest in spontaneous patterns of urban vegetation also segues into a focus on individual species or "sentinels" that can play a key role in the interpretation of environmental change. In some cases, specific species have acquired symbolic significance within the field of urban botany, such as the flourishing of sticky goosefoot (*Dysphania botrys*) in the rubble landscapes of post-war Berlin, the purple drifts of rosebay willowherb (*Chamaenerion angustifolium*) in the bomb sites of London, and the spread of the tree of heaven (*Ailanthus altissima*) in post-unification Berlin.[26] There are also plants that have acquired radically different connotations for different communities: mugwort (*Artemisia vulgaris*), originating in Europe and Asia, and now naturalized in North America, has been a focus of frenzied removal by so-called "weed warriors" in some American cities, yet it is also highly valued by Korean-Americans for tea making.[27] These and other "botanical protagonists" illustrate the interweaving of human and other-than-human histories at a global scale.

The cosmopolitan characteristics of urban flora contrast with the nativist preoccupations of earlier approaches to the study of "plant communities" based on idealized conceptions of nature without human influence. Within this rarefied Eurocentric schema, the distinction between "native" and "non-native" species takes on a particular kind of ideological charge. Yet specific botanical terminologies such as "archaeophyte" (pre-1500) and "neophyte" (post-1500), used to determine degrees of naturalization, appear increasingly arbitrary from the context of North America or elsewhere.[28] More broadly, the development of urban botany raises questions about the origins of botany as a scientific field, and the assumptions and purposes that lie behind the production of botanical knowledge.

If we conceive of cities as open-air laboratories for the study of future natures these intricate programmes of research are often highly vulnerable: the practice of urban botany as a "field science" lies at odds with the molecular emphasis of the biological sciences; the need for long-term data sets is difficult to achieve and requires the endurance of complex networks of expertise over time; and many of the key study sites for urban botanists such as wastelands and other types of marginal spaces are often at risk from development pressures. Few cities have yet produced the kind of longitudinal data on spontaneous vegetation that might help us to better understand the implications of urban ecological change under the Anthropocene. The full realization of the scientific potential for cities to contribute to the study of environmental change rests ultimately on the emergence of citizen science and the harnessing of grassroots expertise.

How does urban botany relate to the idea of landscape? Or, more specifically, how do the distinctive discourses of urban botany relate to emerging paradigms in landscape design? Spontaneous urban vegetation has long been the focus of a kind of aesthetic ambivalence driven by the association of "weeds" with abandonment and neglect. In the wake of events such as the North American foreclosure crisis many commentators noted the proliferation of spontaneous vegetation along sidewalks or around boarded-up buildings.[29] By drawing attention to the aesthetic and scientific value of marginal spaces, however, urban botanists have contributed towards a more nuanced understanding of urban ecology.[30] The declining use of herbicides in French cities, for example, has led to greater awareness of the intrinsic ecological dynamics of urban space and the way in which cities "can create their own flora."[31] There has been a significant change in how "wild urban spaces" are perceived within landscape design: the repurposing or reincorporation of "void spaces" within the urban fabric now includes elements of industrial archaeology such as disused railway lines or gasometers and also the distinctive ecological assemblages associated with marginal urban spaces.[32] Fragments of this "wasteland aesthetic" have been preserved, and in some cases artificially created, through the use of specialized substrates such as *Ökoschotter* (eco-rubble) to encourage a profusion of flowers. The ecological discourses associated with "landscape urbanism" have become more sophisticated both in terms of their aesthetic mimicry of existing spaces and their incorporation of scientific ideas derived from botany, entomology, and other fields. At the same time, however, we find that some of these ecological simulacra are in turn connected with the emerging dynamics of "ecological gentrification" and the creation of new kinds of environmental enclaves. But can these newly created spaces, rooted in ecologically inflected models of urban maintenance, ever be more than sophisticated botanical enclaves within a wider landscape of neglect or indifference?

Insights derived from urban botany illustrate the intricate temporalities of urban space, ranging from seasonal rhythms and the ecological dynamics of vacant land to the longer term emergence of "wild urban woodlands."[33] In practice, most forms of urban horticulture seek to maintain states of "suspended animation" whereas an emphasis on spontaneous vegetation opens up a new set of articulations between the human imagination and the independent agency of nature.[34] The distinctive temporalities of spontaneous nature also intersect with perturbations of capital so that urban ecological processes mirror wider economic and political developments.

Time intersects with urban ecology at a number of different levels. The idea of the abandoned city offers a kind of counter-aesthetic to the controlled spaces of modernity. Yet there are continuities here in terms of the romanticist fascination with ruins such as the strange ecologies of Pripyat after its evacuation in the wake of the Chernobyl nuclear accident or the "stilled time" of geopolitical zones in Cyprus, the Korean peninsula, and elsewhere. The cultural trope of a vine-covered urban landscape under transition back to nature is also a recurring motif in the science fiction imagination. These cultural renditions of urban ecology highlight how plants have their own agency irrespective of human intentions: small fissures in roads and pavements become the starting point for seedlings whose roots create yet more opportunities for newer arrivals in a dynamic and often unpredictable sequence of events.[35]

Urban botany is clearly much more than a contributory element to the scientific sub-discipline of urban ecology. The range of aesthetic and methodological questions engendered by everyday encounters with spontaneous vegetation cuts across a series of disciplinary boundaries. A diversity of perspectives—including some surprising juxtapositions—is reflected in this essay collection with contributions from professional botanists as well as anthropologists, architects, artists, geographers, historians, and authors from many other fields. If we take Walter Benjamin's depiction of the modern flâneur as "one who goes botanizing on the asphalt" as a literal invitation to regard cities differently, we can begin to sketch a series of connections between ostensibly disparate fields.[36] For Benjamin, the city represented a vast archive out of which small fragments could serve as an inspiration for wider reflections on different sources of continuity and change. Similarly, every botanical trace in the urban landscape tells its own story, and every sign of life connects with a wider set of socio-ecological entanglements.

1 Betty Smith, *A tree grows in Brooklyn* (London: Arrow Books: 2000 [1943]) pp. 3–4. For a different interpretation of the presence (and attempted erasure) of *Ailanthus altissima* in North America see also Darren J. Patrick, "The matter of displacement: a queer urban ecology of New York City's High Line," *Social & Cultural Geography* 15 (8) (2014) pp. 920–941.

2 See, for example, Pitton Tournefort, *Histoire des plantes qui naissent aux environs de Paris, avec leur usage dans la Medecine* (Paris de l'imprimaire Royale, 1698).

3 Richard Deakin, *Flora of the Colosseum of Rome; or illustrations and descriptions of four hundred and twenty plants growing spontaneously upon the ruins of the Colosseum of Rome* (London: Groombridge and sons, 1855).

4 See, for example, Zdeňka Lososová, Milan Chytrý, Lubomír Tichý, and Jiří Danihelka et al. "Biotic homogenization of Central European urban floras depends on residence time of alien species and habitat types," *Biological Conservation* 145 (2012) pp. 179–184; and Youhua Ye, Shishi Lin, Jin Wu, Jie Li, Jianfeng Zou and Deyong Yu, "Effect of rapid urbanization on plant species diversity in municipal parks, in a new Chinese city: Shenzhen," *Acta Ecologica Sinica* 32 (2012) pp. 221–226.

5 See Erle Ellis and Navin Ramankutty, "Putting people in the map: anthropogenic biomes of the world," *Frontiers in Ecology and the Environment* 6 (8) (2008) pp. 439–447.

6 See Peter Del Tredici, *Wild urban plants of the northeast: a field guide* (Cornell University Press, 2010). See also the typology of weeds provided by Herbert G. Baker, "The evolution of weeds," *Annual Review of Ecology and Systematics* 5 (1974) pp. 1–24.

7 See Livia Cahn, "Rhizome city: tracing knotweed through the soils of Brussels," and Bettina Stoetzer, "*Ailanthus altissima*, or the botanical afterlives of European power" (this volume).

8 Paul Jovet, "Evolution des groupements rudéraux 'parisiens'," *Bulletin de la Société Botanique de France* 87 (1940) pp. 305–312.

9 See Pierre-Oliver Cheptou, O. Carrue, Soraya Rouifed, and Amélie A. M. Cantarel, "Rapid evolution of seed dispersal in an urban environment in the weed Crepis sancta," *Proceedings of the National Academy of Sciences* 105 (10) (2008) pp. 3796–3799.

10 See, for example, Eyal Shochat, Paige S. Warren, Stanley H. Faeth, Nancy E. McIntyre, and Diane Hope, "From patterns to emerging processes in mechanistic urban ecology," *Trends in ecology & evolution* 21(4) (2006) pp. 186–191.

11 See Richard S. R. Fitter, *London's natural history* (London: Collins, 1945). See Seth Denizen, "The flora of bombed areas (an allegorical key)" (this volume).

12 See, for example, Ingo Kowarik, "Vegetationsentwicklung auf innerstädtischen Brachflächen: Beispiele aus Berlin (West)," *Tuexenia* 6 (1986) pp. 75–99; Hildemar Scholz, "Die Veränderungen in der Ruderalflora Berlins: Ein Beitrag zur jüngsten Florengeschichte," *Willdenowia* 2 (3) (1960) pp. 379–397; Herbert Sukopp, "Beiträge zur Ökologie von *Chenopodium botrys* L.: 1. Verbreitung und Vergesellschaftung," *Verhandlungen des Botanischen Vereins der Provinz Brandenburg* 108 (1971) pp. 3–25; Herbert Sukopp, "Die Großstadt als Gegenstand ökologischer Forschung," *Schriften des Vereins zur Verbreitung naturwissenschaftlicher Kenntnisse in Wien* 113 (1973) pp. 90–140; Herbert Sukopp, Hans-Peter Blume, and Wolfram Kunick, "The soil, flora, and vegetation of Berlin's waste lands," in *Nature in cities*, ed. Ian C. Laurie (Chichester,

New York: John Wiley & Sons, 1979) pp. 115–132; and Herbert Sukopp, ed., *Stadtökologie: Das Beispiel Berlin* (Berlin: Dietrich Reimer Verlag, 1990).

13 See Leonie K. Fischer, Verena Rodorff, Moritz von der Lippe, and Ingo Kowarik,"Drivers of biodiversity patterns in parks of a growing south American megacity," *Urban Ecosystems* 19 (2016) pp. 1–19; Divya Gopal, Moritz von der Lippe, and Ingo Kowarik, "Sacred sites, biodiversity and urbanization in an Indian megacity," *Urban Ecosystems* 22 (2019) pp. 161–172; Divya Gopal, Harini Nagendra, and Michael Manthey, "Vegetation in Bangalore's slums: composition, species distribution, density, diversity, and history," *Environmental Management* 55 (2015) pp. 1390–1401; Chi Yung Jim, "Old masonry walls as ruderal habitats for biodiversity conservation and enhancement in urban Hong Kong," in Norbert Müller, Peter Werner, and John G. Kelcey, eds., *Urban biodiversity and design* (Oxford: Blackwell, 2010) pp. 323–347; Udayakumar Muthulingam and Sekar Thangave, "Density, diversity and richness of woody plants in urban green spaces: a case study in Chennai metropolitan city," *Urban Forestry & Urban Greening* 11 (4) (2012) pp. 450–459; Makoto Numata, ed., *Tokyo project: interdisciplinary studies of urban ecosystems in the metropolis of Tokyo* (Chiba University, 1977); John O. Rieley and Susan E. Page, "Survey, mapping, and evaluation of green space in the Federal Territory of Kuala Lumpur, Malaysia" in Herbert Sukopp, Makoto Numata, and Almut Huber, eds., *Urban ecology as the basis of urban planning* (The Hague: SPB Academic Publishing, 1995) pp. 173–183; Stefan Zerbe, Il-Ki Choi, and Ingo Kowarik, "Characteristics and habitats of non-native plant species in the city of Chonju, southern Korea," *Ecological Research* 19 (2004) pp. 91–98; and Shen Zhang, "The forest and urban greening in Shanghai," in Herbert Sukopp, Slavomil Hejný, and Ingo Kowarik, eds., *Urban ecology: plants and plant communities in urban environments* (The Hague: SPB Academic Publishing, 1990) pp. 141–154.

14 See Mara Polgovsky Ezcurra, "The flight of seeds," and Alex Toland, "Dandelions at work: a street corner tale of ecosystem services" (this volume).

15 Oliver Gilbert, *The flowering of the cities: the natural flora of "urban commons"* (Peterborough: English Nature, 1992).

16 See, for example, Sébastien Filoche, Gérard Arnal, and Jacques Moret, *La biodiversité du département de la Seine-Saint-Denis: Atlas de la flore sauvage* (Paris: Biotope, Mèze, Collection Parthénone/Muséum national d'Histoire naturelle, 2006); and Audrey Muratet, Myr Muratet, and Marie Pellaton, *Flore des friches urbaines du nord de la France et des régions voisines* (Paris: Éditions Xavier Barral, 2017).

17 See Mark Spencer, "Discovering and mapping urban plants" and Birgit Seitz, "Mapping the urban flora of Berlin" (this volume).

18 Hans-Helmut Poppendieck, Gisela Bertram, and Barbara Engelschall, eds., *Der Botanische Wanderführer für Hamburg und Umbegung* (Hamburg and Munich: Dörling and Galitz, 2016).

19 Ian Trueman, Mike Poulton, and Paul Reade, *Flora of Birmingham and the Black Country* (Newbury: Pisces Publishing, 2013)

20 Paul Duvigneaud, "Étude écologique de l'écosystème urbain bruxellois: 1. L'écosystème 'urbs,'" *Mémoires de la Société Royale de Botanique de Belgique* 6 (1974) pp. 5–35. See also Jens Lachmund, "The metabolic city and the city of biotopes: Paul Duvigneaud and Herbert Sukopp" (this volume).

21 See Peter Del Tredici, *Wild urban plants of the northeast: a field guide* (Cornell University Press, 2010).

22 See, for example, Peter Del Tredici "Spontaneous urban vegetation: reflections of change in a globalizing world," *Nature and Culture* 5 (3) (2010) pp. 299–315; Ingo Kowarik and Moritz von der Lippe, "Meadows in historic parks and their adaptive possibilities in an age of climate change," in Michael Rohde, ed., *Historic gardens and climate change* (Leipzig, Edition, 2014) pp. 256–261; Herbert Sukopp and Angelika Wurzel, "Changing climate and the effects on vegetation in Central European cities," *Arboricultural Journal*, 24 (4) (2000) pp. 257–281; and Kenneth R. Young, "Biogeography of the Anthropocene: novel species assemblages," *Progress in Physical Geography: Earth and Environment* 38 (5) (2014) pp. 664–673.

23 S. Clemants, "A short bibliography of urban floras," *Urban Habitats* 1 (1) (2002) pp. 25–29.

24 See, for example, Youhua Ye, Shishi Lin, Jin Wu, Jie Li, Jianfeng Zou and Deyong Yu, "Effect of rapid urbanization on plant species diversity in municipal parks, in a new Chinese city: Shenzhen," *Acta Ecologica Sinica* 32 (2012) pp. 221–226.

25 See Bhavani Raman, "The curious disappearance of the Ennore Creek" (this volume).

26 See, for example, Seth Denizen, "The flora of bombed areas (an allegorical key)" (this volume). On the role of plants as sentinels see also Jennifer Gabrys, "Sensing lichens: from ecological microcosms to environmental subjects," *Third Text* 32 (2–3) (2018) pp. 350–367.

27 Zachary J. S. Falck, *Weeds: an environmental history of metropolitan America* (University of Pittsburgh Press, 2010).

28 See Peter Del Tredici, *Wild urban plants of the northeast: a field guide* (Cornell University Press, 2010). See also Peter A. Coates, *American perceptions of immigrant and invasive species: strangers on the land* (Berkeley, CA: University of California Press, 2006).

29 Falck, *Weeds: an environmental history of metropolitan America*.

30 See Matthew Gandy, "Marginalia: aesthetics, ecology, and urban wastelands," *Annals of the Association of American Geographers* 103 (6) (2013) pp. 1301–1316; and Charles-François Mathis and Émilie-Anne Pépy, *La ville végétale: une histoire de la nature en milieu urbain* (Ceyzérieu: Champ Vallon, 2017).

31 Patricia Pellegrini and Sandrine Baudry, "Streets as new places to bring together both humans and plants: examples from Paris and Montpellier (France)," *Social and Cultural Geography*, 15 (8) (2014) p. 881.

32 See, for example, Nigel Dunnett and James Hitchmough, *The dynamic landscape: design, ecology, and management of naturalistic garden design* (London: John Wiley, 2008); and Jennifer Foster, "Off track, in nature: construction ecology on old rail lines in Paris and New York," *Nature and Culture* 5 (3) (2010) pp. 316–337.

33 See Ingo Kowarik, "Wild urban woodlands: towards a conceptual framework," in Ingo Kowarik and Stefan Körner, eds., *Wild urban woodlands: new perspectives for urban forestry* (Berlin: Springer, 2005) pp. 1–32.

34 There is growing interest in the nature of plant agency and its relations to biopower, materialism, and existing scientific epistemologies. See, for example Matthew Hall, *Plants as persons: a philosophical botany* (Albany, NY: State University of New York Press, 2011); Luce Irigaray and Michael Marder, *Through vegetal being: two philosophical perspectives* (New York: Columbia University Press, 2016); Michael Marder, *Plant-thinking: a philosophy of vegetal life* (New York: Columbia University Press, 2013); and Jeffrey Nealon, *Plant theory: biopower and vegetable life* (Stanford, CA: Stanford University Press, 2016).

35 See, for example, Alan Weisman, *The world without us* (London: Virgin, 2007).

36 Walter Benjamin, *Charles Baudelaire: a lyric poet in the era of high capitalism*, trans. Harry Zohn (New Left Books, 1973 [1923]) p. 36. On the city as a botanical archive see Moritz von der Lippe, "Vegetation as testimony: botanical traces of the past" (this volume).

Histories and taxonomies

Part 1

Signs of life: interview with Herbert Sukopp

Herbert Sukopp is one of the key figures in the post-war emergence of urban botany as a distinctive scientific field. We bring together excerpts from three interviews undertaken in November 2012, March 2013, and July 2015.

Matthew Gandy How did you discover the field of urban botany?

Herbert Sukopp Slowly, from outside to inside, so to speak. My dissertation was an examination of the moors of Berlin that were furthest away from the city. Historically, Berlin had a surprising number of lakes and moors stemming from the ice age, and this was my first field of research. After that, I became interested in the reedbeds of the Havel river and the conditions of the riverbanks and lakesides. From there, I moved on to study urban parks, and finally the *Stadtbrachen* (urban wastelands) in central Berlin.

Matthew Gandy In the 1950s a specific interest in Berlin's *Trümmerlandschaften* (rubble landscapes) emerged. Could you tell us more about it?

Herbert Sukopp This interest developed not only in Berlin but worldwide. The city became a large-scale experiment, comparable in scope only to the first colonization of bare ground covered in volcanic ash and rubble. There was an astonishing abundance of species that spread phenomenally fast. This was nothing new in itself, but the scale across so many cities was unusual.

Sandra Jasper How did you begin studying these urban sites?

Herbert Sukopp Travelling by tram, I often saw something interesting. I knew there had to be something there because of the structure of the surface. I started to select and examine twelve quadrats that were further systematically analyzed by my colleague Wolfram Kunick. At first, we only sought out the most interesting discoveries. This developed into a methodical programme, with a certain number of field sites in densely built-up areas, loosely developed areas, and so on, to be representative of Berlin as a whole. However, this proved difficult with field sites of one square kilometre in size that were simply too large and internally heterogeneous to allow for comparative analysis across the city as a whole.

Sandra Jasper With whom did you collaborate in Berlin?

Herbert Sukopp I mostly worked with Hildemar Scholz, who began to identify unfamiliar and often non-native plants to figure out what they were. In the beginning, we could only identify two-thirds of the plants with one third completely unknown to us.

Matthew Gandy How did you manage to identify these plants without the help of the necessary books and scientific knowledge? How difficult was it back then?

Herbert Sukopp We were lucky in that we had access to a large herbarium in the Botanical Museum in Berlin, where specimens of almost every species from across the world were available. More difficult cases could also be handled by specialists. *Chenopodium botrys*, for instance, was given to Paul Aellen in Switzerland, and other examples of the Chenopodiaceae to Russian colleagues. Many things are only possible through international collaboration.

Matthew Gandy How would you describe the science of urban botany at the time, compared to its forms in earlier periods, such as plant sociology for example? Did urban botany differ from previous work?

Herbert Sukopp Yes. Berlin has a long botanical tradition that also acknowledged plants growing in the city centre. Our oldest flora by Carl Ludwig Willdenow was written in 1787. It mostly focuses on plants of the surrounding countryside, which was very rural at that time with vineyards, fields, and meadows. But this flora includes a remark in Latin, *in urbe ipsa*, which means that a plant can be found in the city itself, and not only in the wider circle surrounding the city that the flora was usually comprised of.

The 19th of March 1953 marks the beginning of urban botany in Berlin. On that day, my colleague Hildemar Scholz began studying the flora of Lützowplatz, and made his first notes about plants that were already sprouting in early spring including *Chenopodium botrys*. He studied the flora and I studied the vegetation patterns. One could say that this is the starting point for urban botany after the war.
A pivotal point in Berlin was the shift from a purely botanical analysis to an inquiry that mattered to people. This beautiful analysis of flora that we take pleasure in was "dead material" for urban planners and policy makers: the data was filed in cabinets and simply forgotten. Only when we established the connection between specific land-use types, urban development, and plants could we then foster a wider interest in urban botany.

Sandra Jasper Could you tell us a bit about the significance of the Red List for endangered plants in an urban context?

Herbert Sukopp Surprisingly, the recent editions of the Red List have stood up in court, so that one has something tangible to argue with. Previously, with the earlier versions, people would not consider it as legally relevant evidence. Currently, we have the fourth edition of the Red List for Berlin. When you look at them side by side, you can demonstrate historical disparities and prove that changes are taking place. People can't claim that things have stayed the same and that nothing has changed. In this sense, it is astonishing how the Red List, which initially only served as a scientific argument, was later taken up by nature conservatists to be utilized effectively as a legal instrument.

Matthew Gandy What is the history of the Institute for Ecology at the Technical University in Berlin?

Herbert Sukopp Formerly, we were a Faculty of Agriculture. After the German Science Council decided to close down the Berlin faculty, we had to think about how to continue. We were then three separate institutes—the Institute of Applied Botany, where I worked, the Institute of Soil Science, and the Institute for the Cultivation of Ornamental Plants. We applied to establish a new Institute for Ecology. Three institutes were at its core, with the later additions of Bioclimatology, Ecotoxicology, Limnology, and a small unit of Animal Ecology.

Matthew Gandy Are there plants that are characteristic for Berlin?

Herbert Sukopp Yes, we have mentioned some of them already. *Chenopodium botrys* was a typical plant for a long time. *Parietaria pensylvanica* occurred only in Berlin, and a number of plants were typical for the city centre such as *Herniaria hirsuta*, *Amaranthus blitoides*, *Amaranthus albus*, and *Chenopodium strictum*.

Matthew Gandy And for your own research: are there specific species that act as a symbol or inspiration?

Herbert Sukopp *Chenopodium botrys* was an exciting discovery at the time. It is a very old garden plant. It occurred in Renaissance Germany and was a very rare and much-loved plant because of its remarkable scent. And suddenly in post-war Berlin, in the open rubble areas with a warmer urban microclimate, the plant began to spread widely.

Matthew Gandy Do you have specific memories of your time as a scientist in the divided city of Berlin?

Herbert Sukopp At first, East Berlin had been accessible. We could usually enter the city without any border controls. After the city was divided, however, it became difficult to carry out research in the East. So we had to limit our first Red List to West Berlin because we could not visit the other parts of the city often enough to include it.

Sandra Jasper Did you sometimes travel to East Berlin to visit specific sites, even though it was not possible to study them in depth? Which of these areas were the most interesting?

Herbert Sukopp The border strip was particularly interesting, especially the "death strip" along the Berlin wall, which was deliberately contaminated [to prevent the growth of plants that might provide cover for people trying to escape the GDR]. But some plants flourished despite the toxicity of the ground. This strip was pure yellow with *Sedum acre*, which can survive the toxicity and also benefit from the destruction of other vegetation. If you travelled with the S-Bahn from Lehrter Station to Friedrichstraße, you could see the stretch of *Sedum acre* growing in the so-called death strip.

Sandra Jasper Were you in contact with urban ecologists in East Berlin?

Herbert Sukopp No, I was not, because few ecologists worked in East Berlin. I had connections with ecologists based in Potsdam, Eberswalde, and Halle (Saale) that lasted throughout the time of the Wall. I was invited to give lectures, and there was considerable interest because I was allowed to raise ecological concerns about environmental damage that they could not openly address.

Sandra Jasper Which of the rubble landscapes were most important to you in the 1950s?

Herbert Sukopp The most important sites were a square called Lützowplatz and the open spaces in its vicinity, the train stations, the surroundings of the Anhalter and Potsdamer train and freight stations, and later, the ecological changes observed in the abandoned freight stations such as the Schöneberger Südgelände.

Matthew Gandy Was there a chance to protect these sites or was that very difficult?

Herbert Sukopp That was difficult. We once tried to protect the Lützowplatz. We said it was our model site [for scientific research] that we had been working on for many years, and that such sites are worth protecting simply because people have been studying them intensively over a long time period. But everyone just shook their heads, and now there is a big hotel there. Our demands were in vain.

Matthew Gandy It must be sad to experience the loss of key study sites.

Herbert Sukopp Yes. But I am also a Berliner and an urbanite, so I tell myself that this is the usual sequence of development for a city. It is indeed a bit sad, sometimes even tragic, but also simply urban. It is a familiar pattern that urban spaces will undergo a process of change.

Sandra Jasper We have many different words for what we might call *Brache* (wasteland) in German. Could you tell us a bit about when a site was still a *Trümmerlandschaft* (rubble landscape) and when it then became a *Stadtbrache* (urban wasteland)? What words would you use for spaces that are difficult to define? What do you think of these words?

Herbert Sukopp The question is, is it just a matter of describing something or making a claim? After all, naming is not just about analyzing what exists; it also contains a hope, or an expectation, or a claim for the site that you want to see realized. Therefore, the discourse concerning spontaneous vegetation, "wild growth," or simply "weeds" depends on what one wants or who might benefit or be harmed.

The metabolic city and the city of biotopes: Paul Duvigneaud and Herbert Sukopp

Jens Lachmund

The shift of biological field ecology towards the city which has taken place since the 1970s has been closely associated with the work of two botanists: the Belgian Paul Duvigneaud (1913–1991) and the German Herbert Sukopp (born 1930). Both reconceived the city as an environment that is profoundly shaped by humans, and both developed related research programmes and made suggestions for an ecologically oriented form of urban planning. As is generally the case with science, this turn to the city did not simply follow some intrinsic universalizing logic.[1] Each of the two botanists mobilized quite specific epistemic practices, socio-political resources, and place-specific affordances. Even if this has never led to an explicit controversy, both botanists followed different trajectories, and hence formulated distinct versions of the botanical city. In this essay, I want to highlight some of these differences and thereby shed light on the extent to which seemingly universal knowledge about the botanical city embodies the local and historical conditions of its production.[2]

Duvigneaud turned to the city as his research object relatively late. He had studied biology and chemistry before receiving a PhD in biology from the *Université Libre de Bruxelles* (U.L.B.) in 1940.[3] During the German occupation, he worked as a researcher at the Brussels-based Institute of National Parks in the Congo. In 1952, he became an extraordinary professor, and in 1956 an ordinary professor, at the U.L.B. During his early career, his work focused on the systematics of lichen and on phytosociology (that is, the classification and surveying of so called "plant societies"), notably in his fieldwork in the Congo. When the Congo became independent in 1960, he shifted his interest to the forests of the Ardennes. In this period, he took increasing inspiration from the new "systems-ecology" as developed by Howard Odum and other American ecologists.[4] These ecologists conceived ecosystems as functionally integrated wholes that connect organisms with each other and with their non-biotic environment, and they sought to unravel the mechanisms (e.g. food chains, cycles of energy, water etc.) that keep such systems in a steady state. Duvigneaud's work was directly aligned with the International Biological Program (IBP) (1964–1974), a research initiative of the International Union of Science which aimed to understand the "biological productivity" of different ecosystems.[5] In 1962, he published a programmatic report on systems ecology for the Belgian government (published later as *La synthèse écologique*), and lobbied successfully for the launch of a state-sponsored Belgian subprogramme of the IBP (which happened in 1968 under his directorship).[6]

Duvigneaud's turning to the city was apparently motivated by an attempt to expand the reach of systems ecology to an ecosystem-type that so far had only received marginal attention. Duvigneaud was thereby also able to link ecology to mounting concerns about the environmental consequences of urbanization and the deterioration of the living conditions in cities. As his writings suggest, he was particularly worried about the situation in his own hometown, Brussels, which was characterized by population growth, urban sprawl, and architectural transformation (the 1958 world fair and the establishment of EEC institutions led to many new building and infrastructural projects).[7] At least for a short period, he acted as an expert advisor to the "Agglomeration of Brussel/Bruxelles," which was founded in 1971 to coordinate the governance of the 19 independent municipalities of the Brussels city region. He plainly benefited from his membership of the F.D.F. (*Front Démocratique des Francophone*)—a French-speaking language party which dominated the elected Council of the Agglomeration—and from his support by the F.D.F's new alderman for environment, Pierre Havelange.[8] The agglomeration sponsored an international workshop on urban ecology (which took place in 1974),[9] and appointed Duvigneaud as a member of a committee on green planning for which he conducted a planning-oriented survey. The agglomeration, however, never gained much regulatory strength, and in 1984 Duvigneaud's supporter Havelange was replaced. Notwithstanding his subsequent marginalization in the planning system, the city remained Duvigneaud's central research object until his death in 1991.

In contrast to Duvigneaud, Sukopp spent his entire academic career on botanical field studies in Berlin, or more specifically in the western part of that divided city, and he was also much more firmly established in the local governance system. One reason for this was the geopolitical situation in West Berlin, where newly erected political borders, and as of 1961 even a wall, prevented field botanists and other naturalists from exploring their traditional fieldwork sites in the adjacent countryside. His early focal points included the fens that existed at the outskirts, yet still within the confines of the walled city, and the vast rubble areas that were left from WWII bombing raids, which soon became covered by new plant species and vegetation patterns. He received a doctorate for a case study of the fens,[10] and became assistant professor at the Technical University Berlin. Following his habilitation and an intermediate period as a *Privatdozent*, he became a professor in 1969. Based at a newly founded Institute of Ecology (as of 1973), he promoted urban ecology as an interdisciplinary research field.[11] Sukopp acted as a political protagonist, creating networks between scientists, conservationists, and policy-makers. As an advisor for the West Berlin Senate—and as of 1975 even as its official appointee—he provided input for nature conservation policies, including a comprehensive landscape and species protection programme which he developed with his research team between 1979 and 1984.[12]

As these brief biographical sketches have shown, quite different career trajectories drew each of the two botanists into conducting research on their own city. In the remainder of this essay, I will trace how these biographical and other local circumstances played out in their fieldwork practice, in the ways in which they represented their cities, and in their political visions of a greener city.

Sukopp's fieldwork proceeded through a long-term process of repeated surveying, often of the same sites, in which a continuous and progressively densifying record of the vegetation cover was produced. The resulting records documented the loss of many plant species which had suffered from the negative influence of the urban environment. At the same time, they revealed that other species were attracted by the city, notably in the urban wastelands or "ruderal areas" that were widespread in the bombed and economically marginalized West Berlin. He identified many neophyte species, which benefited from the attenuated climate of the urban area.

This extended long-term mapping of an entire city was only possible through close cooperation with students who conducted site surveys during their study projects or for qualification theses, and with the broad network of academic and amateur naturalists that existed in Berlin. Additionally, surveys for planning purposes often drew on already existing material, and in turn contributed to the wider densification of spatial knowledge. In terms of field methods, Sukopp and his group shifted from traditional phytosociological site surveys (where a small patch of ground was taken as representative of a stable type of plant society) to a more open "floristic" approach. This method of simply aggregating data at species level was much better suited to studying the city's dynamic vegetational development.[13]

Duvigneaud was not able to build on such an entrenched local tradition of fieldwork. He began his research on Brussels almost from scratch, and relied almost exclusively on a small group of assistant professors and PhD students in his own departmental unit. This work included vegetation surveys; for example, Duvigneaud and his co-workers studied "semi-natural" landscapes in order to make recommendations for planning purposes.[14] His deeper ambition, however, was to use Brussels as an exemplary model for quantitative ecosystem research. In line with the core theme of the IBP, he was especially concerned with the "biological productivity" of the urban ecosystem—that is, with its ability to transform matter and sunlight energy into biomass. It is telling that, even when discussing the ecology of wastelands, he emphasized their enormous "productivity," in contrast to Sukopp's focus on their high degree of species diversity.[15] Much more than Sukopp's, his research also relied on laboratory analysis (e.g. of urban water and air pollution) and climatological measurement.[16] Although this approach was clearly modeled after his earlier fieldwork in the Ardennes, the city proved to be a much more unruly and complex environment than the forest. In the Ardennes, he worked in well-selected field stations where he could perform all kinds of instrumental manipulations (e.g.

cutting trees for measuring biomass, placing measuring devices), but the urban metabolism was rarely accessible to field methods of this type. His group therefore relied on a much more piecemeal approach, and notably on the data that the local administration collected on waste streams, traffic, or population patterns.

The way in which the two botanists represented the city as an ecological entity also differed in interesting ways. For Sukopp, the city was basically a mosaic of structurally different ecological "living spaces" or "biotopes," each of which he associated with the impact of a dominant form of "human influence."[17] Duvigneaud, by contrast, developed a functional understanding of how the city operates as an integrated ecosystem type with its own distinct metabolism. This difference is clearly visible in the schematic cross-sections which each of them produced of their city, and which later became emblematic of their distinct approaches.[18] Sukopp's model distinguished the structural morphology of the city (which is clearly identifiable as Berlin) horizontally into various zones of human influences: forests, rubble heaps, landfills, railway areas, gardens, and various types of development. Below the cross-cut, he added several horizontal lines, which each characterized how features of the vegetation, the animal population, and abiotic factors such as climate, soil and water varied between these zones. At times, Duvigneaud made use of a similar visual language. His most well-known figure, however, was a visual and quantitative model of the main streams of urban metabolism. It showed a cross-section of Brussels surrounded by a plurality of arrows and numbers, which were meant to display the city's precise intake and output of various kinds energy (on top) and materials (at the bottom).

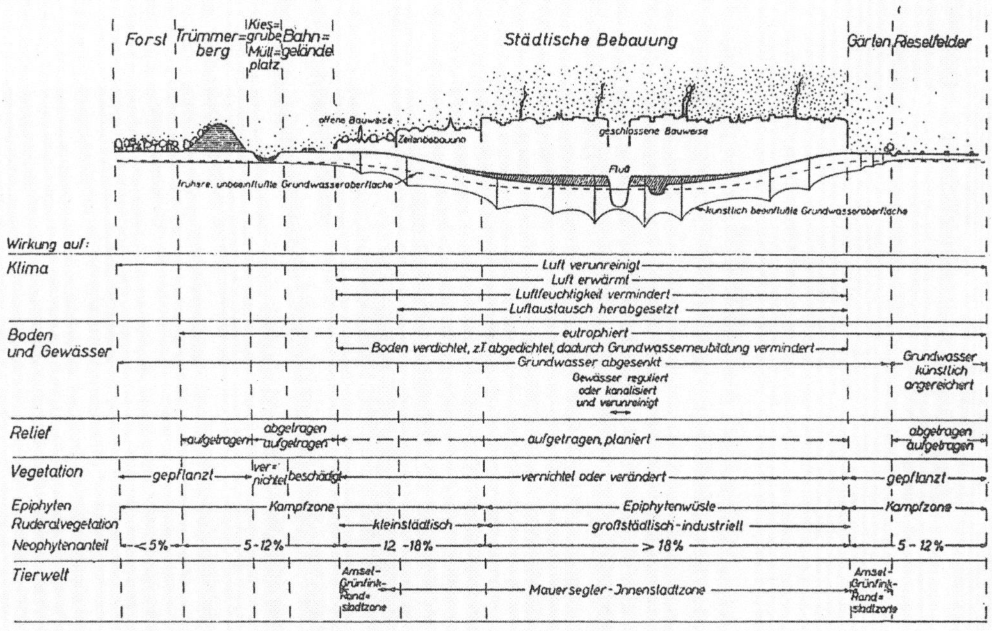

Cross-section of Berlin showing the different zones of "human influence." Source: Herbert Sukopp, "Die Großstadt als Gegenstand ökologischer Forschung" (1973).

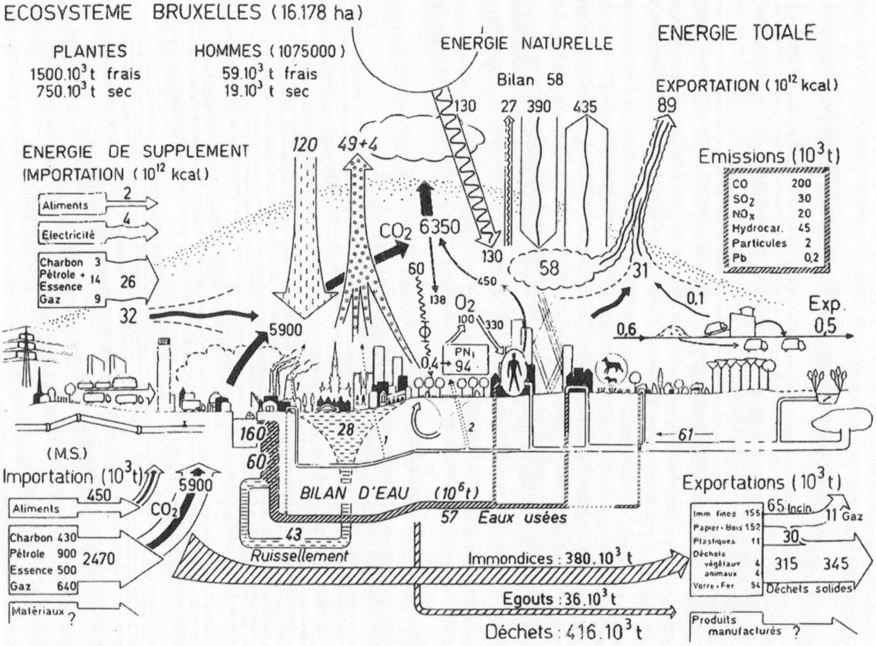

Cross-section of Brussels. Source: Paul Duvigneaud, Simone Denaeyer-De Smet, and Martin Tanghe Carte écologique de l'occupation du sol et des degrés de verdurisation de l'agglomération bruxelloise (Brussels: Service de l'énvironnement, 1977).

The visual and classificatory techniques that Sukopp and Duvigneaud employed in their maps likewise emphasized quite different themes. As part of a "biotope mapping project" for the Berlin Senate, the Sukopp approach created various maps which depicted Berlin as a mosaic of 57 "biotope types."[19] Each biotope type referred to an area of one dominant land use that was associated with a characteristic assemblage of plant species. Besides open spaces such as fens, forests, and wastelands, this also included different development types, which were neatly differentiated according to their spontaneous and planted vegetation. The map of Brussels, which was also produced for local planning purposes, divided Brussels into five "zones of greenness" (*verdurisation*) which stretched more or less concentrically from the "grey zone" of the inner urban area to the "green zone" on the outskirts.[20] "Greenness" was thus understood as the sheer density of "biomass" of the plant coverage, so that "biological productivity" can be seen as the ultimate theme of this map.

Which political visions were associated with these two approaches? One should not overestimate the differences, as both botanists agreed about the value of green spaces for the improvement of urban living conditions. Sukopp, however, understood greening efforts of this type as an urban version of nature conservation. While traditional nature conservation had often treated the city and nature as opposites, Sukopp posited that cities harboured diverse and valuable species, and that it was specifically this diversity of species which was beneficial for urban inhabitants. He claimed that typical urban biotopes such as parks, garden areas, and, notably, wastelands were just as worthy of preservation as the allegedly pristine landscapes of the countryside. He therefore sought to align his research with a comprehensive policy of urban landscape planning, notably through his work for the Berlin Senate's Species Protection Programme. Consequently, this programme made detailed recommendations for how species diversity in each of the 57 biotope types could be improved.

Duvigneaud was much more assertive than Sukopp in linking his ecology to a broader moral and political vision. Ecology, he wrote in 1970, should take a leadership role in a "permanent green revolution" and a "renewed socialism."[21] In contrast to the Marxist associations that these terms might evoke, what he was describing was a rather technocratic project. Accordingly, it included more efficient management of natural resources to help combat hunger in the developing world, and better integration of industrial society with the cycles of nature. Additionally, with regard to cities, Duvigenaud considered ecology primarily as a means to rationalize urban planning. Thus, Duvigneaud drew a direct link between his urban ecology and the modernist urbanism of Le Corbusier and the Athens Charta, which he characterized explicitly as "urban ecological."[22] In accord with Le Corbusier, he considered fresh air, sunlight, and recreation spaces to be preconditions of any livable city. In addition, he also made some (not very developed) suggestions for how the urban metabolism could be improved, for example by promoting collective transport, the use of the underground for traffic, the creation of pedestrian streets, and the greening of the city with parks and planted façades. The concept of biological productivity lost its original link with the issue of food production in these treatises on the city, but remained politically significant in that it expressed the vitality of the urban ecosystem and its ability to provide various benefits (what is now referred to as "ecosystem services"). While the mapping of Berlin's biotopes went hand-in hand with the stipulation of very concrete space-specific conservation and management measures (which were often watered down during the actual planning), Duvigneaud's elaborated ecosystem model had a much more indirect political effect. It served mainly as a means of framing the environment as a public problem and of legitimating future measures, while providing little instrumental guidance for the actual implementation of such measures. Interestingly, those parts of Duvigneaud's work which actually did have a direct impact on planning decisions were in fact those in which he was least ambitious in his application of ecosystems theory, and in which he relied more on classical vegetation analysis.[23]

Thus, while both botanists wanted to make their cities greener, "green" meant quite different things to each of them. For Duvigneaud, urban green was an expression of the biological productivity of an urban ecosystem and part of its complex metabolic mechanisms. For Sukopp, greenness was a question of biological diversity, both in terms of the kind and number of urban species and of the varieties of "biotopes" in which these species assemble. The distinctiveness of these two projects of urban ecology clearly reveals how the ways in which we know the botanical city are entangled with different political visions of how such a city should be shaped and managed. Besides the insights that it provides into the contextual embeddedness of these two visions, this essay therefore suggests a need for a reflexive approach of urban policy-making and public discussion, which focuses not only on the object of the botanical city itself, but also on the choices and normativities that are implied in the ways in which we know that city.

1 See also Peter Galison and David Stump, ed., *The disunity of science: boundaries, contexts, and power* (Stanford University Press, 1996).

2 This chapter combines findings from my previous work in which I have dealt with Sukopp and Duvigneaud separately, and which may be consulted for more empirical detail and references: Jens Lachmund, *Greening Berlin: the co-production of science, politics, and urban nature* (Cambridge, MA: MIT Press, 2013), and "The city as ecosystem: Paul Duvigneaud and the ecological study of Brussels," in *Spatializing the history of ecology*, ed. Raf de Bont and Jens Lachmund (London/New York: Routledge, 2017) pp. 141–161.

3 On Duvigneaud's biography see Pierre Meerts, "Duvigneaud, Paul," in *Nouvelle biographie nationale* (Brussels: Académie Royale, 2013) pp. 130–132.

4 Chunglin Kwa, *Mimicking nature: the development of system ecology in the United States* (PhD thesis: Amsterdam, 1989); Sharon E. Kingsland, *The evolution of American ecology*, 1890-2000 (Baltimore: Johns Hopkins, 2005); David Coleman, *Big ecology: the emergence of ecosystem science* (Berkeley: University of California Press, 2010).

5 See Paul Duvigneaud and Patrick Kestemont, eds., *Productivité biologique en Belgique* (Brussels: Duclot, 1977).

6 Paul Duvigneaud, *La synthèse ècologique* (Paris: Doin, 1974).

7 Paul Duvigneaud, "L'écosystème urbs: Études écologiques de l'écosystème urbain bruxellois, no 1, *Mémoires de la Société Royale de Botanique de Belgique* 6 (1974) pp. 5–35.

8 The F.D.F notably opposed new laws which gave more rights to the Dutch-speaking minority in Brussels.

9 Pierre Havelange, Paul Duvigneaud, and Simone Denaeyer-De Smet, eds., *L'écosytème urbain: Application à l'Agglomeration bruxelloise; Colloque international organisé par l'Agglomeration brusseloise*; *Colloque international organisé par l'Agglomeration de Bruxelles, 14 et 15 septembre 1974* (Brussels: l'Agglomeration de Bruxelles, 1975).

10 Herbert Sukopp, *Vergleichende Untersuchungen der Vegetation Berliner Moore unter besonderer Berücksichtigung anthropogener Veränderungen* (Doctoral thesis, FU Berlin, 1958).

11 Herbert Sukopp, "Die Großstadt als Gegenstand ökologischer Forschung" in *Schriften zur Verbreitung wissenschaftlicher Kenntnisse* 113 (1973) pp. 90–140.

12 Arbeitsgruppe Artenschutzprogramm Berlin, *Grundlagen für das Artenschutzprogramm Berlin*, Vol. 1–3 (Berlin: TUB, 1984).

13 See, notably the thesis which Kunick produced under Sukopp's supervision: Wolfram Kunick, *Veränderungen von Flora und Vegetation einer Großstadt* (Berlin: TUB doctoral thesis, 1974)

14 Martin Tange and Paul Duvigneaud, "Études phyto-écologiques de la Woluwe dans la region bruxelloise: Comme base de son aménagement; Études écologiques de l'écosystème brusselois no 12," *Revue Belge de Géographie* 102 (1978) 1 pp. 5–31.

15 Paul Duvigneaud, "Structure, biomasses, minéralomass, productivité et capitation du plomb dans quelques associations rudérales: Études écologiques de l'écosystème brusselois no 6," *Bulletin de la Société Royale de Botanique de Belgique* 108 (1975) pp. 93–128, and Paul Duvigneaud, *Friches et terrains vagues: La végétation adventice et rudérale dans la ville* (Brussels: Centre Paul Duvigneaud, 1996) p. 30. For a contrasting point of view, see, for example, Herbert Sukopp and Martin Launhard,

"Spontanvegetation in Berliner Stadtgebiet und auf der Bundesgartenschau," *Gartenpraxis* 5 (1985) pp. 16–18.

16 For example, Duvigneaud, "Structure, biomass."

17 Sukopp, "Die Großstadt." See also his "Der Einfluß des Menschen auf die Vegetation," *Vegetatio: Acta Geobotanica* 17 (1969) pp. 360–371.

18 See Sukopp, "Die Großstadt," and Duvigneaud, "L'écosystème urbs."

19 Arbeitsgruppe Artenschutzprogramm Berlin, *Grundlagen*.

20 Paul Duvigneaud, Simone Denaeyer-De Smet, and Martin Tanghe, *Carte écologique de l'occupation du sol et des degrés de verdurisation de l'agglomération bruxelloise* (Brussels: Service de l'énvironnement, 1977)

21 Paul Duvigneaud, "La Revolution verte, IV.," *Espaces vertes—art des jardins,* 13 (1970) pp. 10–22, pp. 20–21.

22 Paul Duvigneaud, "L'écosystème urbs," pp. 31–32.

23 E.g. the landscaping along the Woluwe River. See Martin Tange and Paul Duvigneaud, "Études phyto-écologiques."

Urban granaries, planetary thresholds

Nigel Clark

In the distance, we catch sight of the walls, tall and sheer as escarpments but boasting straight edges such that only a god would dream up. We have come "here" because we no longer have a "there." ... When the rains retreated, we wandered farther and wider, until our cattle grew lean and our own bones showed through our hides. Finally, when hope abandoned us, we rounded up our remaining stock and shouldered what we valued too much to leave to the locusts and the winds. Our bearings we took from the gossip of merchants, our route was a spattering of wells strung together by hoof prints. The last of our livestock and our small treasures we traded along the way, leaving us with only the dwindling strength of our backs. Descending from the plateau to the river valley, we saw for the first time multitudes of stooped bodies worrying at tall golden stems sprung from muddied water ... Finally, we arrive at a break in the wall, a gateway guarded by soldiers whose gazes weigh up our tired limbs as we once eyed the gaunt flanks of our cattle. Though we try to stand tall, fear curdles with the hunger in our bellies. If the guards permit us to pass through, who can say what will happen to us—we who know everything about herding cattle and nothing of tussling with overgrown grass? And we cannot but wonder—have those great walls been built to keep out strangers like ourselves? Or are they intended to keep in the kind of people we may be about to become?

"Thresholds," observes geographer Clive Barnett, "are the very scenes for the drama of responsiveness, hospitality and responsibility."[1] In the opening decades of the third millennium, city life seems once more to hinge upon the timeworn, troublesome presence of walls and gateways, barriers and breaches. Today, it is not only a matter of who is entitled to enter and share our urban spaces but an issue of how cities will cope with critical transitions in climate and the greater earth system. Or rather, it is the challenge of both of these at once: the question of how to organize our cities "responsively" at a time when transgressing limits in the very operation of our planet looks ever more likely to estrange, unsettle, and mobilize large numbers of people.

And in this context, for all that the "complete subordination of the agrarian to the urban" may have been accomplished, as Henri Lefebvre proposed,[2] we would do well to keep our granaries stocked. For there is neither sharing nor withholding without the stuff of livability.

In the midst of a discussion on the way that social-spatial relations have become not only world-wide but "planetary" in their scale and consequences, Lefebvre paused to meditate on the way so much of the language we still use to make sense of the world has "a peasant and artisan origin."[3] The term "threshold" clearly invites such a reading. As linguist Anatoly Liberman teases out:

> Most probably, the threshold was a place where corn was threshed (a threshing floor). The word contained a root and a suffix. That suffix has undergone numerous changes, for people tried to identify it with some word that could make sense to them. What remains unclear is not this process but the semantic leap. We are missing the moment at which the threshing floor, however primitive, began to denote the entrance to the room.[4]

I want to take the agrarian origins of the threshold, in all its obscurity, as a provocation to probe the idea of "planetary urbanization." Elaborating on Lefebvre's notion of "the planetarization of the urban," contemporary theorists have destabilized the idea of cities as discrete objects and explored how urban socio-spatial processes are transforming the entire surface of the earth.[5] In the course of subjecting the concept of the city to a thorough interrogation, however, it is not always so clear what these urban thinkers make of the earth's own boundaries, properties, and dynamics.

While Lefebvre deserves credit for recognizing the environmental significance of the urban, his later writings come just in advance of scientific claims that there are critical thresholds in the functioning of the earth as a whole. The idea that global climate is capable of moving abruptly over a limit into an entirely new regime or state emerged in the 1980s from research into polar ice cores and other proxies of past climate—though it also built on studies of smaller-scale shifts in ecological systems.[6] Over the intervening decades, geoscientists have been piecing together how the different components of the earth system interact—and exploring how these tight relationships or "couplings" make it possible for the entire planet to shift abruptly from one "operating state" to another.

This possibility is conveyed by the thesis that human activities may be nudging the earth out of the geological epoch of the Holocene—11,700 years of relatively stable conditions following the last ice age—into a novel state referred to as the Anthropocene.[7] The idea of the Anthropocene raises difficult questions about what kinds of human impact matter most—and about when members of our species first started to have cumulative impacts on earth and life processes significant enough to leave planet-scaled traces. Although this is currently a minority position among geologists, some strands of Anthropocene science propose that the spread of intensive agriculture thousands of years ago—situated deep within the Holocene as currently defined—was already impacting global climate.[8] Closely associated with Anthropocene science more generally is an approach that seeks to identify thresholds in a range of subcomponents of the earth system—including climate, biodiversity and major biogeochemical cycles. In the process, it delivers stern warnings about abrupt shifts "into states deleterious or even catastrophic to human well-being."[9]

However is it defined, the "urban" is on the frontline of the transitions in question. Even if earth system change remains gradual, cities can expect rising temperatures, inundation, accelerating rural-urban migration, and significant food security problems.[10] But contemporary geoscience does more than map out potentially hazardous planetary transitions. Increasingly high-resolution data sets of past climatic and other environmental change can help situate urban histories in the *longue durée* of a variable and volatile earth. New ways of thinking with and through the earth can also encourage us to disrupt disciplinary boundaries—by considering the ecological, geological, or mineralogical properties and potentialities that human agents share with other terrestrial actors. As geologist Jan Zalasiewicz observes, for example, "(b)oth skyscrapers and coral reefs are basically large masses of biologically constructed rock."[11] Or as he and his co-authors write elsewhere, "we live in and drive on Anthropocene rock constructions that we call houses and roads."[12] However, we should not forget that the philosopher Michel Serres also initiated a certain geological thinking of the social when he encouraged us to view conurbations as "enormous and dense tectonic plates of humanity."[13]

Alongside new developments, there are precedents for putting formative moments of sedentary human life in a "planetary" context. It has long been understood that the emergence of agricultural societies was bound up with the end of the last Pleistocene Ice Age. More recent inquiry proposes that prerequisites of plant and animal domestication—including species selection through human application of fire—were already well underway during late ice age conditions.[14] It has been proposed that prior to intentional selection of favourable plants, foragers were drawn towards those exceptional plants that did not drop their mature seeds on the ground; in this way unintentionally selecting for the kind of plants that would require humans to do the work of seed dispersal but with the benefit of higher yielding, more harvestable grains.[15]

In the Middle East, the warming temperatures and increased rainfall of the waning ice age helped the spread of wheat, oats, barley and other cereals. As these wild—or already partially domesticated—grains needed winnowing, grinding, and cooking to render them edible, their consumption required a toolkit of basic agrarian practices. New discoveries indicate that well before full cereal domestication, temporary harvest camps that included stone or mud-brick structures to both store and process grain began to embed themselves into villages.[16] We might say that global climate and the built environment passed over a threshold in tandem.

For all that most versions of the Anthropocene thesis accentuate the comparative stability of the previous epoch, it is important to remember that the Holocene was far from tranquil. It was not until 6000 years ago, about halfway through the Holocene as currently defined, that the sea-level rise precipitated by the break-up of the great Pleistocene ice sheets came to a halt. Equating to a rise of 120–130 metres since the last glacial maximum, advancing seas would have progressively swamped nutritionally rich coastlands and estuaries—pushing human foraging bands inland and uphill to where the wild grasses flourished.[17]

Further global environmental change was to come: a threshold that has been implicated in the shift from small, relatively egalitarian, and subsistence-based villages to large, fortified and stratified urban centres. Climate scientists propose that the Middle Holocene witnessed what was probably the most dramatic climate change of the last 10,000 years. As a result of cyclical changes in the earth's axis of rotation, global climate proceeded through a series of step-by-step changes. Then, around 5200 years ago, the climate system passed over a tipping point, resulting in a long-term shift from the warmer, more humid conditions of the early Holocene to a cooler regime characterized by enhanced aridity in the tropical latitudes.[18]

Correlations between the Middle Holocene Climatic Transition and the rise of city states have been most fully researched in Mesopotamia, but similar patterns have been documented as far apart as north-central China, the central Sahara, the Indus region and coastal Peru.[19] In Southern Mesopotamia, research suggests that significantly drier conditions led to the abandonment of many smaller farming villages and pastoral communities—and the rapid growth of settlements on the riverine lowlands. Functioning much like refugia—the exceptionally fertile sites that ecologists credit with sustaining biodiversity during rapid environmental change—the annually refreshed alluvial soils of the floodplains could support much more dense human and botanical populations than any other agro-ecosystems. In this way, anthropologist James Scott proposes, alluvium and the crop yields that it can sustain provide a condition of state formation. "It is hard to imagine the early state without grain as a basis for its sinew and muscle," as he puts it.[20]

This is not an argument for the climatic necessity of grain-fed city-states. Some communities, it appears, adapted to Mid-Holocene aridity not through urban agglomeration, but by means of enhanced mobility—and these non-sedentary peoples continued to coexist with their urban neighbours for thousands of years.[21] But where alluvial state formations prevailed, common patterns emerged—a template that included monumental architecture and fortification, pronounced social hierarchy and division of labour, a king-centred polity and centralized administration, record-keeping, and taxation.[22]

Many critical commentators now insist that a life bound to arduous labour in the fields was rarely adopted willingly by those accustomed to more free-ranging existence. The materiality and affordability of grain itself were crucial in what was most likely a highly coercive forging of labour, taxation, and distribution into a workable assemblage. "(V)isible, divisible, assessable, storable, transportable, and 'rationable,'" cereal grains were ideal from a tax official's point of view.[23] In this regard, urban built form effects a kind of doubling of containment: a brick and stone-chambered granary for the safekeeping of the precious agricultural produce and a city wall to keep the labouring, tax-paying populace in its place. Each had its own threshold.

Scott contends that the record-keeping that is key to the grain/labour/land nexus of the ancient Mesopotamian alluvial state signals the inauguration of a new kind of legibility or visualization.[24] "Follow the grain," it could be said, is an imperative around which the city-state formed itself. But there is another side to "seeing like a state." We might call it "geologizing like a state": the city-state increasingly acting as an earth process. Just as the earliest systems of notation record the resources and outputs of agricultural production, so too does the physical act of inscribing clay tablets reiterate the cutting of channels or the plowing of fields. On a grander scale, the increasingly extensive irrigation works at the heart of alluvial grain cultivation can be seen as a human capture and embellishment of sedimentation—one of the great geologic forces shaping the earth's crust.

Sedimentary processes involve the transportation and depositing of particulate matter by flowing water—or, in the words of the old geologists' quip, "mud moves from here to there and then from there to here."[25] Zalasiewicz suggests that sedimentation is so important for the earth that, in terms of comparative planetology, "one might ... denote this planet as the muddy planet, for it is the only one to be encased in a thick shell of mud and mudrock."[26] The irrigation that enabled mid-Holocene urbanization can be taken as a significant moment in the ascending geological agency of our species. As we have seen, the manipulation of mud also had a structural or vertical dimension. Anticipating the idea of "Anthropocene rock constructions," philosopher Manuel De Landa described the durable brick and stone formations of the ancient city as a re-enfolding of geology into the living world. This "sudden *mineralization*," he argues, helped to modulate the unprecedented concentration and mixture of humans and other animals, and especially "the movement of human flesh in and out of a town's walls."[27]

We should also heed the biogeographer Léon Croizat's assertion (made at a much earlier date) that "plantlife ... is a geological layer of the earth."[28] If we acknowledge that terrestrial plants have been a significant force in shaping the outer earth for at least 450 million years, then the selective breeding and extensive redistribution of botanical life at the crux of the urban-grain assemblage could itself be seen as a threshold not only in *human* but in *geologic* history. In this regard, we should keep in mind the "early Anthropocene" hypothesis which suggests that intensive agriculture—inevitably accompanied by dense urban settlements—may have already impacted the global climate sufficiently thousands of years ago to delay the return to glacial conditions that the rhythms of the earth's climate could be expected to bring.[29] But even if we settle for the later Anthropocene, it is hard to imagine the contribution made to earth system change by modern industrialized planting, fertilizing, harvesting, processing, transportation, and storage of grains without the innovations of the ancient cereal-fed city.

As we consider the growing impact of industrial grain production on atmospheric concentration of greenhouse gases, it is worth remembering that the spread of grasslands across the terrestrial globe over 40 million years was in large part a botanical response to carbon dioxide *depletion* in the earth system.[30] Today, we face the prospect of human-induced climate change reducing global grain production, with estimates that wheat yields will fall by 6 percent for each degree of further temperature increase—though this will be highly variable over space and time.[31] As well as keeping our national stockpiles of "critical commodities" in a healthy state, policy analysts recommend that food-insecure countries should cultivate good relations with cooler nations whose grain production is benefitting from warmer climate."Ensuring good trading relationships with those countries best positioned to supply wheat and barley in the long term," we are advised, "will help to offset some of the negative effects that climate change will have as other regions."[32] Meanwhile, current international climate policy promotes the idea that "resourceful" people in less well-resourced regions who are vulnerable to climate change could make a valuable contribution to the international labour force by choosing to migrate to wealthier nations—where they would be expected to perform whatever work is available.[33]

For all that it makes sense to think of the urban as currently passing a critical point into full "planetarization," I have suggested that we might also consider the urban to have been deeply implicated in geological or planetary processes from the outset. If we use the genealogy of the threshold as a means to move from the fine-grained to the global, we might see "planetarity" as an originary complication of the city as much as a recent achievement. City formation is intimately connected with planetary dynamics, most notably through the impacts of global environmental change on the other living things upon which human life depends. However, starting with its most primordial forms, urbanization can be seen as a geological process—not least because botanical life is itself a planetary force, one that cities channel, proliferate, and transform in directions that are new in the history of the earth. And, just as the early Anthropocene hypothesis indicates, we may still be discovering just how much—and for how long—the urban-grain assemblage has been impacting on planetary processes.

There is a great deal that might still be learned from the *longue durée* of geological and botanical urbanism that would help us to cope with the earth system change to come, whether gradual or sudden. However, perhaps the most troubling lesson is how little the script we use in enacting our responses to the threshold has been revised over the course of five thousand eventful years. After all, there is no urban geology that is not also a sedimentation of ethical and political relationships—and a substrate of alternative possibilities.

1 Clive Barnett, "Ways of relating: hospitality and the acknowledgement of otherness," *Progress in Human Geography* 29 (1) (2005) pp. 5–21.

2 Henri Lefebvre, *The urban revolution* (Minneapolis: Minnesota University Press: 2003 [1970]) p. 15.

3 Henri Lefebvre, *State, space, world: selected essays* (Minneapolis: Minnesota University Press: 2009) p. 198.

4 Anatoly Liberman, *Our habitat: threshold*, OUP Blog, 11 February 2015 https://blog.oup.com/2015/02/threshold-word-origin-etymology/ (accessed 1 August 2018).
5 Henri Lefebvre, "Dissolving city, planetary metamorphosis," in Neil Brenner, ed., *Implosions/explosions: towards a study of planetary urbanization* (Berlin, JOVIS, 2014) pp. 566–570, 569.
6 See Wallace S. Broecker, "Unpleasant surprises in the greenhouse," *Nature* 328 (9 July 1987) pp. 123–126.
7 See Jan Zalasiewicz, Mark Williams, Will Steffen and Paul Crutzen, "The new world of the Anthropocene," *Environmental Science and Technology* 44 (2010) pp. 2228–2231.
8 William Ruddiman, "The Anthropogenic greenhouse era began thousands of years ago," *Climatic change* 61 (2003) pp. 261–293; Simon Lewis and Mark Maslin, *The human planet: how we created the Anthropocene* (London, Pelican, 2018) pp. 140–142.
9 Rockström, J., Steffen, W., Noone, K., Chapin, F. S. III., Lambin, E., Lenton, T., Scheffer, M., Folke, C., Schellnhuber, H., Nykvist, B., De Wit, C., Hughes, T., van der Leeuw, S., Rodhe, H., Sörlin, S., Snyder, P., Costanza, R., Svedin, U., Falkenmark, M., Karlberg, L., Corell, R., Fabry, V., Hansen, J., Walker, B., Liverman, D., Richardson, K., Crutzen, P., and Foley, J., "Planetary boundaries: exploring the safe operating space for humanity," *Ecology and society* 14 (2009) p. 32.
10 See Stephanie Pincetl, "Cities in the age of the Anthropocene: climate change agents and the potential for mitigation," *Anthropocene* 20 (2017) pp. 74–82.
11 Jan Zalasiewicz, *The earth after us: what legacy will humans leave in the rocks?* (Oxford: Oxford University Press, 2008) p. 171.
12 Zalasiewicz et al., "The new world of the Anthropocene," p. 2230.
13 Michel Serres, *The natural contract* (Ann Arbor: University of Michigan Press, 1995) p. 16.
14 See Johan Goudsblom, *Fire and civilization* (London: Allen Lane, 1992) p. 446.
15 Lewis and Maslin, *The human planet*, pp. 121–122.
16 See Michael Balter, "Ancient waves of (wild) grain," *Science magazine*, June 22 (2009). http://www.sciencemag.org/news/2009/06/ancient-waves-wild-grain (accessed 1 August 2018); Yuval Noah Harari, *Sapiens: a brief history of humankind* (London: Vintage Book 2011) pp. 95–96.
17 See Colin Tudge, *Neanderthals, bandit and farmers: how agriculture really began* (London: Weidenfeld & Nicolson, 1998) pp. 35–38.
18 See Nick Brooks, "Beyond collapse: climate change and causality during the Middle Holocene Climatic Transition, 6400–5000 years before present," *Geografisk Tidsskrift-Danish Journal of Geography* 112 (2) (2012) pp. 93–104.
19 See Brooks, "Beyond collapse"; Douglas Kennett and James Kennett, "Early state formation in Southern Mesopotamia: sea levels, shorelines, and climate change," *The Journal of Island and Coastal Archaeology* 1 (1) (2006) pp. 67–99.
20 James C. Scott, *Against the grain: a deep history of the earliest states* (New Haven, CT: Yale University Press) p. 134.
21 See Scott, *Against the grain*, pp. 222–227; Brooks, "Beyond collapse," p. 100.
22 See Scott, *Against the grain*, p. 23; Kennett and Kennett, "Early state formation," pp. 79–80.
23 Scott, *Against the grain*, p. 129.
24 Scott, *Against the grain*, pp. 139–140.
25 David Waltham, *Lucky planet* (Icon Books: London, 2014), p. 199.
26 Jan Zalasiewicz, *The earth after us* (Oxford: Oxford University Press, 2009) p. 22.
27 Manuel De Landa, *A thousand years of nonlinear history* (New York: Swerve, 1997) pp. 26–27.
28 Leon Croizat, *Space, time, form: the biological synthesis* (Caracas: N.V Drukkerij Salland, 1962) p. 90.
29 See W. Ruddiman, D. Fuller, J. Kutzbach et al., "Late Holocene climate: natural or anthropogenic?," *Reviews of Geophysics* 54 (2016) pp. 93–118; Lewis and Maslin, *The human planet*, pp. 140–142.
30 See Iain Stewart and John Lynch, *Earth: the power of a planet* (BBC Books, London, 2007) pp. 221–223.

31 See S. Asseng, F. Ewert, P. Martre, R. P. Rotter et al., "Rising temperatures reduce global wheat production," *Nature Climate Change* 5 (2015) pp. 143–147.

32 Kirsty Lewis and Claire Witham, "Agricultural commodities and climate change," *Climate Policy* 12 (2012) pp. 53–61.

33 See Nigel Clark and Giovanni Bettini "'Floods' of migrants, flows of care: between climate displacement and global care chains," *Sociological Review Monographs* 65 (2) (2017) pp. 36–54.

The flora of bombed areas (an allegorical key)

Seth Denizen

Just days after Germany's surrender in May of 1945, the English botanist Edward James Salisbury gave a lecture in the Queen's Chapel of the Savoy in London. Salisbury had made the trip from Kew Gardens, where he was director, in order to report his recent findings on the botanical diversity of London's bomb craters in the aftermath of the Blitz. In particular, it was the rosebay willowherb (*Chamaenerion angustifolium*) that interested Salisbury. It "empurpled" London's ruins every year between June and September with large conical inflorescences,[1] and was clearly a subject of broad popular interest. The Green Cross Society (a.k.a the Women's Reserve Ambulance) had organized the lecture, and *The Times of London* sent a reporter to cover it.[2] Salisbury presented the material as a standard botanical survey, filled with long species lists and careful statistics, but in 1945 it sounded like an allegory. The war was over, and, to a room full of survivors and ambulance drivers, Salisbury reported that new life had sprung from the ruins of the past. These were ruins that the audience found themselves sitting in, as the Savoy Chapel had been hit four times in a bombing raid that flattened the adjacent Savoy Hospital. If Walter Benjamin was correct in saying that "allegories are, in the realm of thoughts, what ruins are in the realm of things," then it was from within the physical space of allegory that Salisbury invited his audience to see the broken Savoy Chapel as the rosebay willowherb saw it: as pure futurity.[3]

The strong allegorical undertow of London's post-war ecology also pulled at R.S.R. Fitter. Another of London's great war-time ecologists, Fitter wrote about the "Flora of bombed areas," adding Salisbury's observations on the botany of war to his own extensive accounting in *London's Natural History*.[4] For Fitter, the spirit of the blitz also stirred in London's fauna, like the nightingales (*Luscinia megarhynchos*), who Fitter noted "are well known for their indifference to gun-fire," and could be heard singing over the cacophony of London's bombing raids. Like Salisbury's plants growing vigorously in the ruins, Fitter celebrated the mallard ducks who began flying farther inland to enjoy the return of a tidal cycle to the Thames after the bombing of the Teddington Lock. "Animals," Fitter observes, "being more mobile, have

Chamaenerion angustifolium a.k.a. rosebay willowherb, fireweed, bombweed (formerly Epilobium angustifolium), "Flora of London Bombed Sites" (1950). Source: London Natural History Museum, Department of Botany.

probably suffered less than plants from the bombing, apart from the innumerable invertebrates that have been blown sky-high along with the soil and turf."[5]

While Fitter's natural history described a Panglossian ecology in which animals and plants thrived (or suffered less) in the traumatic aftermath of World War II, Salisbury's project did the reverse: it was an Uexküllian ecology that tried to see the world from a plant's point of view.[6] Bombs were soil-forming events. Ruins were light-gaps. Shoes were dispersal mechanisms. For the common dandelion (*Taraxacum officinale*) or shepherd's purse (*Capsella bursa-pastoris*), London's bomb sites were not unlike the raw glacial till they had evolved to colonize, chasing the glaciers north as they retreated 12,000 years ago.[7] Or maybe, to the few tender shoots of Sycamore (*Acer pseudo-platanus L.*) that Salisbury found, the bomb sites looked more like tree-fall events in a closed-canopy forest, bringing light into formerly dark areas, mixing new nutrients into the soil from the debris, and initiating a race for succession.

The observation that bombs are, among other things, botanical experiments in ecological succession was one that Salisbury was in a very good position to make. Early in his lectureship at East London College (now Queen Mary) he had discovered a chronosequence of dunes on the north coast of Norfolk where plant succession was driven by soil differences. Each dune was older than the last, offering Salisbury the opportunity to enjoy the (very Victorian) pleasure of strolling back in time as he made his way inland from the water. The age of the dunes correlated nicely with diminishing calcium as the soils acidified over time, causing changes in the species composition of the plant communities. Here, the ecological sequence was produced not by dispersal or plant competition, but by changes in the properties of the soil over time, something he termed "edaphic succession."[8]

The bombing of London turned out to produce a remarkably similar kind of edaphic succession. The fire and ash introduced carbon and nitrogen into the soil, while the pulverized lime mortar used in masonry construction mixed calcium into its surface layers. For citizens, the bombs punched holes into the space of the city, but for Salisbury, the bomb sites were holes in time. Where bombs had fallen, the soil was returned to a state of youth, in which its horizons had been mixed into homogeneity with the parts of the city the bombs had mineralized. The resulting mixture was "young" in the technical sense that this new mixture showed no signs of weathering. It was also "poor" in the agricultural sense that few plants could grow there. To Salisbury, the coarse, dry, calcareous rubble of London must have looked remarkably similar to the young sandy dunes he encountered on the coast of Norfolk.

The species composition of the bomb craters not only registered changes in the soil but were also an archive of key historical shifts in the urbanization of London. Salisbury was surprised by the overwhelming abundance of the rosebay willowherb (*Chamaenerion angustifolium*), since William Curtis's *Flora Londinensis*, published in 1777, had described it as rare in the London area. After the Great Fire of London in 1666, Salisbury reports that it was London rocket (*Sisymbrium irio*), rather than the willowherb, that grew in the ruins.[9] Speculating about what might

Old Montague Street bomb site, 1964. Photo: Richard Lansdown.

account for this change in London's disaster flora, he suggests that the increase in heath fires caused by locomotives and discarded cigarettes opened up new habitat for the rosebay willowherb, which followed these fires along roads and railway embankments like a warm purple afterglow. The willowherb produces a tiny seed surrounded by a plume of light filaments that allow the seed to easily catch the wind. As the seed encounters moist air, its filaments swell and the seed begins to drop out of the air column, increasing the chances it will find moist soil in which to germinate.

On over half of the bomb sites, Salisbury also found Oxford ragwort (*Senecio squalidus*), whose origins he traces to the volcanic slopes of Etna, in Sicily. There's a record of a specimen being sent to Linnaeus from the Oxford Botanic Garden, suggesting that its method of dispersal from Sicily was not the wind, but the botanists themselves.[10] The presence of Oxford ragwort and rosebay willowherb suggested a pattern of plants that are tolerant of the byproducts of combustion left in the soil. However, not all the plants in the survey had some clear connection to fire. English oats were found growing in a number of the sites, prompting Salisbury to speculate that their seeds had been dispersed by the feedbags of London's carriage horses. The soft fluffy seeds of Canadian fleabane (*Conyza Canadensis*; a.k.a. *Erigeron Canadensis*; a.k.a horseweed) were similarly dispersed not by fire but by transatlantic mail, as they were used as stuffing material in seventeenth-century taxidermy. According to Salisbury, "Patient Zero" was a stuffed parrot sent from Canada to Germany in 1686. The dispersal of Canadian fleabane was a botanical allegory that the Times of London couldn't resist so close to VE day; in reporting on Salisbury's lecture, that newspaper described it as subsequently arriving from Germany "by its own parachute."

If Salisbury's report on the *Flora of Bombed Areas* seems to continuously court allegorical interpretation, it is surely this compelling cast of characters that is to

Rosebay willowherb and Canadian fleabane in a ruined City church. Photo: Eric Hosking. Published in Richard S. R. Fitter *London's natural history* (London: Collins, 1945).

blame. There is the carriage horse that broadcasts seeds from it's feedbag as it eats, the careless smoker who starts a heath fire with a cigarette flicked from a moving car, dozens of botanical curiosities who have somehow escaped captivity, a men's fashion for trousers that may be to blame, and a taxidermied parrot known as Patient Zero. Narrative seems to spring from the soil of Salisbury's terse scientific prose like a weed, but unlike Fitter, Salisbury resists these allegorical eruptions. His attendees may have been invited to sit in the ruins of the Savoy Chapel, but his botanical lecture leads them quickly and firmly away into the rigor of his methods, the nomenclature of his plants, and the numbers he has verified. If in Fitter's *Natural History* we were left feeling patriotic, or saddened by war's casualties, how should we read Salisbury's *Flora of Bombed Areas*? To put the question another way, if Salisbury was asking us to see London as the rosebay willowherb saw it, the question still remains: what were we supposed to see?

Salisbury provides us with no hermeneutic key, as this is precisely what he is forbidden from doing as a scientist, as a Fellow of the Royal Society, and as an inheritor of the Enlightenment prohibition against subjectivity in the labour of interpretation. Metaphor, allegory, and above all politics are the negative image of scientific objectivity, against which good science is judged to be good. As Peter Galison and Lorraine Daston put it, "Objectivity is related to subjectivity as wax to seal, as hollow imprint to the bolder and more solid features of subjectivity."[11] What Salisbury can say objectively is directly related to what he cannot say, and must not say, about his work in London's bomb sites. Like the scientists on the Intergovernmental Panel on Climate Change, Salisbury can spend years describing his data in detail, but is prohibited from saying what the data should *mean* to us, and can only watch helplessly as the task is taken up enthusiastically by journalists. In the capable hands of *The Times of London*, Salisbury's scientistic title "The flora of bombed areas" is transformed into the melancholy headline "Flowers on bombed sites." In the allegorical gap between these two titles, Salisbury finds himself in the position of Herman Melville, insisting that it's just a story about a guy and a fish.[12] In taking this position, Salisbury rigorously adheres to the aesthetic requirements of scientific objectivity, effectively shifting the burden of interpretation onto the reader, who can make of his evidence what she will.

Of course, metaphor and allegory are not the only ways to say *what something means*, but historically, these have been among the most powerful tools for doing so. Without these tools available to him, Salisbury's "The flora of bombed areas" was left to be allegorized by writers who had only a passing familiarity with his work. Today, Salisbury's war-time ecology deserves a better allegory than *The Times of London* was willing to write.

A far better allegory would begin with the assertion that "The flora of bombed areas" is not a story about hope, or new life springing from the ruins. The "Flowers on Bombed Sites" did not grow *in memoriam* of the dead. We know this because the first thing Salisbury shows us is that the bombing of London was a continuation of processes that were already ongoing in London since the seventeenth century. The urban transformations of London's industrialization had already produced fire, ash, and bare soil, and for this reason the rosebay willowherb was already in London when the bombing started. In Salisbury's study, the flora of bombed areas is revealed as simply the flora of modernity. This is to say that modernity was always a botanical project, and not simply an accidental one: botany was an engine of the modernizing project. As Donna Haraway writes: "My definition of modernity is that it is the period of the intensified transportation of seeds and genes."[13]

This is why Salisbury's title, "The flora of bombed areas", should sound more striking to us than the headline *The Times of London* replaced it with. *Places* have always had a flora, in the geographical sense that every country or region has its own specific "flora." However, Salisbury was offering a botanical survey not of a *place* but of a *process*. This is the flora that bombs make, re-read as the flora that modernity makes. Salisbury is showing us a botany that has been unmoored from the specificity and provincialism of the regional botanical survey. Instead, London's bomb craters should be read as Salisbury's Chimborazo profile; they are a site-specific microcosm of forces that determine botanical relationships at the scale of the Earth.[15]

The specificity of this flora should also mean something to us. What emerges from Salisbury's survey is not simply a list of plants, but rather a list of environments, or plant-milieus. Salisbury doesn't describe Oxford ragwort growing in London so much as Oxford ragwort growing in a set of conditions that the city has come to resemble. What we should see, therefore, is not a plant growing in some ruins, but rather a plant for whom London resembles a Sicilian volcano. In general, the discovery that the flora of modernity is interpreting our most beautiful cities as a glacial or volcanic aftermath should give us pause, because these are places that people in London don't want to live.

That the director of Kew Gardens should be the one to deliver this message also means something. The colonial project of Kew Gardens is founded on the belief that all of the world's environments can be approximated in London, through a mixture of botany, chemistry, and architecture. The Palm House, badly damaged in the bombing raids of '40 and '41, was one of Salisbury's first restoration projects. If "The flora of bombed areas" had anything to teach Salisbury as he began his directorship of Kew Gardens, it would have been that palms can grow in London and that tropical environments are reproducible within the architecture of modernity—but only until someone bombs the palm house. This is to say that the relationship between a plant and its milieu is not deterministic. One plant does not belong to one environment forever. Oxford ragwort is not indexical of a volcano *per se*, but of all the things that happen on a volcano over thousands of years. If anything had ever happened on the volcano that the species couldn't survive, then it would never have appeared in Salisbury's survey. In this sense, a plant-milieu is not a *place*, but a set of environmental conditions over time; it is a *process*. If we can't grow palms in London, it is because the systems that palms depend on to live in London are fragile over large timescales.

The allegorical lesson, then, of "The flora of bombed areas" is that we should aspire to live in cities capable of providing a milieu for plants as disinclined to catastrophe as we are. Surrounded by the 157 species on Salisbury's survey, we are staring not at the Arcadia of Stowe but at the Hippocratic face of that Arcadia, at plants who specialize in catastrophe and are far better at it than the cities they live in.

1 Salisbury identifies rosebay willowherb as *Epilobium angustifolium* in his paper; however, it is now more commonly identified as *Chamaenerion angustifolium*. This is the nomenclature that appears in the London Natural History Museum collection "Flora of London Bombed Sites" (1950).

2 See "Flowers on bombed sites," *The Times*, no. 50133, May 3, 1945, p. 2.

3 For Walter Benjamin, ruins share an essential structure with allegorical thought. Like ruins, allegories appear in the aftermath of a process of destruction, in which the specificity or individuality of the world is broken apart in order to be reconstituted within a new narrative. In a ruin, as Benjamin notes, "history has physically merged into the setting," see Walter Benjamin, *The origin of German tragic drama*, trans. John Osborne (London; New York: Verso, [1928] 1998), p. 177. Salisbury's invitation to see the ruins as futurity is therefore an invitation to allegorize something which is already (for Benjamin) an allegory.

4 See Edward James Salisbury, "The flora of bombed areas," *Nature*, no. 151 (April 24, 1943). Fitter published Salisbury's complete list of plants that germinated in the bomb craters—157 species—as an appendix, in: Richard S. R. Fitter, *London's natural history: the new naturalist a survey of british natural history* (London: Collins, 1945).

5 Richard S. R. Fitter, *London's natural history,* (London: Collins, 1945) p. 229.

6 See Jakob von Uexküll, *Streifzüge durch die Umwelten von Tieren und Menschen (A foray into the worlds of animals and humans)* (Berlin: Verlag von Julius Springe, 1934), translated by Joseph D. O'Neil as *A foray into the worlds of animals and humans* (Minneapolis: University of Minnesota Press, 2010)

7 Salisbury makes this claim in Sir Edward James Salisbury, *Weeds & aliens: the new naturalist a survey of British natural history* (London: Collins, 1961) p. 25.

8 "Edaphic succession" refers to changes in the composition of plant communities that occur as a result of changes in the soil over time. The term was not taken up by Salisbury's contemporaries, nor is it in use today. At the time when Salisbury was writing, plant succession was theorized as a process driven by modifications that plants themselves made to the environment. An example would be Frederic Clement's theory of succession, in which trees convert a meadow into a forest over time by intercepting the light required by grasses, and thereby changing the pH of the soil. By using the term "edaphic succession" Salisbury is shifting causal agency from plants to soils. Today, this would be called "allogenic succession," meaning succession driven by something other than living things. See Edward James Salisbury, "Note on the edaphic succession in some dune soils with special reference to the time factor," *Journal of Ecology* 13 (2) (1925) pp. 322–328.

9 Job Edward Lousley was working at the same time as Salisbury and also reported on the flora of bombed areas. Lousley noted that in the aftermath of the Blitz in 1943 the *Daily Mail* exhorted its readers to "Watch for Fire Flower," which since the Great Fire of 1666 had referred to *Sisymbrium irio*, a.k.a London rocket. However, by 1945 it was what Salisbury termed *Epilobium angustifolium*, a.k.a fireweed (now *Chamaenerion angustifolium*) that had become the new fire flower in London. See Job Edward Lousley, "Flora of the bombed sites in the City of London in 1944," *Report of the Botanical Society & Exchange Club of the British Isles* 12 (1946) pp. 875–883.

10 Salisbury also found the "turn-ups" of trousers to be a possible dispersal mechanism, at least since they became a popular menswear fashion in the early twentieth century. Salisbury boasted that he once germinated 300 seeds collected from a single pair of pants. See Salisbury, *Weeds & aliens*, p. 105.

11 As Daston and Galison explain, the result of this is that the history of objectivity is inextricable from the history of the self. See Lorraine Daston and Peter Galison, "The image of objectivity," *Representations* 40 (1992) pp. 81–128.

12 Melville famously warns us against reading Moby Dick as an allegory: "So ignorant are most landsmen of some of the plainest and most palpable wonders of the world, that without some hints touching the plain facts, historical and otherwise, of the fishery, they might scout at Moby Dick as a monstrous fable, or still worse and more detestable, a hideous and intolerable allegory." See Herman Melville, Hershel Parker, and Harrison Hayford, *Moby Dick* (W.W. Norton, 2017) p. 195.

13 See Donna Haraway and Thyrza Nichols Goodeve, *How like a leaf: an interview with Thyrza Nichols Goodeve* (New York: Routledge, 2000) p. 88.

14 See for instance, Peter Sell and Gina Murrell's 2010 *Flora of Great Britain and Ireland*, or John Pruski and Harold Robinson's 2018 *Flora Mesoamericana*.

15 In 1807 Alexander von Humboldt published a map of Mount Chimborazo, which he had climbed five years earlier in Ecuador. The mountain is drawn in section (or profile) and every plant that Humboldt found on Chimborazo is labeled at the altitude at which it grows. Humboldt was interested in Chimborazo because it was thought to be the highest mountain on earth, as well as the furthest geographical point from the earth's centre given the earth's equatorial bulge. For Humboldt, this location made Chimborazo a microcosm of all of the earth's climate zones, from the equatorial tropics at the base of Chimborazo to the polar arctic at its summit. The plants that Humboldt found growing on Chimborazo were, in this sense, representative of botanical relationships at the scale of the earth. See Alexander von Humboldt, Aimé Bonpland, and Carlos Montúfar, "Journey towards the summit of Chimborazo, attempted on the 23rd June 1802," translated by Helen Maria Williams, in *Personal narrative of travels to the equinoctial regions of the new continent, during the years 1799–1804* (London: Longman, Rees, Orme, Brown, and Green, 1822).

Vegetation as testimony: botanical traces of the urban past

Moritz von der Lippe

It was just as the total renovation of the *Heimstättensiedlung* in Jena (a city of about 100,000 inhabitants in the federal state of Thuringia, Germany) was about to begin that I discovered wildgrowing forest violets, orchids, and devil's claws in the hedges of its front gardens. These species are not rare in the forests around Jena, but I had never seen them in a housing estate before. In Germany, these species are considered indicator species of ancient woodlands.[1] The *Heimstättensiedlung*, an early Garden City[2] of the 1920s, was also old, but was it really possible that such sensitive forest species had spread from the forests into developed areas? My curiosity was aroused, and I sought out historical pictures of the settlement from the town museum. By bringing together historical documents, and through an understanding of how plants are distributed now, it became clear that these ancient woodland species were primarily found where an overgrown embankment had stood in the early urban development. This discovery was only the beginning of a deeper botanical-historical investigation into the hidden traces of garden history to be found in current vegetation patterns.[3]

What kind of clues might we look for? To begin with, urban vegetation is known to be highly adaptive to rapid transitions in the urban environment. However, another feature of vegetation that is often neglected in an urban context is its persistence in adapting to land use change. Frequently, some components of plant communities that were adapted to previous land uses will persist even decades after the land use has changed. In addition, species that have escaped from horticultural cultivation by spreading out into adjacent vegetation can survive for a long time in certain plant communities, even if the original plantings have long since disappeared. This tenacity of vegetation elements can lead to an accumulation of traces of the past that can be read by experienced botanists. This was first demonstrated in studies on the vegetation of historical parks, where "feral" ornamental plants from previous eras can still be found in old meadows, perennial borders, and other vegetation, proving their high testimonial value.[4]

These traces of history include plants whose origins have a clear human cultural explanation, although their current occurrence is not intentional. Even when the original plantings have long since been replaced, some specimens can survive in the same area or nearby for decades, or even centuries. This phenomenon has been introduced into the botanical literature by Dutch botanists under the term "*Stinzenplanten.*"[5] In such cases, spontaneous vegetation documents a part of a garden's history as an "indicator with memory."

Areas of vegetation can also present evidence of the history of gardens and settlements beyond naturalized populations of ornamental plant species. Spontaneous vegetation can offer indirect evidence of garden practices, tracing the changes in open spaces over the course of their development history. The types of vegetation present in an area can depend on the form and duration of gardening activities or on certain forms of use and maintenance, and thus can be historically conditioned. The vegetation composition of historical settlements can therefore be read as a clue to the degree of care practised over decades, such as the infrequent mowing of meadows.[6] In such cases, the spontaneous vegetation itself represents a historical document that should be included in conservation efforts when a settlement is recognized as protected according to monument or heritage protection laws. Plant species that are dependent on long development periods and continuous forms of use or maintenance can also be used to determine dates in the inventory of historical open spaces, and thus supplement archival research. In the case of several settlements, it has been shown that certain species are bound to residential quarters of different ages.[7] Existing vegetation can lead to a more complete picture of garden history, especially in connection with written or pictorial sources.

A further group of vegetation elements that provide a historical testimony are the remnants of the original vegetation that have been carefully integrated into newly created gardens or settlements, which thus indicate the long-lasting history of a site. As long as the intensity of urban use has not led to a complete change of species, relic occurrences of plants can indicate historical patterns of use. Plants that are typical of agricultural landscapes or forests, and that do not have the ability to spread widely, for example, often indicate the earlier uses of their present settlement sites. In the ecological literature, these relics are often referred to as a result of land use legacies, i.e. the legacy of a former land use that is still visible in the current vegetation.[8]

Does the vegetation of open spaces within developed areas represent a historical document that makes the history of their origin and development legible, in a similar manner to what we see in historical gardens? This question has barely been investigated at all in the context of settlements listed as protected monuments, where expert assessments of the significance of vegetation are mostly limited to an inventory of planted trees and shrubs. Results from urban ecological research indicate that the suitability of spontaneous vegetation as a historical document, especially for landscape gardens, can in principle be transferred to open spaces in settlement areas.[9]

The initial question for the present investigation was therefore whether vegetation elements can be identified as important historical testimonies in the case of Jena's *Heimstättensiedlung*, which is listed as a protected monument because of its typical development as a Garden City and was strongly affected by redevelopment measures after German reunification.

Against the background of the poor housing conditions of the tenements of the late nineteenth century and the housing needs arising from Jena's expanding optical industry, the turn of the twentieth century saw a wide variety of cooperative housing construction activities take place in the city. A housing cooperative was established in 1897 with the express aim of promoting the construction of inexpensive single-family houses with gardens for workers and employees. The model for the "Heimstätten idea" was the Garden City movement,[10] which manifested itself (among other things) in the membership of the Heimstätten cooperative in the German Garden City Society.

A rapid increase in the number of members enabled the construction of the settlement to begin in the spring of 1913. The chosen building site was a hillside on the former outskirts of the city. The hillside location necessitated a serpentine-like main development, to which elongated courtyards were attached parallel to the slope. Due to financial pressures on the cooperative, the ideal of a single-family house with its own garden had to be deviated from again and again. As a result, much of today's housing stock consists of multi-storey apartments. These are partly assigned to tenant gardens in the inner courtyards, but partly also to green areas that can be used jointly (e.g. laundry areas). The coherent overall picture of the settlement is essentially determined by the uniformly designed front gardens.[11] The front gardens are always surrounded by a cut hedge, the composition of which varies from section to section, and within the hedges are lawns and meadows. In the area of single-family houses, garden beds laid out by the tenants are usually integrated into the lawns.

The *Heimstättensiedlung* and its open spaces were designated as a historical monument in 1995. A decisive factor for the designation was the settlement structure, which in this region of Thuringia is rarely found in such a complete state of preservation. As a coherent urban ensemble with a high design and with socially significant open spaces, it closely reflects the principles of the Garden City movement.

Some open spaces within the settlement feature more than 80 years of development. This is mainly due to the largely unbroken continuity of their use. As no comprehensive renovation work took place on the open spaces until the restoration work was initiated in 1996, forms of vegetation dependent on a long continuity of location and specific conditions of use developed in many parts of the settlement. In addition, the long development period also favoured the natural spread of numerous ornamental and functional plants from their original locations.

The extent to which the age of the open spaces, their historical use, and the gardening practices of the inhabitants can be seen from the vegetation is illustrated by the following three examples. In the areas where the earliest construction took place, some demanding forest species grow in the margins of hedges; these

Violets (here: *Viola riviniana*) in the margins of hedges indicate vegetation stands with a long development period. Photo: Moritz von der Lippe.

species are otherwise rarely observed in the settlement area. Violets from forest groves and woods (*Viola riviniana* and *V. reichenbachiana*) even dominate the margins of many hedges. In addition, there are occasional bush anemones (*Anemone nemorosa*), golden crested buttercup (*Ranunculus auricomus*), common lungwort (*Pulmonaria officinalis*), moschatel (*Adoxa moschatellina*), spike-like devil's claw (*Phyteuma spicatum*), and hollow larkspur (*Corydalis cava*).

All these species are primarily spread by ants. Due to the limited mobility patterns of ants, the plants can only overcome barriers, such as the surrounding roads and paths, over very long periods of time. Their presence thus indicates long-lasting site continuity. Moschatel, bush anemone, and golden-crested buttercup are also regarded as indicator species for old forests. It is unlikely that these were intentionally planted, since they are not typical garden plants, and their growth locations do not suggest any horticultural purpose. Reconstruction using historical photographs makes it possible to see that, in the areas where most of the forest species occur today, an old stock of trees and shrubs from the time before the construction of the settlement had been integrated into the open space concept of the landscape design. Obviously, the species mentioned here are relics of vegetation that were present on the site before the construction of the settlement. As these are all species found in undisturbed forest locations, they could probably only survive due to the fact that the hedges are only lightly maintained. All in all, the conspicuous species reflect the largely undisturbed maintenance of the open spaces over a long period of time.

The meadows in front of the houses are an unusual design element of the *Heimstättensiedlung.* With a few exceptions they determine the appearance of the front garden. The meadows are the only vegetative cladding on the generous embankments in front of the apartment buildings. This type of greening was obviously intended to require little maintenance at the outset. This was made clear in a statement by the *Heimstätten* housing cooperative to the State Tax Office, in response to an attempt to revoke its non-profit status by reason of the high expenditure on horticulture in 1933: "The front gardens and grounds are the natural additions to the dwelling and form the natural decoration of the estate, which makes living in the estate healthier and gives the residents joy and love of nature. The complexes are not luxury gardens. The preservation of the gardens will not amount to more than about RM 2000 in the future, since the facilities are so simple that the maintenance costs can be kept to a minimum."
Photographs from the founding period of the settlement illustrate the height of the vegetation in the meadows, indicating that the front gardens were maintained relatively lightly even in the first years after their construction. Until the fall of the Berlin

Embankment in front of the houses of the first construction phase around 1919. The historical record proves that extensive meadow maintenance was already practised in the front gardens during the founding period of the settlement.
Source: Jena City Museum.

Wall in 1989, all meadows that were not assigned to single-family houses were maintained by cooperative gardeners. According to residents, mowing was carried out with the scythe until then. Lawn-like care was thus excluded at the outset.

This maintenance, when practised over decades, results in a species-richness for meadows that is unusually high for human settlements. The species composition corresponds roughly to that of lean agricultural meadows. As time passes, the sites became increasingly nutrient-poor due to the continuous removal of the mown material and the simultaneous lack of fertilization. Over the long development period, the vegetation adapts to the site conditions of the different meadows in a very differentiated way, so that variations in shading or soil moisture are expressed in different species combinations.

The third example illustrates how differentiations below the species level can be helpful in obtaining valuable information on the historical use of plants. In the first construction phase of the *Heimstättensiedlung* in particular, wooden trellises were attached to the front sides of the houses, which were planted with pears shortly after construction. According to older residents, the planting material came from the cooperative nursery. This was privately managed on a specially designated site on the edge of the settlement, and was closely linked to the garden history of the settlement until its dissolution in the 1960s. According to residents (and also deduced from the trunk size of the trees), most of the espalier pears can be dated to the time when the settlement was founded. A determination of the still-existing pear varieties resulted in an unexpectedly high diversity of historical pears. More than half of the pears are very rare regional varieties, which are hardly available commercially anymore and only rarely occur in the numerous orchards surrounding the city. The preservation of this range of varieties is not just important for the protection of rare cultivated plants. It is also a testament to the self-sufficiency concept of the Garden City movement, and the special form of organization of plant procurement in this specific settlement.

The *Heimstättensiedlung* shows in an exemplary manner how historical processes, and the precise development of open spaces can be determined through a study of their vegetation. A prerequisite for this is a lengthy age and a long continuity of similar uses. The redevelopment of the existing buildings and the outside facilities of the *Heimstättensiedlung*, which began in 1996, represents a break in the decades of development continuity for the vegetation.

Protective measures are indeed being taken for the woods. The renovation of the building foundations, however, requires excavations that usually destroy a large part of the front garden vegetation. After the damage caused by the renovation work, the meadows are largely dug up and then sown again. In addition, the particularly valuable old trellises cannot be preserved due to the subsequent external insulation of the façades.

After German reunification, the traditionally minimal care of the meadows and hedges also changed. Maintenance services are now carried out by external caretakers. Meadow mowing takes place at shorter intervals and, with four to five cuts per year, reaches a frequency at which many of the higher-growing meadow species will cease to survive in the long term. The verges of the hedges are now cut regularly with a motorized scythe.

Against this background, a question arises as to how to handle the vegetation in a manner appropriate to the protected historic site. Extensive protective measures during the restoration work which go beyond the protection of individual trees are difficult to communicate to property owners and are not usually required by law. Is it nonetheless worthwhile to preserve herbaceous and partly spontaneous settlement vegetation for reasons of historic preservation? Since this depends on the quality of the individual historical testimonies, individual case decisions are necessary.

The frequently advanced argument that spontaneous vegetation is subject to constant change anyway and therefore does not need to be preserved can be refuted with the example of the settlement vegetation of the *Heimstättensiedlung*. Its characteristic feature is its constancy, due to decades of continuity in care. The fact that it does not survive on its own is illustrated by pieces of meadow that were broken up two years ago as part of the redevelopment. Numerous meadow species which shape the image of the remaining settlement and contribute to the special character of its vegetation were not able to regenerate. The example of the espalier pears clearly shows that the originally planted varieties cannot be easily replaced by replanting. Replacing the rare pear varieties (which are closely linked to garden history) with current nursery stock would greatly reduce the importance of espaliers as historical sources. One solution could be to preserve the historical diversity of varieties by grafting new pear rootstocks with grafts that have been recruited from the settlement.

For the *Heimstättensiedlung* and similar historical settlements, the consideration of vegetation in its entirety could serve to support historical character, and thus documentary value. The idea of the Garden City is closely connected with the goal of self-sufficiency through gardens close to houses, and also with a characteristic garden and care culture. Evidence of this can inevitably be found more in the vegetation itself than in the building structures. With the current practice of monument preservation, however, botanical information that does not relate to relicts of historical plantings is only rarely used as a source of historical information, or as the basis for conservation measures. This case study, which can be transferred more generally to conservation areas that are strongly shaped by historical gardening practices, exemplifies how planted *and* spontaneous vegetation can contribute to the study of garden history—and how both should sometimes be given equal consideration in the conservation of gardens as sites of historical interest.

1 Ancient forest indicator species were identified through the floristic analysis of forest fragments where a long historical continuity of the forest formation is detectable. See, for example, Monika Wulf, "Plant species as indicators of ancient woodland in northwestern Germany," *Journal of Vegetation Science* 8 (5) (1997) pp. 635–642.

2 Although this settlement is not a separate city, the term "Garden Cities" is frequently used for settlements that were developed according to the concept of "Garden

Cities" that was introduced by the British urban planner Ebenezer Howard in his book *Garden cities of tomorrow* from 1898. Even though Howard formulated his idea of the Garden City as independent satellite cities at the periphery of large cities, the realized examples are usually larger uniform settlements in already existing cities.

3 The full study was first published in German, see Moritz von der Lippe and Ingo Kowarik, "Die Vorgärten und Anlagen sind die naturbelebte Ergänzung der Wohnung. Historische Vegetationselemente einer Gartenstadtsiedlung in Jena," in Erik A. de Jong, Erica Schmidt, and Brigitt Sigel, *Der Garten – ein Ort des Wandels: Perspektiven für die Denkmalpflege* (Zürich: vdf Hochschulverlag, 2006) pp. 101–116.

4 On the testimonial value of old park meadows, see, for example, Klaus von Krosigk, "Wiesen-, Rasen- und Blumenflächen in landschaftlichen Anlagen," in Dieter Hennebo, ed., *Gartendenkmalpflege* (Stuttgart: Ulmer, 1985) pp. 205–253.

5 The term "Stinz" stems from the Frisian word *Stins* and refers to a former Frisian stronghold or country estate, where the first investigations into the phenomenon of *Stinzenplanten* were carried out. For an overview, see Piet Bakker and Evert Boeve, *Stinzenplanten* (Zutphen: Uitgeverij terra, 1985).

6 The frequency and timing of the mowing regime is one of the predominant factors shaping species composition in grasslands and has recently been shown to affect urban grasslands in a similar manner, see Simon Chollet, Charlotte Brabant, Samson Tessier, and Vincent Jung, "From urban lawns to urban meadows: reduction of mowing frequency increases plant taxonomic, functional and phylogenetic diversity," *Landscape and Urban Planning* 180 (2018) pp. 121–124.

7 For example, Wolfgang Aey, "Historisch-ökologische Untersuchungen an Stadtökotopen Lübecks: Floristisch-vegetationskundliche und bodenkundliche Untersuchungen unterschiedlich alter Stadtbereiche," *Mitt. ArbGem.Geobot. Schlesw.-Holst./ Hamb.* 41, (Kiel, 1990).

8 See Davis Foster, Frederick Swanson, John Aber, Ingrid Burke, Nicholas Brokaw, Davis Tilman, and Alan Knapp, "The importance on land-use legacies to ecology and conservation," *Bioscience* 53 (1) (2003) pp. 77–88.

9 On differences in species composition between urban areas of different age and historical formation, see, for example, Laura Celesti-Grapow, Giulia Capotorti, Eva del Vico, Edda Lattanzi, Agnese Tilia and Carlo Blasi, "The vascular flora of Rome," *Plant Biosystems* 147 (4) (2013) pp. 1059–1087. On land-use legacies in urban vacant lots see, for example, Joan Iverson Nassauer, and Julia Raskin, "Urban vacancy and land use legacies: a frontier for urban ecological research, design and planning," *Landscape and Urban Planning* 125 (2014) pp. 245–253.

10 On the early history of the garten city movement, see Mervyn Miller, *English garden cities: an introduction* (Swindon, 2010).

11 The early development of this garden city is well-documented in *Die Heimstätten-Genossenschaft Jena 1911–1931* by M. Sänger (Düsseldorf: Lindner Verlag, unknown year).

The curious disappearance of the Ennore Creek

Bhavani Raman

Before landscapes die, they first vanish in the imagination.[1]

Thermal power infrastructure, Ennore Creek (2017). Photo: Bhavani Raman.

The Ennore (Ennūr) Creek in North Chennai began to disappear in the 1980s. Things accelerated in the 2000s when, contrary to laws passed to protect coastal zones, large portions of the wetlands were given over to thermal power plants and to the Ennore port. Now, rivers of fly ash and intolerable levels of untreated pollutants are killing the wetlands and dispossessing those who live intimately with the sea, creeks, and canals.

The creek, however, has already disappeared entirely from the imagination. The Coastal Resource Centre released an official map they received in response to a Right To Information application filed in 2017, in which a full 6,569 acres of the creek are missing.[2] The official map covers up an astounding crime. The government of India, aided by the agencies of Tamil Nadu, is undertaking the greatest possible violation of the law protecting our wetlands. The map wipes out this illegal encroachment. It "disappears" the creek in a backdated map. If the paper map bears no trace of the water, there is no water, so goes the reasoning. There is nothing to protect. No writ of *habeas* can be issued for a missing body of water.

There is something dire in this story of an official effort to disappear nature. The falsifying map exposes the imagination that made it. We ourselves also share in this official imagination which values turning landed property into water. Its tools—walls, earthmovers, and diggers—are a part of our everyday life.

This is what official encroachment looks like. A small blue board appears in a marsh. Earthmovers move in. Projects are approved on the basis of a corporation's project maps.[3]

View from Kattukuppam, Ennore (2017). Photo: Bhavani Raman.

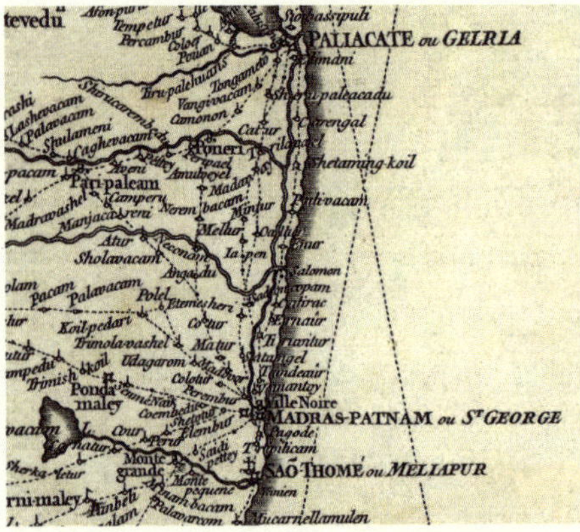

Koromandel (southern sheet).
Atlas map by D'Anville, re-issued by Franz Anton Schraembl, 1800.
Source: David Rumsey Historical Map Collection.

An old "choultry" at Ennur, near Madras, 1786.
Copyright: British Library.

For a long time now, waterscapes like this have been treated as swampy waste, as receptacles of garbage, and as a site to which we banish those we refuse to house. We value water only when it is bottled, stored, piped, or pumped, and we can control it and sell it. However, waterscapes like Ennore are difficult to own. They disappear seasonally, and they defy legal categories because they appear in many interconnected forms such as marshes, floodplains, and ponds. The wrong sluice gate or a wrongly placed wall or culvert brings floodwaters swirling into homes. As the citizens of Chennai know too well from the 2015 floods, small shifts in gradient can make a huge difference to water levels.

Disused Lock, VLC Bridge, Ennore (2017). Photo: Bhavani Raman.

Tamil Nadu's coast is dotted with small blue boards. The raging battle with nature in the city's backyard is in effect part of a war being waged all along India's coasts. How has this landscape come to be, and what imaginaries does it disclose?

The shifting landforms of Ennore integrate features made by ebbing tides, gently flowing rivers, and humans—fishers, salt workers, crabbers, gatherers, and pickers of all kinds who enjoy "use rights" to the waters and its shores. These activities, and hence this landscape, have historically been managed by the conventions of *poramboke*, a Tamil term denoting land that is uncultivated, unassessed, or otherwise not privately owned. Arrangements of usufruct dominate *poramboke*, and are often a point of intense power struggle.

Ennore's salt and fish workers were here before the British canals arrived. An eighteenth-century European map sketches the creeks and settlements on the Madras coast, and locates "Enur" between the sea and the small, unmarked rivers that make up the Kosasthalaiyar drainage system.

About 30 years later, in 1786, the boats and water of Ennore reappeared as a setting for a colonial landscape painting. A painting in the Colin Mackenzie Collection held by the British Library portrays Ennore with the obligatory ruined "choultry," a traveller's rest house, surrounded by trees, glistening waterways, and busy boats. The depiction of Ennore as a place of transit anticipated public works improvements along these *poramboke* watercourses. The British cut new canals and deepened channels to link the backwaters with Pulicat Lake. Boats carried salt from Ennore to faraway Calcutta and Chittagong. Like other manmade plans and imagined futures, this too had a shelf life. Railway lines crossed the creek. From the 1960s, the canal economy dwindled.

Disused waterway, Seppakkam Ashpond, Ennore (2017). Photo: Bhavani Raman.

This shattered infrastructure has since been rewilded. Mangroves, and saline flora combined with the omnipresent but exotic mesquite variety *Prosopis juliflora* (Veli Kaattan) are taking back the lock gates. Mangroves are growing.

Other imaginations endure, sustained by labour or necessity. Ennore's fishers and salt workers continue to fish in the fresh water canals. The remnants of this life still mark borders of the dying river. Freshwater rims the edges underground and feeds the wild grass.

As living by the wetlands becomes increasingly impossible, the peculiar entwining of marine and fresh water flora where sea, river, and land become one is kept alive in the words and imagination of those who did not, or could not, leave. As Nityanand Jayaraman and Pooja Kumar write, the communities in Ennore remember 23 canals or *kaalvai.* The names are a lyrical mix of nature, human, and machine: the deer, yellow machine, broomstick plant. Jamarangal, Karukumaram, Vellamaram, Manjal Machine, Sori Kallu, Maan, Vazhukutharai, Thodappakuchi, Aruvai Munai. Only three Kattur, Eachanchedi, and Karunkali, survive.[4] Seven were submerged by Vallur power plant's 300-acre fly ash dump. This *paraval* or backwater, once rich with fish, crab, and prawn, is now a private shrimp farm. The canals—important *poramboke* fishing grounds—are buried under energy and transport infrastructure. The word *poramboke* holds ambivalent meanings. The Tamil Lexicon describes "*purambōkku*" as land that is uncultivable or set aside for common use. But it also describes the word as meaning "public woman." The Lexicon notes that the verb *purambōkkutal* means "to remove." As with most things in an imagination where the outside operates as the residual category, violence begins with the woman's body and with the right to banish. And yet the ancient Tamil classical poetry of the seashore, *neidal*, reminds us that landscapes inscribe us even as we leave our mark on that which surrounds us. The seashore is a state of mind. It enters us as we recognize the moods of the water. It blooms in us, when we train our eye to that delicate struggle between nature and us. The *neidal* can manifest as an all-out battle. It can also appear in the tone of the *akam* or "in-ness," as the longing for a lover's return. Among the many luminous poems of the seashore, one translated by M. L. Thangappa captures this movingly:[5]

When the waters receded
from the creek
hosts of storks
came down to feast on the lusty fish
in the slushy bed
and perched on the dunes
they moved about
like the king's soldiers
brightly attired.
Go, my friend
and tell my lover
living beyond the creek
that I am wasting away.
And like the holders of the cattle raided
by the king of Mullur
my loveliness is lost.

The earthmovers have come and the bunds walls are enclosing the waters. But landforms change slowly. The saltpans are silent but still visible by satellite. The fly ash cannot obscure the land shaped by centuries of barefoot walking by bent bodies raking salt.

Where the salt and freshwater meet, Ennore (2017). Photo: Bhavani Raman.

Treelines, Ennore (2017). Photo: Bhavani Raman.

The ambit of those who lived with the wetlands is shrinking fast. Roads cut across the water and culverts squeeze flows to rivulets. Tree lines that once marked the boundaries of small fields and let the waters move now lie behind stonewalls. There is no planting.

But those who continue to live here resolutely make life, refusing to yield to the imagination that deems the wetlands to be waste. With no salt to work, no water, no land to maintain or fish to sell, kitchen gardens thrive in *kuruvimēdu* painstakingly handwatered by water brought by tanks and pipes.

Aloe is grown in broken plastic water pots. Jasmine winds over trellises made of salvaged wood and metal. Clothes are hung on lines of leftover wire propped by fallen branches.

Kuruvimedu, Ennore (2017). Photo: Bhavani Raman.

Our fate lies with the fate of the creek and that of the users, keepers, and makers of Ennore's place-words. Our language and our gaze make them invisible to us. As long as we refuse to acknowledge this battle of imaginations, our future also hangs in the balance. As we deplete the ability to denote and imagine particular aspects of our places, to see and hear the wetlands as they call from the canals and the nullahs in our cities, to recognize ways of making life in what we dismiss as waste, we deplete our ability to imagine a different future. The disappearing Ennore creek marks a crisis in our imagination.

1 A version of this essay first appeared in *The Wire* in November 2017.

2 "RTI reveals Chennai's largest estuary Ennore Creek missing in the latest CRZ map," *DNA India* 22 July 2017, see https://www.dnaindia.com/india/report-rti-reveals-chennai-s-largest-estuary-ennore-creek-missing-in-the-latest-crz-map-2510179 (accessed 30 September 2019).

3 "Illegal map used to clear port plan in Ennore creek," *The New Indian Express* 25 July 2017, see http://www.newindianexpress.com/states/tamil-nadu/2017/jul/25/illegal-map-used-to-clear-port-plan-in-ennore-creek-1633204.html (accessed 30 September 2019).

4 "A Venice that no longer is: remembering the canals of north Madras," *The Hindu* 29 August 2017 https://www.thehindu.com/news/cities/chennai/a-venice-that-no-longer-is-remembering-the-canals-of-north-madras/article19577538.ece (accessed 30 September 2019).

5 Kapilar, *Nattrinai* 292, M. L. Thangappa, *Love stands alone* (2010) p. 78.

Phoenix canariensis in Lisbon's new ecologies: a post-phenomenological tracing of a palm tree in a disused gasworks

Daniel Paiva

A dead palm tree in a ruined garden. The top of the tree is cut off. Its trunk is slightly blackened, as if it had burned, and it is surrounded by a green field of grasses and bushes. Its dried-out leaves are still visible under the grasses. The top of the trunk lies upside down behind the dead tree. There are grasses growing inside it. Not far away, the vivacious leaves of a young palm tree stand out in a concrete ditch. Nearby, one can see a couple of slightly older palm trees mixed with other vegetation. Along this area, several young palm trees can be seen facing south on floodable areas near colluviums, walls, and gasometers. Both these scenarios were found at the site of a disused gasworks called Matinha in the eastern part of Lisbon. Most of the site has been demolished, and has remained abandoned for the last two decades. The palm trees shown in the photographs are specimens of *Phoenix canariensis* (Chabaud), a palm tree (family: Arecaceae) endemic to the Canary Islands in the Atlantic Ocean. In this landscape, *Phoenix canariensis* plays multiple roles. It dies alongside the process of ruination of the human constructions of the site but also sprouts among the new ecologies that grow in these vacant lands.

It is my objective to understand how *Phoenix canariensis* has come to participate in the new spontaneous ecologies of the Matinha site. This requires tracing its trajectory in the history of Lisbon's landscape. I understand this tracing as post-phenomenological, meaning that it is attuned to how *Phoenix canariensis* as a body interacts with other bodies in Lisbon's urban ecology, and to the intertwining of biological, cultural, and political matters in the making of Lisbon's contemporary urban landscape. My approach connects the work of art history, politics, and science with insights from ecological studies to explain the performativities of *Phoenix canariensis* in the Matinha landscape that I encountered during fieldwork. I am concerned with how *Phoenix canariensis* is both an object and a subject in the Lisbon landscape. While *Phoenix canariensis* was introduced in Lisbon's urban landscape

Dead *Phoenix canariensis* at the Matinha gasworks site (2018). Photo: Daniel Paiva.

as an object for contemplation, as part of an attempt to engineer an atmosphere of tropical empire, its history also illustrates the role that non-human subjects can play in the transformation of both urban space and culture as their bodies grow, adapt, host, reproduce, and decay.

Palm trees have been present in Portugal for a long time. There is only one native species—*Chamaerops humilis* (Mediterranean dwarf palm)—which is endemic to the Southern Portuguese Algarve region. However, during the Islamic occupation of the Iberian Peninsula (eighth to thirteenth centuries) palm groves were planted in several towns. *Phoenix canariensis* was introduced to mainland Europe in the seventeenth century; its seeds have been found in archaeological sites in Portugal dating from this period.[1] However, the palm tree only became a common feature of the Portuguese urban landscape in the nineteenth century, when it became an important imperial and colonial symbol. Science historian Ana Duarte Rodrigues has shown that the interest in palm trees was initially an economic one.[2] Palm trees such as *Elaeis guineensis* (African oil palm), *Arenga pinnata* (sugar palm), or *Cocus nucifera* (coconut palm) began to be intensively explored in African colonies by the British, Dutch, and Portuguese for the production of oil, starch, coconuts, and fibers. In the case of the Portuguese, the exploration of palm trees in the colonies was mainly done with the exportation of products to other European countries in mind. Interest in palm trees as ornamental plants emerged in the second half of the nineteenth century, linked not only to the appreciation of palm trees as symbols of colonial prosperity, but also to the palm as an esoteric symbol of

Young *Phoenix canariensis* sprouting next to a cemented wall at the Matinha gasworks site (2018). Photo: Daniel Paiva.

exoticism. Rodrigues highlights the research by art historian Katherine Manthorne on the relationship between the rising popularity of palm trees in the nineteenth century and discourses of the epoch on tropical landscapes as paradise. Manthorne notes that the association between tropical landscapes and paradise is not solely due to the beauty of the tropical world; it also stems from the association of the fertility of the tropical landscape with the paradisiacal Garden of Eden.[3] Moreover, the Tree of Life of the Garden of Eden, often associated with the date palm (*Phoenix dactylifera*) in Middle Eastern landscapes, became associated with the coconut palm (*Cocus nucifera*) in South American landscapes during this period. These trees were widely referenced in literary and artistic representations of tropical landscapes up to the nineteenth century.[4]

When first brought to Europe, palm trees were accommodated in large greenhouses, the first and most popular being the one in Kew Gardens, England, constructed in the 1840s. However, palm trees were easily acclimatized in Southern Europe, and quickly became common in the French Riviera. *Phoenix canariensis* became the most popular palm tree species for gardens in the Riviera region between 1870 and 1880. Before long, it was extensively used in regions with similar climates, such as Portugal, or California and Florida in the United States.[5]

Other species of palm trees were also used as ornamental plants in all sorts of spaces in Portugal, including gardens, greenhouses, and streets. However, they were most notoriously used to flank entrance ways to palaces and to line avenues.

In these cases, *Phoenix canariensis* was the most widely used tree, although at least 20 species of palm trees were reportedly acclimatized in outdoor urban settings. Although several of these species of palm trees were native to colonies of the Portuguese Empire, a significant number of palm trees used in urban greening were brought from other parts of the world such as North America, through the networks established between European botanical gardens and horticulturalists. Palm trees remained a common feature of the Portuguese urban landscape during the twentieth century, especially in the capital city Lisbon.

The Estado Novo dictatorship (1933–1974), which placed great emphasis on the colonial project, often used palm trees in major public space projects to convey the unity of Portugal as a multiracial and multicontinental nation.[6] This is exemplified by the Exhibit of the Portuguese World, a large exhibition that took place in 1940 in Belém, located in the western riverside area of Lisbon. The exhibition was intended to portray the modernization of Portugal combined with the cultural identity of Portugal and its expansion in the world. It included a series of themed pavilions in a regenerated public space.[7] Palm trees were ubiquitous in the exhibition, including the public space project. Most notably, the main square of the event was decorated with a line of *Phoenix canariensis*, and the colonial ethnography section was housed in the Colonial Garden (today named the Tropical Garden) which contains a large outdoor collection of palm trees, most notably the species *Phoenix canariensis* and *Washingtonia filifera* (desert fan palm). Moreover, the Brazil pavilion was also partially made from palm tree trunks.[8]

A further emblematic example in Lisbon is the Fonte Luminosa at the Alameda Dom Afonso Henriques, a large fountain and garden inaugurated in 1948 to commemorate the new water supply infrastructure of the eastern part of Lisbon. The fountain contained a number of statues and ceramic icons referencing Portuguese history and mythology.[9] The garden was placed above the fountain, and while the tree species were mainly native, its central piece was a *Phoenix canariensis*.

Throughout the twentieth century, *Phoenix canariensis* appeared in Lisbon's most emblematic public spaces, contributing toward an urban atmosphere of tropical empire. It also became a common species for private and industrial gardens, due to its association with power and economic prosperity. The dead palm tree in Matinha is one of these cases. The Matinha gasworks was one of the main industrial endeavours of Estado Novo's modernization of Lisbon, providing gas for the whole city from coal brought from the colony of Mozambique. The palm tree was planted in the 1940s in a small garden with an arboretum where the gasworks' chief engineer's house was located. As the gasworks' production increased during the 1950s, the house was demolished to give way to additional industrial paraphernalia, but the garden was retained.

Coincidentally, in 1948, *Phoenix canariensis* was reported as naturalized in Portugal.[10] Since then, new palm trees have started appearing in Lisbon near the neglected courtyards of abandoned houses and palaces, especially in the city's periphery. Recent research has discovered that wild *Phoenix canariensis* have been found mainly in "humid colluviums, dry ravines with temporary water flow, or near watercourses, palaeochannels and springs" on the Iberian peninsula.[11] This description matches the landscape of Matinha. In addition to the palm tree in the garden, younger *Phoenix canariensis* would later be planted around some of the gasworks buildings, where the ground is susceptible to flooding. In these conditions, the naturalized *Phoenix canariensis* was able to spread among the new ecologies of these sites in which native and exotic species sprout side by side. However, it was not until the 1990s, when production stopped and demolitions started, that its wild spread in the gasworks site was made possible.

The predilection for palm trees in urban projects in Lisbon persevered past the end of the colonial empire in 1974. In 1998, Lisbon held the World Expo. The theme was "The Ocean." The event was largely a way to reframe the Portuguese expansion in a post-colonial context, by highlighting the economic, technical, and scientific achievements of Portuguese discoveries and expansion, instead of issues related to colonization, extraction, and slavery. Lisbon's largest urban development project in the democratic period—the Parque das Nações—resulted from the reconversion of the event area. Although the public space project emphasized native tree

An avenue of *Phoenix canariensis* at the Campo Grande garden (Lisbon) in the early twentieth century. Source: Arquivo Municipal de Lisboa.

species of the genera *Quercus* and *Pinea*, some areas devoted to the theme of the Portuguese discoveries also contained several types of tropical and Mediterranean palm trees, including *Phoenix canariensis*.[12] After the Parque das Nações project was concluded, the Matinha site was deactivated; it was supposed to be the next large urban reconversion area, but lack of investment hindered the project. The abandoned and devastated landscape of the site, however, has provided a prime location for the *Phoenix canariensis* to spread. The site was very quickly covered by wild vegetation, which attracts many birds to this placid landscape. *Phoenix canariensis* spreads by means of seeds, which are disseminated by the birds that pick up the dates and move them to other parts of the site. Additionally, the colluviums and dry ravines of the site provide excellent conditions for the sprouting of new individuals. Without human intervention, *Phoenix canariensis* participated in the creation of new ecologies and new atmospheres of wildness and abandonment in which native and exotic species sprout side by side.

While new individuals sprouted across the site, the oldest palm tree started to die. Like many others in Lisbon, including emblematic specimens in botanic gardens, historical gardens, and main avenues, it was affected by the arrival of an Asian weevil to the Iberian Peninsula during the 1990s, a consequence of the increasingly intensive and globalized plant trade. This weevil is *Rhynchophorus ferrugineus*, commonly known as the red palm weevil, from the *Curculionoidea* superfamily and the *Dryophthorine* subgroup. It has been considered a *Cocos nucifera* (coconut tree) pest since the beginning of the twentieth century in its native area, which is monsoon Asia, ranging from India to the Philippines. It was also reported in the Mesopotamian region in 1920. However, it was not until the 1970s that it rapidly spread to other geographies, where it has plagued coconut trees but also other palm trees.

The species was first reported in Japan in 1975. In the late 1980s, it was reported in several countries in the Middle East. In this region, it mainly affected *Phoenix dactylifera*, the date palm tree, which is an important agricultural species. Later, in 1994, it was reported in Spain. The species was most likely introduced into Spain through the importation of the ornamental *Phoenix canariensis* and *Phoenix dactylifera*, which were in great demand throughout Southern Europe. Between 1999 and 2011, the species had spread to most countries of the Mediterranean, and it has been found in farther sites such as the Caribbean, China, and Australia. The species spread slowly in the north Mediterranean until 2004, but since then its expansion has been remarkable.[13] The species was first reported in the south of Portugal in 2007 and it has since spread to the whole country.[14] *Rhynchophorus ferrugineus* became a regulated quarantined pest in the European Union in the same year, which means it was acknowledged as a pest in some member states and that measures to control its spread were enforced. Since then, palm trees have been subject to strict regulations regarding importation and commercialization.[15]

Most host plants of *Rhynchophorus ferrugineus* belong to the palm tree subfamilies *Arecoideae* and *Coryphoideae*, but the weevil has also been reported in species other than palm trees such as *Agave americana* (American aloe) or *Saccharum* sp. (sugar canes) Some palm trees species are less susceptible to the weevil, such as *C. humilis, W. filifera, W. robusta* (Mexican fan palm), or *T. fortunei* (Chinese windmill palm).[16] Consequently, these have been increasingly used as ornamental trees in Lisbon over the last two decades.

The spread of *Rhynchophorus ferrugineus* is related to the difficulty in observing its presence, as the weevil spends its entire life cycle on the host plant, and often at the top of large tall plants. The *Phoenix canariensis* not only houses the *Rhynchophorus ferrugineus*, but also allows the weevil to withstand Lisbon's Mediterranean winter. *The Rhynchophorus ferrugineus* can tolerate temperatures as low as 4.5 degrees Celsius. During January—the coldest month in Lisbon—it is common for temperatures to fall below this limit during the night, but as the weevil spends its entire life cycle deeply inside the tree, the living tissues of the plant protect the weevil's premature stages from the coldest periods, maintaining a temperature higher than that of the air. It is extremely rare for the interior of palm trees to reach temperatures below 4.5 degrees Celsius, and the plant's reaction to infestation, coupled with local warming due to the concentration of weevils, reinforces this thermal protection.[17] Despite this, Lisbon's Mediterranean climate does slow down the life cycle of the weevil; it has been reported that its life cycle can be completed in just 45 days in the Philippines, whereas in Spain it lasts at least 139 days.[18]

The weevil *Rhynchophorus ferrugineus* has had a profound impact on Lisbon's landscape, as a great number of palm trees across the city have perished due to it. The imperial landscapes of Lisbon, some of them already facing the material decay of their buildings, are now faced with the quite visible death of their symbol of prosperity. In Matinha's old garden, the *Phoenix canariensis* persevered until the twenty-first century, but it was unable to spread due to the dry concrete ground. Eventually, it was affected by the weevil, which infiltrated the tree, lived in it, and fed off it, eventually leading to its death, with the weevil still protected from the cold by the shelter provided within the trunk. While this specific palm tree and several others in Lisbon have died, or have been cut down for safety reasons at some point, there are afterlives. In Matinha, the dead *Phoenix canariensis* trunk is slowly being covered by epiphytes, mostly *Oxalis pes-caprae* (also known as sourgrass or Bermuda buttercup), which are dyeing it green.

The long history of *Phoenix canariensis* in Lisbon is materialized in the abandoned landscape of Matinha, which is a sort of accumulation of atmospheres and subjectivities. By this, I mean that the atmosphere of Matinha emanates the affectivity of different historical and political periods: the nineteenth-century imperial project, the early twentieth century nationalist dictatorship, and the late twentieth century abandonment of the industrial areas of the city. While the landscape of Matinha was constructed by human subjects during the period when the gasworks was active, the landscape has been transformed by non-human subjects since its deactivation. As the bodies of new *Phoenix canariensis* reproduced and grew, and the old body of the first palm tree hosted the parasitic *Rhynchophorus ferrugineus* and died, the material transformations of the landscape that the palm tree and the weevil instituted had profound consequences for the atmosphere of the factory.

No longer a site of colonial and industrial economic prosperity, the landscape of Matinha now speaks of the material and biological ruination of the past, but also of the emergent ecologies of cities in a globalized world. The *Phoenix canariensis*, once a symbol and an object for contemplation, now plays multiple roles in these new ecologies of Lisbon's abandoned sites, where human, vegetal, and animal subjectivities coexist and co-generate atmospheres that are at once biological, cultural, and political.

1 Paula F. Queiroz, Jose E. Mateus, and Jose P. Ruas, Santa Clara-a-Velha: o quotidiano para além da ruína—Frutos e sementes recolhidos nos trabalhos de escavação arqueológica (1996–2001): Trabalhos do CIPA nº. 111 (Lisboa: Instituto Português de Arqueologia, 2007).

2 Ana D. Rodrigues, "Between usefulness and ornamentation: palm trees in the Portuguese empire in the second half of the nineteenth-century," in Maria J. Castro, ed., *Empire and colonial art: an anthology of essays* (Lisbon: ArtTravel, 2017), pp. 209–232.

3 Katherine Manthorne, "The quest for a tropical paradise: palm tree as fact and symbol in Latin American Landscape Imagery, 1850–1875," *Art Journal* 44 (4) (1984) pp. 374–382.

4 Ana D. Rodrigues, "Humboldt's trip to South America and a new idea of landscape: its impact on Eschwege," *Memorias* 25 (2015) pp. 104–143; A.D. Rodrigues, "Brazilian landscape perception through literary sources (16th–18th centuries)," in José Vicente Serrão, Bárbara Direito, Eugénia Rodrigues, and Susana Münch Miranda, eds., *Property rights, land and territory in the European overseas empires* (Lisbon: CEHC-IUL, 2014), pp. 31–34.

5 Jared Farmer, *Trees in paradise: a California history* (New York and London: W. W. Norton & Company, 2013).

6 In Portuguese, "nação pluricontinental e multirracial," as defined by the 1930 Colonial Act. See C. Castelo, "'Novos Brasis' em África: desenvolvimento e colonialismo português tardio," *Varia Historia* (30) (2014) pp. 507–532.

7 Aquilino Machado, *Os espaços públicos da exposição do mundo português e da Expo 98* (Lisbon: Parque Expo 98, 2006).

8 Margarida Acciaiuoli, *Exposições do Estado Novo 1934/1940* (Lisbon: Livros Horizonte, 1998).

9 Jakob Hartmann, "Visual politics of the Estado Novo realized on the Alameda Dom Afonso Henriques in Lisbon. The construction of ideal citizenship?," *Revista de História de Arte* (11) (2014) pp. 291–303.

10 Joao Domingues de Almeida and Helena Freitas, "Exotic naturalized flora of continental Portugal: a reassessment," *Botanica Complutensis* (30) (2006) pp. 117–130.

11 C. Obón, D. Rivera, F. Alcaraz, E. Carreño, S. Ríos, E. Laguna, J. Sánchez-Balibrea, M. del Arco, E. Bergmeier, and D. Johnson, "What are palm groves of Phoenix? Conservation of Phoenix palm groves in the European Union," *Biodiversity and Conservation* 27 (8) (2018) p. 1915.

12 Machado, "Os espaços."

13 M. Ferry and S. Gómez, "The red palm weevil in the Mediterranean area," *Palms* 46 (4) (2002) pp. 172–178; J.R. Faleiro, "A review of the issues and management of the red palm weevil Rhynchophorus ferrugineus (Coleoptera: Rhynchophoridae) in coconut and date palm during the last one hundred years," *International Journal of Tropical Insect Science* 26 (3) (2006) pp. 135–154; A. El-Sabea, J. R Faleiro, and M. Abo-El-Saad, "The threat of red palm weevil *Rhynchophorus ferrugineus* to date plantations of the Gulf region in the Middle East: an economic perspective," *Outlooks on Pest Management* 20 (3) (2009) pp. 131–134; O. Dembilio and J.A. Jacas, "Basic bio-ecological parameters of the invasive red palm weevil, *Rhynchophorus ferrugineus* (Coleoptera: Curculionidae), in *Phoenix canariensis* under Mediterranean climate," *Bulletin*

of Entomological Research (101) (2011) pp. 153–163; Didier Rochat, Oscar Dembilio, Josep Jaques, Pompeo Suma, Alessandra La Pergola, Rachid Hamidi, Dimitris Kontodimas, and Victoria Soroker, "*Rhynchophorus ferrugineus*: taxonomy, distribution, biology, and life cycle," in Victoria Soroker and Stefano Colazza, eds., *Handbook of major palm pests: biology and management* (London: Wiley, 2017) pp. 69–104.

14 EPPO (European and Mediterranean Plant Protection Organization) Reporting Service, 2008. First Report of *Rhynchophorus ferrugineus* in Portugal. 2008/022, No. 2; C. Soares, J.E. Fernandes, N. Ramos, A. Pacheco, and C. Boavida, *Rhynchophorus ferrugineus (Olivier) uma nova praga da palmeira em Portugal* (Lisbon, DGADR, 2008).

15 EC, Commission Decision 200773657EC on emergency measures against the introduction and spread within the EU of *R. ferrugineus* (Olivier) (notified under document number C (2007) 2161), European Commission, Brussels. *Official Journal of the European Union* (L:139) (2007): 24–27.

16 Rochet et al., "*Rhynchophorus ferrugineus.*"

17 Rochet et al., "*Rhynchophorus ferrugineus.*"

18 Faleiro, "A review."

Urban plants and colonial durabilities

Henrik Ernstson

The long legacy of colonization that is rooted in how plants are known is mostly out of sight.[1] The earliest memories of plant knowledge I remember from growing up in a working-class Swedish town is a botanical field book that was sometimes thrown into the *Kånken* back pack (long before that item became a world brand) as I joined the past-time adventure of the young group of *Frilufsare* ("free-strollers") led by my father and his friend. While I was not particularly interested in plant life, encountering the detailed hand-drawn images and the names of the flowers enticed me because of their detail, order, and overview.

At times, however, the colonial legacy of botany becomes all too apparent. While making the film *One Table Two Elephants* (2018) with my colleague Jacob von Heland, we followed a group of amateur botanists up Elsie's Peak on the Cape Peninsula, lying south of the city of Cape Town.[2] It was not a very arduous walk, and Pat Holmes, Biophysical Specialist of the City of Cape Town, had invited us to join her Botanical Society group. This was part of the leisure walks to popularize botanical and ecological knowledge that she has guided over the last 30 years or so, ever since she first arrived at the Cape from Scotland. A very knowledgeable, commanding woman with a joy and care for plants, she led our little party of five middle-aged and elderly women, all of us with different backgrounds—one of Italian descent, one Australian, and three English South Africans. Walking through gusty winds but pleasant sunshine, we made our way towards the peak, Pat stopping us every now and then to point out different plants, giving their Latin and popular English names before continuing with Jacob, myself, our photographer Johan (also from Sweden), and sound engineer Jonathan (South African) into tow. Closer to the top, our guide happens to meet an old friend. An elderly South African lady with a British accent greets us with a brisk smile. It becomes apparent that she used to work as a guide at the world-renowned Kirstenbosch Botanical Garden, located on the slopes of Table Mountain in the very affluent areas between Tokai, Constantia, and Kirstenbosch. She is enthralled by our film's focus on describing different ways of knowing urban nature in Cape Town, and we ask if we can film her and her company. She agrees, and provides us with a little lecture about our countryman Carl Thunberg, an "apostle" of the great eighteenth-century Swedish botanist Carl

Linnaeus. She informs us that Thunberg arrived in the Cape in 1772, a full century after the Dutch East India Company had built a fort there, and says: "He learnt Dutch, or our version of Dutch, then." Turning to Pat, she asks rhetorically, "How many Ericas did he discover? Two hundred, three hundred Ericas [which is a family of indigenous flowers, Ericaceae]." And, in summing up, she adds: "He [then] went off to Japan. Having become the Father of South African botany, he became the Father of Japanese botany [as well]."[3]

This was a harmless, even pleasant encounter. It was great material for the film, as it so effectively, in a short span of a few minutes, introduced the genealogy of a particular way of knowing plants, one based in a Western colonial adventure and a geography of expansion and control, not just of lands, resources, and people—but of knowledge too. Certainly, our own white maleness, the camera and microphone at hand, and, on top of this, the fact that we were Swedes (with myself having lived and worked in Cape Town for seven years) played a complicit role in the performance of this story.

However, it points towards a more general argument that is often forgotten when the history of urban ecology and "urban nature knowledge" is written up. The now taken-for-granted version of this history is one where modern urban ecology emerged in West Berlin in the 1950s around Herbert Sukopp, or possibly with Paul Jovet in 1930s Paris.[4] It then exploded and expanded rapidly in the late 1990s in the big cities of the USA and Europe, where it became couched in the widely ambitious but quite amorphous "complex systems" theory, followed by efforts to consolidate urban ecology as that global, even planetary knowledge project for urban sustainability that it strives to represent today.[5] But, there is a lack of knowledge of how colonial and imperial forms of science influenced urban botany, how it became constituted within expanding European powers, settler colonial societies, and racial capitalism. Few have asked: What are the remnants of colonialism, if any, within urban ecology and urban environmental knowledge today?

Historians have taken an increasing interest in studying botany as an imperial science in the early modern period. This has included investigations into how "race" emerged from botany—featuring for instance Linnaeus' simplistic "[skin-]colour scheme" of "human varieties" from 1735[6]—and studies of "colonial botany," which is defined by Schiebinger and Swan as "the study, naming, cultivation, and marketing of plants" that intimately supported and emerged from "European voyages, conquests, global trade, and scientific exploration" in the eighteenth-century.[7] There is, however, little explicit focus in this literature on the role of cities and urban processes in the emergence of this colonial science. Closer to the field of urban ecology, and more recently, there have been calls to decolonize urban ecology, drawing on land disputes and collaborative conservation practices in urban areas in Australia, Canada, and South Africa.[8] These have sought to push beyond the recognition of how botany, rather than being a simple "European" construction, has always drawn upon and exploited indigenous knowledge for its own benefits.[9]

The focus here, in this short essay, is to trace a very particular colonial legacy of botanical knowledge in settler colonies. I will draw on a few ethnographical observations to sketch out an analysis of the performative role in social and cultural terms that botanical knowledge has in contemporary Cape Town, and I will argue that this comes from botany's longer genealogy as an imperial and colonial science.[10] This argument is based on how botany became deeply lodged within the settler colony, enmeshed with white elite and middle-class associations and pastime habits, especially in the Western Cape,[11] which still structures social relations and imaginaries and conditions how urban nature can be conceived, engaged, and known. This is despite the victory of the Black liberation movement in the 1990s, and despite botany's more modern and contemporary forms within ecology, conservation, and biodiversity protection. Starting with the scene at Elsie's Peak, I want to use South African historian Premesh Lalu's notion of the "settler public sphere"[12] to outline how the residues of racism and colonialism within botanical knowledge have travelled into present Cape Town as something akin to what Ann Laura Stoler calls "duress" or "imperial durabilities in our time":

> Colonial pasts, the narratives recounted about them, the unspoken distinctions they continue to "cue," the affective charges they reactivate, and the implicit "lessons" they are mobilized to impart are sometimes so ineffably threaded through the fabric of contemporary life forms they seem indiscernible as distinct effects, as if everywhere and nowhere at all.[13]

For Lalu, this quality that colonial pasts have of being "threaded through the fabric" of social life without their genealogy being recognized or called into account can be traced to how the constitution of a normalized order emerged in settler colonies. This included how to view the natural world—and, clearly, also the issue of racial superiority. In his book *The Deaths of Hintsa*, which questions the colonial archives as modes of evidence and seeks a new approach to writing history in post-apartheid times, Lalu recounts the formation of a settler town that lies within what is still known as the Eastern Cape. After decades of warfare with the Khosa people, British settlers arrive by boat to create an English town in Africa, a sphere of civility founded upon—but effectively also silencing, rendering uncodifiable—the social, epistemic, and physical violence of the frontier wars, including the original (and economic) crime of stealing land. Certain qualities of the foundation of living together in community among the settlers could not be represented within this settler public sphere. In Fanon's words, this circumstance structures a Manichean world and "produces the colonised subject as incomplete, as not quite a subject."[14] This settler public sphere expanded in physical and territorial forms—towns, farms, and sugar plantations, and later factories and cities, as well as social and epistemic forms—to develop a particular foundation for representing agency and ways of knowing the world. Only white settlers were properly capable of agency, thought, and knowing.

The argument here is that when we approach "the botanical city," and urban ecology more broadly, these histories of and histories from settler colonies become a

A meeting on Elsie's Peak, Cape Peninsula, with a woman who formerly worked as a guide at Kirstenbosch Botanical Gardens, February 2015. Photo (cropped) taken from the film *One Table Two Elephants* (Von Heland and Ernstson 2018).
Photo: Johan von Reybekiel.

springboard for a different reading of the archives of botany and its mode of evidence. Who were the people travelling and ordaining the ways of knowing plants? How were the original strata created upon which the scientific means of producing global urban ecological knowledge are constructed today? What was the constitutive outside to this knowledge structure and its mode of evidence? Given the constraints of a short essay, I will focus on the third question: on the constitutive outside of the botanical city. That is, I will focus on understanding how botanical knowledge has been structured by that which has been rendered invisible.[15] The argument I will outline is that botanical knowledge has travelled as the remnant of a settler public sphere, functioning as one form of "civil" knowledge (among others) that talks about the world while hiding away violence, inequality, and subaltern histories. Within its realms, in talking about plants, wildlife, and "the environment," we can all come together and "be civil," rendering silent that which divides us. In order to do so, and drawing on a post-colonial tactic to situate the telling of the world from a particular place, I will not provide a "global" overview. Instead, I will continue with two shorter and contrasting stories from Cape Town, both of them taken from my field notes from some years back.

First story: just before Kelvin Cochrane, a baker born in 1960s Cape Town, receives his award at the Kirstenbosch Botanical Garden in 2009, he turns to me, a person he has known as a researcher for about two years, and says: "Last time I was here they would not let me in because I was not white. And see today, the only coloured people here are those serving us." Kelvin's relationship to the location of the venue, the botanical garden, and to the Wildlife Association of South Africa that has awarded him a distinction for being an "environmental champion," is fraught with uneasy and complicated tensions. Indeed, the main reason that Kelvin has been invited lies in his tireless work in his Grassy Park neighbourhood.[16] There he has mobilized people, resources, and spaces to re-plant indigenous *fynbos*, a low growing bush-vegetation[17] known since imperial botany and Linnaeus's days as highly diverse and now under threat from urban development and faster-growing introduced species like Port Jackson wattle (*Acacia saligna*), but also pine and gum tree, all imported from Australia under British colonization.[18]

This civic-led ecological rehabilitation project is novel, mobilizing at wetlands and community parks on Cape Flats, the vast expanse of land onto which the apartheid state forcefully displaced all non-whites from the historical city centre, starting in the 1950s. Now an "environmental champion" and recipient of an award from the Wildlife Association (a few years later, he also received a prize in Johannesburg live on television as an "environmental steward"), Kelvin's comment on that day recognized the spatial and racial legacies of his city and the traditional whiteness of environmentalism in South Africa.[19] More importantly for this essay, it shone a light on the constitutive outside of this meeting—that the same people of colour who were marginalized then are still marginalized now. While certain things had changed and transformed, other things remained more or less the same.

The active remains here of a settler public sphere—the constitutive outside of the botanical city—only become visible if we view this scene from an oblique angle. The extending of recognition to a person of colour in the form of a prize, couched within a green sentiment of caring for the city's plants and wildlife, is far more than that. It *also* smacks of "connectivities to those colonial histories that bear on the present [and which] can escape scrutiny."[20] It is not the prize that should be in focus here, but the stage from whence the gesture of giving a prize comes. Once again, it is a settler colonial institution that invites the other and provides recognition. The structuration of this stage, the institution from which it draws its own recognition and privilege has little to do with plants, wildlife, or environmental concerns. Rather, as critically developed by South African environmental historian Lance van Sittert, the building and the botanical garden that had been constructed along the foothills of the majestic Table Mountain in 1913 *also* represented the physical codification of the home and sanctity of elite and middle-class British white families.[21] Within these walls, then connected to Imperial and later to Commonwealth networks of botanical knowledge, and today connected to wealthy international tourist flows, Kelvin became recognized as a "good environmentalist."[22] Based on the logic from within this sphere of civility (a durability I would claim comes from the past), he had proven his worth and could be let in.

Although the award was not unimportant to Kelvin, it also represented, as I saw it (and also as he sometimes saw it), a way of policing his efforts, placing it within a particular way of thinking about environmentalism, specifically a way that had a lot to do with plants and little to do with social transformation and addressing root causes to injustices. In fact, only a portion of the mobilizing that Kelvin and others had been involved in was about the plants or the wetland. Instead, it used creative forms of mobilizing memories of oppression through planting indigenous fynbos plants, as a way to stake a political claim beyond mere environmentalism, a claim that "we are still here";[23] our schools still lack resources, unemployment is still high, the racialized segregation is still intact, and *our* history and claim to this city are still ignored. Viewed from this subaltern basis of reasoning, the award ceremony was *also* a way of disciplining subaltern agency, enrolling an environmentalist of colour within an established configuration of how to handle the environment while excluding his wider social and political motivations and reasoning. This is how the settler public sphere operates.

My second story (from a couple of years after the award ceremony): in a full-page advert that depicted sad faces painted at the end of logged pine trees, the "Shout for Shade" group entered the Capetonian public sphere in 2010, as part of the debate on whether to chop down pine and gum trees or to rehabilitate fynbos shrub vegetation at the Cecilia Forest on Table Mountain.[24] Pouring out their discontent with how they had been treated by conservation biologists employed by the South African National Biodiversity Institute (SANBI) at Kirstenbosch (or the "fynbos fanatics" as they were nicknamed by the campaign), the advert helped to create an image of two groups at loggerheads in their opinion of what was of value at Cecilia: trees for shade, or fynbos for biodiversity, and whether the site was to be called a "forest" or a "park."

Although the advert to some extent caricatured the conflict that had been ongoing for years, it provides another aspect of how the settler public sphere travels as a remnant within botanical and environmental knowledge. While on the surface it can be seen as a heated dispute over the use of mountain land for *these* plants in preference to *those* (apparently aligning Kelvin with the "fynbos fanatics"), it also constitutes the staging of privilege, which makes plants, both indigenous fynbos and "alien" trees, into props. In this case, the love for trees can be explained by the establishment of forest plantations between 1884 and 1902, with Cecilia being one of the last remaining plantations.[25] This included roads and "zigzag cross-paths-cum-firebreaks" making the mountain and the growing forests on its lower reaches accessible to a wider white elite and middle class who used it for leisure hikes, dog walks, and horse riding.[26] Growing up and using these forests over generations, exclusively surrounded by wealthy areas classified whites-only under apartheid, forged a strong sense of place between elites and the trees, which fynbos conservationists at SANBI now had to contend with. With verbal tirades that framed "a bureaucratic minority [referring to the Table Mountain National Park and conservation botanists] as imposing their will on the majority of the public [those supporting trees for shade]," the high-octane dispute peaked in 2011 in leading newspapers, local magazines, and social forums (but was back again in 2016) and with the mayor of Cape Town weighing in to settle it through a public participation process.[27] The outcome in 2011 was that most of the ("alien") trees in a 600-hectare area were allowed to be felled by commercial companies, but a "transition area" with non-invasive pine and indigenous Afro-montane trees to provide shadow was introduced, covering only 8 percent of the area.[28]

The important thing here is how this dispute lays open another enduring aspect of the settler public sphere, and how botanical knowledge plays a clear role in its constitution. From an oblique view, what is *not* important are the plants and the associated arguments and counter-arguments, but rather the stage that this

Workers taking a rest at Kirstenbosch Botanical Gardens in February 2015. Photo (cropped) taken from the film *One Table Two Elephants* (Von Heland and Ernstson 2018). Photo: Johan von Reybekiel.

Image of felled trees at Cecilia Forest/Park, which lies close to Constantia Nek on Rhodes Drive, Cape Town. The image was published as part of a media campaign with the attached message "It's too late to cry about the trees. It's time to shout for shade." Published as an advert (cropped) in *Cape Times*, 11 March 2011.

dispute launches into the contemporary public sphere and how this performs and distributes expertise about plants, but also of governance and civic duties. The contenders are all privileged in one way or another. Those shouting for shade, claiming to represent "the public," are clearly so. Easily funding a full-page ad in the leading newspaper, most would be among the top-10-percent earners of the city. The fynbos conservationists, more mellow in their responses, represent leading institutions and the knowledge expertise that structures the debate, most originating from a higher education system that still privilege whiteness. Reading through the news articles from 2005 to 2011, one gets a sense that feelings at times boil over. However, what this debate is *not* about—or, to put it more strongly, what it crowds or blocks out—are the underlying historical relations that made this way of reasoning and feeling about plants, trees, and the mountain possible.

Here we are approaching something that is extremely difficult to lay bare, while this conflict can be seen as a nuisance within the wider context of attempts to transform an unjust city. Really, why should anybody care about these rich folks? However, what this dispute does indeed do, its discursive work, is to pull the struggle of Kelvin at Cape Flats into the same governmental field of biodiversity protection and fynbos conservation that tends to map disputes onto cartographical and spatial distributions of plants, effectively cutting off the social world from what is being known, the plants. The remnant, the enduring aspect of colonial and imperial science that resides in botany is complicit in this alignment. It offers no resistance, makes no taxonomic distinction as to whether plants grow among the wealthy or among the poor. As imperial science, it suited the settler colony not only because it provided early schemes for "race" or "human varieties,"[29] but also because it functioned as a cultural code within a sphere of civility that was incapable of registering the violence upon which itself and the settler public sphere was founded. It is the durability of this cultural quality of muteness in relation to racialized and capitalist violence that has travelled into contemporary debates about urban biodiversity protection in today's Cape Town.

This has, in conclusion, wider purchase on how to critically approach "the botanical city," or for that matter any naturalization of the social. The botanical city is not simply a city full of plants, or a city where plant life is taken more seriously in order to somehow secure biodiversity or other high-held ideals. Rather, it should *also* be read in terms of how it underpins a still racialized order of the city. After all, if Kelvin's award-winning ceremony was enshrined within the durabilities of a settler public sphere, one dressed up in botanical knowledge and a care for plants, it was his way of speaking, his tongue, and his historical experience as somebody of "mixed-race" descent that was being simultaneously enrolled and excluded from botanical knowledge in the handing-over of the prize. The constitutive outside of Kirstenbosch and its enshrinement of botanical knowledge from elite and middle-class British amateurs and professionals became, if not apparent to everybody, at least uncannily present as a ghost. As the field of botanical knowledge in cities and elsewhere moves on, coded as biodiversity maps or as ecosystem services calculations, the tracing of enduring colonialism in the structuring of urban knowledge is crucial. So, however, is the search for "epistemic rupture."[30] Indeed, the epistemic rupture that Lalu is directing us to search for cannot spring from within the archives of botany, or from within the settler public sphere that evolved alongside botany, biology, or ecology. Instead we need to cast a wider net across wider epistemologies to construct decolonial and emancipatory practices capable of writing new beginnings and finding alternative origins for ways of knowing urban nature.

1 I am grateful to Jacob von Heland, my filming-and-thinking partner and colleague, for continuously enriching my research practice and for our many discussions over the years, which have shaped part of this essay. This essay also benefitted from the people of Cape Town, who have for a long time shared their understanding of the city and its relationship to plants. I also acknowledge the support from the following research grants: *Towards a Visual Environmental Humanities* (VEH; PI J. von Heland) funded by the Swedish Research Council Formas; and *Grounding and Worlding Urban Infrastructures* (GROWL; PI H. Ernstson) funded by the AXA Research Foundation.

2 Jacob von Heland and Henrik Ernstson, *One Table Two Elephants* (84 min, 2018), World Premiere at CPH:DOX, Copenhagen International Film Festival, 2018.

3 Quotes and the scene described here are found 22 minutes and 22 seconds into the film *One Table Two Elephants* (Von Heland and Ernstson 2018). Carl Thunberg published several major works, including *Flora Capensis* (1807) and *Flora Japonica* (1784).

4 See my own contribution in Henrik Ernstson and Sverker Sörlin, "Toward comparative urban environmentalism," in Henrik Ernstson and Sverker Sörlin, eds., *Grounding urban natures: histories and futures of urban ecologies* (London and Cambridge, MA: MIT Press, 2019) pp. 3–53. There we are drawing on, amongst others: Herbert Sukopp, "On the early history of urban ecology in Europe," in *Preslia, Praha* 74 (2002) pp. 373–393; Jens Lachmund, *Greening Berlin: the co-production of science, politics and urban nature* (London and Cambridge, MA: MIT Press, 2013); and Matthew Gandy, "Marginalia: aesthetics, ecology, and urban wastelands," *Annals of the Association of American Geographers* 103 (2013) pp. 1301–1316. Sukopp (2002, 374) points out much earlier examples of urban botany with floral studies of ruins and walls in Rome, Poitiers, Palestine, and Algeria.

5 Ernstson and Sörlin, "Toward comparative urban environmentalism." For a good example on how urban ecology has become touted as planetary science, see the edited volume by Thomas Elmqvist, Xuemei Bai, Niki Frantzeskaki, and Corrie Griffith, et al., *Urban planet: knowledge towards sustainable cities* (Cambridge: Cambridge University Press, 2018).

6 As demonstrated by Müller-Wille, Linnaeus's main preoccupation was with plants, but he refined and reworked his "human varieties" schema throughout his life, while being notoriously unclear as to who and what he based his scheme on. See Staffan Müller-Willie, "Linnaeus and the four corners of the world," in K.A. Coles, R. Bauer, Z. Nunes, and C.L. Peterson, eds., *The cultural politics of blood, 1500–1900* (London: Palgrave Macmillan, 2005) pp. 191–209.

7 Londa Schiebinger and Claudia Swan, eds., *Colonial botany: science, commerce, and politics in the early modern world* (Philadelphia: University of Pennsylvania Press, 2005) p. 2. For similar historical investigations, see also António Lafuente and Nuria Valverde, "Linnaean botany and Spanish imperial biopolitics," in Schiebinger and Swan *Colonial botany* pp. 134–47; Paula De Vos, "The science of spices: empiricism and economic botany in the Early Spanish Empire," in *Journal of World History* 17 (4) (2007) pp. 399–427; Jim Endersby, *Imperial nature: practices of Victorian science* (Chicago: University of Chicago Press, 2008).

8 See Michael Simpson and Jen Bagelman, "Decolonizing urban political ecologies: the production of nature in settler colonial cities," *Annals of the American Association of Geographers* 108 (2) (2018) pp. 558–568; Marnie Graham, "Postcolonial nature conservation in practice: the everyday challenges of on-ground urban nature conservation, Cape Town, South Africa," in *GeoJournal* 82 (2015) pp. 43–62; Von Heland and Ernstson (2018). See also Harry Garuba, "On animism, modernity/colonialism, and the African order of knowledge: provisional reflections," in *E-Flux Journal* 36 (2012 pp. 1–9; Lesley Green, "The changing of the gods of reason: Cecil John Rhodes, Karoo fracking and the decolonizing of the Anthropocene." *E-Flux Journal* 65 (2015) pp. 1–9.

9 For Cape Town and Western Cape, see Lance van Sittert, "The intimate politics of the Cape Floral Kingdom," in *South African Journal of Science* 106 (3/4) (2010) pp. 3–5. See also: Richard Drayton, "Science and the European empires," in *The Journal of Imperial and Commonwealth History* 23 (3) (1995) pp. 503–510.

10 Botany and biology, as the study of plants, and of their evolution and interactions with the physical environment, has a long career in South Africa, with intimate although not always explicit links to colonial and racialized discourse and planning. See Anker's (2001) treatment of the South African Union's first president Jan Smuts, who was a grassland ecologist, and more recent critiques of "eco-gated communities" by Ballard and Jones (2011). See Peder Anker, *Imperial ecology: environmental order in the British Empire, 1895-1945* (London and Cambridge, MA: Harvard University Press, 2001); Richard Ballard and Gareth A. Jones, "Natural neighbors: indigenous landscapes and eco-estates in Durban, South Africa," *Annals of the Association of American Geographers* 101(1) (2011) pp. 131–48.

11 This has been explored in-depth by environmental historian Lance van Sittert at the University of Cape Town; see Lance van Sittert, "From mere 'weeds' and 'bosjes' to a Cape Floral Kingdom: the re-imagining of indigenous flora at the Cape," in *Kronos* 28 (2002), 102–26; "The bourgeois eye aloft: Table Mountain in the Anglo urban middle class imagination, c. 1891–1952" in *Kronos* 2(2) (2003), 161–90; "Elbows over the fence: Rondevlei and the invention of community-based conservation in Apartheid Cape Town," in *Grounding urban natures,* ed. Henrik Ernstson and Sverker Sörlin (London and Cambridge, MA: MIT Press, 2019) pp. 277–302.

12 Premesh Lalu, *The deaths of Hintsa: post-apartheid South Africa and the shape of recurring pasts* (Cape Town: HSRC Press, 2009).

13 Ann Laura Stoler, *Duress: imperial durabilities in our times* (Durham and London: Duke University Press, 2016) p. 5.

14 Lalu, *The deaths of Hintsa* p. 265.

15 I here take the term "constitutive outside" from my reading of Lalu (2009), who himself does not use the term. Similar notions can be found in feminist, Marxist, and postcolonial theory, for instance in Silvia Federici, *Caliban and the witch: women, the body, and primitive accumulation* (New York: Autonomedia, 2004). I am of course also inspired by Jacques Rancière's *The politics of aesthetics: the distribution of the sensible* (London: Continuum, 2004).

16 Henrik Ernstson, "Re-translating nature in post-apartheid Cape Town: the material semiotics of people and plants at Bottom Road," in Richard Heeks, ed., *Actor-network theory for development* (Manchester: Institute for Development Policy and Management, University of Manchester, 2013), paper 4.

17 *Fynbos* is a vegetation type that contains highly endemic and species rich shrub and heath plants that dominate the mountains and coastal forelands of the Cape Province in Southern Africa, sometimes referred to as the Fynbos Biome or the Cape Floristic Region. It contains some 8,700 species, with up to two thirds endemic to the region. Table Mountain itself is said to support some 2,200 species, which is higher than the number of species found on the entire British Isles. A significant number of fynbos species grow in only a few local settings, mainly due to specific soil types (from quartzitic sandstone and limestone soil), making it a challenge for conservation. Over a thousand species are deemed threatened with extinction, and many of these are found within a fast-growing Cape Town. The main factors governing vegetation spread and reproduction are fire, soil types, introduced species, and human use of land.

Fynbos is divided in five key families: Ericaceae, Restionaceae, Proteaceae, Rutaceae and Iridaceae. For accounts by biologists and conservation ecologists: Richard Cowling, *The ecology of fynbos: nutrients, fire and diversity* (Cape Town: Oxford University Press, 1992); Anthony Rebelo, Pat M. Holmes, C. Dorse, and J. Wood. "Impacts of urbanization in a biodiversity hotspot: conservation challenges in metropolitan Cape Town," *South African Journal of Botany* 77 (1) (2011) pp. 20–35.

18 Van Sittert "The intimate politics of the Cape Floral Kingdom."

19 While Kelvin and many others have shown of course that environmental issues can be articulated from various subject positions and identities, and linked to race and class divides, nature conservation and the caring for plants have historically in the Western Cape and South Africa been dominated by descendants of white English settlers. This includes State and civil society organizations such as SANBI, WESSA, Botanical Society, and Kirstenbosch Botanical Gardens. For nature conservation's articulation with white identity in South Africa during nineteenth and twentieth centuries, see in particular Van Sittert (2002, 2003, 2019), but also Anker (2001).

20 Stoler, *Duress* p. 5.

21 Van Sittert, "The bourgeois eye aloft."

22 I sense a certain ironic resemblance here to the phrase "a good Indian," stated, apparently in another settler society around 1869.

23 Ernstson 2013; Von Heland and Ernstson 2018. See also Henrik Ernstson, "The political nature of urban wetlands: speaking from Princess Vlei Wetland, Cape Town," in *Urban Studies* 2 (2014) pp. 2–5; Hanna Erixon Aalto and Henrik Ernstson, "Of plants, high lines and horses: civic groups and designers in the relational articulation of values of urban natures," *Landscape and Urban Planning* 157 (2017) pp. 309–321.

24 For details on this case study, I draw on my former student's work: Jessica Rattle, "Ways of knowing nature: conflicting notions of land use and ecosystem services in Cecilia Forest, Cape Town" (Cape Town: Environmental and Geographical Science Department, University of Cape Town, unpublished honors degree thesis, 2011).

25 Van Sittert, "The bourgeois eye aloft" p. 171.

26 Ibid., 171.

27 Quote from "TMNP barking up the wrong tree," https://www.iol.co.za/capeargus/letter-tmnp-barking-up-the-wrong-tree-2065144, written by Shout for Shade protagonists and published 6 September 2016 in Cape Argus, no page given (accessed on 15 May 2018).

28 Rattle, 2011.

29 Müller-Wille, "Linnaeus and the four corners of the world."

30 Lalu, *The deaths of Hintsa*.

Ailanthus altissima, or the botanical afterlives of European power

Bettina Stoetzer

The forest stood there, green, next to the ruins.
Ursula le Guin[1]

Take a walk along a city's paved arteries and stumble across a botany of concrete. Look for cracks in the sidewalk, the thin gaps in-between the iron rods of gutters, the dry, gravelly soil of abandoned lots, the seams along the edges of buildings, or spaces along the road and train tracks. In the fissures of the city's built structures, nestled between slabs of concrete, you will find a world full of surprise. And if you are lucky, you will catch a glimpse of a small tree pushing its way through the concrete, breaking its surface, reaching skyward. Its dark green, palm-like leaves gently brush up against a wall. Follow the tree, and it will tell you a history of the world that is more than human.

This tree is called *Ailanthus altissima*, or tree of heaven in English. In Chinese, its name is ch'un-shu, which means "stinking or spring tree." For *Ailanthus*, becoming urban is closely linked to the history of empire, industrialization, and climate change. A fugitive for eighteenth-century European gardens and their orientalist legacies, it is a testament to the unruly lives that have persisted in the cracks of cultivation, domestication and imperial power for centuries. While often dormant or invisible, these fugitives continue to assert their presence. And they show us that Europe's cultivated landscapes, including its cities, have always been more than what humans wanted them to be.

For the purpose of this essay, let me take *Ailanthus altissima's* roots and routes as a guide. With their unique suckering abilities, the tree's roots, once cut, quickly grow back and are able to thrive in anthropogenic and seemingly inhospitable environments. Considered both a noxious weed and a wondrous example of resilience in the city, *Ailanthus* convey stories about the entanglements between people, plants, and urban infrastructure. Tracing their intertwined routes and roots, I ask: in what ways might critical engagements with the botany of cities require cultural analysts to do more than simply rethink urban life beyond the human? In other words, how can we methodologically approach the complex and enduring processes of exclusion, violence, and ruination—as well as the seeds for their transgression—embedded in the very ecology of Europe's urban environments today?

A deciduous tree, *Ailanthus* is considered to be native to Northeast and Central China, to Taiwan, and to North Vietnam. With a long winter dormancy, the tree signals the beginning of spring. Its bark and leaves have been widely used for medical purposes—as astringents and to cure various ailments, including depression, baldness, stomach upset, or skin irritations. Attracting honeybees, its honey has a nutty flavor.[2]

According to botanical storytelling, the tree made its first appearance in Europe in 1740, when Pierre d'Incarville, a Jesuit priest who had received a botanical education in the Jardin Royale des Plantes in Paris, shipped its seeds from Beijing to Paris.[3] Soon they were sown in apothecary and botanical gardens, and they also made it to London a few years later. These early travels of *Ailanthus* occurred at the height of "chinoiserie" and its orientalist fascinations—at a time when Europeans were increasingly becoming interested in plants from throughout Eastern Asia. Faring well in warmer climates, these plants, so was the hope, would aid Europeans economically as they cultivated landscapes in the colonies. At a historical moment when Chinese imperial power was in decline, and Europeans were consolidating their colonial expansion in the Americas, *Ailanthus* thus helped shape Europe's "imperial landscapes,"[4] in the metropole and colony alike: they adorned English and French gardens, such as Le Jardin de Plantes in Paris and the Chelsea Physic Garden[5] as well as cities and colonial plantations in the Americas—thus providing the seeds for materializing European cultural and economic hegemony at home and abroad. In this sense, they are part of a larger trend of what Jill Casid has called "imperial landscaping practices"—the making of everything from plantations to cities to island gardens during the eighteenth and nineteenth centuries, when the global circulation of seeds and plants both symbolized and materialized imperial power.[6]

In 1784, when the tree made it to the Americas via the Philadelphia gardener William Hamilton, it was accompanied by the Shantung silk moth, *Attacus cynthia*. In fact, trees of heaven were intermittently used in silk production in North America as well as in Europe, as they had previously been in China (the so-called Shantung silk is more coarse and durable than other silks, and also does not dye).[7] Praised for their beautiful foliage and exotic appearance, as well as their rapid growth and resilience vis-à-vis smoke, pollution, drought and even a large number of herbivorous insects,[8] trees of heaven appeared widely as ornamental street trees throughout Europe and the Americas. They lined city promenades in France and Italy, as well as streets in Boston, New York, and Philadelphia, and they could also be found at the edges of plantations in the Southern United States.[9] In Europe, they were increasingly used for wood production and as a buffer against erosion and wind,[10] thus assisting urbanization and the fortification of transportation infrastructure.[11]

Trees of heaven thus became associated with cities–although, curiously, in China, they mainly appeared in rural areas. This was due to different European pruning techniques and the ubiquity of urban gleaners in Chinese cities.[12] In contrast, in

Europe and the Americas, *Ailanthus* soon spread beyond gardens and street tree cultivation. Easily adapting to the drier and warmer climates of cities, they were able to thrive in urban environments. In the summer, the tree's reddish and green/golden fruits carry abundant seeds that, amplified by wind or by hitching a ride with urban traffic and infrastructure, can migrate large distances later in the year. *Ailanthus* thus began to grow along urban transportation corridors such as highways, roads, train tracks, and canals, or alongside old buildings and fences. Today, with their seeds also being dispersed by water, one can also see these trees along riparian corridors growing at the edges of canals and water runoffs in cities across Europe and the Americas. Nestled in abandoned lots or at the edges of transportation, electricity, water, and sewage infrastructures, trees of heaven hitch a ride on human projects of engineering, and seem rather indifferent to the boundaries of property and value. As artist and critic Matthew Battles writes, by "habit and quality, *Ailanthus* seek out and colonize the margins, where modern concepts of property find their slippery limits: at the edges of public rights of way," and "along the bent and ragged sheets of chain-link fences that quarter the empty lots."[13] One of the most air pollution-tolerant trees, and easily adapting to rising temperatures in the context of climate change, they are able to tolerate high levels of cement dust, ozone exposure, and even fumes from tar operations (their leaves are able to absorb sulphur dioxide).[14]

Escaping cultivated managements across Europe and the Americas, *Ailanthus* thus became something like a trickster figure, both materially and symbolically speaking. In fact, the trees seemed to escape proper botanical classification for decades. Throughout their initial European trajectories, botanists regularly mistook the plants for Chinese varnish or lacquer trees: their light gray trunks and pinnate compound leaves looked similar at a distance. When *Ailanthus* seeds first arrived in Paris, they were marked as the varnish tree (*Rhus verniciflua*), causing botanical confusion for decades to come.[15] As disputes about their identity smoldered, the plants not only went feral but also appeared under different names, thereby troubling European efforts to collect, discover, and properly name new species and to expand imperial power through the domestication of plants.[16]

In German, *Ailanthus* is called *Götterbaum*, which translates as "tree of the gods." In the city of Berlin, these trees were briefly used for silk production in the nineteenth century, and they are abundant today.[17] Once you familiarize yourself with their jagged bright green leaves, you begin to recognize them everywhere. They grow as tiny shrubs, no more than 20 centimetres high, in the cracks of sidewalks or gutters, or as large trees towering 25 metres high into the sky,[18] offering a habitat for many critters, and they are often neighbours to a similarly hardy tree, *Robinia pseudoacacia*.

Walking on the green strip along the former border between East and West Berlin in the city's Kreuzberg district, you stumble across a tree of heaven with an unusual story. Towering 15 metres high above a garden shack, the tree provides shade for gardeners and passers-by alike—hosting a diversity of birds, insects, and even a few squirrels, climbing in its branches. One day in the early 1980s, when the Berlin

Berlin tree house (2018). Photo: Bettina Stoetzer.

Wall stood tall here, Osman Kalin was on his way to prayers at the nearby mosque. Out of the corner of his eye, he saw this little piece of land and had an idea. Osman had migrated from rural East Turkey to West Berlin in the 1960s, when West Germany was contracting migrant labourers—so-called guest workers—from Turkey to rebuild the country after the war. Due to a back injury from years of strenuous labour as a construction worker, he had just retired and was looking for new tasks. Not having access to a garden or balcony in his family's small apartment, he soon began to cultivate onions, tomatoes, and cabbage on this small triangle of land in the wall's shadow. From objects he found across the neighbourhood, he slowly built a two-floor shack. As the cabin expanded over the years, so did a small shrub of *Ailanthus* in its midst. Growing in the cracks of the sidewalk, it had pushed itself through the cabin's wall. Despite Osman's efforts to cut it, it kept growing back, year after year. In the end, Osman gave up. Today the tree towers high above the shack, and indeed has become an integral part of its front wall. Each year as the trunk expands, Osman cut further into the wall to accommodate its growth. Beneath the tree, he and his family placed a bench, a table, and some chairs, offering a meeting place for neighbours and friends from across the neighbourhood. A few years ago, the chairs and table were stolen and the bench was burned down by hostile neighbours. The next day, Osman promptly replaced them. The table and chairs are now firmly cemented to the ground.

While trees of heaven may provide a shelter for some, as the story of the Berlin Tree House illustrates, they are also often unwelcome intruders. Once among the most popular street trees in Europe and North America, they slowly transformed from a much-desired exotic city dweller into a "weed" and nuisance, capturing botanical, literary and social scientific imaginations.[19] In the United States, initial *Ailanthus* enthusiasm turned into aversion when, from the 1840s onwards, the United States found itself in the midst of an economic boom energized by the China trade. While many gardeners and planners at first celebrated the tree's aesthetic and hardy qualities, many horticulturalists quickly began to despise them: by the 1850s, as political tensions with China amplified, many observers pointed out the tree's uncontrolled proliferation, foul odor, and "treacherous" qualities. Framed in a language of invasive species, "*Ailanthus*-loathing" thus attached itself to nationalist and anti-Chinese rhetoric—long before sentiments turned against the tree in Europe.[20] Today, urban residents still regularly complain about the strong smell of the tree's (male) flowers, which develop into clusters of seed pods that scatter across sidewalks or yards by late summer.

Similarly, for many Berliners, *Ailanthus* is a stinky tree, an obnoxious weed that leaves an uncontrollable mess of seeds. Others abhor it because once it has claimed its presence you will not easily get rid of it. With its propeller-shaped seeds travelling long distances amplified by wind, water, and the unique suckering ability of its roots, it multiplies quickly. Local news thus often portrays *Ailanthus* as an unruly weed "from China" invading Berlin's parks and roadsides. These invasive species, so the story goes, displace native urban flora, pose an allergy risk for humans, and also cause infrastructural damage, growing out of gutters and destabilizing walls and sidewalks. As a consequence, local authorities often urge gardeners to detect and uproot the trees from urban lots.[21]

Concerns of this type about invasive species can easily trigger a series of cultural associations, from images of illegal aliens to a language of invasion, embattled borders and nations—at a time of re-emerging nationalisms and claims to purity and exclusion across Europe.[22] In fact, while cities like Berlin are celebrated for their urban nature and promoted as green cities, anxieties around "foreign" bodies, both human and non-human, abound. These fears echo larger debates around migration and the presence of migrants in cities across Europe and contemporary North America—debates that have deeply transformed the political landscape on both continents in the past decade. For example, depictions of Berlin's urban environment are often heavily infused with metaphors of wilderness and natural disaster encroaching upon urban life.[23] Coupled with a sense of embattled national borders, these images of unruly nature express colonial fantasies of the return of the subjugated coming to haunt the metropole. This occurs at a time when Europe's attempt to shore up its borders, as well as capitalism's ability to infinitely extract resources and labour, are increasingly confronting their own limits.[24]

These scenarios of urban invasion are not merely symbolic; they have material consequences, setting the parameters of political debate and decision-making regarding migration, and urban planning in contemporary Europe.[25] However, as the story of the Berlin Tree House illustrates, the very material presence of *Ailanthus* and its entanglements with other unexpected neighbours also point to an opening:

the fact that plants are more than a passive background of human schemes of order or resource extraction. Recognizing this opening requires alternative modes of approaching the ecology and botany of cities—beyond a binary attention to the wild or domesticated—ideas that are deeply rooted in the history of capitalism and colonialism. Ironically, we can find such forms of "doing [urban] ecology otherwise"[26] in Berlin's blasted landscapes after WWII.

In 1945, the city of Berlin lay in ruins. Heavy bombing toward the end of the war had destroyed close to half of the city centre's built environment. And yet, as with Ursula Le Guin's passage at the beginning of this essay, chronicling the aftermath of imperial destruction, soon a forest stood there, next to the ruins. As political tensions increased and Berlin was divided into East and West, plants from all over the world emerged in the city's rubble—and people took notice. While many Berliners sorted through the rubble in search for edible plants, botanists also began to turn their eye toward the flora of the city. With access to their usual fieldsites in the countryside becoming more difficult due to Berlin's partitioning, these hobbyists and scientists began to study the ecology of Berlin's abundant rubble vegetation in detail. *Ailanthus altissima* was one of the plants that lured their attention, guiding them toward so-called "ruderal ecologies" in the city. The word ruderal comes from the Latin term "rudus," which means rubble. A common term in urban ecology today, it refers to organisms that spontaneously grow in "disturbed environments" usually considered hostile to life—the sides of train tracks, for instance, or roads, waste disposal areas, or literal rubble.[27]

In studying ruderal plants like *Ailanthus*, the botanists encountered a world of cosmopolitan urban nature: many of these plants were non-native species. Their seeds had followed the routes of global traffic, migration, and trade and thus had entered the city—sometimes, this was anticipated by humans, as in the case of *Ailanthus*, and at other times, it was by chance—through packaging materials of goods or fodder for animals, or on the boots of soldiers and refugees. Ruderal plants were not simply a nuisance, but provided possibilities for new ecosystems to flourish in the city—e.g., by offering shade and organic matter, or a habitat for birds, or by enabling new wetlands to emerge.[28] Mapping the occurrence of the tree of heaven and other species in relation to different temperature zones in the city, the botanists were able to demonstrate that these cosmopolitan botanical worlds were not just the traces of global connection, nationalism, urbanization, and war—they were also indicators for pollution and rising temperatures in Berlin and across the globe.[29]

As Jens Lachmund has shown, the knowledge of the unique botany of cities generated by this research was integrated into Berlin's conservation practices and urban planning in enduring ways.[30] But what if we move beyond the boundaries of science and consider the different ways of approaching nature in the city that materialized in the encounters between botanists, ruderal plants, and other Berlin residents, such as Osman Kalin? How might we be able to utilize these encounters for a cultural analysis of urban life on an increasingly inhospitable planet?

In a world shaped by environmental destruction, climate change, and extraction of natural resources and labour, as well as fear of invasive others, trees of heaven and other ruderal plants assert their presence in cities. If we follow their history, we can begin to see a "ruderal city"[31] in which nature is not independent but an integral and unruly part of the city. Tracing *Ailanthus*' trajectories from China to Europe and the Americas, we can also see how the story of this tree is intimately linked with the history of colonization, urbanization, and imperial power—as well as with its transgression. If we think of urban environments as ruins in a broader sense—ruins that emerge from environmental destruction, as well as Europe's history of colonialism, nationalism, and racialized exclusions—then the history of *Ailanthus* and other ruderal plants can be a guide in understanding the lives that appear in their midst. Trees of heaven can inspire, reshape, and queer sensibilities toward urban nature[32] by directing attention to the unexpected neighbours that inhabit today's "disturbed" and inhospitable environments—while being alert to new connections across existing structures of violence and inequality that may erupt in a city's material fabric.

Above all, as a fugitive of Europe's landscaping practices, *Ailanthus* requires us to sharpen our peripheral vision: emerging by chance, these trees easily escape structured observation. You never know exactly where to find them. An analytic that tracks ruderal ecologies in the city can therefore cultivate modes of attention that utilize chance and gleaning as a practice of social inquiry rather than focusing on bounded units, predictable political economies, and coherency. As urban worlds today are becoming increasingly inhospitable, crowded with unexpected toxins, reemerging nationalisms, and often invisible forms of violence, engaging with multiple things at once will be key for understanding the complexities of urban lives in what many call the "Anthropocene."

While *Ailanthus* and other ruderal ecologies may be prime examples of survival and the resilience of life in the midst of damage, they are also cautionary tales about deeply ambivalent and uncanny worlds amid harm, as well as future threats of violence and ecological destruction. In times of an uneven loss of hospitable environments for both people and non-human beings—due to a rise of nationalism across the world, increasing racialized violence, displacement, and global environmental change—we can, by studying the botany of cities, renew the question of which bodies, human or non-human, are able to flourish or become disposable.[33]

Ailanthus remind us of the fugitives, the border crossers and the illegal hitchhikers of European domestication projects and their disastrous planetary effects. While the cultivation of plants has been an integral element in the creation of Europe's imperial power,[34] Europe's gardens have also always carried within them unpredictable seeds for change. Attending to the unintended neighbours and dormant fugitives that appear in these cultivated landscapes might thus be a first step towards decolonizing the ways in which we imagine urban environments. Beyond a deeply fraught fascination with the urban "wild," *Ailanthus* instead cautions us to be attentive to practices that transgress the legacies of European power and metropolitan exclusions today.

In the midst of many cities across the globe, there is a little tree pushing itself skyward. Its growth signals both the possibility of connection *and* the dangers of destruction. Its botany of concrete indicates a city abundant with unruly cosmopolitan lives and uncertain futures. While *Ailanthus*'s trajectories across the New World and Europe, including Berlin, might be a story of vital persistence, let's not forget that the bench placed in the shadow of the *Ailanthus altissima* in the story of the Berlin Tree House was burned down.

1 Ursula le Guin, *The word for the world is forest* (New York: TOR, 2010 [1972]) p. 25.

2 Shiu Ying Hu "Ailanthus," *Arnoldia* 39 (2) (1979), and Ingo Kowarik and Ina Säumel, "Biological flora of Central Europe: *Ailanthus Altissima* (Mill.) Swingle," in *Perspectives in plant ecology, evolution and systematics* 8 (4) (2007) pp. 207–237.

3 Pierre d'Incarville was a Jesuit priest who had been a member of the China mission since 1740. D'Incarvile regularly sent herbarium specimens and seeds to Bernard de Jussieu, who was superintendant at the Jardin Royal des Plantes in Paris, see Hu "Ailanthus," 32ff.

4 Indeed, Chinese traditions played a key role in the formation of British landscape and gardening practices at the very moment when England became a centre of imperial power. In this context, the term "imperial landscapes" refers to material and aesthetic landscaping practices becoming tools of imperial power and thus the fortification of cultural, economic, and political expansion—practices that are never stable or homogenous across historical and geographic contexts; see William J.T. Mitchell, "Imperial landscapes," in *Landscape and power* (Chicago, University of Chicago Press, 1994) p. 9. See also Ann Stoler's discussion of imperial formations as ongoing processes of displacement, racialization, and domination that affect bodies and landscapes, Ann Stoler, "Imperial debris: reflections on ruins and ruination," in *Cultural Anthropology* 23 (2) (2008) pp. 191–219. As Frantz Fanon has pointed out, the process of imperial expansion always involved the domestication of seemingly unruly bodies and landscapes, see Frantz Fanon, *Wretched of the earth* (New York: Grove Press, 1968) p. 182.

5 Behula Shah, "The checkered career of *Ailanthus altissima*," *Arnoldia* (Fall 1997) p. 22.

6 As Casid writes, "landscaping functioned as an imperial mode that defined and transformed the 'heartlands' of nations as well as the conceived national borders, contact zones, and colonial peripheries ... (xxi-xxii)." Transplanting vegetation from the metropolis thus became a key tool in making claims to land and enabling a future in the colony—a practice that always nevertheless also contained the seeds for alternative futures, see Jill Casid, *Sowing empire: landscape and colonization* (Minneapolis: University of Minnesota Press, 2005) p. xix.

7 Hu "Ailanthus," 43, and Ingo Kowarik and R. Böcker, "Zur Verbreitung, Vergesellschaftung und Einbuergerung des Goetterbaumes in Mitteleuropa," in *Tuexenia: Mitteilungen der floristisch-soziologischen Arbeitsgemeinschaft* 4 (1983) pp. 4–29; and Darren Patrick, "Queering the urban forest: invasions, mutualisms, and ecopolitical creativity with the tree of heaven (*Ailanthus altissima*)," in L. Anders Sandberg, Adrina Bardekjian and Sadia Butt, eds., *Urban forests, trees and greenspace: a political ecology perspective* (London: Routledge, 2014) pp. 191–206.

8 Kowarik and Säumel, "Biological flora," pp. 207–237.

9 On his first "Southern journey," visiting a tobacco plantation in Virginia, Frederick Law Olmsted commented on a row of *Ailanthus* trees lining a plantation street—and he also later promoted the cultivation of *Ailanthus* in Central Park, New York, see Kenneth Mc Farland, "The awful Ailanthus.' A love to hate story," in *Magnolia: A Publication of the Southern Garden History Society* (Spring 2017) pp. 1–6.

10 Cultivated *Ailanthus* was also used, for example, in the production of steamers in East China, see Hu, "Ailanthus," p. 40.

11 See Hu, "Ailanthus," p. 49; Kowarik and Böcker, "Zur Verbreitung, Vergesellschaftung und Einbürgerung des Götterbaumes in Mitteleuropa," pp. 4–29; and Darren Patrick, "Queering the urban forest," pp. 191–206.

12 Trees were not able to spread in most Chinese cities because gleaners regularly searched out the streets for plant materials, for use as firewood or also medicinal purposes. In contrast, applying different cutting and pruning techniques, gardeners in Europe cut feral trees to the ground, thus inadvertently triggering further growth into large bushes. Left alone, the trees would grow into stands with thick aggregates, see Hu, "Ailanthus,"p. 39.

13 Matthew Battles, *Tree* (New York/London: Bloomsbury, 2017) p. 6.

14 Peter Del Tredici, *Wild urban plants of the northeast: a field guide* (Ithaca/London: Cornell University Press, 2010) p. 104.

15 Hu, "Ailanthus," p. 33.

16 These contestations around the name led to various versions, from Moluccan, to ailanto, and then tree of heaven, via the botanist R.L. Desfontaines in 1785, and later in 1916 via Walter Swingle of the United States Department of Plant Industry, who applied an earlier epithet of Philip Miller's and created a new scientific name *Ailanthus altissima*, (Miller) Swingle, see Hu, "Ailanthus," pp. 33ff.

17 See http://www.wildesgrueninberlin.de/content/goetterbaum (accessed 8 February 2019).

18 Growing rapidly, (with annual growth rates up to 150 centimetres and the ability to grow from severed roots) *Ailanthus* often reaches heights up to 30 metres.

19 See e.g. Betty Smith, *A tree grows in Brooklyn* (New York: Harper and Row, 1947).

20 Behula Shah, "The checkered career of *Ailanthus altissima*," p. 24.

21 Christian Hönicke, "Götterbaum-Plage bedroht Parks," *tagesspiegel* (3 August 2018), available at: https://www.tagesspiegel.de/berlin/sorge-um-gartendenkmal-goetterbaum-plage-bedroht-parks/21048732.html (accessed 8 January 2019).

22 See also Miriam Ticktin, "Invasive others: toward a contaminated world," in *Social Research* 84 (1) (2017) pp. xxi-xxxiv.

23 Bettina Stoetzer, "Wild barbecuing: urban citizenship and the politics of (trans-) nationality in Berlin's Tiergarten," in Jeffrey Diefendorf and Janet Ward, eds., *Transnationalism and the German City* (London: Palgrave Macmillan, 2014) pp. 73–86.

24 Ghassan Hage, "*Etat de siege*: A dying domesticating colonialism?" in *American Ethnologist* 43 (1) (2016) pp. 38–49.

25 Bettina Stoetzer, "Ruderal ecologies: rethinking nature, migration and the urban landscape in Berlin," *Cultural Anthropology* 33 (2) (2018) pp. 295–323.

26 Natasha Myers, "Ungridable ecologies: decolonizing the ecological sensorium in a 10,000 year-old natural-cultural happening," *Catalyst* 2 (3) (2017) pp.1–23.

27 These forms of disturbance can range from use of herbicides, to vegetation removal or drought, fire, and soil erosion, see J.P. Grime, "Evidence for the existence of three primary strategies in plants and its relevance for ecological theory," in *American Naturalist* 111 (982) (1977) pp. 1169–1194.

28 Because of their large compound leaves, trees of heaven contribute to air renewal in the city, and could potentially provide an important source for use of firewood due to their rapid growth. See Hu, "Ailanthus," p. 48. They also contribute to soil building on degraded land and slope stabilization. See Peter Del Tredici, *Wild urban plants of the northeast*, p. 104.

29 Herbert Sukopp and Angelika Wurzel, "The effects of climate change on the vegetation of Central European cities," in *Urban Habitats* 1 (1) (2003) pp. 66–86.

30 Jens Lachmund, *Greening Berlin: the co-production of science, politics and urban nature* (Cambridge: MIT Press, 2013).

31 Bettina Stoetzer, *Ruderal city: ecologies of migration and urban life in Berlin* (Durham: Duke University Press, forthcoming).

32 See Matthew Gandy, "Queer ecology: nature, sexuality and heterotopic alliances," in *Environment and Planning D: Society and Space* 30 (4) (2012) pp. 727–747; and Darren Patrick, "Queering the urban forest," pp. 191–206.

33 Judith Butler, *Bodies that matter: on the discursive limits of sex* (New York: Routledge, 2011).

34 Jill Casid, *Sowing empire*.

Seeing, surveying, and sorting urban trees: the 1970s street tree project in Dresden

Sonja Dümpelmann

Park departments in many major cities today use geographical information systems and digital maps to record and document their street trees. On these maps, the trees are georeferenced; information on their species, age, planting date, trunk and crown caliper, height, and location is just a mouse-click away. In some cities, urban foresters and arborists use a GPS-equipped device in the field to record these characteristics, together with tree damage and maintenance instructions. The data flow afforded by these new technologies has increased the flexibility and speed with which urban trees can be surveyed and managed. In a process that has lasted for over a century, the methods and tools for surveying street trees have developed from handwritten lists on paper to computer-generated datasets that can be adjusted in split seconds. The means of controlling trees have developed to accommodate trees' inherent malleability and changeability, revealing a struggle to come to terms with the less tangible, or even inherently ephemeral, characteristics of urban trees. While computerized bureaucracy has frequently been criticized for its mechanized abstract processes—which often go hand in hand with processes of alienation and depersonalization in the case of human data collection—in the case of street trees, it can be argued that methods and technologies facilitating data management have also been able to call greater attention to individual trees, their character and their needs.

Once it had become clear in the second half of the nineteenth century that the systematic planting of trees along streets could do much to alleviate the ills of the industrial city by improving its climate and urban aesthetics, the impulse to plant trees was accompanied by efforts to control their growth and development through efficient and standardized management and care. As the trees "naturalized" the city, they themselves were "urbanized." The Departments of Gardens kept lists of trees. They established best management practices for planting and maintaining trees, began to spray them to keep insects, fungi, and diseases at bay, and even built watering systems for the street trees they planted. Tree nurseries sought to produce the ideal street tree, and began to breed new cultivars that were expected to be more resistant to the vagaries of urban life. However, extreme weather events (such as storms that uproot and damage trees) and inherent characteristics of various species that proved to be a nuisance in urban environments (such as brittle wood and certain branching habits that rendered maintenance extremely labour-intensive; and fruit and seeds that cluttered sidewalks) also led to an increasing recognition that the trees' own life force could not be controlled entirely. City foresters and garden architects realized that, while bureaucratic management and care was necessary to guarantee the implementation of comprehensive street tree systems in the first place, the more flexible the management could be, the better the city's green canopy would fare. In the best case, the cities' street tree control and surveillance included the trees' cartographic documentation and representation.[1]

In socialist East Germany, some cities' Departments of Gardens had begun to survey their street trees and document them on index cards in the 1960s, but a first attempt at a thorough comprehensive model project for the documentation of street trees that included cartography and other paper technologies was only undertaken in the early 1970s in the city of Dresden. As one of the German cities that was heavily destroyed by the air raids of WWII, Dresden lost over 20,000 of around 60,000 street trees registered in 1932. More trees were lost after the war, when tree-felling and wood theft were a common occurrence despite official prohibitions.[2] Dresden's citizens were desperate for firewood. In 1950, over 1,000 new street trees were planted; this number was not achieved again until after the fall of the Wall.[3] Given the lack of nursery stock in the immediate post-war years, it was common to dig up trees that had established themselves spontaneously on the city's rubble and plant them along streets.[4] By the early 1970s, the city counted around 36,000 street trees, of which a third were damaged.

This situation called for change, and Dresden soon became the testing ground and laboratory for a new system of street tree management. The city found an ideal working partner in Siegfried Sommer; at the time, he was a young landscape architect and lecturer at the Technical University's landscape architecture programme. Saxony's nominal capital had become home to the German Democratic Republic's (the GDR's) only academic landscape architecture programme in 1970, when the programme was moved from the Humboldt University in Berlin to the Technical University in Dresden.[5] At the same time, the VEB Kombinat Robotron also established its seat in the city on the river Elbe. With the VEB Kombinat Zentronik, it had developed out of the VVB Datenverarbeitungs- und Büromaschinen (the association of the GDR's manufacturers of electronic and mechanical data-processing and office machines, including sorting machines and hardware punch card systems). Dresden and some smaller towns in Saxony and Thuringia had long been Germany's centres of research into and production of early data-processing machines, preoccupations that were pursued again in these regions after the foundation of the GDR. In 1951, an office for data-processing in industry and research was also established in the Institute of Applied Mathematics at the Technical University

Dresden.[6] The edge-notched cards that Sommer would use to keep track of Dresden's street trees were thus a data-recording and processing technology that was omnipresent in the region, if not in the city itself. Even if the technology was already outdated in general terms at the time, it signified an innovation in the realm of street tree management.

Sommer, who had moved to Dresden from Berlin, had a long-standing interest in roadside trees. Having undertaken an extensive research project on their impact on adjacent vegetation at Berlin's Humboldt University, and having researched tree planting and care in urban environments, Sommer had already proposed the use of card systems to survey street trees and their condition during his years in Berlin. In the early 1970s, he finally found a willing partner in this endeavor in Dresden's municipal government.[7]

The government's objective was to increase and improve its tree canopy through an increased efficiency of tree care and the planting of more resistant species. The central aim of this new tree management system was a paper database and documentation system which could be updated easily, and which provided a basis for an ecological and aesthetic tree-planting concept—that is, a citywide street tree planting plan that responded equally to aesthetic design criteria and environmental conditions. To protect the city's trees and to promote its afforestation, Sommer and his students at the Technical University Dresden developed a system for a citywide street tree survey, using city maps and edge-notched cards. The latter was a paper technology originally invented at the beginning of the twentieth century and widely used between the 1940s and 1970s by scientists, engineers, and administrators in Europe and the United States.[8] City maps on a scale of 1:5.000 were used to indicate the survey units represented by street trees of the same species or cultivars that stood along a street, or on a plaza or median. The maps also indicated the respective trees' life expectancy through hachures drawn along streets. For example, a full thick line indicated high life expectancy, a cross hachure signified medium life expectancy, an inclined hachure stood for low life expectancy, and no hachure was used when the trees were dead and should be felled. This information could also be retrieved from the edge-notched cards, where it was recorded in Roman numbers as well as through notches along the cards' edges (notches in the numerical sorting field "M"). Street tree data recorded on the cards also included their species, age, location, and the formation or type of planting (standalone; row; allée; mix of diverse species). Besides the use of punched notches to register the specifics of the trees' location (notches in the numerical sorting fields "A," "B," "C," "D"), species (notches in the numerical sorting fields "E," "F," "G"), and age (notches in the numerical sorting fields "N," "O," "P"), the cards were also number-coded, corresponding to a particular numbered location on the city maps.

As with any edge-notched cards, Dresden's mechanical card sorting system facilitated both the organization and analysis of a large amount of information. Data was extracted from the cards by passing one or more slim needles through selected holes in a group of cards. By lifting the needles, the cards that were notched in the hole positions where the needles were inserted would be left behind while the

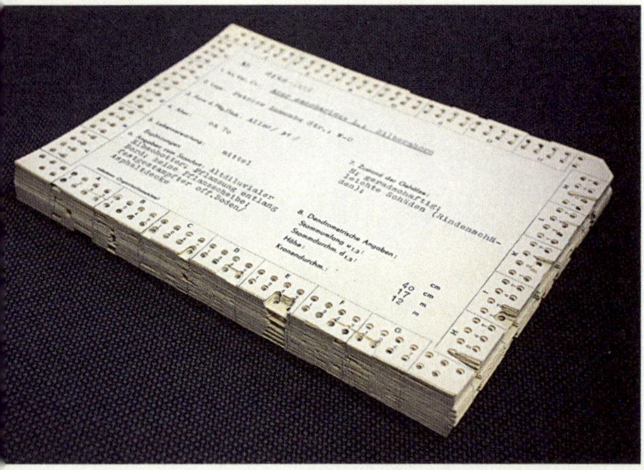

Edge-notched cards used in Dresden to record street tree data in the 1970s. Photo: Sonja Dümpelmann. Courtesy Amt für Stadtgrün und Abfallwirtschaft Dresden.

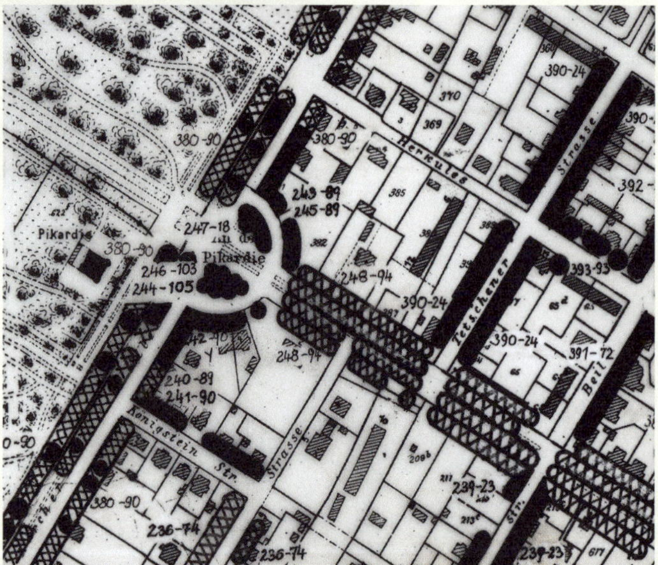

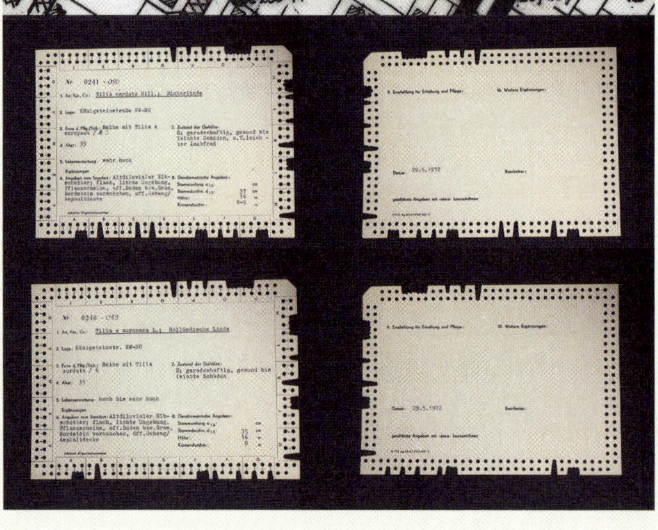

Top: Map detail illustrating data from the street tree survey in the early 1970s. Source: Stadtarchiv Dresden.
Below: Front and back of two edge-notched cards recording the data of street trees along Königsteinstraße which can be seen on the bottom left of the map detail. The card numbers "0241-090" and "0241-089" can be found indicated on the map. "0241" describes the location, "090" and "089" stand for the tree species, *Tilia cordata* and *Tilia x europaea* respectively. Photos: Sonja Dümpelmann. Courtesy Amt für Stadtgrün und Abfallwirtschaft Dresden.

rest of the cards were lifted by the needles. This procedure facilitated the search for particular tree data and eliminated the time-consuming job of refiling cards in any exact order.

Building on the survey work, in the second half of the 1970s, students from the Technical University drew up tree-planting concepts for the city. On the basis of these preliminary studies, in the 1980s, the city itself finally developed a new comprehensive tree-planting concept.[9] The idea of these concepts was introduced by East German landscape architects in the 1950s and 1960s to provide a planning tool for green urban infrastructure. Underlying this idea was the general belief that trees in the city were as important as buildings. Architecture and landscape were to be treated as equally important components of urban design, and trees were to be integral components of any urban plan rather than ornamental afterthoughts. Landscape architects in East Germany drew up tree-planting concepts for both new and existing cities, and for many new residential neighbourhoods featuring mass housing. These tree-planting concepts were based upon the geographical classification of soils and landscape types, as well as the climatological and aesthetic functions provided by the different tree species.[10] Tree-planting concepts were a means to divide cities into recognizable and characteristic planting units and to standardize street tree planting on a city-wide scale. Their objective was also the facilitation of tree production plans in East German tree nurseries. These goals were clear and efficient, but the reality often looked different. Given that East German tree nurseries were selling many of their best trees to West Germany as part of the state's effort to balance its debt through foreign exchange, plant material was often lacking for East Germany's own needs.

However, despite these shortcomings, Sommer's and his students' work ultimately facilitated the revitalization of the tree canopy in Dresden. The renewed attention paid to street tree planting in the city also inspired nurseries to cultivate resilient species that could resist many of the shortcomings of urban environments, such as *Tilia tomentosa*, *Sophora japonica*, *Platanus x hispanica*, *Ginkgo biloba*, *Corylus colurna*, *Sorbus latifolia*, and *Sorbus intermedia*, as well as several species with small tree crowns that could be planted in narrow streets. In 1976, the student Anne-Kathrin Knepel drew up a tree-planting concept for Dresden's main streets in the city centre. Besides providing ideas for species selection and planting patterns, her objective was to achieve a phased planting plan, so that existing trees could be replaced over time depending on their condition and age, and trees could be grown and prepared in the nurseries beforehand. Another objective was to provide Dresden with a characteristic "vegetation image" (*Vegetationsbild*), or "plantscape," and to turn its main thoroughfares into orienting guidelines for traffic. Based on soil composition that was considered more "natural" the further one moved away from the city centre and species resilience against urban stress factors, Knepel's tree-planting concept determined that, as one moved outward from the centre, more and more tree species belonging to the "potentially natural vegetation" (PNV)[11] should be planted. Depending on their adaptability to more or less artificial soils, Knepel sorted the various species into three groups that could then provide the basis for tree planting in the various environmental zones of the city (also based upon hydrology and air quality). Whereas Knepel proposed species like the tree of heaven, ginkgo, honey locust, and pagoda tree for the city centre, moving outside of the city, her suggestions included species that could typically be found growing in the region, like maples, oaks, and lindens. In the 1980s, building upon this student work, the city developed its own tree-planting concept for the centre and expanded the concept's reach across its entire territory. The comprehensive plan was accompanied by detailed plans for the main thoroughfares. To diversify the tree canopy, the idea was also to test new species and cultivars for their urban resiliency by planting them along side streets, thus turning less-trafficked areas into an urban laboratory. In 1986, the city also invited Sommer to serve in an honorary capacity on the city's tree protection committee. Based upon the GDR's 1981 tree ordinance, the committee had been supervising urban tree conditions and tree removal since 1982. By 1986, however, new work rules and the committee's reform appeared necessary. By this time, Dresden's street tree inventory was already showing deficiencies, as it had not been updated regularly. In consequence, Sommer argued for the use of a computer with efficient storage capacity, and his university colleague Wolfgang Fischer was charged with finding possibilities to update the street tree inventory with the help of aerial photography. However, although aerial photographs were put to use in the late 1980s, it was not until 1990 (after the fall of the Wall) that Dresden's street tree canopy began to undergo another phase of substantial renewal, which was then boosted by 20,000 German marks provided by its West German twin city Hamburg for another aerial tree survey, for ground truthing, and for soil samples.[12]

Dresden's street tree work in the 1970s was spurred by the socialist state's urge to connect research and practice, and to systematize and industrialize work processes. This took place in connection with the housing programme that was announced by Erich Honnecker in 1971 and was set in motion in 1973 during the ninth congress of the Socialist Unity Party's Zentralkommittee, with the objective of solving the housing question by 1990. In speeches and documents, the autocratic state and its functionaries attributed value to trees and to green open space. At the tenth convention of the Zentralkommittee in October 1973, building minister Wolfgang Junker called for "a new quality of greening residential areas … with picturesque tree groups, … tree plantings in the form of friendly allées, continuous groves, and parks that offer shade and improve the microclimate and the experiential quality of urban areas."[13] He reminded his audience that in previous times many architects, and not the worst of them, had used tree plantings as full-fledged urban design element.[14] It appeared that a total of three million trees and 90 million shrubs would be needed in order to realize the housing programme, and that existing trees would also need protection.[15]

In Dresden, the edge-notched cards and the set of city maps provided a system for the surveillance, management, and maintenance of one of the most important non-human natural elements in the city: street trees. But the use of edge-notched cards for surveillance purposes had been approved in the GDR since the 1960s, albeit in a different context. Since 1965—and until around 1980 when it was replaced

Tree-planting concept for Dresden's city centre, 1984–88. Source: Stadtarchiv Dresden.

by digital information systems—the GDR's Ministry of National Security had used a larger version of edge-notched cards for personal registers—for example, to document informal collaborators and record their profession, party affiliation, habits, hobbies, and other personal interests and inclinations. The edge-notched card system encoded this information and provided a means to facilitate the internal communication and interpretation of data, which the socialist state functionaries considered vital for their autocratic, repressive leadership.[16]

With regard to trees, however, Dresden's 1970s street tree survey marked both a high point and a turning point for the management and control of street trees.

It had been established before cities in East and West Germany began managing their trees with the help of computers. Analog cartographic and indexing systems like Dresden's edge-notched cards and maps anticipated the flexibility that was ultimately provided by computers and geographical information systems. In the 1960s and 1970s, East and West German cities alike struggled to keep adequate records of their street trees, and for the most part they were losing more trees than they were planting. Dresden's comprehensive card and map system was an exception. Although it turned street tree data into abstract numbers and mechanized its management, it provided a way to promote adequate care of the trees and prevent their neglect. The information collected on the edge-notched cards also included "dendrometric" data, such as trunk diameter and circumference, height, and canopy diameter, notes on soil and tree conditions, as well as suggestions for maintenance and care. An additional column was provided for observations that did not fall into any of the given categories. Although "dendrometric" information and suggestions for maintenance and care were seldom provided, additional comments on the cards sometimes included the history of plantings on the respective site. Dresden's 1970s street tree project therefore sought to see, survey, and sort the trees depending on both their individual character traits and the spatial effects created by their type of planting as single tree, row, or allée, or in a group of diverse species. It was a method of tree control, but it was also a method of tree care.

1 For the history of street tree planting and topics related to this article, see Sonja Dümpelmann, *Seeing trees: a history of street trees in New York City and Berlin* (London and New Haven: Yale University Press, 2019); Sonja Dümpelmann, "Trees, wood, and paper: materialities of urban arboriculture in modern Berlin," *Journal of Urban History* 46 (2) (2020) pp. 310–333.

2 Steffen Löbel and Siegfried Sommer, "Dresdner Straßenbäume. Vom Ende des Zweiten Weltkrieges bis zum Jahre 2012. Zweiter Teil," in Stadtmuseum Dresden, ed., *Dresdner Geschichtsbuch* 18 (Altenburg: DZA, 2013) pp. 193–223 (193–194).

3 Ibid. pp. 193–223 (195).

4 Ibid., pp. 195–196.

5 For notes on the education of future landscape architects at the Technical University Dresden and the history of the landscape architecture programme, see Helmut Giese and Siegfried Sommer, "Die Dresdner Schule," *Garten + Landschaft* 103, no. 1 (1993) pp. 8–11.

6 In an interesting twist of history, many offices of Dresden's city government, including the office for street trees, are today housed in the former Robotron buildings on Grunaer Strasse. The VVB Datenverarbeitungs- und Büromaschinen had been founded in 1964 in the wake of the ministerial council's enactment of a "program for the development, introduction, and realization of machinic data processing in the GDR in the years 1964 until 1970." For the history of data processing and computer science in the GDR, and the role of Dresden, see Erich Sobeslavsky and Nikolaus Joachim Lehmann, *Zur Geschichte von Rechentechnik und Datenverarbeitung in der DDR 1946–1968* (Dresden: Hannah-Arendt-Institut für Totalitarismusforschung, 1996); Matthias Judt, "Zur Geschichte des Büro- und Datenverarbeitungsmaschinenbaus in der SBZ/DDR," in Werner Pumpe and Christian Kleinschmidt, eds., *Unternehmen zwischen Markt- und Macht: Aspekte deutscher Unternehmens- und Industriegeschichte im 20. Jahrhundert* (Essen: Klartext, 1992) pp. 137–153.

7 See Siegfried Sommer's research report "Der Einfluss der Gehölzpflanzungen an Landstrassen auf die Vegetation des angrenzenden Geländes" (Berlin: Humboldt Universität, 1966); Siegfried Sommer, "Probleme der Gehölzpflege," *Deutsche Gartenarchitektur*

12 (4) (1971) pp. 79–80; Ernst Kürsten, "Das Strassenbaumkataster," *Das Gartenamt* 33 (4) (1984) pp. 245–52; S. Sommer, "Erfassung des Strassenbaumbestandes—Grundlage für Erhaltung und Rekonstruktion," *Landschaftsarchitektur* 4 (4) (1975) pp. 113–14; Siegfried Sommer, "Zur Auswertung der Strassenbaumerfassung im Stadtgebiet von Dresden," *50 Jahre Landschaftsarchitektur, Schriftenreihe der Sektion Architektur, Technische Universität Dresden*, 14 (1979) pp. 149–54; Harald Linke and Horst Burggraf, "Sektion Architektur, Übersichtsbericht zur Forschung 1975," Universitätsarchiv Dresden, S 18 no. 96.

8 For edge-notched cards and punch card techniques and their application in science and industry, see Robert S. Casey and James W. Perry, eds., *Punched cards: their applications to science and industry* (New York: Reinhold, 1951); Martin Scheele, *Punch-card methods in research and documentation with special reference to biology* (New York: Interscience, 1961); Allen Kent, James W. Perry, and Robert S. Casey, "Introduction," in Robert S. Casey, James W. Perry, Madeline M. Berry, and Allen Kent, eds., *Punched cards: their application to science and industry* (New York: Reinhold, 1958) pp. 3–11. Dresden's 1970s edge-notched card survey is currently still kept in the Department of Gardens. But over the years, updating the cards and the survey proved a challenge. Initially, the project had relied on student labor and it appears that already in the late 1970s the survey was no longer updated systematically and was used for reference purposes only.

9 See Anne-Kathrin Knepel's report "Bepflanzungskonzeption für die wichtigsten Hauptverkehrsverbindungen im Zentrum Dresdens," Technische Universität Dresden, Sektion Architektur, Fachstudienrichtung Landschaftsarchitektur, 1976, Stadtarchiv Dresden, VEB Grünanlagen, 9.1.5. no. 991.

10 For comprehensive tree-planting concepts, see Sonja Dümpelmann, *Seeing trees: a history of street trees in New York City and Berlin* (New Haven and London: Yale University Press, 2019) pp. 165–175.

11 PNV is an ecological concept–today increasingly criticized–that was developed in the 1950s by phytosociologist Reinhold Tüxen to describe the vegetation that would be expected on a particular site given its particular environmental conditions if this site was undisturbed by human interventions or particular hazardous events.

12 See documents, especially "Jahresarbeitsplan der Baumschutzkommission 1987"; Mutscher in a letter to Prof H. Linke, 7 January 1986; "Protokoll Sitzung der Baumschutzkommission am 23.5.1990" in Universitätsarchiv der TU Dresden, B.7, Sektion 18-Architektur, 8.6.114. See also Wolfgang Fischer, "Möglichkeiten zur Ermittlung des Bestandes und des Zustandes der Vegetation in städtischen Teilgebieten," *Landschaftsarchitektur* 17 (4) (1988) pp. 110–112.

13 Wolfgang Junker, *Das Wohnungsbauprogramm der Deutschen Demokratischen Republik für die Jahre 1976 bis 1990, 10. Tagung des ZK der SED*, 2. Oktober 1973 (Berlin: Dietz, 1973) pp. 24–25.

14 Ibid. pp. 24–25. Also see *Programm der Sozialistischen Einheitspartei Deutschlands, einstimmig angenommen auf dem IX. Parteitag der Sozialistischen Einheitspartei Deutschlands, Berlin, 18. Bis 22. Mai 1976* (Berlin: Dietz, 1984).

15 See Junker, *Das Wohnungsbauprogramm*, pp. 24–25; Walter Délenk, "Planung und Gestaltung der Freiflächen in der Stadt," in Bauakademie der Deutschen Demokratischen Republik, ed., *Aufgaben des Städtebaus zur Erfüllung des langfristigen Wohnungsbauprogramms als Beitrag zur Lösung der Hauptaufgaben des VIII. Parteitages der SED*, Schriftenreihen der Bauforschung, Reihe Plenartagungen der Bauakademie, no. 8, (Berlin: Bauinformation, 1975) p. 51.

16 See "Befehl Nr. 299/65 über die Organisierung eines einheitlichen Systems der politisch-operativen Auswertungs- und Informationstätigkeit im Ministerium für Staatssicherheit" from 24 July 1965, available at https://www.bstu.de/informationen-zur-stasi/quellensammlungen/die-grundsatzdokumente-des-ministeriums-fuer-staatssicherheit/ (accessed 31 October 2018). For the GDR's surveillance system in general, see, for example, Jenny Krämer and Benedikt Vallendar, *Leben hinter Mauern: Arbeitsalltag und Privatleben hauptamtlicher Mitarbeiter des Ministeriums für Staatssicherheit der DDR* (Essen: Klartext, 2014).

Vertical ecologies: the balcony biotopes of Berlin

Dorothee Brantz

In Walter Benjamin's memory, his family's loggia was "the cradle in which the city bedded its new citizen."[1] It was an auspicious place where young Walter started to explore his hometown Berlin around 1900. Setting out from here, he discovered seasonal variations, and the different ways his neighbours lived. It was a space for curiosity and respite in a city characterized by an increasing pace and blasé anonymity.[2] The balcony was both a place of participation and withdrawal; people gathered there to contribute to the vertical livelihood of streets, yet it remained removed from its openly public realm.

Architecturally, a loggia is not the same as a balcony. While a loggia is incorporated into the façade, a balcony protrudes from the wall of a multistory building. Both are valuable architectural contributions to urban apartment buildings because they add an outside dimension to urban housing. Balconies come in many different shapes and sizes. Some, like the Juliet balcony, hardly protrude from the wall at all, while others offer large, richly decorated platforms. Their balustrades pay tribute to the broad spectrum of architectural design, featuring materials ranging from brick to cast iron to concrete or glass. Sometimes they attest to the stratification of wealth and social class within a single building, with the bel étage style traditionally featuring the most elaborate structural and decorative elements.

The Juliet balcony might be the most acclaimed given its Shakespearean origin, but other balconies have also become historically significant stages. They have offered a setting for important speeches like the competing declarations of the first German Republic by Philipp Scheidemann and Karl Liebknecht in November 1918. When Hans-Dietrich Genscher appeared on the balcony of the West German embassy in Prague in September 1989, it marked the immanent demise of the GDR. More generally, kings, queens, popes, and pop stars use balconies to demonstrate their alleged dedication to those below; but balconies are also places of display for personal politics, national allegiances, or sexual preferences. As such, balconies are cultural signifiers. In apartment buildings they serve as an extension of private interior homes. To some, their balcony is a place to dry laundry or to store stuff

Spring balcony (2019). Photo: Dorothee Brantz.

like bicycles, ladders, and beer crates. For others, the balcony serves as a satellite receiving station for news and media from homelands far away. Many also utilize it as a spot for gardening. Even emptiness can be read as a statement.

As spaces of transgression, balconies dissolve the conventional boundaries between inside and outside, public and private, up and down, as well as nature and culture. A balcony is a private space open to the publicity of the streets below. It is an outdoor space serving as an extension of the indoor apartment to which it belongs. Around the turn of the twentieth century, one Berlin woman declared that "the balcony replaces many things. It serves as a children's room, pantry, garden restaurant, study, and summer home. It often encompasses all the natural elements big city inhabitants want to bring into their daily lives."[3] Balconies offer distinct biotopes that add to the diversity of urban life through the range of human activities, plants, and animals that abound there. Surprisingly, however, the balcony is still rather invisible in the field of urban studies despite being a quite ubiquitous space of urbanity, and a rather peculiar one to boot. One exception is the boom in gardening literature, including "how to" guides on planting out the balcony as a kitchen garden or explorative permaculture. But why has the balcony not garnered more attention from urban scholars? Has it simply been overlooked? Even in the growing literature on urban verticality and vertical greening, it is hardly mentioned despite its long tradition as part of urban architecture, gardening, and sociable biodiversity. Henri Lefebvre described his Paris balcony as the perfect vantage point for the study of urban street rhythms.[4] For him it served as a protected space for the

Couple on a Berlin balcony, ca. 1930s. Source: Susann Hellemann and Lothar Binger, *Von Balkon zu Balkon: Berliner Balkongeschichte(n)* (Berlin: Verlag Dirk Nishen, 1988).

observation of the theatrics of urban life below. But the balcony itself also presents a site for socio-natural spectacle—as was demonstrated by a special exhibition at a local Berlin museum a number of years ago.[5] Based on private photographs taken over several decades, the exhibit presented a fascinating tableau of how Berliners have used their balconies across time; how they sat there to read, eat and drink; how they played on their balconies; and, of course, what they planted.

In the early twentieth century, the balcony was a space for cultivated togetherness. It would be fashionably decorated with tablecloths—and, of course, plants. Interestingly, while fashions have obviously changed, the kinds of flowers and greenery that people plant have remained much the same. Then as now, ivy, pelargoniums, and petunias were among the most popular. For years, the Central German Gardening Association has put together a list of the most popular garden and balcony plants; and for decades the pelargonium has taken first place.

Pelargoniums are colourful, grow quickly, and carry a touch of the exotic. They add a luscious appearance even to a small space. Other popular plants include begonias, pansies, summer heath, primroses, and chrysanthemums—all of them pretty and easy to grow. Garden centres and balconies abound with them throughout the summer months. They certainly add flair and colour to the city, but ecologically most of them have some serious disadvantages. To be ready for spring planting, they have to be grown in energy-intensive green houses. Since most of them are only perennials, they will bloom for one season only, and then end up in the trash. More importantly, however, the fact that they are not indigenous means that most insects cannot feed on them because their probosci are too short to reach the flowers' nectar. Hence, these plants are pretty, but unfortunately, they are not good for much else. Environmental organizations like Nabu (Germany's largest nature conservation NGO) currently discourage their use, recommending that people plant native wild flowers and herbs instead.

Can balconies actually make a difference to the ecological outlook of cities? The answer is that they might. Balconies have potential as significant contributors for the proliferation of urban biotopes. Taken together, planted balconies account for a substantial amount of vertical green in the city. Thus, the private oasis of the balcony could and indeed should serve as a space for political botany or botanical politics. It could add to urban botanical diversity by helping to feed insects, butterflies, and birds. While the actual effect of balcony greenery on urban biodiversity and its impact on a street's micro-climate remain to be investigated, commonsense observation certainly suggests positive effects. Green balconies feel cooler, and bee-friendly plants attract all kinds of little flying creatures. Perhaps this could even be a field of investigation for citizen science. However, even without the aspect of scientific inquiry, the balcony certainly offers a space to increase people's awareness for the intricacies of urban nature and for the potential of cultivating the botanical city right outside one's own apartment.

More than any other private living area, the balcony is a seasonal space. As I am writing this, two seasons—winter and spring—are wrestling with one another. Of course, we know which one will win out in the predestined course of time. For now, however, Berlin's balconies provide the stage for a fascinating spectacle. Plants bud and blossom, flowers bloom and wilt, all at their own distinct pace. Weeds break through the ground. Insects, birds, and other animals turn up to suck nectar and to pollinate plants. Birds are chirping and building nests for their young. But there is also a distinct human element. In spring, people reemerge on their balconies. As it gets warmer, voices suddenly emerge along the façades of houses. People are opening their doors again, sitting outside to take in the sun or enjoying the mild evenings. Many of them embark on gardening activities. Just as some people cannot wait to exchange their winter wear for shorts and t-shirts, there are balcony gardeners who will use the first rays of the sun to clean up the ravages of winter, to start planting this and that, and to transform their balcony from one seasonal display to another. Out go the twigs that protected the perennial plants from wintery frosts. It's cleanup time. Winter had turned most balconies into mere storage spaces. Spring is a time of new beginnings, soft colours, and brightening days getting three minutes longer every day.

Winter balcony (2019). Photo: Dorothee Brantz.

In Berlin, March and April are transient times because both types of seasonal balconies persist. On many balconies, pine twigs still dominate, while on others pansies, narcissi, and hyacinths are already in bloom. No pelargoniums and petunias yet. They are too sensitive to frost, which could still return at any time in early spring. The garden centres are slowly filling up their outdoor spaces with plants as customers grow ever more eager to purchase flower boxes, dirt, and all kinds of flowery and green plants. Early spring weekends are among the busiest times of year for home supply stores. Garden centres have long been highly commercialized spaces of an astounding eco-globality in the midst of cities. Here one can purchase plants from all over the world. Japanese cherries stand next to

Mediterranean olive trees, boxwoods next to citrus plants. Oleanders are lined up next to rose bushes of all kinds. These days, there are also a growing number of specially-bred miniature fruit trees. All of them end up on balconies across the city. Spring holds the promise of a summer harvest—of urban agriculture in miniature. After all, balconies embody the philosophy of the "edible city." Often, they are described as a private oasis amidst the bustle of the urban or as a little paradise and safe haven in times of planetary demise. Very likely, this is just an illusion. We will see when spring turns to summer. If 2020 turns into another European summer of drought, what will happen to the city's planted balconies? Will they become another site of drought, or will they attest to the excessive use of water? Both would present problematic sights, and sad signs of our changing environmental and political climate.

In a recent shift towards a more phenomenological perspective on the corporeal and sensory dimensions of cities, scholars are looking at the complexity of urban atmospheres to uncover the prevailing mood or cultural representations of a place. Matthew Gandy writes that atmospheres of this kind always connect to "a persistent material or meteorological presence, either real or imagined, which envelopes or unsettles the human subject."[6] Balconies embody the transitory nature of urban atmospheres and how they affect various living creatures. Walter Benjamin called his loggia a protected place where time and place melted together, where impressions of life amalgamated and where life slowed down to a sense of *carpe diem*.[7] Balcony life is not just about *carpe diem*, but it encapsulates numerous temporal dimensions such as time of day, seasonal time of year, memory, and history. It embodies change and continuity, both of which are exemplified in the lifecycle of plants that blossom, bloom, and wilt to reemerge the following year (if they are frost-resistant). Plants also participate in historical processes through their continuous existence either as individual plants, in their persistent succession (such as roses and pelargoniums), or in their distinct presence at specific historical moments (consider vegetables in the immediate post-war years or miniature fruit trees today). Recognizing the whole urban temporal spectrum opens up a deep perspective on the botanical city—both in specific geographic (climatic) locations and with regard to species diversity. The balcony offers a stage where these urban atmospheric distinctions manifest themselves. This is not only a matter of perceptions and impressions; it also translates into a profit margin. If one is to believe real estate advertisements, a balcony oriented towards the sun contributes substantially to the monetary value of an apartment. In Berlin, a south-facing balcony is by far the most desirable because it provides the largest amount of sunshine while the north-facing balconies are considered the least attractive option. The existence and size of balconies as well as their sun exposure are important factors in determining real estate values, but not simply as a matter of hype.

Alignment towards the light matters with regard to sun exposure, which in turn has a direct effect on what can be planted. Plants, as we know, influence the atmosphere of a place, not just with regard to human leisure but also with regard to its ecology—which plants will grow, which birds and insects might come to visit (or not), and how engaged one needs to be with one's plants. Thus, balconies can create distinct botanical atmospheres, both for individual homes and for cities at large. To put it another way, balconies can contribute to the larger ecological make-up of urban environments. This potential is increasingly recognized, but much remains to be done. In light of the increasing pressures on urban ecosystems, city administrations could do a lot more to educate and encourage inhabitants to convert their balconies into botanical spaces. Some gardening stores have already recognized the business potential of such biodiversity. Numerous plants are marketed as bee-friendly, and many shoppers happily respond to these offers. In the neoliberal city, businesses might be more sensitive towards the need for and profitability of change than politicians, who are tied to bureaucratic and legislative circumstances. The city of Berlin is currently drafting a "Charter for Berlin's Urban Green,"[8] which does mention balconies, even if only in a very general way. More to the point, some current citizen initiatives seek to enforce political action. Following the astounding success of a Bavarian citizen initiative to protect bees and insects, there are also attempts to mobilize Berliners to participate in a similar referendum and also to take concrete action, including on their balconies.[9] Nabu and other environmental organizations are campaigning for a more ecologically conscious planting of balconies, with wildflowers and herbs instead of pelargoniums and bamboo. Another current initiative seeks a referendum to declare a local "climate emergency" for Berlin in order to force the government to act in accordance with the Paris climate accords. Even if only in a small way, balcony greenery could also be integrated into these initiatives to improve Berlin's urban climate and biodiversity. Moreover, balconies are drawn into more representational efforts for political change. For instance, the Fridays for Future movement is organizing a campaign entitled "one million balconies," which aims to place banners across balconies calling for climate action.[10] More important than symbolic statements, however, are concrete actions that enhance ecological viability and foster urban biodiversity. Sensibly planted balconies might make a small but meaningful contribution to the vertical appearance and environmental impact of cities.

1 Walter Benjamin, *Berliner Kindheit um neunzehnhundert* (Frankfurt: Suhrkamp, 1987) p. 11.
2 Georg Simmel, *Die Großstädte und das Geistesleben* (Frankfurt: Suhrkamp, 2006, originally 1903).
3 Cited in Johannes Böttner, *Balkongärtnerei und Vorgärten* (Frankfurt, 1904) p. 1.
4 Henri Lefebvre, *Rhythmanalysis: space, time, and everyday life* (London: Bloomsbury, 2013).
5 Susann Hellemann and Lothar Binger, *Von Balkon zu Balkon: Berliner Balkongeschichte(n)* (Berlin: Nishen, 1988).
6 Matthew Gandy, "Urban atmospheres," *Cultural Geographies* 24 (3) (2017) p. 355.
7 Walter Benjamin, *Berliner Kindheit*, p. 13.
8 https://meingruenes.berlin.de/ (accessed 10 May 2019).
9 The Bavarian initiative garnered more than 1.7 million signatures in less than two weeks. Only a month later the Bavarian state government turned this petition into law.
10 https://parentsforfutureberlin.de/1-million-balconies (accessed 10 May 2019).

Drying greens, commons, and the possibilities of the botanical (in one quiet corner of London)

Marcus Nyman

Plants can help modest spaces tell bigger stories. This story concerns the anomalous spaces in which apparently discrete urban ecologies collide, with "modest" being an apposite term for the often hidden politics and practices of domestic life. A city such as London, with its fractured, palimpsest landscapes, does not always make easy reading, and its awkward comings-together of people, material, and other forms of life often require careful ambulatory navigation. It is through one small tract of Blackheath—itself one small tract of southeast London, England—that this essay leads: to a peculiar form of vernacular space and the confluent themes of drying clothes, spontaneous vegetation, and urban commons. "Drying greens" are the idiosyncratic spaces in question. These small patches of fenced-off, concreted ground that are attached to blocks of social housing and intended for the air-drying of clothes, while *seemingly* disused, bristle with emergent vegetation and possibility. My train pulled into Blackheath station a few minutes after the allocated start time of four o'clock in the afternoon, but I was not far behind the others. Upon exiting the eastbound platform, I quickly located the two recorders already at work, peering over the low wall fencing the station car park from the adjacent gardens, scribbling down notes on each species of wildflower encountered. Our task was to help to record data for the London Flora Project survey, an ongoing initiative to update the city-wide records of the "ever-changing urban flora" of London's "complex mosaic of land surfaces and uses."[1] The last iteration of this survey was undertaken over 30 years previously, and was published in the *Flora of the London Area*.[2] Nominally, the task was to record but, in my case, this was more a case of trying to follow along, to make use of my limited botanical identification skills, to ask some (but not too many) questions, and to try and learn as much as possible. With Latin names pinging back and forth between the two experienced recorders, I hoped, where possible, either to pick out the more commonly recognizable plants

Former drying site, Blackheath, London (2017). Photo: Marcus Nyman

or to provide another pair of eyes to spot something novel and as yet unnoticed. I had by this point become somewhat accustomed to the peculiar rhythms and embodiments of this form of botanical surveying. When the focus is species occurrence—rather than, say, abundance or richness—walks tend to move only a little in the first hour or so. As the more common species are noted down, their occurrence later on in the route becomes incidental and the overall pace increases. And yet urban landscapes are far from smooth, and a stop-start pattern is only further complicated by disrupted and fractured terrain. This is not so much a question of the physical capacity to traverse city spaces (although in some cases, soil, rubble, and detritus can present precarious footing[3]), but the form and focus of a survey concerned with wild and self-sown plants offers a re-reading of such spaces. This form of surveying is atlas-based. It divides an area of interest—in this case the whole of Greater London—into grid reference squares, and surveys each of these for the number of species occurring within each of them (on several different occasions). It constitutes a "transect" inasmuch as it is based around a linear, walked route rather than making use of quadrats, but it is not itself a form of representative sampling.[4] Routes are largely dictated by the local knowledge and experience of the meeting leader and by connecting the spaces in which one would be most likely to encounter wild plants, rather than their domesticated and cultivated cousins. Although selectively walked routes may well confer certain biases,[5] urban environments, with their mosaic-like landscapes, do not provide smooth, unimpeded terrain upon which to record. It is estimated that around 24 percent of Greater London is private, domestic garden.[6] While typically populated by cultivated species, these gardens are also locations in which the wild and the self-sown thrive. And yet domestic gardens are beyond the practicable purview of this kind of survey. Although classically, a transect—as a rigorous sampling method—can be useful for assessing species change across different land types and zones of transition, such transects would likely prove unfeasible and inappropriate for surveying the variegated landscapes of a city such as London, at this scale.

We worked our way back westward through the car park, parallel to the railway, noting down as we went not the ornamental or monumental but the bit-part vegetal players, growing from cracks in the pavement, occupying the edges of paths, and encroaching on otherwise carefully managed spaces. The back fences of the gardens we passed and the presence of tomato plants (*Solanum lycopersicum*) hinted at the possibilities of botanical escape that urban density and diversity engender—an unintended invitation for plants to cross human-imposed boundaries. We squeeze between cars and brush past oddly-shaped alkanet (*Pentaglottis sempervirens*) reaching out from the loosely-soiled pavement edges and the base of trees, while discarded bedsprings offer an improvised growing frame. Meanwhile, woody nightshade (*Solanum dulcamara*) makes use of chain-linked fencing for support in its circuitous growth upwards, catching the tree-dappled light on its crimson-red berries. Blackheath is a largely affluent neighbourhood, approximately ten kilometres southeast from the centre of London. Once a suburb *proper*, the city's urban expansion has long since engulfed everything but the Heath itself. Like many such areas of London, despite its sometimes grand architecture and obvious wealth, Blackheath contains pockets of public housing, and it is contiguous with areas such as Charlton and Woolwich to the north, Lewisham to the west and Kidbrooke to the east, that contain higher levels of socio-economical disadvantage. The somewhat anarchic growth of the city did not always leave room for the strict segregation of the rich from the poor. The railway arrived here in the 1840s, linking the metropolis with this newly sprung-up suburb lining the southern edges of the sizeable expanse of common land known as Blackheath. Heading east, the railway continues to the Thames estuary, the Medway, and the north Kent coast. As local historian Neil Rhind points out, unlike many of the ancient villages ultimately subsumed in the expansion of London, Blackheath village was not especially old. Indeed, "it was never, in the true sense, a village at all, for when it finally came into being it was sited at the meeting point of four parishes."[7] Like many extant areas of metropolitan common land, the semi-rural vistas that the heath afforded the owners of its large new residences provided a factor in motivating and shaping its preservation and protection from development[8]. The aesthetic and the botanical aspects also brought people from further afield, while the railway provided the practical means for new forms of visitation. An 1881 "Half-Holiday Handbooks" guide to the district of Greenwich and Blackheath notes how distinctive the heath is from the nearby wooded parklands of Greenwich Park by virtue of its open, elevated position and gravelly subsoil. While the heath's preservation as a public amenity ("against the unscrupulous lords of the manor") was established via the mechanism of the 1871 Metropolitan Commons Supplemental Act, this touristic guide laments some of the Metropolitan Board of Works' management and "ridiculously irksome" bylaws. It notes:

> Under these regulations, a child picking daisies, or a botanical class studying the grass flora of our heaths, are compelled by keepers to throw down their specimens, under pain of apprehension for non-compliance ... regulations are, of course necessary, but it is an insult to put the well-conducted naturalist on the same level as the "rough," who breaks down trees and sets fire to acres of furze.[9]

The nineteenth century had seen a shift in how common land such as Blackheath, increasingly surrounded by the city, was used and understood. Manorial lands—specifically common or manorial wastes[10]—upon which various formal and customary "rights of common" had traditionally been exercised by parishioners, were increasingly enmeshed in changing metropolitan politics, demographics, and development. Commons had previously played an important role in the rural economy and village life, offering subsistence to some of the poorest and spaces of relative freedom and respite.[11] However, by the mid-nineteenth century, "urbanization had removed many of the traditional function of commons ... those who derived benefits from them such as gypsies, cottagers, or the poor, were politically weak."[12] With demographic changes and the expansion of the urban fabric, large and relatively unmonitored tracts of green space accommodated a range of people and activities, including political meetings, sports and games, hawking and begging, religious preaching, donkey riding and animal grazing, carpet beating and clothes drying. These green spaces were also notorious for robbery and assault.[13] For affluent, more genteel residents—exemplified by many of the political campaigners of the Commons Preservation Society—there was an intrinsic tension between controlling such informal, "undesirable" usage and maintaining the "wild" aesthetic—the *rus in urbe*—of these open spaces. As the historian David Reeder points out, "the commons had to be tamed but without making them too park-like."[14] It was not only a question of regulating behaviour; there were also aesthetic and landscape issues that applied to the commons, generated by overgrowth and ecological succession. As Neil Thornton, writing on the history of London's commons preservation, explains: "if not the haunts of dangerous people, commons were often undrained, overgrown and impassable."[15] Blackheath was particularly known for its prevalence of gorse (*Ulex europaeus*), commonly called "furze," which was one of the plants gathered under "estovers"—the common right to collect fuel. In addition to its utility, the furze was also an aesthetic, vernacular, and botanical curiosity, spurring an apocryphal tale of Carl Linneaus falling to his knees on a visit to the heath as he saw the dazzling sight of the plant in yellow flower.[16] Commons such as Blackheath had long been spaces for subsistence *and* recreation, maintained by both legally recognized rights and customary practice. Urban expansion brought nearby commons into the auspices of emerging metropolitan authorities and generated diverse perspectives on their proper function. The debates that surrounded commons preservation were not solely populated by powerful landlords and disenfranchised commoners. Many users for whom sites such as Blackheath were crucial to their livelihoods were not recognized rights-holders. Indeed, commoners themselves may have been keen to profit from rights they no longer practiced but which were held in perpetuity. These debates were often parochial in nature but, in the case of Blackheath, the lords of the manor were quite willing to hand management of the land over to the city. At the time of Blackheath's formal preservation for the public by the Metropolitan Board of Works (MBW) in 1871, it was reported that, "the Heath was rapidly being destroyed by the number of costermongers and others who almost constantly took possession of it."[17] While "taking possession" could refer to the permanent extraction activities of materials such as soil or gravel from the heath, it more likely means the use of space for a specific and singular purpose (temporarily, and without implying theft or enclosure). One such documented purpose was the use of Blackheath as open-air drying and bleaching grounds by local laundresses. It is not altogether clear how long clothes drying had occurred on Blackheath, but the practice long predated both its formal preservation and the emerging regimes of public sanitation and cleanliness associated with the late Victorian period. The area on the southern edge of the heath, next to the Royal Parade and All Saints Church—the section closest to Blackheath village itself—was known locally as Washerwoman's Bottom because of its use by local laundresses and the topological scars of gravel and sand extraction.[18] A row of small cottages once lined this section of the Heath and was known colloquially as "Washerwoman's Row," named after the occupation of many of its inhabitants.[19] While drying and bleaching clothes in public presented well-to-do Victorian residents with an uncomfortable and immodest reminder of the dirt and corporeal reality of everyday life and the presence of otherwise hidden (and mainly female) domestic labour, these residents also valued the services the washerwomen provided. As Rhind notes, there had been concerted effort by some parties (from the 1860s onwards) to lobby the Board and Lord of the Manor "to remove the drying rights for the laundresses and thus the eyesore of the washing poles."[20] However, not everyone agreed. "The washerwomen, for as long as anyone could remember, had dried clothes on the Heath and there was no doubt the clothes had to be dried somewhere."[21] The Board inherited these features and functions of the Heath, drying posts and all, when it took over its management. While the byelaws it introduced proscribed the drying of clothes on the Heath's furze, it compromised and issued licenses to the local laundresses with various provisos attached, such as no drying on Sundays.[22] In 1877, the Board tasked its superintending architect with assessing the number of posts on the heath and checking whether all licensees were still alive.[23] While some complained of the nuisance caused by carpet beating in the vicinity of their properties,[24] others lobbied the Board to uphold the rights of laundresses to use the heath to undertake their work. In May 1877, William George Lemon—a member of the Lewisham District Board of Works—wrote to the Metropolitan Board on behalf of a local laundress, Mrs Ann Greer, on account of the imminent removal of her license to dry clothes on the heath following the death of her mother, Mrs Coppin. They had lived and worked in Bath Place—likely another toponymical indication of the professions of its inhabitants—for many years but the license was not transferable.[25] The Metropolitan Board was somewhat ambivalent to the plight of the laundresses continuing to use the heath for their livelihoods, resolving in 1879 to revoke all existing licenses and reissue them on an annually renewable basis, rendering them "revocable at pleasure." The clerk of the Board—a Mr Wakefield—noted that "by securing the receipt of each woman every year there would be no difficulty in checking correctly any who may die off."[26] No further licenses were issued after 1893, and the practice had ceased a few years later.[27] However, the ceasing of drying on the Heath was not solely a consequence of middle-class preference and spatial ordering by metropolitan authorities—it was also a response to changing economies and technologies.

That drying clothes requires space seems at first glance a remarkably banal observation. Yet the demands for space by an ever-present activity must, by definition, shape the domestic and the built environment and its use. For anthropologist Sarah Pink and others, by "foregrounding the background," laundry—and clothes drying in particular—can help illuminate the materialities and organizing processes of everyday life.[28] In the drying of clothes, we find the intertwined threads of geography and space, family and gender, aesthetics and cleanliness, and of weather, temporality and routine. Concerns relating to the environmental impacts of indoor clothes drying, particularly in social housing with limited access to outside space, are pertinent to contemporary questions of public health, and energy and water consumption[29] but are not novel. As historian Patricia Malcolmson explains, laundry work in Victorian England ("doing the wash") "was almost everywhere an activity that caused major dislocation of domestic life."[30] Indeed, the various laundry processes, when undertaken in domestic dwellings, created a rhythm of textures and senses through the week, including the way that "dripping clothes democratically dampened the heads and shoulders of all." Weather and the city's pollution would dictate whether the heat and humidity generated by domestic laundry could be relieved by opening windows and allowing in fresh air. By the end of the nineteenth century technological advancements and economies of scale had largely superseded the need for laundry to be done by hand at a small local scale—or by domestic servants, for whom Blackheath provided a practical amenity.[31] By way of an example, one of the early large-scale laundry factories in London was established in 1869 in Rushey Green, Lewisham—just three kilometres southeast from Blackheath. It served businesses in the growing financial centre of the City of London.[32]

We sidle our way along the roadways that ultimately slope up towards the heath, passing a school named for the radical priest John Ball—one of the figureheads of the Peasants Revolt of 1381, which saw royal representatives meet rebels at Blackheath on their march to London from Kent. The quiet, sun-beaten roads lined with blocks of medium-density twentieth-century social housing seem alien to such conflagrations of the city's past. And yet, these blocks, constructed in the aftermath of WWII, were likely intended to meet the escalated demand for housing in the post-war period, and to fulfill modernist ideas for communal life. Three or four stories in height and constructed with the topography in mind, these blocks are dissimilar to the taller, denser towers with which post-war reconstruction is often associated. Following the national government's Right to Buy scheme of the early 1990s, a number of these flats are now likely to be at least partially privately owned. Just behind them, the rear elevations of the substantial houses lining the heath can be glimpsed, along with the walls of their extensive gardens—some of which appear to have been extended at some point at the end of the nineteenth century. The area is well shaded by the verdant tree canopy emerging from private gardens and the public realm, along with the abundant vegetation abutting the nearby train tracks. The lead surveyor, familiar with the area, brought us down a footpath in front of the flats, and we soon came across a small patch of concrete—approximately five metres by eight metres in area—enclosed by chain link fencing. Although the space was not altogether inviting, the rusted latch opened easily, allowing us to enter. This was, he informed us, an outside communal drying area, associated with the adjacent flats. At first glance, it appeared unused, as spontaneous vegetation had taken hold of many of the edges and surfaces of stone. No clothes were visible, although rusted posts and lines remained in situ. For some time, we paced this small patch, recording what was present. Although external to the buildings, this communal space could hardly be described as "public" or "visible"—it was set back from a quiet side road, at the end of a path with no thoroughfare, and shaded by tree cover. Before widespread access to tumble dryers, a vernacular built form of this kind served the needs of this particular form of public housing. The scale of the buildings would not warrant segregated internal facilities, while such an outside space would be insufficient and inconvenient for residents of higher-occupancy tower blocks. This was a deliberate design intervention to serve the needs of domestic life, one based around common access. These were common spaces, not designed and directed towards a general or abstract public, but designed with particular people in mind. Botanical walking may offer new framings of urban space, but, like any form of observation, it is partial. It cannot tell you how life unfolded in these drying spaces, or what they meant to residents. However, it is not too much to imagine that such places of domestic encounter contained not only the functional activities of drying clothes but also various modes and textures of social life—spaces of dwelling and coexistence. Across the road and towards the heath, we come across another so-called "drying green." Larger and more open, this one is nestled on the south-facing slope, and is flanked by the back walls of gardens on two sides and garages to the other. The surrounding concrete surfaces form a sun trap, within which a surprising quantity and variety of vegetation grows. It is immediately clear why such a space would also be valuable for drying clothes. Some of the plants appear cultivated (although little maintained), while others are wild or escapees. As we enter the fenced but unlocked area, I mistake the distinctive leaflets of a sumac tree (genus *Rhus*) for those of the tree of heaven (*Ailanthus altissima*), notable for its capacity to thrive in the concrete-dominated climes of the city and its transgression of ecological and cultural boundaries.[33] Our focus was on self-sown and wild species, but the distinction does not always hold. From the thin cracks of the laid concrete, ground-covering plants spring up. The relatively untrammelled nature of the ground enables ruderal species to occupy it.[34] Buddleia (genus *Buddleja*) is present but is far from dominant, while brambles (*Rubus fruticosus*) and nettles (*Urtica dioica*) have not had the chance to crowd out other species. Gleaming amid the greenery, closer to the ground, are the ruby red fruits of wild strawberry (*Fragaria vesca*) and raspberry (*Rubus ideaus*). The former, much smaller than the more familiar cultivated species, is soft to the touch and powerfully sweet to taste. Their arrival may have been facilitated by the variegated mosaic of the surrounding urban space—like their ragwort neighbours (*Senecio* spp.)—but it is the micro-geographies of the site that have enabled their flourishing.

Several months after my first visit, I returned to the site. I wanted to photograph it in better quality than I had been able to during my first encounter of the survey. The summer heat was excessive and had clearly taken its toll on much vegetation. Contrary to my prior belief, the first small drying green now appeared to be in use for its designated purpose of clothes drying. The mossy ground blushed in one corner with the pink sweep of fallen blossom. Back up the slope, I found an additional concrete patch I had missed the first time around. Larger than the others but lacking vegetation, it was almost completely in shade. Painted on the ground were markings for children's games. The planting surrounding the third space was still abundant, if a little ragged, but the area itself was now locked and inaccessible. My presence soon caught the attention of two residents, a father and son. They asked me, in an altogether friendly but inquisitive manner, what my interest in the space was. They explained that they were in the process of organizing and cleaning it up, aiming to repurpose it as a community area, as well as responding to requests from older female residents who wished to use it for drying again. They were surprised by the idea that there might be anything of botanical interest in the site, and even more so that wild edibles could be growing amid the asphalt. They told me how slow and unwilling the council was to offer support, and that they had taken it upon themselves to make it a useable space, particularly for children on the estate. One of the tasks they had set themselves was to clear out the weeds. With a certain glee, the older of the two showed me the herbicide they had acquired to excoriate the area of its existing plant life.

An urban botanical transect survey is quite distinct from the kinds of botanizing encouraged by the "Half-Holiday Handbook" mentioned above. The guide extols the route to nearby Eltham as, offering "good hunting ground for the botanist," with "great toad flax, golden rod, and many other wild flowers."[35] Similarly, it lauds the marshes of Plumstead to the northeast: "to those of our readers who are botanists or microscopists, they afford one of the best collecting grounds near the metropolis."[36] It lists a host of botanically and medicinally interesting species that might be encountered, including sea wormwood (*Artemisia maritima*), wild asparagus (*Asparagus officinalis*), and flowering rush (*Butomus umbellatus*). Although London has many areas that are protected for nature conservation, the urban landscape offers fewer such opportunities for botanizing. Although this was not its primary purpose, the format of surveying for the London Flora Project, with the value it places on *occurrence*, rather than rarity or diversity, meant that it paid attention to plants that grow in the margins, in wall cracks and in otherwise overlooked spaces. It provides an opportunity to learn about the common and unexceptional alongside the valuable or beautiful. The discrete ecologies of spontaneous urban vegetation and domestic laundry collide in the small drying greens of Blackheath, but they are not contained there. These spaces are not restricted to those found during this one botanical walk, and, although not "typical" of metropolitan social housing per se, they are not uncommon. In the tenement housing of cities in Scotland, open-air drying spaces are more recognizable and culturally valued architectural vernacular, providing a design solution to the spatial requirements of both laundry and communal life.[37] In many cases, the image of domestic clothes drying on balconies and other repurposed spaces provides an ambiguous motif for the continued presence of the urban poor and the informal strategies with which people get on with the task of living in cities. To see clothes drying is a reminder of the bodies that otherwise inhabit them and the women (usually) who wash and hang them. The relative usefulness of a drying green is affected by social and technological change; thus, the advent of the tumble dryer and the ability to dry more efficiently elsewhere create conditions in which wild or feral plants can make a quiet vegetative claim to otherwise abandoned spaces. The proximity of these isolated patches of concrete to the common land at Blackheath is not merely convenient or coincidental. Geographical and temporal adjacency is a fundamental condition of urban life and quality of urban space, forcing together people and things in sometimes awkward congress. Proximity enables botanical escape. It structures microclimates, it can foster regimes of both care and nuisance, and, significantly, it frames who or what is present, and who is invested in the life of a place. As London's planning and development strategies increasingly focus on higher levels of density to meet high demand, even purportedly unused space has potential value. It may be that the small size and awkward location of these drying greens mean they are overlooked in the speculative dynamics of development in London, and all the more reason for residents to take an active part in maintaining and protecting them. Although these spaces are publicly owned, it is a mistake to imagine these as "public spaces" in a meaningful sense. The extent to which they "belong" to an identifiable community (rather than an abstract public) and function within the realms of domestic and communal life suggests they are rather more like "commons" in the traditional sense than the officially designated common land of Blackheath lying only a few metres away. While "common rights" played a pivotal role in the protection of sites such as Blackheath, its preservation and subsequent management was ultimately undertaken in the interests of the "public" who, as the Commons Preservation Society itself outlines, had no previous stake in the legal status of common land.[38] A *public* interest meant the prohibition of enclosure, encroachment, or activities that prevented others' enjoyment of the common. Inevitably, this meant the erosion of subsistence practices, such as clothes drying, the materiality of which did not suit changing aesthetic preferences and could not be conducted without dedicated space. The space ultimately "preserved" at Blackheath was in reality something quite different to the forms of common that had preceded it. Where once the commons blurred the distinction between the public and the private, offering resources through which the poorest were able to cope with the material demands of everyday life, their preservation meant that everyone had a legitimate claim to the common, no matter their individual need or interest. While metropolitan authority ultimately maintained the cartographic presence of common land, urbanization dissolved the social relations that had formerly filled it with meaning. The pits at Washerwoman's Bottom to the south of the heath, where laundry once hung, appear to have been infilled with bombsite rubble, covered with soil, and seeded with ryegrass (*Lolium perenne*) some time after 1945.[39] This coverage enables low-cost, easy maintenance with mowing, and facilitates surveillance and the perception of public safety on the site, but offers little of botanical interest. Kempt perennial ryegrass, while ecologically dull, might be the most apt indication of a particular form of once-common public space. While serving a leveled public interest, it enables certain forms of aesthetic enjoyment, leisure, and easement but curtails other possibilities for dwelling and subsistence. This management rests on state or metropolitan delegated authority, enforced through bylaws and bureaucratic structures. It is in contrast to the *getting on with* ethos of historic commoning practices of subsistence, whose legitimacy rested on local social and economic ties and customary uses, rather than explicitly-granted permission. Rights by prescription—continued visible and demonstrable use—were also (and continue to be in some cases) a mechanism through which informal and customary practice acquired legal status and protection. Today, the heath remains privately owned but managed as a publicly accessible space in perpetuity. The southern portion of the heath is managed by Glendale, a private company, on behalf of Lewisham Borough Council, as is the case with much of the borough's green space portfolio. One of the few online references to "Washerwoman's Bottom" at "Blackheath" arises in the parochial news blog *The Blackheath Bugle*, and concerns council-backed plans for the erection of a temporary public entertainment area during the London Olympic Games in 2012.[40] Comments on the article reflect the ongoing local and wider disagreement about how these "common" spaces should be accessed and used, and in whose interest. Some support the proposal, while others lament the increased noise and traffic, the effects of long hours of licensed alcohol sales, and the principle of "enclosing" (even temporarily) sections of the heath for profit. Debates of this kind echo controversies unfolding elsewhere around the "borrowing" of urban public space for events which, although purportedly temporary, have "enduring effects ... on the ways spaces and places are used, interpreted, and imagined."[41] Urban researcher Andrew Smith has written extensively on how the official Olympic events staged in neighbouring Greenwich Park, including the equestrian and modern pentathlon (which appealed to particular audiences over other user groups) have acted as a precursor for further "festivalization" of spaces. He notes that while "Some legitimate arguments are used to justify event projects ... these are no consolation to those who feel their everyday spaces have been appropriated and/or violated."[42] The sites this essay has explored offer novel and interesting assemblages of plants and spaces, enabled by the ecologies and economies in which they are enmeshed. Just as human denizens make claims on spaces through political lobbying or commoning practice, so too plants make claims on urban spaces through their material growth and reproduction. To occupy, to be present is—in some sense at least—to make a claim. In the absence of other communicative capacities, plants may well make claims simply by being present. However, such a botanical claim to a common can only be partial and precarious. To survey spaces for the occurrence of different plants is ostensibly to record and to register, and is not to articulate a normative vision for what a site should be, and what should be present. When confronted by the idea of local, informal recommissioning—or *re-commoning*—of drying greens for other communal or shared uses, we might consider what it would mean to try and advocate the value of plants or ecologies already in situ amid residents' legitimate desire to order and make use of the scarce resource of open space in a city such as London. A defence of the botanical in this context might be better framed through the natural history of plants, their uses and values, and the encouragement of co-habitation and care instead of eradication, rather than the articulation of this defense through rights claims.

1 London Natural History Society, 2018, *LNHS sections: botany*, London Natural History Society [Webpage]. Available at http://www.lnhs.org.uk/index.php/about-us/lnhs-sections/botany (accessed 2 October 2018).
I would like to thank Nick Bertrand of the Creekside Discovery Centre, Deptford for leading the botanical walk featured in the essay and for his generous thoughts and contributions.

2 Rodney Burton, *Flora of the London area* (London: London Natural History Society, 1983).

3 See Tim Edensor, "Walking through ruins," in Jo Lee Vergunst and Tim Ingold, eds., *Ways of walking: ethnography and practice on foot* (Aldershot & Burlington, VT: Ashgate) pp. 123–142.

4 Stephen T. Buckland, David L. Borchers, Alan Johnston, Peter A. Henry, and Tiago A. Marques, "Line transect methods for plant surveys," *Biometrics* 63 (4) (2008) pp. 989–998, p. 989.

5 T.C.G. Rich & E.R. Woodruff, "Recording bias in botanical surveys," *Watsonia* 19 (1992) pp. 73–95

6 Chloe Smith, *London: Garden City? Investigating the changing anatomy of London's private gardens, and the scale of their loss* (London: London Wildlife Trust, 2010), Greenspace Information for Greater London and the Greater London Authority, see https://www.wildlondon.org.uk/sites/default/files/files/London%20Garden%20City%20-%20full%20report.pdf (accessed 2 October 2018).

7 Neil Rhind, *The Heath: a companion volume to Blackheath Village and Environs* (London: Bookshop Blackheath Ltd, 1987), p. v.

8 Neil P. Thornton, *The taming of London's commons*, (PhD Thesis, University of Adelaide, 1988). Available at https://digital.library.adelaide.edu.au/dspace/handle/2440/18841 (accessed 2 October 2018).

9 Half-Holiday Handbooks, *Greenwich and Blackheath: a handy guide to rambles in the district, with a map and nine illustrations* (London: Marshall Japp & Company, 1881) p. 28.

10 Blackheath common is split between the manor of the Earl of Dartmouth and the Crown Estates. The term "wastes," while culturally connected to contemporary meanings of "wasteland" (see Vittoria Di Palma, *Wasteland: a history*, New Haven, CT: Yale University Press, 2014), referred more technically to areas within the manorial estate considered unproductive, uncultivable, or uncultivated. Customary rights of pasture—as well as the collection of various materials for fuel, food and crafts—were often practised in these areas.

11 J.M. Neeson, *Commoners: common right, enclosure and social change in England, 1700–1820* (Cambridge: Cambridge University Press, 1994).

12 Thornton, *The taming of London's commons*, p.44

13 David Lambert and Sally Williams, *Commons, heaths and greens in Greater London Report*, Research Report Series 50–2014 (London: English Heritage, 2005). Available at http://www.parksagency.co.uk/wp-content/uploads/2014/10/commons-heaths-and-greens-in-greater-london.pdf (accessed 2 October 2018).

14 David A. Reeder, "The social construction of green space prior to the Second World War," in Peter Clarke, ed., *The European city and green space: London, Stockholm, Helsinki and St Petersburg, 1850–2000* (Aldershot & Burlington, VT: Ashgate Publishing, 2006) pp. 41–67, p. 49.

15 Thornton, *The taming of London's commons*, p. 44

16 During his only visit to England, Linnaeus is unlikely to have spent time in Blackheath. Putney Heath in southwest London may provide a more probable setting due to the time he spent at the nearby Chelsea Physic Garden, although the dates of his visit do not match when the gorse would have been in flower. See Frederic Dawtrey Drewitt *The romance of the Apothecaries' Garden at Chelsea* (Cambridge: Cambridge University Press, 2010).

17 Times, "Metropolitan Board of Works.-The usual-," *The Times*, 19 April 1896, p. 7. Available at The Times Digital Archive (accessed 6 Nov 2018).

18 Right of soil was itself another right of common, although this extent of damage was likely a result of unscrupulous and illicit activities.

19 Neil Rhind, *Blackheath village and environs 1790–1970: Volume I, The village and Blackheath Vale* (London: Bookshop Blackheath, 1976), p. 2.

20 Ibid.

21 Ibid.

22 Ibid, p. 3.

23 Metropolitan Board of Works, "Parks, Commons and Open Spaces Committee Minutes, Volume 11," 21 March 1877, p. 604. Document: MBW/0987 (London: London Metropolitan Archives).

24 MBW, "Parks, Commons and Open Spaces Committee Minutes, Volume 11," 28 June 1876, p. 111. Document: MBW/0987 (London: London Metropolitan Archives).

25 Metropolitan Board of Works, "Parks, Commons and Open Spaces Committee Minutes, Volume 11," 2 May 1877, p.669–671. Document: MBW/0987 (London: London Metropolitan Archives).

26 Metropolitan Board of Works, "Parks, Commons and Open Spaces Committee Minutes, Volume 13," 22 January 1877, p. 497. Document: MBW/0989 (London: London Metropolitan Archives).

27 Op. cit. Rhind (1976), p.3

28 Sarah Pink, Kerstin L. Mackley, and Roxana Moroşanu, "Hanging out at home: laundry as a thread and texture of everyday life," *International Journal of Cultural Studies*, 18 (2) (2015) pp. 209–224.

29 Rosalie Menon and Colin Porteous, *Design guide: healthy low energy home laundering* (Glasgow: MEARU, University of Glasgow, 2011). Available at http://www.gsa.ac.uk/media/486640/mearu_laundry_design_guide.pdf (accessed 2 October 2018).

30 Patricia Malcolmson, *English laundresses: a social history, 1850–1930* (Chicago & Urbana: University of Illinois Press, 1986), p. 23.

31 Ibid.

32 Ibid, p. 8

33 Darren Patrick, "Queering the urban forest: invasions, mutualisms, and eco-political creativity with the tree of heaven (*Ailanthus altissima*)," in L. Anders Sandberg, Adrina Bardekjian, and Sadia Butt, eds., *Urban forests, trees, and urban green space: a political ecology perspective* (New York, NY: Routledge, 2014) pp. 191–206; Matthew Gandy, "Unintentional landscapes," *Landscape Research*, 41 (4) (2016) pp. 433–440.

34 Peter Del Tredici, "Spontaneous urban vegetation: reflections on change in a globalized world," *Nature & Culture* 5 (3) (2010) pp. 299–315.

35 Half-Holiday Handbooks, *Greenwich and Blackheath*, p. 57.

36 Ibid, p. 63.

37 See Jim Johnson, "Sustainability in Scottish cities: two case studies of local management," in Mike Jenks, Elizabeth Burton, and Katie Williams, eds., *The compact city: a sustainable urban form* (London: Chapman & Hall, 1996) pp. 318–327. Iron drying posts still stand in Glasgow Green, Glasgow—the city's largest park—along with a plaque commemorating the centuries old practices of washing and drying clothes on the site.

38 Common Preservation Society, 1876, *Report of Proceedings of the Commons Preservation Society, 1870–1876*. Document: CLA/078/09/01 (London: London Metropolitan Archives).

39 Lewisham Borough Council, 2013, "Habitat changes and ecological decline of Blackheath, [Archived webpage]. Available at https://archive.is/ccJ0e (accessed 2 October 2018).

40 Blackheath Bugle, "The Olympic washerwoman's bottom," *The Blackheath Bugle*, 5 January 2012 [online news blog]. Available: https://blackheathbugle.wordpress.com/2012/01/05/the-olympic-washerwomans-bottom/ (accessed 2 October 2018).

41 Andrew Smith, "Animation or denigration? Using public spaces as event venues," *Event Management*, 21 (5) (2015) pp. 609–619, p. 618.

42 Andrew Smith, "'Borrowing' public space to stage major events: the Greenwich Park controversy," *Urban Studies*, 51 (2) (2014) pp. 247–263, p. 260

Botanizing the asphalt

Part 2

The flight of seeds

Mara Polgovsky Ezcurra

> If the world be connected ...
> then *thinking in terms of stories* must be shared by all mind or minds, whether ours or those of redwood forests and sea anemones.
> Gregory Bateson, *Mind and nature*[1]

Recently, looking out from my college window in Cambridge, I was struck by a small flying object that resisted immediate identification. For several minutes, it was spinning at full speed at least seven metres above ground level, choreographing soft waves and full circumferences in a seemingly unpredictable manner. What exactly was this gravity-defying creature? Was there a child playing with a tiny kite in the garden? Was this a minuscule UFO? Or, rather, the latest piece of surveillance technology?[2] Was this object recording my movements or my heat? My imagination soared as I let myself be carried away by the awe-inspiring flight of this creature, its resistance to falling, and its apparent capacity to indulge in pleasant journeying without a clear direction, allowing its body to swing freely in the errant winds. I was most certainly deceived by my desire for wonder, for it is unlikely that I had witnessed anything other than a winged seed being transported by the eddies of air along the river Cam. Yet the memory of this seed's airborne drift continues to astound me; and, enthused by a desire to revisit such patterns, I have failed to find records of such boundless sense of flow in the vast archives of online moving images. Seeds travel all too little on the Internet; we tend to imagine them, like we imagine most plants, as passive and static. Their migrating patterns and forms of flight remain little known outside the realm of botany. Even in literature and art, as literary scholar Alan Bewell suggests, we have tended to conceive of seeds as fundamentally terrestrial, rather than flying, creatures, for "we assume that mobility and travel are a human privilege. Nature is local ... something that is visited and revisited, not something that itself travels, coming across the seas."[3] Might a better understanding of seeds' forms of flight return us to a different history of both human and non-human experiences of exile and migration?

In 2001, having recently moved to Berlin, Brazilian artist Maria Thereza Alves found herself pursuing this question as she reflected upon her own sense of displacement in a city visibly layered by colonialism, war, partition, and migration. The city was also being rapidly reshaped by a real-estate furore that was laying open extensive plots of land that would have been otherwise covered by concrete. As if confronted with a newly opened historical archive awaiting categorization, Alves visited seventeen of these construction sites in order to collect soil samples from each one of them and then attempted to "awaken" the seeds that she had found, both as a means to perform their (dormant) aliveness and as the starting point to trace back the histories behind their presence in Berlin. While pursuing this project, Alves interviewed botanists, visited libraries, and rescued historical documents from a number of sources, thus engaging in a form of artistic research akin to what curator Mark Godfrey calls "the artist as historian."[4] However, she also belatedly erased or "lost" the references of each one of these documents, casting doubt on their authenticity and making visible her own hesitations as to whether the work of primarily white, male botanists from former empires could offer an account of urban nature uprooted from a nationalist and/or colonial past. Her research thus became both a performance of the challenges of a decolonial history of urban ecology and an invitation to attend carefully to the travelling histories of urban nature. For the artist, urban nature is more than a means to embellish the city; it is a living archive of biocultural and biosemiotic entanglement.[5]

Alves's *Wake* accompanied her iterative project entitled *Seeds of Change*. This project aimed to locate colonial ballast sites in European ports (including Marseille [1999–2000], Reposaari [2001], Liverpool [2004], Exeter and Topsham [2004], Dunkirk [2005], and Bristol [2007]) in order to identify ballast flora that may have been transported by merchant sailing ships.[6] Both projects involve an exploration of the histories of seed banks as a means of unveiling the presence of colonial histories; the various ways in which colonial exchange has refashioned local landscapes; and how, effectively, the experience of colonization has been repeatedly masked by mythologies of national purity. In both of these projects, the artist found herself asking similar questions: at what point do seeds become "native"? What are the socio-political histories of place that determine the framework of belonging? The political conviction fueling both projects in turn fostered the idea that a closer engagement with the journeying of seeds has the potential to alter our perceptions of the identity of a place—displacing, in particular, notions of purity, fixity, and biological or cultural authenticity. This seemingly simple proposition is far from secondary at a time of rising xenophobia and right-wing nationalism. And yet the truly fascinating aspect of Alves's artistic research is the extent to which it shows how the long-distance migrations of plants and humans are impossible to disentangle: they have mutually enabled one another, as humans and plants have become tied together by forms of co-habitation and agency that exceed the human will and the evolutionary choices of biological creatures. From this perspective, the history of the natural world is always a history of culture to begin with, and vice versa. Moreover, the human-aided migration of plant species that we have come to imagine as "native" can potentially become the basis of a novel conception of (national) belonging, one rooted not in any sense of purported blood purity but rather in the nomadism, hybridity, and dynamic adaptability of the migrant subject,

Maria Thereza Alves removing samples of earth in Berlin, 2000. Photo: Jimmie Durham.
Courtesy of Maria Thereza Alves.

organism, and/or system. This ecological reshuffling of the politics of citizenship and belonging, based upon a different approach to human-non-human relations, is what forges Alves's aesthetico-political vision.

In *Wake for Berlin* (2000), the artist collected soil samples from seventeen construction sites around the German city, seeking to identify the "seed banks" present in each one of them, their singularities, origins, and the ways in which they might speak for the agitated history of the metropolis. She gave dormant seeds—some of which could have been a number of decades old—the chance to germinate, and then planted them.[7] Having recently arrived in Berlin after living for a number of years in Mexico, the artist struggled to find a place where she could cultivate the samples. It was the middle of winter, and her original idea of keeping them on a public, open-air terrace would not work. The artist therefore tried to place them in the foyer of the German Academic Exchange Service (DAAD),

Maria Thereza Alves removing samples of earth in Berlin, 2000. Photo: Jimmie Durham.
Courtesy of Maria Thereza Alves.

which was supporting her project. However, the building's architect found them unfitting—or even too ugly—for the site, and asked Alves to remove them. The collected seeds finally landed in the Natural Conservancy of the Tiergarten. Once they arrived there, having received sixteen hours a day of artificial light in midwinter, a third of the seeds sprouted. The other two-thirds were eaten by snails. In addition to the variety of plants that Alves found in each of the sites, these awakened seeds were the carriers of multiple histories of travel, conquest, trade, exploitation, and defeat. They also carried testimonies of human-aided botanical drift and adaptation that exceed the anthropocentric desire to dominate any given land.

Alves developed her artistic research in close dialogue with botanist Heli Jutila, who had for years carried out an extensive investigation on emergent flora in the Finish port of Repossaari, where ballast had been recurrently dumped. One of Jutila's recommendations was to take samples from different depths, as the

Maria Thereza Alves: *Wake for Berlin* (1999–2001) (detail). Photo: Maria Thereza Alves.

topsoil can include "similar species in many places."[8] Carefully following this advice, Alves's research on the seventeen sites resulted in a 400-page document containing not just the botanical drawings of the plants that did germinate—and of others found on the site—but also a large assortment of historical documents, including photographs, photocopies of botanical treatises, personal annotations, and records of exchanges with various botanists and ecologists.[9] The richness and scope of these materials is truly striking, even if, as I suggest above, they simultaneously perform the act of historical investigation and disavow it by treating each finding as a "found object" or "text" to be rapidly stripped of its references—i.e. to be decontextualized and treated as an index of a larger narrative of a globalizing colonialism.

In the important boulevard Unter den Linden (German for "under the linden trees"), which runs from the City Palace to the Brandenburg Gate in Mitte, Alves collected a soil sample 2.7 metres below street level, where a hole had been dug out in order to do some piping work. The artist was drawn to this site by its immediate relationship with the history of war, given the inevitable crossing of the Brandenburg Gate by marching soldiers—those who travelled to conquer, and those returning from victory or defeat. In recalling some of these wars, Alves mentions Napoleon's multi-national army of one million soldiers (coming from Poland, Sweden, the Netherlands, Prussia, and France), a section of which were garrisoned in Berlin on their way to Russia in 1812. She also recalls their return to Berlin after their colossal defeat, having first crossed the Berezina and Neman Rivers into Poland. In moments of triumph and celebration, Unter den Linden was decorated with greenery, including the symbolic laurel and oak wreaths, and was also filled with celebratory flowers presented by women along the routes. Alves identifies species of all these provenances and varieties as potentially located in the site's seed bank, together with seeds brought to Berlin as a result of international trade. She mentions, too, the increased presence of luxury goods in Unter den Linden towards the beginning of the twentieth century—with diamonds coming to Germany from Namibia "where German soldiers were stationed."[10] New varieties of flowers arrived on the site during times of protest and unrest in the 1930s, even if during the early days of his rule Hitler ordered the linden trees that had given a name to the boulevard to be cut down, only to replant them in 1936. The soft street surfacing used at that time allowed "seeds to easily settle into the seed bank."[11] This policy changed in 1961, with the replacement of soft materials by concrete slabs that would seal access to the soil beneath. The potential consequence of this change in urban policy is a gradual diminution of diversity in the seed bank with the passing of time.

During her research on this site, Alves conversed with botanist Herbert Sukopp, whose work has shown that two non-native plants have become characteristic of the area: the *Sisymbrium irio*, originally from the Mediterranean, and the *Parietaria pensylvanica*, first found in the state of Pennsylvania in the United States. The former was first seen in Berlin within the confines of the Moabit Prison; so it is likely that its seeds spread via the management of soil by prison workers, and the subsequent use of this soil to plant tree saplings in the city. The second one may have spread in the mid-nineteenth century from samples brought to the botanical gardens of Schöneberg and Humboldt University. The seemingly unintentional dispersion of these plants in Berlin is significant in a context in which the acquisition and loss of plant varieties as a result of warfare was an object of botanical interest, as Alves shows in her research on another of these sites (a construction site in the corner of Charlottenstraße 33 and Französische Straße 42/44). Here, she includes among her "found documents" a photocopy of a French botanical study listing the plants lost by Germany after the annexation of Alsace-Lorraine by France in 1918—and those, in turn, gained by France. This treatment of plants as spoils of war shows how problematic the nationalist appropriations of plant species ultimately are. It also serves as a reminder of the ways in which the desire to own, appropriate, and domesticate "foreign" plants animated the colonial imagination.

Just as Gregory Bateson suggests in this article's opening epigraph, stories are links—bonds between humans as well as non-humans. They frame the distribution of our perception of the world, and, correspondingly, our perception of our sense of selfhood. The seeds Alves awakened during *Wake for Berlin* are not, therefore, mere residues, but signifiers of systems lying silent beneath layers of city concrete. Moreover, the artist's evocation of an awakening is not limited to facilitating the germination of seeds; rather, it involves the historically conscious act of recuperating a history and finding ways to act upon it. This is how, according to Teobaldo Lagos Preller, *Wake* generated a global archive of local memories and a composite of images, stories, and plants blended together by the synchronic temporality of the seeds' awakening.[12] And yet positing the seeds as objects to be collected, classified, and archived rather than as fully fledged actants limits the artwork's epistemic and eco-critical potential. As I will suggest here, Alves's work could also be seen as a way of challenging us to conceive of the seeds as belonging to an embodied and extended mind, per Bateson's innovative reconception of the notion of ecology.

Indeed, while Alves's gathering of historical and botanical evidence seems at times to be scattered and driven by chance encounters, it contrives a holistic appraisal of nature-culture relations that return us to early cybernetic and ecological thinking, and in particular to the writings of British anthropologist Gregory Bateson. Bateson brought information and systems theory to the study of ecology after his immersion in post-War cybernetic theory.[13] His radical conceptual and methodological reframing of this field involved questioning ecology's traditional focus on energy and material flows. This was in order to suggest that "ecosystems had

Potted samples of earth with seeds sprouting, 2000. Photo: Maria Thereza Alves.

to be considered to be communicating and informational systems, and even as mental systems, as minds," and that "we are constantly participating in cognitive [and semiotic] systems that extend throughout our environment."[14] For Bateson, therefore, the travelling of seeds involves more than the movement, redistribution, or reshuffling of species. The local circulation of meanings itself becomes transformed. Informed by a cybernetic approach to all living and non-living (open or dynamic) systems as communicative systems, he wrote: "Insofar as living things contain communication, and insofar as they are, as we say, 'organized,' they must contain something of the nature of message, events that travel within the living thing or between the living thing and others."[15]

What Bateson describes as a travelling "event" can also be understood as the constitution of new relations between entities (or agents) which triggers "differences that make a difference"—i.e. new information inputs—in the semiotic worlds of humans and non-humans. Moreover, the realm of the living, the ecological and biosemiotic interactions among its agents, and these agents' relationships with cultural forms, are better described as a densely interconnected mind than as a series of discrete encounters between ontologically distinct creatures. From this perspective, the mind is an immanent system of relations within a system whose boundaries exceed the body and the self to encompass the environment.[16] As Evan Thompson puts it, one can speak of a radical continuity of mind, whereby "the roots of mental life lie not simply in the [human] brain, but ramify through the body and the environment."[17] According to this framework, refashioning or "awakening" nature has far greater consequences than what one might envision from a strictly humanist or anthropocentric perspective. It focuses not just on the historical co-creation of human and non-human entities, but also on our semiotic co-dependence and cognitive co-constitution. In light of that, Alves's *Wake* becomes a call to recognize the ultimately frail and disabling borders setting individuals, cultures, and living systems apart. Moreover, it invites reflection on the dense interactions between the multi-species elements that constitute urban life.

As mentioned, the title of *Wake for Berlin* originally referred to the artist's intention to awaken seeds in a condition of dormancy. However, the dual meaning of the notion of "wake" is also present in this work, which can be imagined as a vigil for complex and ephemeral histories of human and non-human travel and communication that have become almost impossible to recover. Alves's art is in this sense a form of ecological art that goes beyond the simple engagement with plants and other living forms as artistic materials.[18] It reveals what art historian Richard William Hill describes as "natural and social histories so inextricably entwined as to challenge the foundational Western ontological distinction between nature and culture."[19] This could be further elaborated as a repositioning of ecological art that moves beyond past attempts to raise awareness of an impending ecological crisis, inspire environmental change, or imagine practical solutions to these problems. Cast in a multi-species epistemology, Alves's ecological art performs the necessity to *shift thought* about the relationships between living and the non-living, the human, and its many co-constitutive others.

1 Gregory Bateson, *Mind and nature: a necessary unity* (New York: E. P. Dutton, 1979) p. 13.

2 On small drones, see n.a., "Living dragonfly drones take flight," *BBC News*, (7 November 2017), https://www.bbc.co.uk/news/av/technology-40508099/living-dragonfly-drones-take-flight

3 Alan Bewell, "Traveling natures," *Nineteenth-Century Contexts* 29 (2–3) (2007) p. 89.

4 Mark Godfrey, "The artist as historian," *October* 120, no. Spring (2007) pp. 140–72. See also Claire Bishop, "The Fifty-Sixth Venice Biennale," *Artforum*, no. September (2015), https://www.artforum.com/print/201507/claire-bishop-54492.

5 Italian biologist Marcello Barbieri defines biosemiotics as a synthesis of biology and semiotics, the purpose of which is "to show that semiosis is a fundamental component of life, i.e., that signs and meaning exist in all living systems." Marcello Barbieri, "A short history of biosemiotics," *Biosemiosis* 2 (2) (2009) p. 221.

6 For further detail about this project, see the artist's website: http://www.maria-therezaalves.org/works/seeds-of-change?c=47. *Wake* also became an iterative project when Alves carried out a similar investigation into the seed banks of Guangzhou (2008) and Dubai (2015).

7 In correspondence with Alves in December 1999, botanist Heli Jutila wrote that seed banks can survive in deep soil for years, "and even decennia." Maria Thereza Alves, *Wake: A Project for Berlin* (s.l.: s.n., 2001) p. 10.

8 Alves, p. 10.

9 Alves self-published an excerpt of her much longer investigation as *Wake: A Project for Berlin*. I was able to access the (homonymous) complete version to write this article. The project was also exhibited as an installation in the Jewish Museum Berlin in 2011.

10 Alves, p. 3.

11 Alves, *Wake. A Project for Berlin* (s.l.: s.n., n.d.) p. 6.

12 Teobaldo Lagos Preller, "'Wake' de Maria Thereza Alves: Palabra y proceso vegetal, saberes en expansión," *Revista de Estudios Globales y Arte Contemporáneo* 3 (1) (2015) p. 442.

13 Post-war cybernetic theory was first developed by American mathematician Norbert Wiener in collaboration with, among others, Mexican physiologist Arturo Rosenblueth. It was then appropriated by academics from various fields through what are known as the Macy Conferences in New York (1946–53). These conferences were attended by Wiener, Rosenblueth, Bateson, W. Ross Ashby, Julian Bigelow, Margaret Mead, Heinz von Foerster, John von Neumann, and others.

14 Jon Goodbun, "Gregory Bateson's ecological aesthetics—an addendum to urban political ecology," *Field: A Free Journal for Architecture* 4 (1) (2010) pp. 41–42.

15 Gregory Bateson and Mary Catherine Bateson, *Angels fear: towards an epistemology of the sacred* (New York: Macmillan, 1987) p. 61.

16 Gregory Bateson, *Steps to an ecology of mind: collected essays in anthropology, psychiatry, evolution, and epistemology*. (Northvale, NJ: Jason Aronson, 1987).

17 Evan Thompson, *Mind in life: biology, phenomenology, and the sciences of mind* (Cambridge, MA: The Belknap Press of Harvard University Press, 2007) p. ix.

18 In her article "Ecological art," Ruth Wallen presents a survey of ecological art practice since the 1960s. She describes early environmental art, including land art and earthworks, as fundamentally interested in challenging the definition of art by using "natural materials" and working directly on the landscape. By contrast, she suggests, "practitioners of ... ecological art conceived of themselves as engaged citizens or public intellectuals responding to the call of the activist movements of the day." Ruth Wallen, "Ecological art: a call for visionary intervention in a time of crisis," *Leonardo* 45 (3) (2012) p. 235.

19 Richard William Hill, "Borderless Histories," *Third Text* 32 (2–3) (2018) p. 273.

Dandelions at work: a street corner tale of ecosystem services

Alexandra R. Toland

A hot afternoon in August, I steered my bike to a stop along a busy street in Kreuzberg to inspect a proliferation of especially large dandelions in an empty tree pit with my four-year-old daughter, Tilia. For several minutes, we immersed ourselves in the natural history of the sidewalk, examining the miniature field of wildflowers that occupied the space where a tree once stood.[1] "Many street trees have a hard time in the city because of water stress and pollution," I explained, "but other plants find a comfy home in such tiny forgotten spaces and seem to do just fine. These spaces are called ecological niches. And the plants we see here are ambassadors of what's called spontaneous vegetation, or plants that plant themselves." We marveled at the yellowness of the dandelion florets amid the otherwise dusty sidewalk surroundings and picked a few delicate globelike seed heads, as all children do. I allowed her to pick a few flowers for the ride home but not to taste or smell them. "Why not?" she wondered, having recently picked bags full of the golden flower heads to make sweet syrup and dandelion tea on an excursion to the countryside. "Flowers that are edible, sometimes even medicinal, do *other* things in the city," I explained. "They are beautiful spots of color to make people happy; they are food and shelter for other creatures who live on this street; but more importantly they are busy filtering tiny particles from all those cars going over the bridge, so that our daily bike ride is a little less dusty."

Flowering plants are not only a source of nectar, aesthetic pleasure, and mental well-being, but also help reduce harmful residues of city life. One such residue is of particular interest here: the accumulation of particulate matter (PM), otherwise known as dust, from natural sources such as pollen, and anthropogenic sources such as industrial and vehicular emissions and tire abrasion. These airborne substances present a huge threat to human health, especially in cities where there is relatively more pollution and less vegetation to filter it.[2] Dust filtration is an example of an *ecosystem service*, or a special service provided by non-human entities such as plants, soil, and water for the benefit of humans, and effectively other

Taraxacum pappus with captured airborne microfibers and dust.
Photo: Alexandra Toland, 2016. Courtesy of the artist.

creatures as well. Ecosystems services are described by the UNEP (2009) as the provisional, regulative, cultural, and supporting services provided by nature for human recipients.[3] Säumel et al. (2015) discuss a number of specific examples and management strategies for ecosystem services (as well as disservices) provided by roadside vegetation in an argument for more liveable urban habitats.[4] Dandelions, like all flowering plants in the city, contribute to some of these ecosystem services, such as providing joy to children with their seed pods (a cultural service), providing food and nesting niches for insects (a supporting service), and stabilizing the soil, shading the surface, and to some extent filtering dust (all regulating services).

To date, much research has been conducted on the dust filtration capacity of trees[5] and herbaceous vegetation[6] along roadsides, where the source of traffic-induced PM is at its greatest.[7] While the filtering capacity of plants has been linked to various morphological features of *leaves*, such as hairy or wrinkled surfaces,[8] there

Taraxacum models made with microfiber cleaning products.
Photo: Alexandra Toland, 2016. Courtesy of the artist.

is very little known about the filtering capacity of *flowers*. Because the presence of plant leaves, required for photosynthesis, is relatively greater than the seasonal presence of flowers, required for reproduction, and the bulk quantity of leaves exceeds that of flowers, leaf structures have been seemingly singled out for study in determining the dust filtration capacity of urban plants. The complex, three-dimensional structures of flowers, however, make them interesting allies in dust filtration. Since that fateful afternoon in August, I began to focus my attention on all the flowers, fruiting bodies, and seeds in my neighbourhood. Which species bloomed the longest? What kind of flower shapes made the best filters? Which surfaces captured the most dust? What kinds of dust were the flowers and seeds picking up? And how could the questions that are relevant to urban ecologists be investigated with artistic means? I sketched out an artistic ecology research plan, started experimenting with forms, and promised my daughter that we would have better answers come next August. With a flood of questions, tiny seeds took flight.

Installation view of *DUST BLOOMS* at the 2017 Ars Electronica Cyber Arts Exhibition (with reference to Dürer's 1503 "Great Piece of Turf"). Photo: Alexandra Toland, 2017. Courtesy of the artist.

The *DUST BLOOMS* project, which has had several iterations under several titles,[9] is an ongoing transdisciplinary artistic research experiment in multiple parts that aims to better understand the role that roadside flowers play in making cities healthier, happier places. Using a synthesis of artistic and scientific methods, the project juxtaposes the beauty and function of urban flora to comment on the very idea of ecosystem services in cities. It is both a systematic investigation and a practice of embodied everyday curiosity. As an art project, *DUST BLOOMS* does not provide answers but rather raises questions often avoided by scientists in ESS discourse: Should plants be seen as "service providers" in a larger service society? What moral responsibilities do humans have towards plants in return for their services? Can the services provided by plants be seen as phyto-technologies in a multi-species democracy? And how can new human technologies be used to improve relationships between plants and humans under the environmental strains of the Anthropocene?

The burden of answering these questions I place upon the speechless dandelions clustered in an empty tree pit on my busy street in Kreuzberg. Consider the dandelion, with its dense radial structure (both as a flower and as a seed pod). Note the looseness of the individual achenial seeds with their hairy pappus "wings," the length and straw-like hollowness of the stem, and the browning, curling phyllary leaves pushed downward towards the base. The dandelion speaks as a "model species" widely referenced in ecological research because of its highly adaptive

Installation view of *DUST BLOOMS* at the 2017 Ars Electronica Cyber Arts Exhibition. Photo: Alexandra Toland, 2017. Courtesy of the artist.

morphological and genetic properties.[10] Dandelions can adjust their size, shape, and metabolic properties to better deal with stress factors such as being grazed in rural locations[11] or with pollution in urban ones.[12] Its super adaptability makes the dandelion a super-species—a complex group of species so closely related that, taxonomically, they are nearly impossible to tell apart. If in real life the morphological potentialities of the dandelion escape conclusive specification, then I am emboldened to study its likeness with different combinations of materials and compositions in order to get to know the species better. To model the dandelion is to honor 30 million years of subtle shape shifting through sculptural research. To model the dandelion is to have a conversation about the Anthropocene without spoken words.

Biologist, Gerhard Scholz (2015) recognizes that "models, like all cultural objects, are reflections of their time in terms of materiality and aesthetics but also in terms of scientific knowledge, viewpoints and concepts represented."[13] The materials used in *DUST BLOOMS* are sourced from the very world they seek to understand. Unique inventions of consumer society—plastic dental brush-sticks, microfiber wipes, polycarbonate screws, beading wire, plastic clay, glitter, rubber bands, and granular resins—are fused together as glorified bricolage of the Anthropocene. What is in other contexts used to clean, decorate, or hold things together can be repurposed to measure environmental phenomena. Sculptural prototypes based on the morphological features of the *Taraxacum* (Dandelion) family are developed using materials sourced from household cleaning and hygiene products. The botanical models made out of microfiber cleaning wipes and disposable toothbrushes playfully suggest a form of reverse-biomimicry by using human inventions to model nature, as it appears in a very humanly altered state. In a roadside ecosystem, the native dandelions ask the makeshift models, "what can we learn from the likes of a Swiffer?"

"A model," write historian Kathrin Grotz and biologist Dirk Kruger, curators of the exhibition *modelSHOW* at the Botanical Garden of Berlin "regardless of whether it is an intellectual concept or tangible object, always relates back to a specific prototype, namely the phenomenon or original. In this sense, it is always a model *of* something. On the other hand, every model is also intended to have some kind of use. And in this sense, it is a model *for* something."[14] There is a fine line of intention between model and sculpture, whose interstice I attempt to navigate with my *DUST BLOOMS*. The botanical sculptures of dandelions are made in the spirit of scientifically driven botanical illustration, but in three-dimensional form. They are obviously a representation *of* something—roadside flowers. But they are also made *for* something—the understanding of dust accumulation and possible adaptation to place by flowering plants in urban areas, the contemplation of beauty and function inherent in one source object, and the recognition of a certain absurdity of the anthropogenic forces that I must somehow explain to my children. While a sculpture is a free form determined by the artist and variously appreciated by the art public which is to receive it, Kruger (2015) explains that a model can take the form of "a work of art (plants made of bronze, wall charts), a concept (biomembrane model), a pattern (apple and pear models), a scaled reproduction (poisonous mushrooms, plants in a model railway landscape), a teaching aid (flower models), an investigational object (explosive mechanism in meadow sage), a living creature (the model plant *Arabidopsis thaliana*, or thale-cress), a research object (DNA model), or an abstract representation (kinship relations in a cladogram)."[15] Intended as conceptual research objects in an artistic production context, the dandelion objects in my ongoing *DUST BLOOMS* are decidedly both–models and sculptures.

The first step in modelling is observation. In the summer of 2016, together with urban ecology students at the Technical University of Berlin instructed by Dr Ina Säumel and myself, a measuring campaign was carried out to examine dust from the flowers of several species at multiple locations in the city of Berlin.[16] Ten flowers per species were picked from major roadways with an average daily traffic rate of more than 50,000 motorized vehicles. Five petals were then examined from each flower. Using light microscopy, it was possible to quantitatively estimate the surface area of a flower and qualitatively describe the morphological characteristics of individual flowers, as well as determine the type and amount of dust particles captured on the petal surfaces. In a second step, special Arduino-powered sensors were placed in locations with and without vegetation. At this very moment, atmospheric dust levels are being measured with sensors hiding among the wild vegetation at Prinzessinnengarten Berlin on busy Moritzplatz. Having just been granted the rights to use the former brownfield site turned urban garden as a lively multi-species community space for another 99 years, long-term measurement is intended to document important information on any changes (positive or negative) in the local environment. Incoming data is transferred to the open knowledge platform, luftdaten.info, creating a link between socially engaged urban green space, open-source data visualization, art, and citizen science.

As it turns out, our microscopic observations showed that the dandelion captures most dust on the outer third of its petal surfaces. The barbed hairs of its achene seeds also trap dust effectively. In addition to dust, free-floating microfibers get entangled in the joyous seed pods of the dandelion. The sensitive dust sensors show that there is not much difference in filtration between the real dandelions and the hidden sculptural prototypes at Prinzessinnengarten. The important thing is that there is something present to do the work of filtration, and the examples of spontaneous vegetation in cities ask little for their services (they plant and maintain themselves, after all). The dandelion is in other words not a superhero of dust filtration, but simply one of many foot-soldiers working in a rather dusty environment. As a protagonist of the street, it captures the imagination as a model service provider and symbolic "companion species" of the plant kingdom. Only a generation ago, the seeds of my dandelion neighbours might have been the only organisms to freely parachute across the Oberbaum Bridge into the East German district of Friedrichshain just paces away. The dandelion is a mascot of biological and cultural diaspora, a comforting friend from the plant world for many people from around the world who have come to the city of Berlin (or any city), including myself, who find themselves far away from "home" but surrounded by familiar "faces" in the flower and seed heads. This symbolic gesture, I suppose, can be described as a cultural ecosystem service, if companionship can ever be narrowed down to such terms.

1 This essay is in large part an edited version of the essay, *DUST BLOOMS: a research narrative in artistic ecology*, written for the exhibition catalogue, *Lasst Blumen Sprechen* (Let flowers speak) published in 2016 by Museum Schloss Moyland. A special thanks goes to Dr Ina Säumel of the TU Berlin, whose ongoing research on the topic of ecosystem services in the city and the dust filtration function of roadside plants significantly inspired the trajectory of this project; to Prof Dr Ulrich Szewzyk and the Department of Environmental Microbiology for the enthusiastic help with macro- and microscope photography; to Ulf Kypke-Burchardi and Rajko Zschiegner (luftdaten.info) for support with dust filtration instrumentation; and to my daughter, Tilia, now eight years old, whose curious spirit leads me to new ways of questioning and understanding the world we live in.

2 See reports in UNEP, 2007, "Global environment outlook: environment for development (GEOe4)" and WHO, 2007, "Improving public health responses to extreme weather/heat-waves," e EuroHEAT.

3 UNEP, 2009, "Ecosystem management programme: a new approach to sustainability" (Division of Environmental Policy Implementation).

4 Ina Säumel, Frauke Weber, and Ingo Kowarik, "Toward livable and healthy urban streets: roadside vegetation provides ecosystem services where people live and move," *Journal of Environmental Science & Policy* (available online 29 November, 2015).

5 C. Y Jim and Wendy Y. Chen, "Assessing the ecosystem service of air pollutant removal by urban trees in Guangzhou (China)," *Journal of Environmental Management* 88 (2008).

6 See, for example, Frauke Weber, Ingo Kowarik, and Ina Säumel, "Herbaceous plants as filters: immobilization of particulates along urban street corridors," *Journal of Environmental Pollution* 186 (2014); and Joshi Nitesh, Bist Bharati, Mule Prachiti, and Joshi Ambika, "Importance of common roadside plants as dust collectors in Tarapur industrial area," *Int. Res. J. of Science & Engineering* 2 (2) (2014), pp. 31–36.

7 Tom Litschke and Wilhelm Kuttler, "On the reduction of urban particle concentration by vegetation: a review," *Meteorologische Zeitschrift* 17 (3) (2008) pp. 229–240.

8 Huixia Wang, Hui Shi, and Yangyand Li, "Leaf dust capturing capacity of urban greening plant species in relation to leaf micromorphology," *International Symposium on Water Resource and Environmental Protection (ISWREP)*, Conference Proceedings Volume 3 (2011).

9 *Dust Blooms* in the group exhibition, *Let Flowers Speak* at Museum Schloss Moyland (2016); *Dust Blooms* in the group exhibition, *Himmel und Erde* (Kreuzberger Salon, 2016); *Dust Blooms* in the Prix Ars Electronica exhibition, *Cyberarts* (2017); *Dust Blooms* at the group exhibition, *Stories for a More Than Human World* (2018); *The Unbearable Heaviness of Dust* in the *On Plants and People* exhibition at the German Hygiene Museum (2019); and *Probing the Planthroposcene: Excerpts from a Disservice Society* in the *Shared Habitats* group exhibition at Ars Electronica (2019).

10 Alyabyev, A. Yu., Khamidullin, A. F., Ogorodnikova, T. I., Vorobyev, V. N., and Vorobyev, G. V., "Adaptive properties of the dandelion (*Taraxacum officinale* Wigg. s.l.) under conditions of air pollution by motor vehicle exhausts," *Russian Journal of Ecology* 45 (2) (2014) pp. 90–94.

11 Noboru Fujita and Ryosuke Koda, "Capitulum and rosette leaf avoidance from grazing by large herbivores in *Taraxacum*," *Journal of Ecological Research* 30 (3) (2015) pp. 517–525.

12 See again: Vorobyev et al., "Adaptive properties of the dandelion."

13 Gerhard Scholtz, "Morphological models of animals and plants: outdated or about to flourish again?," in Kathrin Grotz, ed., *modellSCHAU: perspectives on botanical models* (Berlin: BGBM Freie Universität Berlin, 2015) p. 64.

14 Kathrin Grotz and Dirk Krüger, *modelSHOW: perspectives on botanical models* (Berlin: BGBM Freie Universität Berlin, 2015) p. 92.

15 Dirk Krüger, "Models plant knowledge!," in Kathrin Grotz, ed., *modelSHOW: perspectives on botanical models* (Berlin: BGBM Freie Universität Berlin, 2015) p. 86.

16 Unfortunately, not enough data was collected to conduct a statistical analysis. The collection protocols were rather presented as exhibition materials along with a detailed photographic journal.

Plants in the urban night

Bergit Arends

A lush, green Hollywood juniper tree is swaying in the Californian night, its undulating motion thrown into contrast against a grey concrete wall and wire fence. The elastic trunks of palm trees bend in a rising wind, their large leaves brushing through the air. The branches of an oak tree are silhouetted against the lit windows of a brick building in the winter's night. These are some of the scenes of urban plants observed in *Nightlife* (2015), a video and sound installation by French artist Cyprien Gaillard (b. 1980). The film captures the plants in mesmerizing reveries. However, there are also complex histories of violence underlying this hallucinatory portrayal of urban botany. The histories of the plant species presented closely intertwine with human histories, making the urban plants works of history as much as works of nature. Gaillard creates a slow-motion film narrative that links black histories and the migration of plants into North America by connecting different moments in time and space. In the curating or discussion of cultural works such as this one, political contexts, including experiences of exclusion, violence, and self-empowerment, that are directly connected to migration and colonialism have hitherto remained largely unaddressed and absent.[1] In this essay, I shall start by exploring some conceptual aspects of the relationship between plants, migration, and histories through a number of artworks exploring different political contexts. I use the artwork *Nightlife* to show how plants are expressions of human interventions into nature, and how plants can shadow histories of racism and race conflicts. The study of urban flora in contemporary artists' representations often start with seeds, which offer a route into complex histories of nature-making. Seeds are highly mobile and accompany the migration of people, plants, and cultural ideas. Brazilian artist Maria Thereza Alves's (b. 1961) ongoing project *Seeds of Change* studies colonialism, slavery, and the global commerce of goods by looking at displaced seeds in ballast—the material historically used to balance ships engaged in maritime trade. Dumped in ports at the end of the voyage, ballast often carried dormant seeds taken from their place of origin, which remained in the soil for many years before germinating and growing. Alves identifies seeds and plants as a way of studying the inadvertent displacement of people and soil from the transatlantic slave trade routes. Artists have also created interventions in the public structure of the botanic gardens often found in cities to critique the deliberate economic mobilization of plants such as poppies.[2]

Contemporary artists' practices draw our attention to human relationships with urban flora by noticing plants that are often overlooked in urban environments because of their size or non-ornamental status, or because of the urban site itself. The geographer Doreen Massey has shown that "nature" can be endlessly geographically mobile, thereby enabling and problematizing notions of intrinsic indigeneity and belonging. Massey emphasizes "place and landscape as *events*, as happenings, as moments that will again be dispersed." She evokes place as an open meeting place that is in ongoing production.[3] This notion can be observed in the projects by Austrian artist Lois Weinberger (b. 1948), who speaks of ruderal "wild vegetation," specifically from south-eastern and eastern Europe, and migration. A project (1997–ongoing), entitled *Das über Pflanzen ist eins mit ihnen* (What is beyond plants is at one with them), is sited at Kassel Kulturbahnhof in Germany. Weinberger planted fast-spreading neophytes, which he had collected himself, along a stretch of a 100-m track in order for these plants to mix with the (so-called) native flora. The artist considers his interventions in vegetation communities to be metaphors for social processes. By considering the processes of "nature" into which the artist intervenes, he hopes to support the viewer in getting a better understanding of a mobile human society. Equally, Weinberger not only ascribes metaphoric readings to vegetation communities, but also considers single plants, such as *Wegwarte* (chicory, i.e. *Cichorum intybus*), as a metaphor for human migration. Plants—intentionally or unintentionally—can thus become part of events in places and landscapes in the enacting of human societal histories, but they can also become actors within political and social movements. For example, the 1980s grassroots environmental movements focusing on forests in Brazil, India, and Kenya saw plants begin to affect national politics through either civil disobedience or official channels. These movements were embedded in social struggle and in a context of countercultural critique.[4] Since the 1970s, the environmental art movements espoused by Western artists have been expanding their practices into intervening in the landscape itself, be it rural or urban. Within the urban environment of Kassel, then a provincial town near the East German-West German border, artist Joseph Beuys' project *7000 Oaks* (1982–1987) was a gesture towards green regeneration. Beuys considered an oak tree to be a piece of sculpture defining a place. Each planted tree was paired with a basalt stone, serving as a marker for a beginning in time and offering an alignment between geological and biological temporalities. Drawing attention to specific plants within landscapes can reflect political change. Artist William Kentridge's print *Staying Home* (1999) counteracts colonial landscape fantasies of "wilderness" as they apply to his native South Africa. His image of a landscaped garden shows a few stand-alone trees—perhaps indigenous fever trees (*Vachellia xanthophloea*)—planted in rectangular containers. Their thin trunks and bushy canopies are set in front of a leafy hedge row—all of these elements are expressions of a human-made environment. *Staying Home* has been printed on a book page, a typical trope in Kentridge's wide-ranging oeuvre. The double page is taken from a Latin text by ancient Roman poet Virgil, headed *P. Virgili Maronis*, possibly expressing Kentridge's unfettered affection for the South African landscape and his sense of belonging, inspired by Virgil's love for his native Italy.

"I was born a loser" is the strangely entrancing refrain of the 1969 song "Black Man's World" by Jamaican rocksteady singer Alton Ellis. The song's lyrics continue: "I was living in my own land. I was moved because of white men's plan ... I was born a loser because I am a black man." The refrain is used to meditative yet unsettling effect throughout Gaillard's 3D film and music installation *Nightlife*. The final repeat of the refrain is not as anticipated, but changes to "I was born a winner," taken from Ellis' re-recording of the song in 1971 by Coxsone label. The song was re-titled "Black Man's Pride." Within two years "loser" had turned to "winner." By combining both recordings Gaillard also played with the spatializing effects of reverb and delay in the soundtrack, creating an overall sensation of echo. Ellis's song is on the cusp of a changing political and social situation in the United States, with the change in the lyrics embodying a shift in subjectivity. In *Phonographies: grooves in sonic Afro-modernity,* Alexander G. Weheliye imagines black life as inhabiting a virtual sounding-space shaped through modern sound technologies.[5] African American studies scholar Weheliye terms it "sonic Afro-modernity," wich he sees as allowing black artists to shape new ideas of subjectivity, temporality, and community. A space of this kind is structurally described in *Nightlife* via the medium of sound recording, lending an insistent visibility to black subjectivity. In their works, both artists, Ellis and Gaillard, create a metaphorical space for change and for freedom: Ellis through his accusation of white man's violence towards black life through the loss of his land and the abuse of the black man's body; Gaillard by historicizing black lives in making connections between events within places.

In *Nightlife* the metaphorical space develops within three places: Cleveland, Los Angeles, and Berlin. For each city a significant episode is visually described and sonically shaped by Ellis's mournful lyrics of injustice and displacement. At the end of this sequence of cities, the film returns to Cleveland, but to a different site to the one in the introductory scenes. The filmic and sound storylines together play out a narrative of entwined plants, places, people, and politics.

In the first images of *Nightlife*, the camera pans over the bronze sculpture *The Thinker* by French artist Auguste Rodin (1840–1917). Initially conceived in 1880, numerous casts of the sculpture at different scales now exist. One of the monumental casts is located outside the Cleveland Museum of Art, where it was installed on the south steps in 1917.[6]

On 24 March 1970, the Cleveland *Thinker* was bombed as a political act. Its foot was blown off and the phrase "[illegible word] the ruling class" was painted on the pedestal. This object in a public place became a site for confrontation, even though no one claimed responsibility and the bombing remains unsolved. As members of the Weathermen, an anti-imperialist underground organization, and Students for a Democratic Society (the SDS) were active in Cleveland, the bombing was likely a symptom of the protests against the American War in Vietnam. Moreover, the explosion took place just a few weeks before National Guardsmen opened fire on protesters at Kent State University and killed four citizens. The museum decided to leave the damage unrepaired as a reminder of the violence and the fragility of our social fabric.[7] The camera encircles the sculpture, and Gaillard recasts *The Thinker* as a virtual projection, a sculpture made from light—maybe to indicate a potential space for a new subjectivity.

The ambiguous scenes of violence, beauty, and transcendence are followed by the introduction of one of the main plant protagonists of the film, the Hollywood juniper. From an elevated perspective, the camera lingers on a juniper tree. The observation of the tree's leafy, irregular, twisted branches rhythmically moving in the nocturnal wind, offers a disconcerting sense of seduction. The Urban Forest Ecosystems Institute in San Luis Obispo, California, cites this tree as *Juniperus chinensis* 'Torulosa' of the *Cupressaceae* family, which may be referred to as male or female.[8] The tree, an imported plant from Asia, is characterized as a desirable, utility-friendly, and drought-tolerant tree. Pervasive in California, the plant adapted well to a new geography, and become attributed to Hollywood through its common name.

Not only is California one of the most cosmopolitan U.S. states, its flora is also among the most varied. Historian Jared Farmer ascribed this to immigrants from across the globe, who in the late nineteenth and early twentieth centuries tried to grow everything in a climate suitable for a variety of plants, including trees from the immigrants' places of origins.[9] This has sometimes caused "botanical xenophobia"

Hollywood juniper tree in Cyprien Gaillard *Nightlife* (film still), 2015, 3D motion picture. Courtesy of the artist and Sprüth Magers. Copyright Cyprien Gaillard.

but this has not—as might have been expected according to Farmer—coincided with "actual xenophobia." The rhetorical device of likening immigrants to weeds was foregone, though many leading conservationists of that time were in fact racists, nativists, and even eugenicists. "Inversely," Farmer states, "in the 1880s when Californians initially turned against eucalyptus trees, they did not compare unwanted specimens to despised foreigners such as the Chinese."[10] In this context, environmental historian Harriet Ritvo also reminds us that "the reconsideration of the morally loaded rhetoric in which discussions of biological migration and transplantation are often couched, might make it easier to identify those causes and even to do something about them."[11]

In the next sequence, the camera rises above a grove of trees. We see the colourful fireworks of the annual Pyronale competition. The spectacular pyrotechnics explode in the airspace above the Olympic Stadium in Berlin. The fireworks' ephemeral shapes of light and smoky tendrils curiously evoke the abiding movement of the Hollywood juniper. Then the film returns to Cleveland for its concluding section. This time it is not *The Thinker*, but a leafless oak tree in winter. In 1936, the German Olympic committee gave each gold medalist an oak sapling. Significantly, four saplings were given to world record-setting American sprinter and long jumper Jesse Owens, whose outstanding achievements had made a mockery of race ideology. In *Nightlife*, a helicopter searchlight illuminates the oak. The building in the background is Rhodes High School, where Owens had trained. The athlete

Oak tree in Cyprien Gaillard *Nightlife* (film still), 2015, 3D motion picture.
Courtesy of the artist and Sprüth Magers. Copyright Cyprien Gaillard.

planted the oak in the school's courtyard as a sapling—the only sapling known to have survived. This arboreal gift to Owens is part of historic German lore, in which the tree is an emblem of strength. In the fascist context of 1930s Germany, the tree was adopted by national-socialist ideology. And yet the winner's sapling was planted and cared for within the Cleveland school yard. The uneasiness of the tree's history is alluded to by the surveying motion of the search light in the concluding sequence of images.[12]

The artists' projects discussed here—projects creating botanical interventions or those representing plants within their urban environments—are works embedded within social, racial, and political histories. Histories of humans and plants are entangled in the artists' uses of seeds, saplings and plants, which were either spontaneously dispersed, intentionally planted, or an effect of human-made infrastructures. In Gaillard's *Nightlife* no people can be seen. The visuals, sounds, and lyrics are used as metaphorical structures to describe migration and the social invisibility of protagonists of Black history. These plants in the urban night provide an oblique mirror of human stories and events within the landscape.

1 See Natalie Bayer, Belinda Kazeem-Kamiński, and Nora Sternfeld, eds., *Curating as anti-racist practice*, vol. 2, *Curating: exhibition, theory & practice* (Berlin: De Gruyter, 2018).

2 See the examples of works by Indian artist Sunoj D and Chinese artist Hu Yun at the Natural History Museum in London in Bergit Arends, "The subversive potential of seeds in three acts (2010, 2013, 2014)," in Khadija von Zinnenburg Carroll, ed., *Botanical drift: protagonists of the invasive herbarium* (Berlin: Sternberg Press, 2017).

3 See Doreen Massey, "Landscape as a provocation: reflections on moving mountains," *Journal of Material Culture* 11 (1/2) (2006) pp. 33–48.

4 John Robert McNeill, "The environment, environmentalism, and international society in the long 1970s," in Niall Ferguson, ed., *The shock of the global: the 1970s in perspective* (Cambridge, Mass: Belknap Press of Harvard University Press, 2010) pp. 263–278.

5 See Alexander G. Weheliye, *Phonographies: grooves in sonic Afro-modernity* (Durham and London: Duke University Press, 2005).

6 The sculpture was first conceived by Rodin for *The Gates of Hell*, a large sculptural doorway commissioned in 1880 by the French government, but later became an independent piece. The sculpture, initially referred to as *The Poet*, represents the medieval Italian poet Dante Alighieri, author of the *Divine Comedy*, the inspiration for *The Gates*. The poet is seen to observe the circles of hell and to meditate on his work. He is considered as both a tortured soul (though in a powerful body) and a free-thinking man who transcends his suffering through poetry.

7 Local newspaper coverage by Steven Litt (31 August 2017), Cleveland Museum of Art shared tip about 1970 bombing of Rodin "Thinker" with FBI. Retrieved from https://www.cleveland.com/arts/index.ssf/2017/08/cleveland_museum_of_art_shared.html (accessed on 15 July 2018).

8 For details on Californian plants, see the web resources by the Urban Forests Ecosystem Institute at San Luis Obispo Cal Poly, for example, *Juniperus chinensis* 'Torulosa' tree record, 1995–2018. Retrieved from https://selectree.calpoly.edu/tree-detail/juniperus-chinensis-torulosa (accessed on 13 July 2018).

9 Owing to human migration and landscaping from the nineteenth century onwards, Los Angeles now has very few native trees, such as the slow-growing coast live oak (*Quercus agrifolia*), a perennial shrub native to California.

10 See the interview with Jared Farmer by Nathan Masters (23 January 2014) "How did L.A. become a city of palms? And other questions about California's trees." Retrieved from https://www.kcet.org/shows/lost-la/how-did-la-become-a-city-of-palms-and-other-questions-about-californias-trees (accessed 13 July 2018).

11 See the environmental humanities lexicon entry by Harriet Ritvo, "Invasion/invasive," *Environmental Humanities*, 9 (1) (accessed 13 July 2018: http://environmentalhumanities.org/lexicon/).

12 See also the research by German artist Christian Kosmas Mayer, who traced the oak sapling given to Olympic athlete Cornelius Cooper Johnson. The African American high jumper planted the sapling in the courtyard of his parents' house in Los Angeles. Mayer's work was shown in the exhibition *Natural histories: traces of the political*, Museum Moderner Kunst Stiftung Ludwig Wien, September 2017 to January 2018.

Toxic tour: Houston's environmental apartheid and institutional liberation

T. J. Demos

Wastelands have increasingly merged with urban sacrifice zones at the frontiers of impoverishment, environmental degradation, structural racism, and police brutality, where containment is no longer fully possible—if it ever was. Still, this situation grows worse and is revealed in city areas formed at the catastrophic convergence of climate change and extreme weather, as in post-hurricane Houston, Texas. As investigated by the U.S. based artist collective Not an Alternative/The Natural History Museum, Houston offers a revealing lens on shifting conditions of resurgent urban gentrification, environmental injustice, and petrocapitalist mythology. They also propose modes of intervention that build on the intersectionalist political ecologies of contemporary art, according to which creative aesthetic sensibility conjugates social justice concerns with multispecies life and more-than-human forms of life in ways that are both critically analytical and environmentally generative.[1] In the case of Not an Alternative's *Mining the NHMS*, a mixed-media installation and social-practice project of 2016, the urban zone of Houston becomes a diorama of socio-ecological connections in which botanical formations intersect with politico-economic divisions.

Urban wastelands have long been the focus of environmental justice (EJ) movements in the United States. These emerged in the 1980s, but extend back to social movements of the 1960s that staged protests against environmental racism. One fundamental insight of EJ analyses, led by African-American concerns for in/equality in environmental health, is that communities of colour (African American, Indigenous, Hispanic), are disproportionately impacted by the urban toxicity of landfills and incinerators and corresponding lack of greenery; consequently, any justice-based solutions to waste management and urban design must take social inequality in exposure and vulnerability into account. The momentum of EJ activism initially built on the1968 Memphis Sanitation Strike over better pay and safer working conditions, and resulted in such key publications as the 1983 congressional study on "Siting of hazardous waste landfills and their correlation with racial

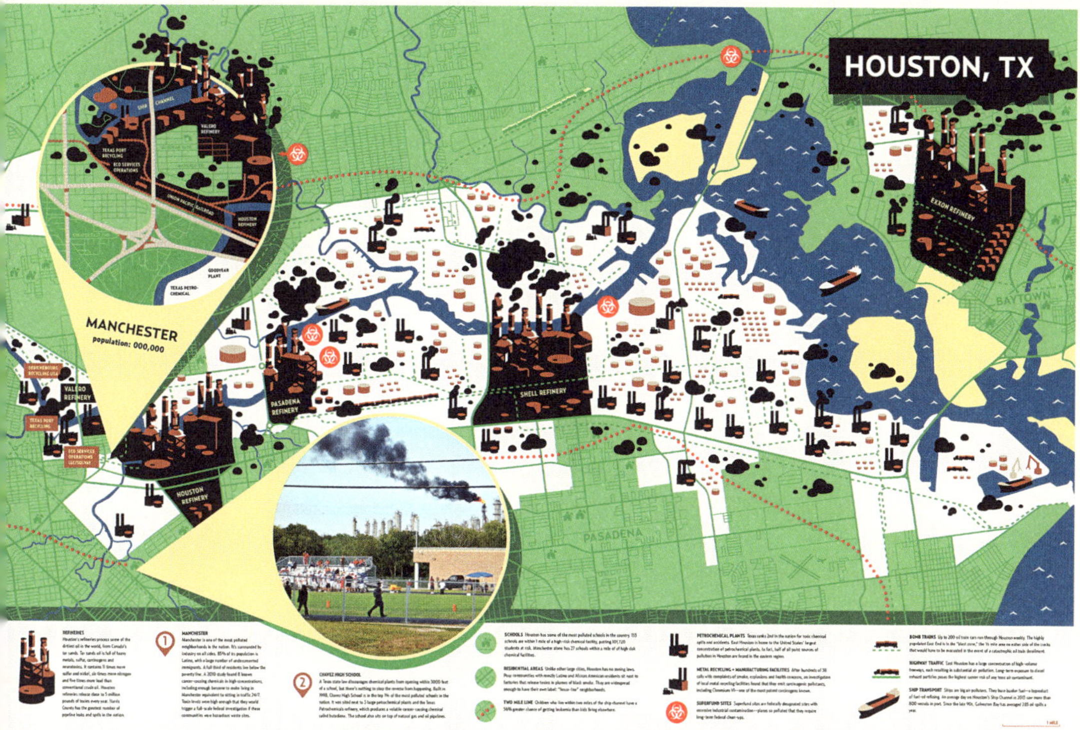

Not An Alternative, *Houston's Fossil Fuel Ecosystem*, map charting Houston's geography of environmental injustice, installed as a lightbox table in the exhibition *Mining the HMNS: An Investigation by The Natural History Museum*, Project Row Houses, Houston, TX, 2016. Photo: Not An Alternative/The Natural History Museum. Courtesy of the artists.

and economic status of surrounding communities," which in turn informed the United Church of Christ's Commission for Racial Justice's 1987 study *Toxic wastes and race in the United States*, and Robert Bullard's 1990, *Dumping in Dixie: race, class, and environmental quality*.[2] These were generally opposed to the tendencies of white, liberal environmentalism, which, beginning in the nineteenth century, directed preservationist policies toward wilderness conservation and wildlife protection, reflecting the interests and privileges of outdoor leisure cultures shocked at the horrors of unregulated extraction, deforestation, and spread of industrial waste that were effects of colonial modernity. That trajectory continues today with the mainstream focus on greenhouse gases and atmospheric carbon. For example, the Sierra Club, founded in 1892 by Scottish-American preservationist John Muir, proclaimed its ambition in its original mission statement as follows: "To explore, enjoy, and render accessible the mountain regions of the Pacific Coast," without mentioning the fact that those lands were premised on Indigenous dispossession. It is precisely this mode of environmentalism—today, implicating the kind dedicated to the ineffectual liberal reformism of recycling and green consumerism, rather than socio-ecological justice—that Indian activist Ramachandra Guha terms the "ecology of affluence."[3]

The affluence at stake is, in the present, the limited definition of what "climate" means, typically signifying prevalent weather patterns over an extended duration, while "environment" tends to refer generally to non-human natures, opting for biogeophysical elements when it comes to the discourse of climate change in much science and in the popular imagination. When mobilized critically, however, the notion of urban wastelands rejects these depoliticized formulations, instead expanding both climate and environment (including botanical elements of resilient green city design) toward relations of power, inextricable from socio-economic and political inequities. Such a definition is indicated in what Katherine McKittrick calls "Black geographies," designating the racialized segregation of urban space and production of (in)security in the U.S. which extends to noxious atmospheres and dirty environments of particulate matter, chemicals, toxins, and degraded water supplied to racialized and disenfranchised communities, as in Flint, Michigan.[4] In these cases, climate and environment stand to be radically redefined along the lines of EJ concerns. Moreover, in the era of climate breakdown, these terms—climate and environment—are pushed together under intensive instability and crisis, where changing climates impact, cause, and exacerbate environmental destruction, measured in ways that intensify socio-political and economic inequalities. While EJ movements have long focused on urban wastelands as sites of uncontrollable contamination, placing vulnerable and disenfranchised communities of colour at risk of uneven exposure to toxicity, and geographical exclusion from green retreats, these risks have expanded and multiplied in the era of catastrophic weather events that create environmental crises of ever greater intensity.

What do these shifting conditions reveal about the character of urban wastelands today, and how might cultural practitioners working at the intersection of ecology and social justice respond?

Not an Alternative/The Natural History Museum addressed these very questions in Houston, Texas, one of the most polluted cities in the U.S. and the nation's largest and most concentrated centre of the petrochemical industry. *Mining the HMNS* was extensive in form, and included three central elements. Firstly, the collective organized public "toxic tours" that surveyed Houston's East Side and industrial waterways in coordination with the city's Latinx-led environmental justice organization t.e.j.a.s. (Texas Environmental Justice Advocacy Services, an organization with connections to Robert Bullard's work). Secondly, they investigated the oil industry's sponsorship of the Houston Museum of Natural Sciences, installing a critical mixed-media installation at the Project Row Houses, a community platform based in Houston's historic Third Ward, one of the city's oldest African-American neighbourhoods, that intends to enhance lives through art with positive impacts on the urban landscape. And thirdly, they created "Operation Dinosaur," a citizen science air-quality monitoring study in neighbourhoods abutting the world's largest petrochemical hub.[5]

One key element of their installation is a map that charts the salient environmental inequities in Manchester, an area of Houston located in the highly industrialized eastern part of the city and a couple of miles from the Third Ward. "Manchester is one of the most polluted neighbourhoods in the nation," the map's explanatory text notes. "It's surrounded by industry on all sides. 85% of its population is Latino, with a large number of undocumented immigrants. A full third of residents live below the poverty line. A 2010 study found 8 known cancer-causing chemicals in high concentrations, including enough benzene to make living in Manchester equivalent to sitting in traffic 24/7. Toxin levels were high enough that they would trigger a full-scale federal investigation if these communities were hazardous waste sites."[6] As a schematic diagram with two enlarged areas of detail, the map shows the Manchester neighbourhood—effectively a hazardous waste site—flanked by the Union Pacific Railroad and Ship Channel (one of the nation's busiest sea ports with a high volume of industrial barge traffic). The Valero refinery, Texas Port Recycling, and Eco Services Operations surround its other sides, with a Goodyear plant and Texas Petro-Chemical down the road, and the Shell and Exxon refineries close by. In the immediate vicinity there is also a Superfund site, a federally designated area containing excessive industrial contamination requiring long-term federal remediation. Dozens more unidentified petrochemical plants are located in the area. We learn from the map's lettering that Houston's refineries process some of the dirtiest oil in the world, including Canadian Tar Sands bitumen containing heavy metals, sulfur, carcinogens, and neurotoxins, and "release close to 5 million pound of toxins every year." A massive petroscape, "Harris County"—the Texas region including Houston—"has the greatest number of pipeline leaks and spills in the nation."

In a second zoom-in, we see an image of Cesar Chávez High School, named after the Mexican American labour and civil rights leader associated with the California farmworkers' struggle in the 1960s and 1970s. We learn from information contained in the map that the school, located a mile and a half from Manchester, was built in 1998 and serves a majority Hispanic population. Next door are three large petrochemical plants and the Texas Petrochemicals Refinery, producing a volatile cancer-causing chemical called butadiene. The school also sits on top of natural gas and oil pipelines and is in the top 1 percent of the most polluted schools in the United States. The image shows the school's sports field hosting a game, with spectators in the bleachers, while a refinery's chimney belches black smoke from a gas flare visible in the background. As such, Cesar Chávez High School offers a classic instance of what Robert Bullard, back in 1990, termed "urban apartheid" in the United States. Designating a system of spatial inequality based on race and class differentials, it also constitutes environmental separation, creating segregated habitats of clean and dirty elements of air, water, and earth.[7] Adding to those physical qualities, the negativity of uneven exposure to toxicity—which in Bullard's study concerns human impacts rather than more-than-human effects, which await the further formation of multi-species justice activism—is compounded by lack of financial resources and health services, characteristic of impoverished communities.

Obviously the situation that Bullard identified persists, continuing to disproportionately affect black and brown communities, which remain situated near toxic

Not An Alternative, Operation Dinosaur, press photograph for an air quality monitoring operation led by The Natural History Museum and t.e.j.a.s. in partnership with scientists from Texas State University, in association with the exhibition Mining the HMNS: An Investigation by The Natural History Museum, Project Row Houses, Houston, TX, 2016. Photo: Not An Alternative/The Natural History Museum. Courtesy of the artists.

waste and Superfund sites, incinerators, and landfills across the United States, communities that lack the resources to move elsewhere.[8] This is the case even as clean urban environments have increasingly become the object of city design and integral to the economics of "environmental gentrification," where the seemingly progressive theory of urban sustainability—entailing schemes of beautification including the planting of trees and edible gardens, soft industry remediation, providing new bike lanes and water catchment systems—have had the effect of driving up property values and displacing low-income residents, some of whom have lived in the area for generations. Coined by Melissa Checker, the term "environmental gentrification" designates the process by which the sustainable cities movement has been instrumentalized by high-end real estate developers at the expense of low-income residents: "While it appears as politically neutral, consensus-based planning that is both ecologically and socially sensitive, in practice, environmental gentrification subordinates equity to profit-minded development."[9] If displacement occurs, then people end up in areas like Manchester, where home values bottom out at $19,000, compared to Houston's median home value of $181,800.[10]

A further aspect of the city's green divide is its botanical inequalities. While the enviro-remediation capacities of plants and trees (of which, in Houston, live oaks, pine, green ash, and Chinese tallowtree are among the most common) are well known, cultivated green spaces are largely absent in the city's most polluted areas.

Indeed, their botanical benefits include carbon storage (Houston's trees absorb approximately 140,000 tons of air pollution per year), runoff and flood risk reduction, and lowering annual residential energy costs by limiting urban heat effects.[11] Yet the majority of trees are located on private lands, and green urbanism is carefully deployed mostly in well-resourced areas of the city, such as Emancipation Park and the Botanic Garden, the recent multi-million dollar renovations of which have drawn accusations of monopolizing city budgets at the cost of the housing and health care needs of lower income communities. Not only this, but the city has dedicated federal funds for buyout programmes for damaged homes in flood-prone areas (whereby houses are demolished, leaving green spaces in their footprints); yet these buyouts tend to exacerbate gentrification, displace poorer community members, and fail to keep pace with or effectively mitigate storm destruction and climate transformation.[12] Not surprisingly, affluent white communities are able to cultivate well-tended gardens and floral displays, whereas buyouts in low-income areas result in vacant lots and green abandonment.[13] Botany thus becomes a site of socio-environmental inequality, and these urban wasteland-wilderness zones await further research into what grows, their petrochemical impacts, and how these green spaces might be productively mobilized in the interests of social justice.

The Manchester case study, as presented in Not An Alternative's *Mining the HMNS*, exemplifies one such urban wasteland, from which we can draw three observations. Firstly, urban wastelands like Manchester's designate areas where disenfranchised communities that exist at the intersection of racial, political, and economic discrimination are consigned to toxic environments as an effect of environmental apartheid. Historically, wastelands signified deserted or barren places inspiring fear or contempt, with waste drawing on the Latin *vastus* meaning vast, void, and unused.[14] With U.S. settler colonialism, the production of wastelands included the violent making of racialized bodies and degraded regions in the country's Southwest through industry and extraction. Indigenous territories have long been targeted for disproportionate exposure to environmental harm, as with uranium mining on Diné (Navajo) land.[15] Applied to contemporary urban contexts like Manchester, however, "urban wasteland" describes neither empty territories or low-density territories beyond urban culture, nor colonial practices of despoliation in frontier zones, but highly populated areas of petrocapitalist industrial activity that consign communities populated by racialized and impoverished bodies (as well as neglected more-than-human natures) to toxic vulnerability and chemical debilitation.

Secondly, urban wastelands designate not simply territories of land and botanies of negligence, but also bodies of people, as petrochemical contamination reaches into the physiologies of inhabitants, creating hazardscapes of bioaccumulation. Chemicals and toxins disperse into circulating air, local water sources, and soil, and are variously ingested into bodies with prolonged exposure to these petrochemical environments, bodies that subsequently show signs of heightened mental illnesses, diseases, and mortality rates. Indeed, new research shows that exposure to toxic air causes an enormous reduction in intelligence in addition to well-known impacts on physical health.[16] This includes several million premature deaths, links to high mortality rates in people with mental disorders, and increased childhood illnesses and risk of dementia. These cycles of debilitation converge with the structural effects of de-capacitation, which, according to the dominant neoliberal political regime, targets and intensifies inequalities of race and class in spaces of systematic infrastructural privation, where subjects are then exposed to the predations of privatized health care services and resulting financial indebtedness.[17] Urban wastescapes are also bodyscapes of socio-environmental injustice.

Thirdly, if contemporary biopolitics is mutating under the combined vectors of ongoing petrocapitalist extraction and catastrophic climate change, then Manchester is an example of its urban conditions, where life connects intimately with environments that are at once biophysical and socio-economic. Beth Povinelli has proposed the term "geontopolitics" in order to update modern biopolitics and to define a new paradigm of late liberal governance that distinguishes between life and non-life, a politics of differential ontologies and Earth elements constructed and policed in the interests of fossil capital accumulation.[18] For disenfranchised communities living near toxic facilities, this means an increasingly limited access to clean, healthy environments as their living and working spaces are contaminated by industrial activities, against which they have little legal or political recourse absent of economic resource. The necropolitical logic at play here—implied in Povinelli's geontopolitical phase shift—is the gradual transition of inhabitants of toxic urban wastelands from the zone of the living to that of the non-living, where toxicity's "slow violence" transitions into "slow death."[19] In sum, Manchester is a case of urban wastelanding, which exemplifies neoliberalism's violent shaping of debilitated racialized bodies in/as degraded landscapes, which defines contemporary geontopolitics of toxic zones of sacrifice.

For an additional part of their project, The Natural History Museum collaborated with t.e.j.a.s. and scientists from Texas Southern University on a series of monthly "toxic tours" (one recorded version is presented in a short hologram video version available on their website[20]). The tour describes the environmental circumstances of tens of thousands of people who live along Houston's Ship Channel, situated opposite the city's gentrified area and its luxury homes and lush greenery, public parks and outdoor recreational areas. The city's impoverished east side lives in the shadow of a mega-complex of industries and transportation networks of ships, rails, and trucks, normally invisible to those not living within it.[21] The video features the voices of Bryan Parras, founding member of t.e.j.a.s. and members of Manchester's community, who offer an overview of life in Manchester. With emergency sirens sounding in the background, we hear from the speakers how kids commonly play in vacant lots that are also Superfund sites (Houston has more than 20, containing a variety of chemicals and toxins). There are no green parks or access to clean water, even though the area borders rivers, which are dedicated to industrial use and abuse. Nor, as Parras explains, are there any edible gardens, owing to the contaminated soil—only refineries and polluted areas, brown fields and neglected green zones, with regular damage to properties caused by industrial sonic explosions, occurring without explanation or prior announcement. Such is the life of a frontline impoverished community living in a toxic "war zone" as Parras observes, with high levels of police surveillance, responding to endemic links to perceived criminality exacerbated by structural racism and resource and infrastructure poverty. While Manchester is surrounded by some of the most profitable companies in world history, none of them invest in their immediate neighbourhood or support community development. Instead, industry's very presence is destructive and debilitating to the living.[22]

Where corporations do invest vast resources, it is in publicity campaigns that seek to legitimate the petrocapitalist economy. Central to the Natural History Museum's Project Row Houses' project is their installation *Mining the HMNS*, referring to the Houston Museum of Natural Sciences, which, following the artists' critical investigation, is seen to figure as a PR front for the fossil fuel industry.[23] Their installation excavates key narratives and displays in the museum and highlights the voices and stories that are excluded from its industry-sponsored galleries—those of low-income and predominantly Latinx and African-American frontline communities living along the Houston Ship Channel. The Natural History Museum also created a critical hologram video tour of the HMNS,[24] narrated by Beka Economopoulos, its co-founder and co-director, who provides analysis of the museum's narrative, in particular considering its educational approach to nature, energy, and the environment. In the video, we learn that HMNS encourages visitors to adopt the perspectives of its corporate sponsors, particularly in the "Wiess Energy Hall." There, the HMNS presents educational media that locate the "origin of energy" in oil and gas (whereas solar and wind power are unmentioned) and thus naturalizes the privileged narrative of the fossil fuel industry. Not surprisingly, there is no consideration of climate change or any of the other negative environmental and socio-cultural impacts of fossil fuel.[25] In this way, the industry positions itself as the "natural" outcome of evolution, an advertising strategy meant to shape the positive cognitive associations of petroculture.

We also learn that the U.S. museums see more visitors annually than sporting events and theme parks combined. While museum institutions have tremendous impact as trusted sources of knowledge and convey cultural norms, the fossil fuel companies that sponsor them manipulate narratives, presenting an industry perspective that naturalizes perception and engineers consent. The exhibiting of drilling heads in a museum gallery causes technology to appear like precious art objects, while there is no mention of oil spills in the museum's Texas wildlife wing. Meanwhile ExxonMobil, one of the museum's sponsors, is under criminal investigation for lying to investors about the negative impacts of climate change and funding denial campaigns for decades. The coastal regions of Texas bear the brunt, as they are the locations of spreading cancer clusters and habitat destruction. This disproportionately affects low-income communities of colour and the region's flora and fauna. While museums all over the world are divesting from fossil fuel wealth and reinvesting in post-petro systems, the HMNS celebrates petrocapitalism. "In this way, the Houston Museum of Natural Sciences functions as a public relations tool for ExxonMobil, Chevron, Shell, and the rest of its many corporate sponsors," explains Economopoulos.

Back at the Project Row Houses, the *Mining the HMNS* installation includes a "Sponsorship Wall" that lists corporate donors, their logos resized according to their respective greenhouse gas emissions: Exxon Mobil, BP, GDF Suez, Shell, and Chevron stand out. One of the installation's dioramas points out that employees of companies that give the museum $25,000 or more get priority scheduling to be trained as docents of the Wiess Energy Hall, where school groups commonly take tours—including, as the display indicates, the children who live within two miles of the Houston Ship Channel where the petrochemical industry is concentrated and where residents have a 56 percent greater likelihood of developing leukemia that those who live elsewhere. Another of the artists' dioramas portrays the Texas Coastal Ecology wing of the museum, including elements excluded from the HMNS's own display such as life-size pelicans standing on petrochemical detritus and bayou plant life behind a barbed wire fence with ExxonMobil signage, and "No Trespassing" warnings. Meanwhile, a light box portrays community members, a number of them children, and Manchester housing next to industry buildings, documenting the area's toxic social environment.

Mining the HMNS describes the normal and everyday socio-environmental conditions in Houston, but what happens under the added pressures of climate transformation and its extreme weather events? In August 2018, a year after the artists' intervention, Hurricane Harvey struck Houston, a category 4 tropical storm, dramatizing how climate change impacts and exacerbates socio-environmental injustice. One of the costliest tropical cyclones on record, and the wettest in the United States, it wreaked $125 billion worth of damage. Some areas, including Harris County, received between 40 and 60 inches of rain during 24–28 August 2017, with the resulting floods inundating hundreds of thousands of homes and displacing more than 30,000 people.[26] While Manchester did not suffer the extensive flooding experienced in other areas of Houston, the rainfall did cause chemical leaks, including an estimated 1,881 pounds of carcinogenic benzene. According to an Environmental Defense Fund report, this represented a fraction of nearly 5.3 m pounds of pollutants released by the storm.[27] The storm brought disaster to industrial facilities and Superfund sites in Houston, allowing dangerous chemicals and toxicants—including polycyclic aromatic hydrocarbons (PAH)—to spill into and contaminate air, water, and ground. Exposure to these materials has been linked to adverse health outcomes, including cancer and diseases of the skin, liver, and immune system. Documented evidence shows that Manchester was particularly hard hit, with high quantities of PAHs due to extreme flooding associated with Hurricane Harvey.[28] While *Mining the HMNS* was created a year before Harvey, it nonetheless proved prescient in terms of the disastrous effects of the petrochemical industry on surrounding communities.

On this basis, we can draw numerous conclusions. Firstly, we cannot restrict the "environment" of urban wastelands to biophysical and non-human natures—rather,

Not An Alternative, Texas Coastal Ecology Installation, critical revision of a diorama found in the Texas Coastal Ecology wing of the Houston Museum of Natural Sciences, installed in the exhibition *Mining the HMNS: An Investigation* by The Natural History Museum, Project Row Houses, Houston, TX, 2016. Photo: Not An Alternative/The Natural History Museum. Courtesy of the artists.

the forcing together of cultures and environments defines the inextricable entanglements of what Donna Haraway calls naturecultures, characteristic of the new geological age of the Anthropocene, in which natural and human sciences become similarly inextricable as a consequence.[29] If so, these naturecultures are striated by racial and economic lines, producing zones of environmental apartheid and climates of anti-blackness. Writing about the aftermath of transatlantic slavery, of life "in the wake," Christina Sharpe alludes to this conception where she describes weather as a vector of racialization: "in what I am calling the weather, antiblackness is pervasive as climate." Whereas ecology defines "the branch of biology that deals with the relations of organisms to one another and to their physical surroundings," it also correlates with "the political movement that seeks to protect the environment, especially from pollution," for some more than others.[30] These entanglements are revealed in Manchester. Anti-blackness as climate proposes ecology as the intersection of biophysical relationalities between organisms and their surroundings, including linkages between human bodies and petrochemical atmospherics, linkages that are integral to the differential construction of race in the U.S., especially in the U.S. as it exists under the conditions of climate breakdown. (If these social ecologies are emphasized over botanical ones, it is likely in recognition of the emergency conditions of Houston's severe environmental racism.)

Secondly, insofar as climates are also changing owing to petrocapitalist causality—what some refer to as the Capitalocene, rather than invoking the liberal-humanist thesis of the Anthropocene[31]—climates are bringing increased unpredictability and intensity to environmental conditions, particularly when it comes to extreme weather events. Climates of anti-blackness, in other words, are intensifying, creating ever more pollution, ever more debilitation, threatening to expand beyond historically designated areas of toxic containment and urban wastelands. With ever more multitudes subjected to politico-economic disenfranchisement and environmental risk in a world of growing resource inequality—dramatized particularly in the post-disaster zones of Houston, Detroit, New Orleans, Puerto Rico, and Haiti, to mention only those sites in the Americas that form an interconnected field of structural and purposeful neglect—we are witnessing a spreading blackout that is socio-economic and structurally unequal in racial terms. Indeed, for Achille Mbembe, this system represents the expansion of the centuries-long conditions of profound dispossession once directed primarily toward those of African origin under the terms of slavery, producing the historical meaning of Blackness. Now called "precarity" and released from strictly racial classification (though this is not to say that racial capitalism does not still persist), we face what Mbembe terms the "becoming black of the world."[32]

This phrase designates for Mbembe the globalized blackout of impoverishment, necropolitics, and dispossession—the dispossession of the power of self-determination, of control over one's future, even of the free access to time and the possible. To this diagnosis of a new norm of precarious existence, I would add the exposure to extraction's waste-zones, befouled elements, colonized atmospheres, toxic externalities, and public health emergencies, where becoming-black is evidenced in urban pollution, degraded water, mismanaged trash, and indebted and diseased bodies. While its zones may be expanding globally, exposure is still based on differential vulnerabilities and unequal resources of protection, with the interconnected relations between the two inspiring further cycles of commodification (targeting health care, education and housing as much as the primary elements of water, air, soil, and plants). Without collapsing the discussion of toxic inequalities into the liberal universalism of some climate change discourse, it's clear that today's urban wastelands, in the era of extreme weather events, are seeing threats expand, even while not equalizing vulnerabilities. Indeed, Hurricane Harvey intensified toxicity in Houston and expanded its zones of contamination beyond containment, in a "worlding" of waste.

Thirdly, these climates at the intersection of the biogeophysical and the socio-economic spheres are being globalized, in places where the urban location of wastelands is giving way to environments of generalization. These in turn create new markets of clean air and water, according to the wider conditions of neoliberalism's individualized systems of commercialized elements, health, education, and infrastructural access. Even as Manchester's inhabitants have no recourse but to breathe the toxic air in the aftermath of a hurricane's stirring together of the environments of Superfund sites and petrochemical facilities and high-density urban areas, companies around the world are experimenting with the commodification of clean air as a luxury good. Thus, urban gentrification—as it exists from Houston to Beijing—is not simply a matter of unequal atmospherics, occasioned by the construction of upmarket real estate and urban greenery in distinction to zones of toxicity, but also extends to the respiratory habitats of the well-resourced who have access to all the clean air they need, whether in air conditioned condos and cars, or in individualized microclimates provided by clean-air commodity paraphernalia like luxury oxygen products.[33]

In relation to these factors, the Natural History Museum project, in coordination with t.e.j.a.s., made one further intervention, this time intervening in systems of visibility and education. Their "Operation Dinosaur" comprised a citizen science air-quality monitoring study conducted in the Manchester neighbourhood abutting the world's largest petrochemical hub. Making reference to HMNS's newly designed dinosaur wing, the project entailed distributing plastic red T-rex models with air quality monitors hanging from their necks to residents, enabling them to observe ongoing levels of atmospheric pollution. In other words, those most debilitated by environmental apartheid could thereby gain the knowledge to resist, forming communities of action, which might influence and redirect public institutions otherwise given over to fossil corporate interests. The motivation was a landmark study conducted by the *Houston Chronicle* ten years earlier which revealed high concentrations of several cancer-causing chemicals in the air of East Houston's fence-line communities. NHM's goal was to push the fossil fuel industry into its own cycle of natural evolution, thus causing it to become an outmoded dinosaur in the present.

In this regard, their project unites environmental justice with revolutionary politics, recalling and updating the words of Franz Fanon in our climate-changed present: "We revolt simply because, for a variety of reasons, we can no longer breathe."[34] Moving beyond Fanon's decolonial politics, what would it mean to expand this revolt to include the more-than-human, to create a multispecies "conspiracy," a revolutionary breathing-together in the demands for respiratory life and justice that would ultimately overcome petrocapitalist destruction?[35] This remains an urgent challenge. In this vein, *Mining the HMNS* forms part of Not an Alternative's larger project of "institutional liberation," through which they aim to contribute to the formation of communities of action to challenge fossil capital itself and its threatened transformation of the earth into an expanded wasteland within and beyond the city. Ultimately, their project is much more ambitious than simply making an intervention in a single museum, neighbourhood, or city, going beyond liberal reformism. As Not an Alternative explains, "institutional liberation isn't about making institutions better, more inclusive, more participatory. It's about establishing politicized base camps from which ever more coordinated, elaborate, and effective campaigns against the capitalist state in all its racist, exploitative, extractivist and colonizing dimensions can be carried out."[36]

1 For more information on this subject, see T. J. Demos, *Decolonizing nature: contemporary art and the politics of ecology* (Berlin: Sternberg Press, 2016); and Yates McKee, "On flooded streets and breathing-in-common: climate justice, black lives matter, and the arts of decolonization," *Strike art: contemporary art and the post-Occupy condition* (London: Verso, 2016) pp. 181–236.

2 See https://www.epa.gov/environmentaljustice/environmental-justice-timeline. United Church of Christ's Commission for Racial Justice, *Toxic wastes and race in the United States*, revealed that "three out of every five Black and Hispanic Americans lived in communities with uncontrolled toxic waste sites." (xiv); Robert D. Bullard, *Dumping in Dixie: race, class, and environmental quality* (Boulder: Westview, 1990). These conditions certainly extend beyond the U.S., with biggest negative impacts in India and China: https://www.theguardian.com/environment/2018/apr/17/more-than-95-of-worlds-population-breathe-dangerous-air-major-study-finds.

3 Ramachandra Guha, *Environmentalism: a global history* (Oxford: Oxford University Press, 2000); and Madhav Gadgil and Ramachandra Guha, "Ideologies of environmentalism," *in Ecology and equity: the use and abuse of nature in contemporary India* (London: Routledge, 1995).

4 Katherine McKittrick, *Demonic grounds: black women and the cartographies of struggle* (Minneapolis: University of Minnesota Press, 2006); also see Lindsey Dillon and Julie Sze, "Police power and particulate matters: environmental justice and the spatialities of in/securities in U.S. Cities," *English Language Notes* 54 (2) (Fall/Winter 2016) pp. 13–23; and Anna Clark, *The poisoned city: Flint's water and the American urban tragedy* (New York: Metropolitan Books, 2018).

5 See *https://projectrowhouses.org/about/about-prh/.*

6 Jennifer A. Horney et al., "Comparing residential contamination in a Houston environmental justice neighborhood before and after Hurricane Harvey," *Plos One* (8 February 2018) p. 4. Further: "Within 1 mile of the Manchester neighborhood, there are 21 facilities that report to the EPA's Toxic Release Inventory: 11 large-quantity generators of hazardous waste; 4 facilities that treat, store, or dispose of hazardous wastes; 9 major dischargers of air pollution; and 8 major storm water discharging facilities ... The population of the Harrisburg/Manchester Super Neighborhood is 90 percent Hispanic and 6 percent African-American, with a median income that is one-third less that of the City of Houston overall."

7 Bullard, *Dumping in Dixie*, p. 6.

8 Environmental racism means that race is the most significant predictor of a person living near contaminated air, water, or soil in the United States. Indeed, 56 percent of the population near toxic waste sites are people of colour; they have 38 pecent higher nitrogen-dioxide exposure; they are two times more likely to live without potable water and modern sanitation; and they have seen 95 percent of their claims against polluters denied by the EPA. See Bryce Covert, "Race best predicts whether you live near pollution," *The Nation* (7 March 2016) https://www.thenation.com/article/race-best-predicts-whether-you-live-near-pollution/.

9 Melissa Checker, "Wiped out by the greenwave: environmental gentrification and the paradoxical politics of urban sustainability," *City & Society* 23 (2) (2007) pp. 210–229. Also see "Environmental Gentrification," https://critical-sustainabilities.ucsc.edu/environmental-gentrification/.

10 See https://www.har.com/pricetrends/manchester-realestate/707; https://www.zillow.com/houston-tx/home-values/.

11 See *Houston's Urban Forest*, 2015, US Department of Agriculture, https://srs.fs.usda.gov/pubs/54109.

12 Lisa Song and Al Shaw, "Buyouts won't be the answer for many frequent flooding victims," *ProPublica*, 1 November 2017, https://features.propublica.org/houston-buyouts/hurricane-harvey-home-buyouts-harris-county/; and Kevin Loughran, James R. Elliott, S. Wright Kennedy, "Urban ecology in the time of climate change: Houston, flooding, and the case of federal buyouts," *Social Currents* (24 September 2018).

13 Loughran et al., "Urban ecology in the time of climate change," p. 16.

14 See Vittoria Di Palma, *Wasteland: a history* (New Haven: Yale University Press, 2014).

15 Traci Brynne Voyles, *Wastelanding: legacies of uranium mining in Navajo country* (Minneapolis: University of Minnesota Press, 2015).

16 See reports on new research from the *Proceedings of the National Academy of Sciences*, https://www.theguardian.com/environment/2018/aug/27/air-pollution-causes-huge-reduction-in-intelligence-study-reveals. Air pollution causes a "huge" reduction in intelligence, indicating that the damage to society of toxic air is far deeper than the well-known impacts on physical health. The research was conducted in China but is relevant across the world, with 95 percent of the global population breathing unsafe air. It found that high pollution levels led to significant drops in test scores in language and arithmetic, with the average impact equivalent to having lost a year of the person's education. "Polluted air can cause everyone to reduce their level of education by one year, which is huge," said Xi Chen at Yale School of Public Health in the U.S., a member of the research team. "But we know the effect is worse for the elderly, especially those over 64, and for men, and for those with low education. If we calculate [the loss] for those, it may be a few years of education."

17 Jasbir K. Puar, *The Right to maim: debility, capacity, disability* (Durham, NC: Duke University Press, 2017).

18 Elizabeth Povinelli, *Geontologies: a requiem to late liberalism* (Durham, NC: Duke University Press, 2016).

19 Rob Nixon, *Slow violence and the environmentalism of the poor* (Cambridge, MA: Harvard University Press, 2011); and Lauren Berlant, "Slow death (sovereignty, obesity, lateral agency)," *Critical Inquiry* 33 (Summer 2007) pp. 754–780: "The phrase *slow death* refers to the physical wearing out of a population and the deterioration of people in that population that is very nearly a defining condition of their experience and historical existence," p. 754.

20 See http://thenaturalhistorymuseum.org/houston-exhibition-video-and-pics/.

21 "Research published in 2016, by the Union of Concerned Scientists and Texas Environmental Justice Advocacy Services (t.e.j.a.s.), found that the concentration of a carcinogen, 1,3-butadiene, was 174 times higher in the Harrisburg-Manchester area than in the prosperous west Houston neighborhood of West Oaks-Eldridge, where the cancer risk is 30 % lower." https://blog.ucsusa.org/science-blogger/new-ucs-report-documents-chemical-pollution-double-jeopardy-for-houston-communities. I do not mention this in order to dismiss urban greening and ecological design initiatives—only to criticize them where they are not advancing the interests of more inclusive, democratic, and egalitarian urbanism.

22 For more information, see also the website of t.e.j.a.s. (http://tejasbarrios.org/), and the "toxic tour" they organized with *Democracy Now!* in the days after Hurricane Harvey: "Petro Metro: a toxic tour of Houston from refineries to superfund sites in wake of Harvey," (5 September 2017), https://www.democracynow.org/2017/9/5/petro_metro_a_toxic_tour_of.

23 The name and museum-critical practice of the Natural History Museum's project recalls Fred Wilson's 1992 artwork Mining the Museum, which excavated race and inequality at the Maryland Historical Society, and represented a defining 1990s contribution to the conceptualist practice of institutional critique. See Jennifer Gonzalez, *Subject to display: reframing race in contemporary installation art* (Cambridge, MA: MIT Press, 2008); and MTL, "From institutional critique to institutional liberation? A decolonial perspective on the crises of contemporary art," *October 165* (Summer 2018) pp. 192–227.

24 See http://thenaturalhistorymuseum.org/houston-exhibition-video-and-pics/.

25 See http://www.hmns.org/exhibits/permanent-exhibitions/energy-hall/.

26 Kara M. Watson, et al., "Characterization of peak streamflows and flood inundation of selected areas in Southeastern Texas and Southwestern Louisiana from the August and September 2017 flood resulting from Hurricane Harvey," *U.S. Geological Survey Scientific Investigations Report*, 2018, https://pubs.er.usgs.gov/publication/sir20185070.

27 See https://www.theguardian.com/us-news/2018/jan/29/houston-manchester-hurricane-harvey-texas-foul-air.

28 Horney et al., "Comparing residential contamination in a Houston environmental justice neighborhood before and after Hurricane Harvey," pp. 3 and 12.

29 Donna Haraway, *Staying with the trouble: making kin in the Chthulucene* (Durham, NC: Duke University Press, 2016).

30 Christina Sharpe, *In the wake: on blackness and being* (Durham, NC: Duke University Press, 2016), 2016.

31 See T. J. Demos, *Against the Anthropocene: visual culture and environment today* (Berlin: Sternberg Press, 2017), and Jason W. Moore, ed., *Anthropocene or Capitalocene: nature, history, and the crisis of capitalism* (Oakland, CA: PM Press, 2016).

32 Achille Mbembe, *Critique of Black reason*, trans. Laurent Dubois (Durham, NC: Duke University Press, 2017) p. 6: "Across early capitalism, the term 'Black' referred only to the condition imposed on peoples of African origin (different forms of depredation, dispossession of all power of self-determination, and, most of all, dispossession of the future and of time, the two matrices of the possible). Now, for the first time in human history, the term 'Black' as been generalized. This new fungibility, this solubility, institutionalized as a new norm of existence and expanded to the entire planet, is what I call the *Becoming Black of the world*."

33 See http://www.aethaer.com/aethaerjars; and https://www.departures.com/lifestyle/technology-gadgets/fresh-air-becomes-luxury-good: A $23 can of Banff air from the Vitality corporation promises about 80 shots of air. Vitality's co-founder Troy Paquette has said he hopes future climate talks will obviate the need for such products but remarked that "if China remains looking like it does right now, then absolutely I can see clean air becoming a commodity."

34 Franz Fanon, *Toward the African revolution* (New York: Grove, 1994 [1970]) p. 51; cited in Sharpe, *In the wake* p. 108.

35 See Natasha Myers, "How to grow livable worlds: ten not-so-easy-steps," in Kerry Oliver-Smith, ed., *The world to come: art in the age of the Anthropocene* (Gainesville: Samuel P. Harn Museum of Art, 2018) pp. 53–64.

36 Not an Alternative, "Institutional liberation," *e-flux* Journal #77 (November 2016), http://www.e-flux.com/journal/77/76215/institutional-liberation/.

Queering the transect

Matthew Gandy

I feel at times a love and joy
For every weed and every thing.
John Clare, "The flitting"[1]

John Clare's poem, first published in 1835, evokes an intense connection with the Northamptonshire countryside, along with the menace of enclosure, and the destruction of human and other-than-human communities alike. The weed in question is shepherd's purse (*Capsella bursa-pastoris*), an inconspicuous plant characteristic of disturbed ground, which has distinctively heart-shaped seed pods. For Clare, shepherd's purse would have been a familiar plant of field margins, along with the many other species of plants and animals that feature in his writing. The poetry of Clare is rooted in the creative alchemy of walking, of stepping outside, of systematically retracing familiar itineraries, of taking time to notice subtle variations; his universe is marked by patience, slowness, and the presence of the political in small things. Though widely considered a Romantic poet, the work of Clare has a contemporary resonance with more elaborate conceptions of agency, and the significance of close observation for the formation of political insights into social and environmental change.[2]

In this brief essay I want to emphasize the significance of the transect as a creative act that transcends the mere application of a botanical method.[3] The argument brings the phenomenological insights of the feminist scholar Sara Ahmed into dialogue with a queered reading of urban botany. A transect is a kind of botanical reverie that connects the practice of walking with the space of thought and creativity itself.[4] Every kind of walk can be considered a kind of transect, or at least a "transection" in the earlier etymological sense of the verb "transect," derived from the Latin *trans* meaning "across" or "beyond" and *secare* meaning "to cut."[5] Having first appeared as a verb in the mid-seventeeth century, the English word transect begins to acquire usage as a noun in the early twentieth century, and becomes closely associated with the emergence of ecological science, the elucidation of vegetation patterns, and the application of modern botanical methods.

The botanical walk known as the "transect" has become one of the most familiar methods used in conducting ecological surveys. Unlike the "quadrat," which involves closely focusing on a small area, and is in essence a stationary method

Shepherd's purse (*Capsella bursa-pastoris*) growing in a London street, September 2019. The plant originates from Eastern Europe, and is considered to be an archaeophyte by European botanists (arriving before 1500). It has now spread through much of the northern hemisphere and beyond. Photo: Matthew Gandy.

to estimate species diversity, the "transect" is a mobile form of data collection that involves tracing a line through a designated area, typically on foot, in order to systematically record what can be found. These static and mobile dimensions to botanical method are complementary, and belie the impossibility of knowing everything: there is only so much human time, knowledge, and concentration that can be applied to any kind of ecological survey. And if the objective is to generate longitudinal data, and assess environmental change over time, then there is a kind of epistemological contract with the future, and the hope that perhaps as yet unknown individuals might assist in carrying on with the work.

A botanical transect typically involves walking in a straight line at right angles to a zone of transition produced by natural features such as coastlines, mudflats, marshes, or altitudinal variations. In 1905, for example, the American ecologist

Frederic Clements simply described the transect as "a cross section through the vegetation of a station, a formation, or a series of formations."[6] From the outset, however, there has been ambiguity over the appropriate scale for a transect, and by implication, how the data derived from this method might relate to broader inferences about the ecological characteristics of a wider area.[7] Hovering between a diagrammatic representation and an analytical tool, it is uncertain whether the purpose of the transect is to reveal identifiable "phytosociological communities" à la Braun-Blanquet and other plant sociologists, or merely to serve as a heuristic device for landscape interpretation. Writing in 1954, for example, the American botanist Dorothy Brown considers how the transect might be used for the exploration of "new territory" but refers to undertaking fieldwork by "road cruising" in a tacit admission that most landscapes are simply too vast to be systematically assessed by walking alone.[8] In the movement from a "walking line" to a "road line," there is an implicit acceleration so that details must be interpreted from more infrequent or distant forms of observation.

Modernity itself can be conceived as a series of lines, ranging from the regularization of space to a teleological understanding of its own historiography. For the anthropologist Tim Ingold, the act of walking in a straight line is an enactment of modernity that connects with the tracing of plotlines, land measurement, and the elevation of linearity to a mode of rational thought.[9] The idea of "straightening" has multiple connotations extending to questions of racial and sexual difference: an emphasis on linearity as a form of power finds echoes in Sara Ahmed's characterization of "the production of whiteness as a straight line."[10] Similarly, the performance of the line as a socio-spatial inscription of power is captured in the psychologist Carl Jung's observation, based on his travels in East Africa, that "the white man's idea is to walk straight ahead."[11] The role of walking as a contrary or dogged display of perseverance emerges as a constitutive element in the spatial imaginaries of European modernity.

Although the term "transect" only begins to appear in botanical literature in the early twentieth century, its practical roots can be traced back to the Humboldtian scientific tradition, the mania for measurement, and methodologies of imperial prospection. The practice of botany is connected with the scientific frontiers of territorial acquisition, including the emerging trade routes of global capital, the inland empires of "white settlerism" after what the Jamaican writer Sylvia Wynter refers to as the "1492 event," and the geo-political imaginaries of European fascism.[12] In the modern age, cartography emerges as a series of "points or dots" with the establishment of "lines of occupation" serving as the logistical precursors to "settlement and extraction."[13] The historiographic unease generated by a botanical itinerary with a purpose necessitates a careful reflection on the utilitarian dimensions to walking methodologies. Indeed, the use of the transect as an experimental method in its own right, as undertaken by artists and writers, serves as a useful counterfoil to the perpetuation of certain kinds of unreflective methodological empiricism.

Does the appearance of the "urban transect," in all its practical and experimental guises, disrupt or merely overlook its complex historical associations with the utilitarian envisioning of nature? There are a number of botanical studies that simply apply the transect method directly to urban areas in order to examine the plant diversity at specific sites.[14] In other cases, a more schematic approach is adopted in order to provide a cross-sectional representation of the urban-rural gradient in terms of variations in the built environment and its characteristic vegetation.[15] The transect has also been adopted within some architectonic formulations as a way of depicting urban topography, or as an urban design tool, yet these approaches are invariably schematic depictions rather than a direct application of botanical method to urban space.[16] More prescient, however, are those botanical surveys that have sought to directly challenge the nativist preoccupations of plant sociology and its colonial underpinnings, by emphasizing the novel socio-ecological assemblages to be found in urban space. In the hands of geographers such as Gerhard Hard, botanical methods not only enable interpretation of the unusual characteristics of urban vegetation but also become a means to interrogate the history of landscape itself, in all its ideological complexity.[17]

Cultural iterations of the urban transect can take several different forms. An urban transect can follow a line produced by infrastructure networks such as roads, canals, or railway lines, as reflected in projects such as the LA-based artist Ed Ruscha's series of photographs entitled *Every Building on the Sunset Strip* (1966). The simple practice of walking is also a significant motif within Land Art, exemplified by Richard Long's performance *A Line Made by Walking* (1967), which records a transitory impression left by the artist walking across a field. In some cases the transect becomes the ecology of the line itself, as in studies of plants growing in the interstitial spaces produced by transport networks such as roadside verges or railway embankments. In other examples a more conventional type of botanical transect is undertaken within a chosen site, as reflected in a variety of works by the French artist Paul-Armand Gette such as his 16-mm film entitled *Le Transect* (1974). In some instances, there is an attempt to transect space directly, as in the performance art of Simon Faithful, where in an homage to Buster Keaton, he scales fences and crawls through windows to follow the meridian line as precisely as possible in *0°00 Navigation* (2008). Similarly, Gordon Matta-Clark's intervention entitled *Splitting* (1974) sees a recently abandoned house cut in half so that the transect becomes an active sculptural intervention in urban space.

Writers have also used the transect as a way to structure a narrative around movement through space. The transect can be conceived as a Perecian literary device, serving to spur heightened forms of observation and creative reflection through the use of an artificial constraint.[18] The idea of the line as a restriction on thought, or a form of conceptual rigidity, is effectively inverted to heighten the experience of space. Examples include the French writer François Bon, who describes the changing landscapes he observes on his regular commute from Nancy to Paris, or the Welsh writer Iain Sinclair's exploration of London's hinterland by tracing the route of the M25 orbital motorway.[19]

A botanical transect is an embodied methodology par excellence: the systematic recording of plant life involves not just training the eye to notice small details,

Richard Long, *A Line Made by Walking* (1967). Photo: Copyright Tate Gallery.

using sophisticated forms of pattern recognition, but also the use of other sensory clues such as smell to help identify specific plants, haptic interactions with leaves to explore their surface textures, and an awareness of small variations in light and shade, to produce an "incidental sensorium" that is open to the unexpected. The completion of a transect introduces a degree of "slowness" to the navigation of space that echoes Isabelle Stengers's appeal for *ralentissement* (deceleration) in scientific practice.[20] Indeed, the very act of slowing down can be likened to a kind of "ecological loitering" that serves as an entry point into the nuance and complexity of urban space.

The transect also resonates with psyschogeographical explorations of the modern city. And yet the situationist excursion or *dérive*, in its classic late 1960s formulation, has little grounding in ecological observations.[21] Methodologically, the *dérive* is a highly impressionistic if not masculinist cultural trope, although we should be cautious over any essentialist form of epistemological critique. For the Paris-based writer Lauren Elkin, it is attentiveness to the shifting and often invisible contours of the "affective landscape" that marks the starting point for urban walking as a form of societal critique as well as critical reflection.[22] Similarly, the geographer

Morag Rose shows how urban walking can "follow lines of desire, curiosity and coincidence but also invisible threads of power and the whispers of ghosts under the pavement." Rose emphasizes how the use of walking as experimental practice can "disrupt the banal" and reveal "minor epiphanies."[23]

The ethnographic transect is rooted in a slow and often painstaking immersion in urban space that points towards the conceptual orientation of the embodied human subject, in an intellectual manoeuvre that questions relations between bodies, objects, and others. To queer the transect is to destabilize this walking methodology from a variety of empirical and conceptual vantage points. The relevant insights from queer theory clearly extend beyond the identification of "queer space," or the use of a transect to encounter traces of human sexuality. In fact, they serve to problematize a series of categorizations, taxonomies, and subjectivities.[24] Queering the transect connects botanical practice with a series of post-human and other-than-human critical discourses. Following the lead of Sara Ahmed we can introduce the significance of "queer phenomenology" as a matter of orientation that operates on different levels: firstly, the orientation of the human subject towards objects and others (in a variety of configurations that extend to other-than-human nature such as plants); and secondly, Ahmed's play on the word "orient" as a geographical and ideological counterpoint to modernity that connects with the recognition of cosmopolitan urban ecologies.[25] The transect invites a reverie of disorientation as the queered observer becomes "lost" within the line. What appears to be simply given, as part of the "taken for granted" world within idealist cosmologies, is rendered off centre or unfamiliar: there is a productive dissonance between the familiar and the unfamiliar. Taking the diasporic dimension to disorientation further, we can characterize cosmopolitan ecologies as a kind of "queer regional imaginary," following the insights of cultural critic Gayatri Gopinath that stands in explicit contradiction to nativist landscape idioms.[26]

The etymology of the word "transect" also connects with recent developments in "trans theory" as a further elaboration on the queering of space, materiality, and the human subject. Drawing on the relational rather than nominal import of trans theory, as a matrix of connections rather than a set of categories, we can connect with "proliferating ecologies of embodied difference." The spatial implications of "transing" the world encompass a series of movements where "the lines implied by the very concept of 'trans-' are moving targets, simultaneously composed of multiple determinants."[27] Implicit within the prefix "trans" is a sense of multiple crossings, not just of walking across, but also of interspecies encounters, including an enrichment of the botanical imagination. Trans theory unsettles the re-inscription of the (modified) human subject within the burgeoning field of post-humanist studies and widens the potential scope of interspecies interactions.[28] The displacement of heteronormative space opens up the affective potentialities of socio-ecological assemblages as well as the multiple sexualities that suffuse the non-human realm, including plant life (to the evident unease of early botanists).[29] The unsettling of existing taxonomies or classification systems holds implications far beyond the confines of urban ecology.

Perennial wall-rocket (*Diplotaxis tenuifolia*) growing in Park am Gleisdreieck, Berlin, September 2019. The plant originates from the Mediterranean region, and is considered to be a neophyte by European botanists (arriving after 1500). It is now a common component of the ruderal flora of many European cities. Photo: Matthew Gandy.

The sense of what is "in place" clearly rests on the operation of repetition, familiarity, and naturalization: a set of ideological coordinates that routinely ignores the complexity of lived space occasioned by the interpolation of difference. The socio-ecological determinants of space comprise a series of lines–both temporal and spatial–that rest on an array of affective and material orientations. If we consider marginal spaces in European cities, one common adventive plant that we encounter is the yellow flowered *Diplotaxis tenuifolia*, which originates from the southern Mediterranean and parts of western Asia. The presence of *Diplotaxis tenuifolia* and other non-native species invites reflection on the ecological lineaments of Ahmed's use of the term "constitutive outside," and the way in which the history of vegetation science in a European context had emerged in the context of anxiety over the perceived inauthenticity of unusual socio-ecological formations. In a German context, for example, pre-war botanists placed particular emphasis on the perceived threat to the "purity" of the central European flora posed by plants from "the East" in an explicit elision of geo-political and ecological imaginaries.[30] This queering of botanical methods connects with a wider set of discourses concerning the human subject, the history of science, and the role of walking methodologies in ecological surveys. I use the term "ecological" in this instance to denote a set of relations that transcend the here and now of site specific observations. The urban transect emerges as a kind of epistemological and ideological disturbance, not only to the historiography of botany and related fields, but also to the boundaries and categories that inhere within modernity itself. The botanical transect is a means to systematically record material differences, but it is also a spur to thought and reflection in its own right.

1 The poem was originally published under the title "On leaving the cottage of my birth," See Jonathan Bate, ed., *John Clare: selected poems* (London: Faber and Faber, 2004).

2 There are parallels between Clare's political awakening through observations of nature and the twentieth-century revelations of Rachel Carson. See Meehan Crist, "A strange blight," *London Review of Books* 41 (11) (6 June 2019) pp. 3–7.

3 Earlier versions of this essay received helpful feedback from Stephen Barber, Yasminah Beebeejaun, and Marion Ernwein.

4 On walking and creativity see, for example, David Evans, ed., *The art of walking* (London: Black Dog Publishing, 2012); and Frédéric Gros, *A philosophy of walking*, trans. John Howe (London: Verso, 2014 [2009]).

5 Oxford English Dictionary (www.oed.com) (accessed 30 July 2019).

6 Frederic Edward Clements, *Research methods in ecology* (Lincoln, Nebraska: The University Publishing Company, 1905) p. 176.

7 R. H. Whittaker, "Gradient analysis of vegetation," *Biological Reviews* 49 (1967) pp. 207–264.

8 Dorothy Brown, *Methods of surveying and measuring vegetation* (Farnham: Commonwealth Agricultural Bureaux, 1954).

9 Tim Ingold, *Lines* (London: Routledge, 2007).

10 Sara Ahmed, *Queer phenomenology: orientation, objects, others* (Durham, NC: Duke University Press, 2006) p. 121.

11 Cited in Blake W. Burleson, *Jung in Africa* (New York: Continuum, 2005) p. 114.

12 Sylvia Wynter, "1492: a new world view," in Vera Lawrence Hyatt and Rex Nettleford, eds., *Race, discourse, and the origin of the Americas* (Washington DC: Smithsonian Institution Press, 1995) pp. 5–57. On plants and empire building see, for example, Londa Schiebinger, *Plants and empire: colonial bioprospecting in the Atlantic world* (Cambridge, MA: Harvard University Press, 2004).

13 Ingold, *Lines*, pp. 85, 87.

14 See Kevin Austin, *Botanical processes in urban derelict spaces* (University of Birmingham, unpublished PhD thesis, 2002).

15 See Herbert Sukopp, ed., *Stadtökologie: Das Beispiel Berlin* (Berlin: Dietrich Reimer, 1990).

16 See, for example, Andrés Duany and Emily Talen, "Transect planning," *Journal of the American Planning Association* 68(3) (2002) pp. 245–266; and Nicolas Tixier "Le

transect urbain: Pour une écriture corrélée des ambiances et de l'environnement," in Sabine Barles and Nathalie Blanc, eds., *Écologies urbaines: Sur le terrain, Economica-Anthropos* (PIR Ville et Environnement, 2016) pp. 130–148.

17 See, for example, Gerhard Hard "Die Natur, die Stadt und die Ökologie: Reflexionen über "Stadtnatur" und "Stadtökologie,"' in *Dimensionen geographischen Denkens* (Osnabrück: V & R unipress, 2003[1994]) pp. 341–370.

18 See, for example, Richard Phillips, "Georges Perec's experimental fieldwork; Perecquian fieldwork," *Social & Cultural Geography* 19 (2) (2018) pp. 171–191.

19 François Bon, *Paysage fer* (Lagrasse: Verdier, 2000); Iain Sinclair, *London Orbital: a walk around the M25* (London: Granta, 2002)

20 Isabelle Stengers, *Another science is possible: a manifesto for slow science*, trans. Stephen Muecke (Cambridge: Polity, 2017 [2013]).

21 On aspects of the dérive as methodology see also Philip Conway's review of Stengers, *Another science is possible,* on the *Society and Space* website (2018) (accessed 30 July 2019).

22 Lauren Elkin, *Flaneuse: women walk the city in Paris, New York, Tokyo, Venice, and London* (London: Chatto and Windus, 2016) p. 288.

23 Morag Rose, "Confessions of an anarcho-flâneuse, or psychogeography the Mancunian way," in Tina Richardson, ed., *Walking inside out: contemporary British psychogeography* (London: Rowman & Littlefield, 2015) pp. 158, 159, 160. See also Stephanie Springgay and Sarah E. Truman, *Walking methodologies in a more-than-human world: WalkingLab* (London: Routledge, 2018).

24 See, for example, Claire Colebrook, "On the very possibility of queer theory," in Chrysanthi Nigianni and Merl Storr, eds., *Deleuze and queer theory* (Edinburgh: Edinburgh University Press, 2009) pp. 11–23.

25 Sara Ahmed, *Queer phenomenology: orientation, objects, others* (Durham, NC: Duke University Press, 2006).

26 Gayatri Gopinath, *Unruly visions: the aesthetic practices of queer diaspora* (Durham, NC: Duke University Press, 2018).

27 Susan Stryker, Paisley Currah, and Lisa Jean Moore, "Introduction: trans-, trans, or transgender?," *Women's Studies Quarterly*, 36 (3/4) (2008), pp. 12, 13.

28 See, for example, Julie Livingston and Jasbir K. Puar, "Interspecies," *Social Text* 106 29 (1) (2011) pp. 1–14; and Camille Nurka, "Animal techne: transing posthumanism," *TSQ: Transgender Studies Quarterly* 2 (2) (2015) pp. 209–226.

29 Londa Schiebinger, "Gender and natural history," in N. Jardine, J. A. Secord, and E. C. Spary, eds., *Cultures of natural history* (Cambridge: Cambridge University Press, 1996) pp. 163–177.

30 See, for example, Gert Gröning and Joachim Wolschke-Bulmahn, "Politics, planning and the protection of nature: political abuse of early ecological ideas in Germany, 1933–45," *Planning Perspectives* 2 (2) (1987) pp. 127–148.

Walking with plants: disrupting the material logics of *degrado* at the banks of Turin's Stura river

Lucilla Barchetta

Walking, as an everyday practice, can be considered one of the most emblematic engagements with everyday living environments–and especially with natural spaces in human settlements, which are the focus of this essay. In recent years, the interest in walking as a research topic in social sciences agendas has significantly expanded, with scholars investigating a variety of issues associated with urban space.[1] Walking has thus been framed as a methodological concern within discussions on ethnographic practice, primarily in the study of how different types of walks (functional, aesthetic, and experiential) may alter phenomenological appropriations and atmospheric experiences of space; however, scholars have also argued that encounters with the vegetal world can alter human thinking during the process of walking.[2]

The emergence of two bodies of research within the field of cultural studies known respectively as strollology (or promenadology) and critical plant studies confirms the renewed attention that walking has received in recent times. The Swiss architectural thinker Lucius Burckhardt was particularly bold, claiming that new design intelligence was not just embedded in everyday life but emerged from taking a stroll. The only aesthetic one can produce is strollological, he argued, for the simple reason that walking is a way in which the human body can explore and build knowledge of place, while also reaching a higher awareness of the close relationship between the human and non-human world.[3]

In this essay I argue that "walking with plants" in marginal urban areas can offer a means to build a collaborative laboratory of environmental change, in that it represents a transformative practice of engaging with the elusiveness that characterizes the processes of ruination in urban settlements that cause places to experience neglect or destruction.[4]

Thus, this essay explores ways of documenting the affective ecologies that connect human subjectivities and spontaneous urban flora in Turin's riverbank area, with the aim of formulating a different language through which to capture the tenacious effects of ruins; rather than speaking of "inert remains" and "privileged sites of reflections,"[5] this essay will focus on their agentive reconfiguration, decomposition and re-composition into the present.

Patrizia stands at the side of the gravel track that was built in 2009 along the left bank of the Stura river. Destined to become part of a river park, the edges of the Stura represent one of the gateways to the recovery and cleaning up of peripheral riverbank spaces. Rows of young maples and willows on each side of the three-km track are palpable marks of a physical intervention. Despite the inauguration of Arrivore Park in 2010, the recovery has been accompanied by difficulty in materializing a systematic project of riverfront rehabilitation. The result is the presence of tracts of riverbank spaces where intermittent developments combined with forms of controlled abandonment have occasioned a peculiar condition of temporal suspension, which is illuminated by the manifestation of peculiar configurations of "waste" and "blight" space.

Two bridges interrupt the trail and delimit a huge open space where cultivated vegetation and spontaneous riparian woods combine. The seasonal changes in the river embankments between spring and summer time have formed gentle slopes, where children and dogs play and chance upon mallards, grey herons, and crested grebes, turning the river's edge into an interspecies playground.

Patrizia is 58 years old and lives in the Barca area, a neighbourhood located on the edge of the city, near the confluence of the Stura and Po rivers in the north-eastern periphery of Turin. As we walk along the river, she recalls how her parents always forbade her to hang out nearby the Stura area, which she remembers as an inaccessible heap of thorny plants and weeds with the remains of a sand extraction site showing along the riverbanks; it was used for the construction of a residential building area during the housing boom of the 1950s and 1960s.

Manuela, 55 years old, has joined us on the walk. Samples of pokeweed (*Phytolacca americana*), dubbed "pest species" by the river park's gardeners, hamper her steps as she rapidly moves towards the flowers of *Robinia pseudoacacia*, a tree commonly known as the "invasive" black locust on account of its rapid growth.

Suddenly, as she loses the perception of contact with the ground, she looks down and unexpectedly finds a group of puffballs (*vescia* in Italian). They remind her of her uncle who used to harvest them there, even though nobody in his family would eat them because they came from a toxic area.

The women's memories speak of the edges of the Stura as a political project of ruination, where territorial stigmatization, industrial pollution, negligence, and administrative mismanagement have imprinted the forms of a socio-spatial marginality, and sedimented a common perception of a no-go area.

Nevertheless, as the documentary *City Veins* suggests,[6] the Stura edges are less an "empty space" than a "crossroads of stories"; the stories of sex workers, stray dogs, drug dealers, and consumers, together with the retired *meridionali* (as Southern migrants were called) who cultivated their vegetable gardens along the river, intersecting with migrants and refugees who—ever since the 1990s—have

Roaming the dried-up riversides, 2018. Photo: Daniele Fazio.

built their shacks in the woods, which are characterized by rushes, alders, and poplars.

Through their botanical encounters, Patrizia and Manuela tell us more than just the historical facts of degradation. They also convey an idea of ruination that touches on the ways in which bodies and spaces become associated with narratives of waste, and thus come to be considered abject, dirty, and out of place. They show, in fact, that ruination is not only a sequential moment of disrepair, but also an evasive and slippery ecology of unanticipated alliances that, as the anthropologist Bettina Stoetzer writes, "traces the ways in which humans and non-humans do not stick to their assigned places amid projects of domestication."[7]

After identifying the processes that have produced this form of wasteland inhabitation at the edges of the Stura, this essay explores the multiple and contrasting experiences that are evoked by following the unexpected traces and "footnotes" left by herbs and plants.

Patrizia, Manuela, and I continue along the gravel track. We see a man in his seventies disappearing into the dense vegetation on the slope that adjoins the river. As the man turns towards us, we realize that he is collecting reeds. The man looks at us suspiciously, and remains silent for a few seconds. The tension builds up, but slowly flows away as he waves at us, while he points at the reeds he is collecting for his vegetable garden. He puts down the reeds and begins to recount his memory of the park, when it was still a wetland. Then he returns to the present: "Look at these rushes! We're not in the Amazon jungle, the mayor doesn't care about

Crafting paths throughout wormwood fields, 2018. Photo: Eleonora Pacciani.

anything other than herself," he adds bitterly. The Amazon jungle thus becomes a geographical metaphor for a bounded idea of pristine nature which, outside of its conventional site of fruition, becomes a marker of disorder. Laying down his head, the man continues: "I just see all this *degrado*, and it's making me feel sad. At least I can use these reeds to fence my vegetable garden."

Over the past decade, the topic of *degrado* (decay, blight) has become a subject of public attention and an integral part of political debates that focus on urban security policy. The proliferation of digital spaces and municipal by-laws for the purpose of tackling *degrado* as a matter of everyday life has had an enormous influence on the creation of particular atmospheres and perceptions of ruination in urban contexts.[8] *Degrado* has become an all-encompassing term, one which aesthetically qualifies persons, things, and environments. It signifies both neglect and exhaustion. Under the aegis of "quality of life policing," marginal communities (especially migrants and homeless people) have experienced the severest security measures, being targeted as bodies that pose threats. However, as the ethnographic descriptions presented here suggest, *degrado* also affects urban spaces, and particularly the vegetation that we expect to see nurtured.

Overgrown unmown lawns in the city's public spaces, from urban parks to roadside verges, have become the object of accusations and the expression of a general uneasiness, in which the lack of maintenance of open and green spaces has played an important part in the association of *degrado* with undesired natural spaces in urban contexts. This process has highlighted the aesthetic roots of *degrado*,

as a particular atmosphere that encloses and presses upon bodies, creating the sense of a city "gone wild."[9]
Arianna is a 37-year-old environmental educator and anti-speciesist activist who, through urban botanical explorations, experiments with the potentials of an imaginative re-interpretation of the urban space as a spontaneous and libertarian place of freedom.[10]
We stop, pausing to look at a lush pile of sweet wormwood (*Artemisia annua*) adjoining the gravel track. Arianna describes this annual plant as "saboteurs of order"; the scent of their leaves and their vast distribution show the forms of a "new nature," thus disrupting normative aesthetic conventions. Weeds can also be considered to be "traces" of a biographical type, to the extent that they tell the stories of those who love and hate them. But how important is it for plants to be recognized? How does this change representations and perceptions of space? Rather than showing the potential of healing (toxic) bodies and places through wilderness, it seems that the sensual experience actuated by roaming shifts the baselines and determines the extent of change by suspending one's anthropocentric judgments; in doing so it occasions rethinking of anthropogenic interventions in urban environments and begins to track our attentiveness and intimacy with places.
The knowledge captured in the walk can thus be compared to the practice of "informal garbage collectors"[11] who take an archaeological look at the convergence and divergence of both organic and inorganic materials.
As my interlocutors join their footprints with lady's thumbs (*Persicaria maculosa*) and yellow mignonettes (*Reseda lutea*), taking the time to stop, observe, and

Encounters with lady's thumbs (*Persicaria maculosa*), 2018. Photo: Daniele Fazio.

touch, they are doing more than simply exploring the material vitality of what would otherwise be disposed of; they also tell alternative stories that urge us to reflect on the messiness of social realities without ever reducing ruination "to an all-too-human by-product in need of rational management."[12] Instead, they show that ruination remains within and continuously flows through bodies and the corporeal dimensions of space.

"Everything gets knotty here!" 60-year-old Fulvio exclaims, while he moves towards the thick vegetation that brings us to the river's edge. Fulvio (Patrizia's husband) notices that, in all of their Sunday walks on the edge of the Stura, they have never left the main path. Crafting new paths therefore not only liberates the body from the performative constraints of the city, but it also provides a way of venturing the possibilities of life processes and creating entanglements without losing the complexity of histories.

Unexpected encounters with corncobs and tomato plants remind us of once cultivated lands, which carried the seeds of Turin's "car empire"[13]—constructed on former areas of subsistence farming—into the present. By looking at the way white bryony (*Bryonia alba*), honeysuckles (*Lonicera japonica*), tree lupin (*Lupinus arborens*) and mock strawberries (*Duchesnea indica*) expand and radiate across space, or even "roam," according to French gardener, botanist and writer Gilles Clément,[14] there emerges the possibility of interpreting the infrastructure of the city as a vegetative system where, as Andrea Brighenti writes, "the manifestation of the urban only or just takes place when the time is ripe."[15] Cities concentrate time and space in "knots," but they also contain gaps, frictions and discontinuities.[16] This is less a celebration of a romantic and universal hybridity than an acknowledgement of the messy actuality and incompleteness of everyday experiences that we, as researchers, often attempt to disentangle.

These topographical explorations approach the urban space as a temporal horizon by aligning with multiple time-spaces and highlighting the way that temporal sedimentations of ruination can be observed through a sensing, rather than a mastering. This dimension is central to an understanding of the uses of *degrado*, especially in the Italian context. *Degrado* is an aesthetic problem that is solved at the level of perceptions towards urban spaces and the bodies that grow in the midst of them. Feelings of disgust and waste spread across the city (the city stinks!), and people also feel abandoned. What does ruination do? How do bodies live with it? How does one describe these phenomenological and atmospheric encounters? The future of ethnographic enquiry has to engage with these questions.

We end the walk by roaming the dried up riverbanks, finding a buried car lying near a sample of *Verbascum thapsus*, known as the great mullein. Daniele is a 45-year-old agronomist, very passionate about learning how plants can help connect fragments of stories to socio-ecological transformations. After foraging information in his plant identification notebook, he recalls how people used to extract a juice from the seeds of the plant, which they then poured into the water in order to poison fish and thus catch them more easily. Patrizia, Daniele, Manuela, Fulvio, and I found ourselves surrounding this plant and wondering to what extent these forms of "post-industrial landscape scars"[17] and their toxic residues, captured both in their physical presence and absence, might tell alternative stories about this place simply by walking along the riverbank. More precisely, by engaging with the difficulties inherent in the creation of entanglements, we as a group have come to acknowledge the importance of less eventful and visible traces, which may challenge the reconfiguration of persons as victims of ruination while highlighting the potentials of ordinary affects and sensory experience in the creation of transformative articulations of publicness and nature-people alliances.

My essay has discussed how botanical walks can help deconstruct the material, catalytic role of "blight" as a traditional pattern of both stigmatization and redevelopment in processes of metropolitan change.

Escaping from urban life by walking into the non-human world of plants can offer an opportunity to construct an experience of sauntering, which provides the basis for a transfiguration of human thinking and, simultaneously, to approach plant life by "thinking without a head."[18]

Nonetheless, as cultural and scientific forms of exploration, botanical walks have their own set of challenges. They can, for instance, encourage forms of "botanical tourism"[19] and Edenic spectacle, which might weaken the possibilities of redefining securitarian and normative politics of nature and public space. In this sense, this essay encourages ways of walking politically, and not voyeuristically, among the silent permanence of plants, by collecting material objects and observing processes of ruination in order to track people's lives and social realities.

1 See, for example, Evrick Brown and Timothy Shortell, *Walking in cities: quotidian mobility as urban theory, method, and practice* (Philadelphia: Temple University Press, 2016).

2 Michael Marder, *Plant-thinking: a philosophy of vegetal life* (New York: Columbia University Press, 2013).

3 Jesko Fezer and Martin Schmitz, eds., *Lucius Burckhardt writings: rethinking man-made environments: politics, landscape and design* (Vienna: Springer, 2012).

4 Matthew Gandy, "Cities in deep time: bio-diversity, metabolic rift and the urban question," *City* 22 (1) (2018) pp. 96–105.

5 Ann Laura Stoler, *Imperial debris: on ruins and ruination* (Durham, NC: Duke University Press, 2013) pp. 9–10.

6 Andrea Deaglio, *City veins: Il futuro del mondo passa da qui* (Babydoc Film, 2010).

7 Bettina Stoetzer, "Ruderal ecologies: rethinking nature, migration, and the urban landscape in Berlin," *Cultural Anthropology* 33 (2018) pp. 295–323.

8 The proliferation of municipal by-laws (*ordinanze*) as a specific feature of the regulation of public spaces in Italy has increased significantly in recent years. Research clearly shows the characteristics of such an instrument, its diffusion and its often arbitrary application by some municipalities, in order to regulate behaviour in public spaces.
On the uses of *degrado* in the Italian context, see Tamar Pitch, *Contro il decoro: L'uso politico della pubblica decenza* (Bari: LaTerza, 2013). See also Carmen Pisanello, *In nome del decoro: Dispositivi estetici e politiche securitarie* (Verona: Ombre Corte, 2017).

9 Mike Davis, *Dead cities and other tales* (New York: The New Press, 2002) p. 384.

10 George McKay, *Radical gardening: politics, idealism and rebellion in the garden* (London: Frances Lindon, 2011).

11 Nick Dines, "Ethnography and waste," *Etnografia e ricerca qualitativa* 1 (2018) pp. 5–10.
12 Joshua Reno, "Waste and waste management," in *Annual Review of Anthropology* 44 (2015) pp. 557–572.
13 Greg Grandin, "Empire's ruins: Detroit to Amazon" in Ann Laura Stoler, ed., *Imperial debris: on ruins and ruination* (Durham, NC: Duke University Press, 2013).
14 Gilles Clément, *Elogio delle vagabonde: Erbe, arbusti e fiori alla conquista del mondo* (Roma: Derive Approdi, 2013 [2002]).
15 Andrea Mubi Brighenti, "The Vegetative City," *Culture, Theory and Critique* (2018) pp. 1–17.
16 Ash Amin and Nigel Thrift, *Seeing like a city* (Cambridge: Polity Press, 2016).
17 Anna Storm, *Post-industrial landscape scars* (New York: Palgrave Macmillan, 2013).
18 Simona Vermeire, *Plant(e)escape* in made of walking (2018) http://www.themilena.com/made-of-walking.html
19 Natasha Myers, "Edenic apocalypse: Singapore's end of time botanical tourism," in Heather Davis and Etienne Turpin, eds., *Art in the Anthropocene: encounters among aesthetics, politics, environments, and epistemologies* (London: Open Humanities Press, 2015) pp. 31–42.

Following mosquitoes into an urban forest

Nida Rehman

In recent years, following a severe outbreak of dengue fever in 2011, entomologists and public health inspectors in Lahore have discovered a unique, and especially concerning, epidemiological threat right in the middle of the city. Land belonging to Pakistan Railways in the historic neighbourhood of Mughalpura appears to harbour dengue-transmitting *Aedes* mosquitoes in large numbers. This 400-acre site, established in the early twentieth century, comprises storage yards for discarded materials awaiting auction (some over several decades old); immense workshops for carriages, locomotives, and other articles; administrative areas; fire brigade ponds; and vast open tracts of railway sidings. Here, overgrown vegetation, heaps of scrap metal, defunct trains and equipment, and dilapidated colonial-era buildings give the *Aedes albopictus*—also known as the tree-hole mosquito—and its more dangerous cousin, the *Aedes aegypti*, ample opportunities to breed and thrive.

On muggy late summer mornings in 2017, I accompanied a health inspector and her team of scouts—railway employees deployed to conduct vector-control activities—into the storage and workshop yards. I followed as they walked the site, carefully seeking out *Aedes* mosquitoes, draining collections of stagnant water, pouring used engine oil into unreachable hollows to suffocate larvae, and identifying areas for more extensive chemical spraying or "fogging." During these visits, the monsoonal weather seemed to intensify the verdant hues of the thick vegetation or "wild growth," which the inspector and scouts suggested was the key challenge of mosquito control in this area. Indeed, it was not the railway infrastructure but vegetal nature—in the form of mature trees, overgrown grasses, and tangled vines—that seemed to be the most imposing presence in the site, absorbing the din of the busy carriage and locomotive workshops nearby as well as the city at large.

In the Mughalpura railway yards, nature is inextricable from the industrial forms and processes normally considered drastically unnatural. And yet it points to the biodiversity of unmanaged or neglected areas. During one of our visits, the scouts pointed out hundreds of dragonflies—natural mosquito predators—swarming over muddy ground, which appeared viscous and tar-like. On another day, we marveled at trees limbering up and through gnarled electricity poles in a particularly remote part of the workshop grounds. Against a backdrop of artificial hills formed by decades of discarded metal shavings, I saw dozens of slow-flying plain tiger (*Danaus chrysippus*) butterflies flitting about in a small "meadow" of the weedy tree daisy (*Montanoa hibiscifolia*). Throughout the railway property, we passed condemned colonial-era buildings where cracks in the brick façades have allowed banyan ediphytes to germinate and thrive. Most significantly perhaps, the presence of hundreds of mature trees of different species, such as the culturally significant *peepal* (*Ficus religiosa*) and *bohr* (*Ficus benghalensis*) as well as mango (*Mangifera indica*) and *gulmohar* (*Delonix regia*) is an encouraging sign of broader ecosystem health. Not only are they good bio-indicators of, and a bulwark against, the increasingly unbearable levels of atmospheric pollution in the city,[1] but they also signal the existence of pollinating insects as well as birds and bats, whose lives are entangled in these arboreal ecosystems.

This area exemplifies many of the properties and processes associated with unregulated, disturbed, or neglected landscapes that scholars in recent years have highlighted as a crucial aspect of contemporary urban nature. These include ruderal and spontaneous vegetation in human-dominated or post-industrial sites, and species which are attuned and adapted to the built environment and polluted soils but which, in many cases, are often considered non-native or invasive.[2] On sites of this type, non-human subjects open up new avenues for engagement, research, and conservation with respect to the complexities of urban ecological processes, while also often disrupting pre-existing cultural and scientific frameworks and aesthetic conceptions of landscape.[3] However, while the unregulated and spontaneous vegetation in Lahore's railway yards—and indeed in other under-managed sites in the city—has become an issue from the perspective of public health, ecological interest has not followed, and these spaces remain neglected by contemporary urban environmental frameworks in Lahore. In this essay, I will propose that this hybrid and unmanaged landscape presents a rich opportunity for critical reflection on normative practices and discourses on urban nature in post-colonial South Asian cities, as well as on some of the conceptual limitations of Anglo-European focused approaches to urban wastelands and marginal sites. Ultimately, it points to alternative possibilities for the aesthetics and politics of urban nature in Lahore.

Lahore's urban landscape has long been associated with gardens and cultivated nature, popularly traced to a legacy of imperial patronage and the construction of gardens and waterworks during the Delhi Sultunate, and, more prominently, the Mughal period.[4] More deliberate efforts to transform the urban landscape on a large scale emerged in the mid-nineteenth century under British colonial rule, linked to agricultural and urban "improvement" across the province of Punjab (as well as the growth of its capital city to house the colonial civilian and military bureaucracies, and upper and middle class Indian residents).[5] This period saw the development of urban parks, private gardens, and tree-lined avenues, spurred by intellectual and practical endeavours such as those of the Punjab Agri-Horticultural Society. This ostensibly private but state-subsidized society was established to introduce new crop species and to disseminate modern cultivation techniques across Punjab. However, its real successes were localized in Lahore, where it

A view of the General Store in the Lahore Railway Yards, 2017. Photo: Nida Rehman.

influenced horticultural pursuits and ornamental gardening through its centrally located garden, featuring didactic displays, plant and flower shows, and a nursery.[6] Post-colonial and contemporary urban development and planning in Lahore have continued to narrowly privilege urban nature practices steeped in historicist rehearsals of the Mughal "city of gardens" and colonial horticultural aesthetics. Today, a preference for water-intensive and exotic trees and flora, highly manicured lawns, and ornamental shrubs is apparent in private elite gardens. Meanwhile, urban managers deploy monocultural planting of economically expedient (and profitable) species such as *Conocarpus* or date palms for urban "beautification" along the city's main arteries and public areas. As rapid urbanization and the expansion of the built environment have decimated swaths of urban forest cover, imported and ornamental species have largely replaced mature, shade-giving trees, contributing to a crisis of deteriorating air quality.[7] The resultant urban landscape exemplifies the unequal and stratified geographies of class in relation to the environmental politics of post-colonial South Asian cities. For instance, the presence of tree cover and access to open areas is far greater in central and suburban elite neighbourhoods than in denser working-class areas, while the health risks of atmospheric pollution are unevenly distributed, disproportionately affecting those who lack access to air-conditioned private spaces and automobiles.[8]

Conversely, concerned citizens and environmental groups decry the use of exotic and invasive species. "Every alien eucalyptus is a tube well, drinking up our precious groundwater," laments Salman Rashid, a prominent columnist and activist, speaking about a much-reviled tree[9] introduced and acclimatized over a hundred years ago for its economic value (and a nineteenth-century belief in its power to "absorb swamps and destroy malaria").[10] Similarly, the presence of invasive species such as mesquite, lantana, and parthenium in wasteland and other neglected sites like cemeteries is a source of concern for ecologists. In recent years, research efforts have focused on the conservation and restoration of native, drought-tolerant plant species.[11] However, discourses privileging the revival of native ecosystems do not account for the historically and culturally constituted diversification of urban landscapes, the impossibility of "turning back the ecological clock," and, notably, the socio-ecological possibilities of cosmopolitan and novel ecosystems,[12] such as those present in Lahore's railway yards.

Despite its proximity to the historic centre of the city, its dense residential communities, and some of the city's busiest arteries (such as the Canal Bank Road and the Grand Trunk Road), the Mughalpura railway land is effectively invisible to and inaccessible from the city, hidden behind tall boundary walls and guarded entrances. In contrast to both the "beautified" and denuded aspects of the urban environment outside the walls, nature operates here outside the limits circumscribed by urban management, while being thoroughly bound up in human-dominated processes over the course of the site's more than hundred-year industrial history.

While the complex ecologies of the railway yards, their industrial uses and toxicities, and their largely neglected status in terms of public perception present interesting overlaps with those of the marginal urban landscapes discussed in literature focused on wastelands and post-industrial sites in the global north, they also raise certain conceptual challenges, and suggest avenues for further research. For instance, urban ecology and landscape design literature on wastelands or "terrain vague" has frequently highlighted their associations with emptiness and lack of productivity. On the one hand, these associations of vacancy and devaluation can be propagated by or co-opted into processes of urban development or land seizure.[13] Conversely, in being "mentally exterior" to the city, wasteland or other marginal spaces also lend themselves to counter-narratives of freedom and play, where the limits of propriety and behaviour normally established in managed landscapes and parks may be transgressed (if only momentarily), giving way to more ambivalent encounters.[14] However, the spaces of "old urban nature" in Global South cities, such as the railway yards in Lahore, index distinct political ecologies and functional dynamics.[15] As an active and controlled landscape of production within an established institutional purview, the railway yards are not (at least at the moment) subject to development pressure, but they are also highly securitized and enclosed. Here, even the more remote areas are actively policed, and access is restricted, as I learnt one morning when our group was stopped and interrogated by a guard patrolling the storage yards. While institutional controls and security of this type may help maintain the state of neglect towards urban nature through protection against urbanization, they also restrict possibilities for public use or informal appropriation. Freedom for trees and weeds to do their own thing does not seem to translate as readily into similar possibilities for people. Resolving this paradox might be crucial for ecological interest in such sites to grow.

The tension between ecological and epidemiological concerns raises further conflicts. That mosquitoes have led us here in the first place is an indication that the site is difficult to fit into the narratives of reclamation and resilience that are

A railway scout searching for stagnant water amidst discarded materials and overgrown vegetation, 2017. Photo: Nida Rehman.

particularly apparent in landscape urbanism, urban design, and planning literature.[16] It is a landscape rife with real and perceived dangers. As we ventured into shady sections of the yards, managers and guards warned us to watch out for snakes and wild dogs hiding in the tall grasses and vines, but the scouts often brushed off the warnings, knowing that their own target represented a far graver danger. The seemingly uncontrollable vegetation, along with large amount of waste and scrap materials, provides numerous breeding opportunities for *Aedes* mosquitoes. From the perspective of public health, these spaces give us pause. Entomologists and health inspectors in Lahore warn against easy narratives of mosquito eradication or complete disease control, and instead emphasize the need for continuous vigilance and maintenance. However, in the railway yards, in areas where the attentive perambulation of inspectors and scouts cannot do the job, this inevitably includes the indiscriminate culling of "wild growth," and the extensive use of chemical insecticides through fogging—practices which pose further challenges to the protection or enhancement of urban biodiversity.

The Lahore railway yards' histories of ecological diversification, species' adaptation to ongoing toxicities and human processes, and seemingly uncontrollable forms of vegetation present an ecological and aesthetic counterpoint to the legacies of colonial urban and landscape improvement as they continue to play out in the managerial impulses of planners, horticulturalists, and botanists in the city. At the same time the site's institutional and political contexts—and, still more so, its epidemiological threats—unsettle Anglo-Eurocentric readings of post-industrial and wasteland ecologies, as well as cultural and scientific frames of understanding, experiencing, and managing landscapes.[17] In these respects, the unruly vegetal and vector ecologies seem to present a post-colonial challenge: as spaces and processes that are unseen or cast as marginal, they compel a revaluation of analytical, methodological, and practical frameworks, from below or laterally.[18] The presence of mosquito vectors is a reminder that infectious diseases are part of the matrix of intertwined urban environmental and political ecological issues endemic not only in Lahore or in cities in South Asia, but also increasingly across northern and southern geographies.

Yet the tension between the imperatives of health, possibilities for ecological diversity, and ways of conceptualizing landscape might be a productive one—in that the "sense of (things) being out of joint" presents opportunities for experimentation and to pursue new ethics, aesthetics, and politics in more-than-human relationships.[19] In my interlocutors' guarded but attentive engagement with nature during their daily walks, we might see hints of alternative approaches for urban managers, citizens, and ecologists. The mundane, daily practices of following mosquitoes into this urban forest suggest an approach to learning from and encountering nature that is concrete and embodied, sometimes joyful—but always tentative, slow, and cognizant of danger. Moving beyond the realities of the city's denuded landscape and the aspirations for exotic beautification on one hand and reclaiming native landscapes on the other, they might signal new or unexpected relationships between old trees, dangerous mosquitoes, and attentive humans.

1 On the tolerance of species such as *Magnifera indica*, *Ficus religiosa*, and *Ficus benghalensi* to the effects of air pollution in urban and industrial settings in South Asia, see D. Sarala Thambavani and Calanit Kamala, "Air Pollution Tolerance Index (APTI) of some tree species growing near rail roads of Madurai, Tamil Nadu (India)," *Journal of Environmental Science & Engineering* 52 (4) (2010) pp. 285–290; Prabhat Kumar Rai and Lalita L. S. Panda, "Dust capturing potential and Air Pollution Tolerance Index (APTI) of some road side tree vegetation in Aizawl, Mizoram, India: an Indo-Burma hot spot region," *Air Quality, Atmosphere & Health* 7 (1) (2014) pp. 93–101.

2 Peter Del Tredici, "The flora of the future," *Places Journal*, April 17, 2014, see https://placesjournal.org/article/the-flora-of-the-future/ (accessed 30 September 2019).

3 Steve Hinchliffe et al., "Urban wild things: a cosmopolitical experiment," *Environment and Planning D: Society and Space* 23 (5) (2005) pp. 643–658; Jens Lachmund, "The making of an urban ecology," in Dorothee Brantz and Sonja Dümpelmann, eds., *Greening the city: urban landscapes in the twentieth century* (Charlottesville, London: University of Virginia Press, 2011); Matthew Gandy, "Unintentional landscapes," *Landscape Research* 41 (4) (2016) pp. 433–440.

4 James L. Wescoat, "Gardens, urbanization, and urbanism in Mughal Lahore: 1526–1657," in James L. Wescoat and Joachim Wolschke-Bulmahn, eds., *Mughal gardens: sources, places, representations, and prospects* (Washington DC: Dumbarton Oaks Research Library and Collection, 1996) pp. 139–170.

5 On the history of "improvement" discourse in colonial India see David Arnold, "Agriculture and 'improvement' in early colonial India: a pre-history of development," *Journal of Agrarian Change* 5 (4) (2005) pp. 505–525. On Lahore's colonial urban history see William J. Glover, *Making Lahore modern: constructing and imagining a colonial city* (Minneapolis: University Of Minnesota Press, 2007).

6 Ian Kerr, "The Agri-Horticultural Society of the Punjab 1851–71," in N. Gerald Barrier and Harbans Singh, *Essays in honour of Dr Ganda Singh* (Patiala: Punjabi University, 1976) pp. 252–272; Nida Rehman, "Description, display and distribution: cultivating a garden identity in late nineteenth-century Lahore," *Studies in the History of Gardens & Designed Landscapes* 34 (2) (2014) pp. 176–186.

7 On urban residents' perceptions about the environmental impacts of diminishing urban vegetation in Lahore, see Safdar Ali Shirazi and Jamil H. Kazmi, "Analysis of socio-environmental impacts of the loss of urban trees and vegetation in Lahore,

Pakistan: a review of public perception," *Ecological Processes* 5 (1) (2016) p. 5. For an analysis of recent transportation infrastructure projects and changes in Lahore's built environment with respect to deteriorating air quality, see Waqas H. Butt, "Distributing destruction," *City* 21 (5) (2017) pp. 614–621.

8 On the politics, class implications, and aesthetics of urban nature practices in South Asia see also Amita Baviskar, "The politics of the city," *India Seminar* 516 (August 2002); Leela Fernandes, "The politics of forgetting: class politics, state power and the restructuring of urban space in India," *Urban Studies* 41 (12) (2004) pp. 2415–2430; Emma Mawdsley, "India's middle classes and the environment," *Development and Change* 35 (1) (2004) pp. 79–103; Franklin Ginn, "Plant politics in Karachi," *Arcadia* 12 (2018), see http://www.environmentandsociety.org/arcadia/plantpolitics-karachi.

9 Salman Rashid, "Why trees matter," *Odysseus Lahori* (blog), (4 September 2017), see http://odysseuslahori.blogspot.com/2017/09/why-trees-matter.html.

10 Edgar Spooner, "Report by the superintendent of the Agri-Horticultural Society's gardens, Panjab, for the year ending 31st March 1876" (Lahore, 1876), 3.

11 Researchers at the Government College Lahore, along with international collaborators, have spearheaded a pilot project for the restoration of dry woodlands in Punjab. See Joachim Gratzfeld and Amin Ulhaq Khan, *Dry woodlands in Pakistan's Punjab province: Piloting restoration of a unique yet vanishing natural resource* (Richmond, UK: Botanic Gardens Conservation International, 2015).

12 Del Tredici, "The flora of the future," introduces some of the broad range of ecosystem benefits of spontaneous urban vegetation.

13 See Erik Harms, "Knowing into oblivion: clearing wastelands and imagining emptiness in Vietnamese new urban zones," *Singapore Journal of Tropical Geography* 35 (3) (2014) pp. 312–327.

14 Ignasi de Solà Morales, "Terrain vague," *Anyplace* (Cambridge, MA: MIT Press, 1995) pp. 118–123; Nina-Marie Lister, "Insurgent ecologies: (re)claiming ground in landscape and urbanism," in *Ecological urbanism* (Baden, Switzerland: Lars Müller, 2010) pp. 524–535; Gandy, "Unintentional landscapes."

15 See Gandy, "Unintentional landscapes," p. 438 on some of the challenges and contestations with respect to spaces of spontaneous urban nature in Global South cities.

16 Lister, "Insurgent ecologies: (re)claiming ground in landscape and urbanism."

17 See Daniel A. Friess and Tariq Jazeel, "Unlearning landscape,'" *Annals of the American Association of Geographers* 107 (1) (2017) pp. 14–21.

18 My use of "post-colonial" here aligns with concerns about decentring the long-held Anglo-European foundations of knowledge production, and for attention to their geographical and conceptual peripheries. See for instance, Warwick Anderson, "Introduction: postcolonial technoscience," *Social Studies of Science* 32 (5/6) (2002) pp. 643–658 in on the use of post-colonial theory to interrogate techno-scientific claims of "universal reason," and Ananya Roy, "The 21st-century metropolis: new geographies of theory," *Regional Studies* 43 (6) (2009) pp. 819–30, on dislocating the centres of urban theoretical production through "an analysis of the heterogeneity and multiplicity of metropolitan modernities." In calling for attention to spontaneous and unwanted ecologies, I also follow Timothy Mitchell's suggestions for thinking through the situated complexities of agency and materiality as avenues for "thinking from the south" and to challenge the deeply rooted "sovereignty of theory" that continues to pervade scientific, social scientific, and developmentalist discourses. See Timothy Mitchell, "City talks | Timothy Mitchell on the materialities of political economy and colonial history, interview by Omar Jabary Salamanca and Nasser Abourahme, November 17, 2015," see https://www.youtube.com/watch?v=0Q3_Bd563M0#.

19 See Steve Hinchliffe, "'Inhabiting'—landscapes and natures," in Kay Anderson, Mona Domosh, Steve Pile, and Nigel Thrift, eds., *Handbook of cultural geography* (SAGE Publications Ltd, 2003). See also Franklin Ginn, Uli Beisel, and Maan Barua, "Flourishing with awkward creatures: togetherness, vulnerability, killing," *Environmental Humanities* 4 (1) (2014): 113–123.

Rhizome city: tracing knotweed through the soils of Brussels

Livia Cahn

Japanese knotweed is a very urban plant that thrives in urban soils and is primarily spread by the movement of soils in the city.[1] Its leaves have a pointed tip and show a dark-red tinge as they unfurl. They grow into flattened, smooth, bright-green ovals that align either side of an upright, red, and speckled hollow and bamboo-like stem that grows out of compact root nodules. This enigmatic knotweed forms dense clusters as it grows. It grows particularly well and abundantly in European cities, where it has been subject to varying degrees of intervention, including policies ranging from supranational to hyper-local and incentives that try to grapple with its growth. Over the course of a century, this plant came into and then markedly out of favour almost everywhere in Europe (including in Brussels). Knotweed features as the star of many lists of invasive species said to threaten biodiversity in Europe, a fact that tends to spur on attempts to eradicate it wherever it grows. Knotweed continues to be classified, qualified, re-qualified, dis-classified and reconsidered. The question of how to halt or limit the growth of this particular plant is a worry for many urban gardeners. This chapter follows the history of the changing ways in which knotweed is drawn into human cultures (and areas lying beyond them) by introducing an alliance with a pair of goats from Brussels.

The characteristics of urban soils (generally covered with paving slabs, asphalt or concrete, often disturbed and as a rule polluted and low in nutrient content), do not deter knotweed plants. Knotweed can grow in hostile places, among cracks, in abandoned plots of land, and on piles of rubble that have been dug up and deposited on building sites.[2] The plant "coexists with disturbances." It grows where other plants do not grow.[3] It can even grow when buried a metre underground, and, in some instances, through asphalt.[4] The growth of the plant is not in antagonism with the urban milieu. Japanese knotweed has become an urban ally.

Knotweed is not alone in growing spontaneously and vigorously in urban terrains. Buddleia (*Buddleia davidii*), for instance, is known for attracting butterflies; and much like knotweed, it grows in the crevices of buildings and along train tracks. Potato weed (*Galinsoga parviflora*) prefers moist soils, and thus grows well, for instance, at the feet of city trees. It is much less well documented than knotweed,

Young knotweed shoots unfurl in early spring (2017). Photo: Livia Cahn.

but its tiny flowers produce millions of seeds that spur on its recent and rapid spread in cities. Dandelions, with their familiar yellow flower, thistles, blackberries, and nettles: all of these flourish in derelict sites. What distinguishes knotweed is that it grows particularly fast. Knotweed can grow up to four centimetres a day and up to three metres tall.

Its tendency to dominate a plot is linked to the plant's particularly effective vegetative reproductive system. In Europe, the plant doesn't even form fertile seeds. It reproduces exclusively asexually. All knotweed plants in Europe are thought to be female clones.[5]

Knotweed blankets the ground with an extensive rhizomatic network of roots that can grow up to three metres deep and up to seven metres away from the parent plant. This extension of the plant that is buried underground constitutes its greatest total mass and its "trickery."[6] While its leaves and stems die in the winter, its roots continue to expand and grow up to 50 centimetres a year. Its rhizomes can lie dormant in soils for up to ten years before sprouting. The presence of the knotweed is as mobile as urban soils: its growth is unforeseeable, ongoing, changing but incessant. There was a time when the fast growth of this plant was celebrated. In the 1840s, Phillipe von Siebold (1796–1866), a doctor and naturalist from Bavaria was stationed in Japan by the Dutch state. He imported a range of plants to Europe for his commercial enterprise in Leiden. A sales list catalogue from Siebold & Cie published in 1848 notes that in the previous year it had been awarded a gold medal by the Society of Agriculture and Horticulture at Utrecht.[7] The medal was awarded to "the most interesting new ornamental plant of the year."[8] At the time,

Fallopia japonica was independently classified as *Reynoutria japonica* by Houttuyn in 1777 and as *Polygonum cuspidatum/sieboldii* by Siebold in 1846. The taxonomical naming of this plant is as changeable as its reception. In 1901, the Japanese botanist Makino realized that the two plants were identical.[9] It was generally referred to as *Polygonum cuspidatum* by Japanese and American authors, followed by Swiss botanist Carl Meissen's 1856 classification as *Fallopia japonica*. Today, these three names are considered to be synonyms for the same plant species in the *Polygonaceae* family. Some propose that it be reverted to Reynoutria based on DNA sequence analysis.[10] "*Reynoutria japonica* Houtt," is cited as the preferred name in "The plant list," 2013, a list of reference for taxonomists. After much hesitation, the European Committee for Invasive Plants decided not to change the name of the plant in its literature. This would set a precedent for keeping up with taxonomists' debates. The reader will have noticed that I refer to plants by their common names. Knotweed has many common names: Japanese bamboo, donkey rhubarb, German sausage, and crimson beauty. Nicknames, whether affectionate or pejorative, express the various relationships constituted between the plant and people. These common names do not distinguish between the different species and varieties of the Polygonum family; they reflect the reality of the usual vernacular urban knowledge of this plant.

The fast-growing qualities of this plant in Europe are easily observed. As a laudatory footnote in the price list points out, the "interest" this plant generated comprised more than its fast-growing qualities.[11]A legacy of the Dutch colonial presence in Japan, knotweed was reportedly originally imported from Japan for its exotic qualities, and planted for its ornamental, aesthetic, utilitarian, and edible virtues too.[12] Gardeners would readily share cuttings. Even accidentally stepping on knotweed or pulling it out from the ground can cause a new plant to grow. Strikingly, even just 0.7 grams of rhizomatic material (10mm in length) can produce a new plant within ten days.[13] Given the characteristics of its roots, human practices have been and continue to be the major factor in spreading the plant (sometimes inadvertently or even in an attempt to eradicate the plant).[14]

From botanical gardens to private gardens, this plant was introduced to European cities, bit-by-bit, step by step. One hundred and fifty years after having been praised in the very same places, the same plant is troubling gardeners, local authorities, and supranational legislations. Today, in the name of biodiversity and on the grounds that the plant severely damages "local" environments, the economy or human health, the knotweed "problem" is tackled by targeted eradication campaigns put in place by local authorities and European-wide listings.[15] Its compact, fast-growing clumps limit the other plants growing around it by shading them. Furthermore, its roots emit compounds that are thought to alter soil chemistry and prohibit other plants from growing nearby. By reducing the plant biodiversity of plots, it also affects animal populations. Compared to other plants, knotweed stems are not particularly difficult to pull out of the ground. Generally speaking, however, gardeners be they communal or regional, are unable to muster the persistence and regularity necessary to eradicate knotweed, and in partiular its rhizome.

The dumping of green garden waste and the movement and piling up of soils are also typical of cities, and exacerbate the spread of the plant further. Shaping the city involves the movement of large quantities of soil, sometimes across great distances. Shifting soils to stabilize or level ground for construction works can disperse rhizome fragments (interspersed among a whole host of micro-organisms, seeds, spoors, and root fragments of other plants) infinitely. Soil moves through complex global circuits that are difficult to trace. In particular, polluted soils are shifted according to changing and differential national and regional norms and regulations that are navigated by a growing industry of specialized companies that import and export huge quantities of soil. The movement of soils, as a market commodity, tends to consider soils to be inanimate matter.[16]

Given that knotweed is already relatively widespread in Europe, this moving of soil creates pathways for fragments of plant rhizomes to keep spreading further. The movements of rhizome fragments are harder to trace than the heavy metal pollutants, which can be analyzed, recorded, measured, and checked. There are no ways of checking a soil for rhizomes (other than to wait and see if rhizomes sprout, which can take up to ten years), but soils with rhizome fragments are increasingly treated like "polluted soils" and regulated.

It can take several displacements of soil "contaminated" with rhizome fragments for the plant to grow. Thus, the shaping of the city can be understood as a primary knotweed dispersal mechanism. In other words, the shaping of the city and the plant's distribution go hand in hand. In Brussels more specifically, big infrastructural works along routes, train lines and waterways since the mid-twentieth century have involved digging up spaces and moving large quantities of soil, bringing a corresponding explosion in the expansion of the plant in the region.[17] Today, when the presence of knotweed is known, it shapes the way construction work is conducted; procedures are built in to limit the spread of knotweed rhizome fragments.[18] If soil components change the way construction work is organized, they are perhaps not such an inanimate matter after all. With wide dispersal of the plants' root fragments, this challenges notions of urban ecosystems, plant classifications, and ways of engaging with knotweeds presence.

Since the 1950s, discourses about human and non-human migration have increasingly been based on notions of "non-native" and "exotic," "alien" species that "invade" an assumed "pristine" landscape that needs to be "preserved."[19] This conception of stable and finite ecosystems is inconsistent with the history of planet Earth, which is entangled with a history of humans and their commerce.[20] Plants and animals travel. They escape from their usual habitats, adapt to new living conditions, survive, and proliferate, and possibly form new alliances with organisms encountered on their forced or accidental journeys and stopovers.

The difficulty of reversing this movement of fragments dispersed through the movement of soils indicates the subtle ways in which life slips through the gaps, spills out through the cracks, and resists being managed. The rhizomes were out of sight and for a long time overlooked by those involved in moving soils. The spreading of rhizome persists.

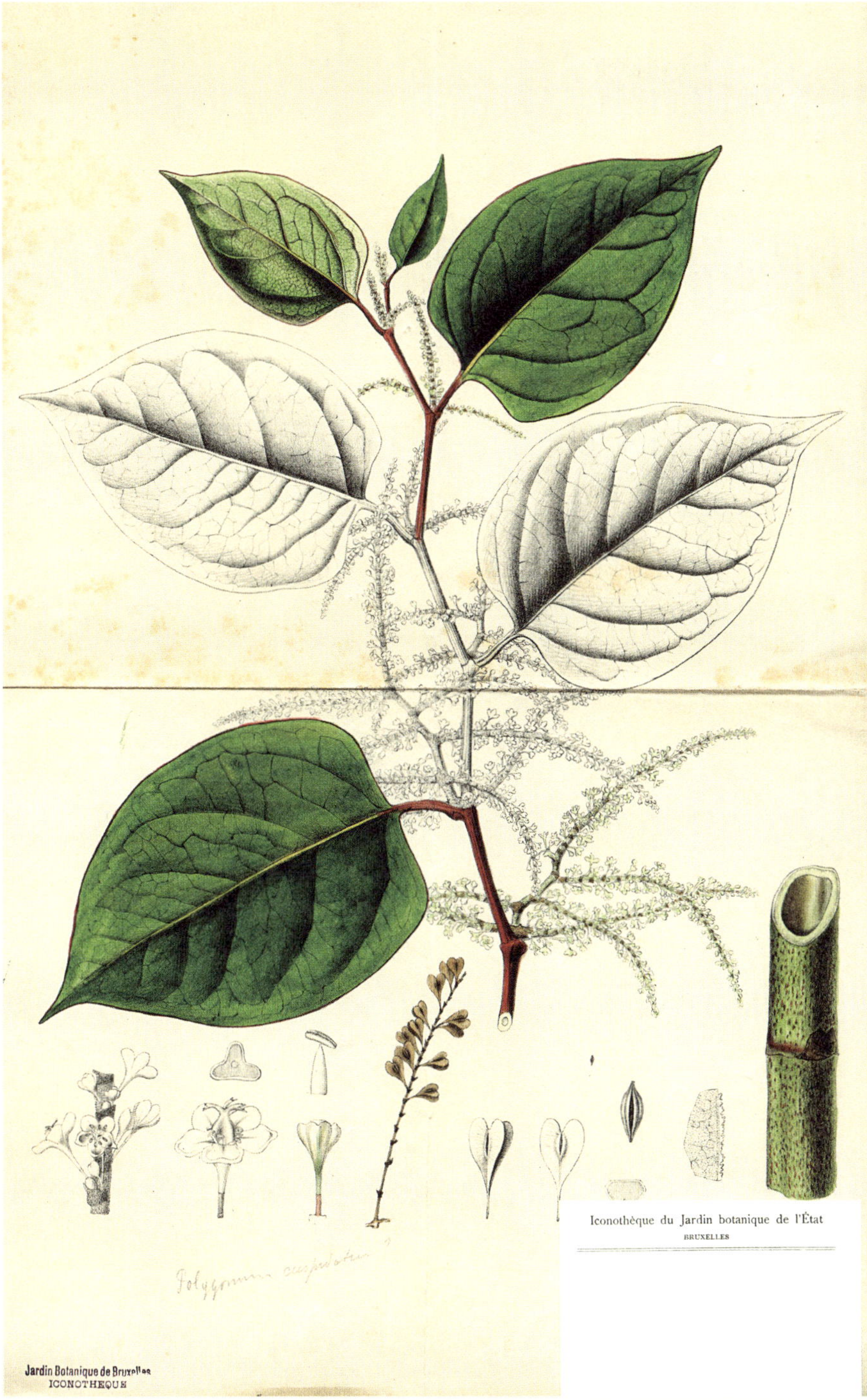

Known as *Polygonum cuspidatum* in the nineteenth century. "Polygonum cuspidatum," *Curtis's Botanical Magazine*, 3rd series vol. 36 [vol. 106], 1880, tab. 6503. Collection of the Belgian Federal State, on permanent loan to the Botanic Garden Meise.

At the European Union level, representatives from member states agreed on a list of "exotic invasive species" that affect the entire European Union.[21] By only listing plants and animals that affect the union as a whole, the legislation binds nations to move together in a united effort, across the very different bio-geographic contexts of the EU: from Mediterranean semi-arid landscapes and high temperatures to the cold winters of the north. Knotweed has spread across Europe. Having topped this list for over a decade, it was recently removed because efforts to limit its growth had little effect.[22] The biodiversity threat posed by knotweed is not resolved by this disqualification, but left up to regional initiatives. Many gardeners, plus local and regional administrations, are busy grappling with how best to limit knotweed's growth.[23]

If knotweed grows so abundantly in Europe's cities, this is also in part because of an absence of direct competitors or predators in Europe. In Japan, in addition to competition from other plants such as miscanthus, wisteria, pueraria, and cuscuta, knotweed is also subject to predation from a whole range of invertebrates and fungi. The UK is currently running field experiments on the effects of introducing the psyllid *Aphalara itadori* (a kind of bug) as a biological control technique to limit the plant's growth. These insects are imported from Japan, where they feed on young knotweed shoots. The insects deform the plant's leaves and reduce its competitive photosynthetic rate: with less leaves, the plant grows slower. So far, however, it seems that on British soil the psyllid populations did not establish themselves "successfully."[24]

If knotweed is considered an invasive plant in Europe, it's not because it is an intrinsically invasive plant, but rather because it was introduced without any of the other organisms that limit its growth in Asia, nor the practices that make use of it. Indeed, in Japan, China, and Korea, knotweed grows smaller and is less dominant. Its leaves are smaller and its stems are shorter.[25] Can we postulate that there is no such thing as an "exotic" species? There are simply living beings that move with forces that lift them. Taken in isolation, without "its world," knotweed was bought to "another world."

Eradication scenarios and biodiversity discourses consider the knotweed itself to be useless and yet, even today, the Internet is a mine of suggestions on how to serve knotweed. Its roots, its shoots, and its stems can be boiled, steamed, stuffed, dried, infused, preserved in sugar or salt, or pickled. In Chinese medicine, knotweed, known as *itadori*, is used to heal because of its high retinol content—something that pharmaceutical companies are beginning to exploit to promote anti-cancerous supplements.[26] The roots are also used as a natural colourant, producing a deep orange, and dried knotweed leaves were used as a substitute for tobacco during WWII in Japan. Its capacity to grow so fast has triggered research into using a cultivar of knotweed as biomass for biofuel.[27] After years of coexisting with it, getting to know the plant has opened up even more uses for it. The attention and trouble this plant has been triggering for some time now brings with it a proliferation of ways of relating to it and its roots. In the same way that the knotweed "problem" is implicated in and entangled with human practices, any attempts to provide general solutions can trigger additional, unexpected situations. Getting to know the plant in the Brussels context, an urban farmer and city administrator recalls a history of animals in green spaces in the city. In a very particular site in Brussels where the knotweed grows abundantly, the overwhelmingly negative reputation of the plant is momentarily reversed. A plant that is dispersed by old and new global trade patterns shapes practices locally, in surprising ways.[28] Under the guidance of a few humans, an uncanny alliance is born between the undesirable and fast-growing plant and goats from an educational farm in the centre of town.

La Ferme Maximilien hosts a range of animals that are selected for their pet-ability and are accustomed to being prodded and stroked—including goats. Dwarf goats are easier for kids to reach and do not grow pointed horns. Goats nibble almost anything: cardboard, left-over food, and clothing. However, they are very picky about what they actually eat. The farm manager relates his observations: the goats won't eat nettles, or the thistles that farm donkeys are surprisingly fond of.

Rather than bring fodder for the goats to the farm, two goats have recently begun to leave the farm. They are led out by farm workers to graze a utility plot at the city cemetery some five kilometres away. The city's teams of gardeners have been dumping grass clippings and undesired weeds on this site since the 1970s. It is overwhelmingly overgrown with Japanese knotweed. At the cemetery the goats get to eat in return for their labour and services rendered. On the farm, the goats have been dubbed: "*tendeuse bio gratuite*" (free organic mower). The goats' habit of grazing insistently and repeatedly on the plant's leaves is a significant mechanical obstacle to the plant's growth. This doesn't tackle the rhizomes in the soil directly. However, with less leaves, the rhizomatic root network has less energy to expand, just as it does in winter when the plant loses its leaves and stems. The goat's grazing results in the plant's gradual demise. Furthermore, the goat's droppings fertilize the soil. This change creates more nutrient-rich soils capable of receiving other plant species.[29]

For the moment, the goats' migration only connects two points on the map of the region, but it opens up many other potential new itineraries, animal leads, and pasturelands in a concrete-dominated urban context. This reactivation of a historical human practice opens up new possible futures for the city, for its soils, and for the animals and plants that inhabit it.

This mode of seasonal migration has become an intriguing means of targeting the perceived "invasion" of a particular plant, while feeding city goats at the same time. The inherently urban expansion of knotweed translates into locally grown fodder for urban goats. The new association that has been formed brings the familiar figure of a goatherder back into the urban context. An interstitial practice gives knotweed qualities that might write a new chapter into the history of this plant.[30]

Goats aren't suitable for every urban terrain because they require regular care and enclosures. "Goat-scaping" simply provides yet another way of relating to this plant in a manner that acknowledges its relentless sprouting in new ways, and gives urban goats a role that is not purely representational. It involves more than human narratives in an often very anthropocentric relation with "invasive species." Following knotweed in its uncanny alliance with goats, offers inroads to reconsider plants, animals, and soils as living beings shaping their behaviours respectively. In this way the (hi)story of knotweed acts as a reminder that living beings are trying, and are not easily reduced to places, categories or listings.

It recalls the histories of overseas journeys and conquests launched from Europe that are still alive today, that the practice of gardening has and had a cultural and economic value,[31] that soils need care, that plant growth depends on the state of soils, that the incessant movement of urban soils causes havoc to ecosystems, that cycles of organic matter that are usually interrupted in the urban ecosystem can be closed locally in situated and creative ways,[32] and that the "management" of urban landscapes is a complex and expensive affair for which there are no ready-made solutions.

The local effects of plant classifications are sometimes quite unpredictable. Making new associations between plants and animals to limit the plant's growth is also a way of no longer seeking to eradicate knotweed but inventing new ways to live with knotweed, its rhizomes and the history of the plant in a context in which it is clearly no longer characterized as a "stranger."

1 This essay is a collaborative work: it is closely based on research conducted for a chapter in a book prepared collectively by members of the research group "Ecologies de Bruxelles" (https://ecobxl.hypotheses.org/) with Chloé Deligne, Noémie Pons-Rotbardt, Nicolas Prignot, Alexis Zimmer, and Benedikte Zitouni: *Terres des villes, enquêtes potagères de Bruxelles aux premières saisons du 21e siècle* (Paris: éditions l'éclat, 2018). It's important to note that this book was co-written, and that the write-up of a first version of this chapter benefitted from discussion, comments, and rewriting from every member of the team. This text was originally translated into English by Livia Cahn for the occasion of a workshop with Anna Tsing organised by Rotor for the Architecture Triennale in Brugges, May 2018. It has been reworked for this edition. I hereby want to thank the other members of the group and Anna Tsing for their input and feedback that has been vast.

2 A. P. Conolly, "The distribution and history in the British Isles of some alien species of Polygonum and Reynoutria," *Watsonia* 11 (1977) pp. 291–311.

3 Anna Lowenhaupt Tsing, *The mushroom at the end of the world: on the possibility of life in capitalist ruins* (Princeton: Princeton University Press, 2015).

4 The plant has been observed to grow through five centimetres of asphalt (http://www.iucngisd.org/gisd/species.php?sc=91). In her book on social movements, Starhawk makes an association between plants that can move cement by growing between the cracks and obstinate acts of contestation that can bring about political change: "*Si se puede!*" (Yes we can!). Could it be that she's referring to knotweed? Their persistence bears resemblance. See Starhawk, *Parcours d'une altermondialiste. De Seattle aux Twin Towers* (Paris: Les Empêcheurs de penser en rond / Le Seuil, 2003) p. 3.

5 Only the closely-related *Fallopia sachalinensis* can hybridize with *Fallopia japonica* to form *Fallopia x bohemica*. This capacity to cross-breed, to reproduce in ways other than through its root system, is not very widespread in Europe.

6 Michelle L. Hollingsworth and John P. Bailey, "Evidence for massive clonal growth in the invasive weed *Fallopia japonica* (Japanese Knotweed)," *Botanical Journal of Linnean Society* 133 (2000) pp. 463–472.

7 P. F. Siebold, "Extrait du catalogue et du prix-courant des plantes du Japon et des Indes-Oreintales et Occidentales Neerlandaises," *Jaarboek van de Koninklijke Nederlandsche Maatschappij tot Aanmoediging van den Tuinbouw*, 1848, pp. 38–49.

8 John P. Bailey and A. P. Conolly, "Prize-winners to pariahs—a history of Japanese knotweed s.l. (Polygonaceae) in the British Isles," *Watsonia* 23 (2000) pp. 93–110.

9 See John P. Bailey, "Breeding behaviour and seed production in alien Giant Knotweed in the British Isles," in M. Richards Moorehead and Ruthin Laing, eds., *The biology of invasive plants; a BES Industrial Ecology Group Symposium*, 1990, pp. 110–30.

10 Based on DNA sequencing (rather than morphological characteristics) of more than a thousand species of Polygonaceae, Fallopia is considered a distinct taxonic group from and Reynoutria, see Galasso et al., "Molecular phylogeny of Polygonum L. s.l. (Polygonoideae, Polygonaceae), focusing on European taxa: Preliminary results and systematic considerations based on rbcL plastidial sequence data," *Atti della Società Italiana di Scienze Naturali e del Museo Civico di Storia Naturale di Milano*, 150 (2009) pp. 113–148.

11 "This knotweed is one of the most important imports from Japan, a perennial, ornamental plant, solid, with glossy leaves and clusters of very gracious flowers, perfect for hedgerow, to protect young plants, to stabilize sandy banks and sand dunes. Can be mowed several times in spring to feed animals that like to eat its flowers that blossom in autumn, and are good for beekeepers because they provide bees with winter stocks. Their bitter root is healthy and used in Chinese and Japanese medicine. Their stalks that die in winter are good for fires and for making matches." Our translation of P. F. Siebold, *Catalogue Raisonne prix courant des plantes et graines du Japon cultivées dans l'établissement de von Siebold & Company* (Leiden: Henry & Cohen, 1856).

12 It didn't take long for these culinary virtues to be questioned. In the same publication that several years earlier published its praise, we read (italics in the original): "*Let's get straight to the point, to put our mind to rest!—We tried, but the results were disastrous! God knows the efforts we went to get the disgusting taste of this famous knotweed off our pallets.*" Our own translation from French from Louis Van Houtte, *Flore des serres et des jardins de l'europe* (Gent: Louis Van Houtte, 1865–67) p. 16.

13 R. R. Locandro, "Weed watch: Japanese bamboo," *Weeds Today* 9 (4) (1978) pp. 21–22.

14 See Marilyn Strathern, "Gathered field: a tale about rhizomes," *Anuac.* 6 (2) (2017) pp. 23–44, for an exploration of philosophers' and gardeners' rhizomes.

15 Claude Lavoie, "The impact of invasive knotweed species (*Reynoutria* spp.) on the environment: review and research perspective," *Biological Invasions*, 19 (8) (2017) pp. 2319–2337.

16 On care for soil, see Maria Puig de la Bellacasa, *Matters of care, speculative ethics in more than human worlds.* (Minneapolis: University of Minnesota Press, 2017).

17 S. Godefroid, "A propos de l'extension spectaculaire de *Fallopia japonica, F. sachalinensis, Buddleja davidii* et *Senecio inaequidens* en Région bruxelloise," *Dumotiera* 63 (1996) pp. 9–16.

18 For the construction of a new train tack in Brussels, when digging up soils, huge budgets were mobilized to lay metal plates on the ground to prevent the spreading of rhizome fragments. See http://www.alterias.be/en/online-publications/video/full-version from 10'34.

19 Notably with the publication of Charles S. Elton, *The ecology of invasions, by animals and plants* (Chicago: University of Chicago Press, 2000 [1958]). Research in this vein attempts to detail the arrival of the plant in Europe. With the plant being actively sold and promoted from Siebold's nursery at Leiden back in 1848, Leiden is widely considered the initial locus of the plant's arrival in Europe, probably between 1823 and 1831 see John P. Bailey and A. P. Conolly, "Prize-winners to pariahs." Botanical garden registers are used to date later movements of the plant through new territories: on the 9 August 1850 an unsolicited package of plants from von Siebold, arrived in the Royal British Gardens in Kew, London. This package supposedly included the Japanese

knotweed. On the 26 April 1856 a sample of the same plant arrived at the Royal British Gardens in Edinburgh, from Jackson's of Kingston, not far from Kew Gardens. In 1869, the plant is registered to have arrived in Chelsea, in 1878 in Erfurt, in 1895 in York and so on, see P. Bailey, "Breeding behaviour and seed production in alien Giant Knotweed in the British Isles."

20 See Christian Lévêque et al., "À propos des introductions d'espèces," *Etudes rurales de l'EHESS* 185 (1) (2010) pp. 219–34; Juliet J. Fall and Laurent Matthey, "Des plantes dignes et d'invasions barbares: Les sociétés au miroir du végétal," in *VertigO—la revue éléctronique en sciences de l'environnement* (2011), Débats et Perspectives (online); and J. Baird Callicott, Larry B. Crowder, and Karen Mumford, "Current normative concepts in conservation," *Conservation Biology* 13 (1) (1999) pp. 22–35.

21 The Environment Commission of the EU's regulation on "Invasive Alien Species," http://ec.europa.eu/environment/nature/invasivealien/index_en.htm.

22 I refer here to an extended conversation with Etienne Branquart that this research has benefited from. Branquart works for the interdepartmental office for invasive species in Wallonia and represents Belgium at the European stakeholders meetings.

23 Although the use of herbicides is increasingly regulated in cities, it is still advocated as a "solution" in some cases because knotweed is sensitive to glyphosate, the active ingredient of Roundup by Monsanto. I won't go into more detail here, except to say that the side effects of the use of such toxins on the environment and animal health are well known. Pollinating insects are declining because of a lack of suitable habitat niches and a decline in food sources. A key factor is the impact of pesticides, herbicides, and fungicide.

24 Richard Shaw et al., "Weed biological control in the European Union: from serendipity to strategy," *BioControl*, 63 (3) (2018) pp. 338–339.

25 Perhaps because of a set of mycorrhizal mushrooms that didn't travel to Europe with the plant? Mycorrhiza form mutualistic relationships with plants: the plant captures energy from the sun and supplies it to the fungus, thereby limiting the plant's growth. The fungus in turn supplies water and mineral nutrients from the soil to the plan. See Gilles Clément and Brigitte Lapouge-Déjean, *Plantes envahissantes, pionnières ou simplemnt expansives? Comment vivre avec au jardin écologique* (Mens: Terre vivante, 2014).

26 See https://www.papillesdetendues.com/renouee-du-japon-source-de-resveratrol-c1200x55214.

27 The utility of a plant that engages with economic value on this scale begs the question of whether a preservation of biodiversity is really what is at stake here, http://www.desertconsult.de/projects/igniscum.html.

28 Here I want to think with Natasha Myers on how develop "forms of knowing otherwise" that stand along science to consider modes of knowing that break with rationalist assumptions, extractivist, colonial and quantifiable logics; see for example, "Ungridable ecologies: decolonizing the ecological sensorium in a 10,000 year-old natural cultural happening," *Catalyst: Feminism, Theory, Technoscience* 3 (2) (2017) pp. 1–24.

29 See Aldo Leopold, *A Sand County Almanac, and sketches here and there* (Oxford: Oxford University Press, 1989 [1949]) pp. 156–159 on how ecosystems reconfigure. Overgrazed native (cheat) grasses in Utah gives way to "new" vegetation that is difficult to protect from fire and too prickly for cows to eat but also turns to out have the positive qualities of reducing erosion and the effects of sheep grazing.

30 Patches as opposed to universalist notions borrowed from Anna Tsing's proposal to consider the Anthropocene as "broken into uneven and unequal patches" experienced in very local ways. See "Earth stalked by Man: towards a feminist approach to Anthropocene" seminar at the Université Libre de Bruxelles, Brussels, 19 October 2016.

31 Despite prohibitions on planting knotweed in Brussels (section 5, article 77 § 1), ironically there does seem to be a customer demand, because plant nurseries continue to sell cultivar varieties of knotweed that grow fast. A *Fallopia japonica compacta,*

summer sunshine, crimson beauty or pink flamingo costs about eight euros for two-litre pot.

32 Other novel exploits have also emerged in Brussels. The fact that Japanese knotweed is fit for human's consumption, too, has not escaped the imagination of artists: the collective Cooking Sections made locally sourced knotweed ice cream to redefine the notion of an "invasive" species (festival Jardin Essentiel, Park Design, Brussels, August 2016) and Gosie Vervloessem made knotweed jam for her audience (*Greeting from Nagasaki—bioterrorist recipe II,* an artist's lecture about Japanese knotweed at Beursschouwburg, Brussels, June 2016).

The art of urban flora

Part 3

Lois Weinberger

51. 稗

别名. 野稗草（湖南、四川）

形态特征. 一年生草本. 茎秆直立, 株高约1米左右. 夏日抽穗, 小穗簇生或密生, 具绿色或紫色的芒.

生活环境. 多生长在水田里与稻混生. 是稻田里很难除尽的一种杂草. 还有一种光头稗子(或称无芒稗)在北方地区很常见. 也可利用.

食用方法. 采集籽粒捣米煮粥, 蒸食或磨作米粉食也可. 籽可酿酒, 制糖.

其他用途. 籽粒和稗草的幼苗都是家畜家禽饲料.

学名. Echinochloa crusgalli (L.) Beauv.
禾本科. 稗属

图51. 稗

41. 葎草

别名. 葛勒子秧, 葛葎蔓, 葛葎蔓, 拉藤(救荒本草), 拉拉藤, 刺人藤(上海)

形态特征. 多年生蔓生草本. 高达1米余. 茎和叶柄, 渐渐变红色, 生有密生短钩刺. 叶对生, 一般为掌形状分裂作五或七裂片, 边缘有锯齿. 叶面粗糙, 有刺毛. 夏季8.9月开淡绿色小花. 果实形似松球.

生活环境: 喜生于荒野, 道旁和垃圾堆中. 常成片蔓生. 各地常见.

食用方法. 采取嫩苗茎叶, 用开水烫过, 清水浸洗后炒食. 或和入面粉蒸食.

其他用途. 与其他饲料混合喂猪. 也可入药.

图41. 葎草.
① 着雄花的枝 ② 着雌花的枝 ④ 雌花 ⑤ 瘦果

学名 Humulus scandens (L.)
桑科. 葎草属

Zheng Bo

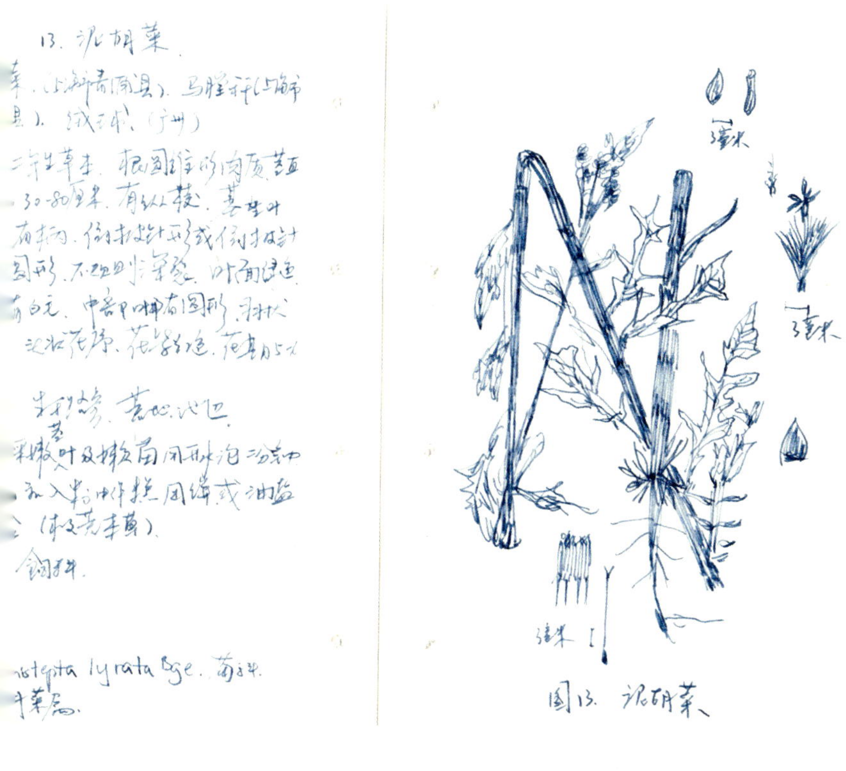

Mona Caron

RECORDING STUDIO

15A
32
ELETROP

落落大方
彬彬有礼

Yan Wang Preston

Uriel Orlow

Lois Weinberger

p. 197 *Das über Pflanzen ist eins mit ihnen* (1997).
Photo: Dieter Schwerdtle © Studio Weinberger.

For this work Lois Weinberger introduced a range of neophytes from Southern and South-Eastern Europe onto a 100 metre stretch of railway tracks at the "Kulturbahnhof" (culture station) as part of the documenta X in Kassel.

Zheng Bo

p. 198/199 *Survival Manual I* (2015).

The complete work consists of 72 sheets hand-copied by Zheng Bo from *Shanghai's wild edible plants* published in 1961. In the wake of the Great Leap Forward (1958-60) widespread famine led to the Communist Party publishing a book of edible plants to help people survive.

Mona Caron

p. 200/201 *Outgrowing*, Kaohsiung, Taiwan.
p. 202 *Swinecress*, San Francisco, California.
p. 203 *Can Masdeu*, Barcelona, Spain.
p. 204 *Aster*, Asheville, North Carolina.
p. 205 *Heliopolis*, São Paulo, Brazil.
All photographs taken by Mona Caron.

In her *Weeds* series the muralist Mona Caron has worked in a variety of cities to display small details of locally occurring spontaneous nature on a larger scale. Caron often works alongside local environmental movements and social justice campaigns to create new representations and vantage points for urban nature.

Yan Wang Preston

p. 206/207 *View from Egongyan Bridge*, Chongqing, China, 2017.
p. 208 *Woodland overlooking Caiyuanba Bridge*, Chongqing, China, 2017.
p. 209 *Allotments under Caiyuanba Bridge*, Chongqing, China, 2017.
All photographs taken by Yan Wang Preston.

In her series of photographs entitled *Forest* Yan Wang Preston investigates some of the oddities and incongruities of urban landscapes in Chongqing, the largest city in southwest China, where there have been attempts to plant trees and create an "urban forest." The transplanting of old trees into urban settings has become a lucrative dimension to landscape design. This process of "uprooting" emerges as a wider metaphor for Chinese urbanization and the destruction of other unseen ecologies.

Uriel Orlow

p. 210/211 Uriel Orlow, *The Fairest Heritage 13*, 2016. © Uriel Orlow.
p. 212 (top) Uriel Orlow, *The Fairest Heritage 1*, 2016 © Uriel Orlow.
p. 212 (bottom) Uriel Orlow, *The Fairest Heritage 15*, 2016 © Uriel Orlow.
All Rights Reserved, DACS 2020.
Stills from *The Fairest Heritage*. Single channel video, 5' 22", 2016.

In 1963, on the occasion of the 50th anniversary of the founding of Kirstenbosch, the national botanical garden of South Africa in Cape Town commissioned a series of films to document the history of the garden, the Cape Floral Kingdom, and the jubilee celebrations with their "national" dances, pantomimes of colonial conquests, and visits of international botanists. The films' protagonists of scientists, visitors etc. are all white – the only Africans featured are labourers. Considered neutral and passive, flowers were excluded from the boycott until the late 1980s and so botanical nationalism and flower diplomacy flourished unchecked at home and internationally. The films have not been seen since 1963 and were found by the artist in the cellar of the library of the botanical garden. Orlow collaborated with actor Lindiwe Matshikiza who puts herself and her body in these loaded pictures, inhabiting and confronting the found footage and thus contesting history and the archive itself. (Text adapted from Shela Sheikh and Uriel Orlow (eds) *Uriel Orlow: Theatrum Botanicum* [Berlin: Sternberg Press, 2018] p. 339).

Experiments in non-design

Part 4

Framing urban landscapes: interview with Susanne Hauser

Susanne Hauser is one of the most innovative contributors to recent thinking on post-industrial landscapes, combining insights from aesthetics, history, and urban design. The interview took place in July 2015.

Matthew Gandy Can we still use the word *Brache*?

Susanne Hauser Yes, absolutely. It depends a bit on what for. *Brache* refers to something that has been used before, usually a piece of land, that is not in this specific use anymore, and is also in no other use that we would understand as such. The term *Brache* implies that no activities are currently happening, but it is not "nature," or just a terrain, or a place prepared for something to happen. Aesthetically, there is a desire to conceive of a *Brache* as an entity, but I find this slightly misleading. It is a very distinctive idea, and also a very specific kind of historical approach, that derives a type of beauty from the *Brachen*. It requires a particular appreciation that is not applied at all times. Even in the current century, it has not been applied for a prolonged period so far.

Matthew Gandy Are there other words that we can use for these distinctive spaces in the city or in industrial landscapes?

Susanne Hauser Most words immediately imply some kind of utilization. For example, *Bauerwartungsland* (land awaiting development) imposes a legal framework; it still might appear as a *Brache* but something else has already happened. *Ruinengelände* (ruin terrain) does not apply to every *Brache*, because with ruins we expect to find remnants of human construction, which means there are traces of buildings.

Matthew Gandy Do *Brachen* have a specific aesthetics? Is there an aesthetics of *Brachen*?

Susanne Hauser Something like that has massively developed when large-scale industrial areas were abandoned in Europe—especially when heavy industries disinvested in northern and western Europe in the 1960s and 1970s. Similar developments happened thereafter in other parts of the world, of course. Industrial wastelands exist globally. At that time, the concept of an aesthetics of *Brachen* was useful, because plenty of land that obviously used to be productive was not in use anymore, so one had to come up with an idea for its interpretation and treatment. Aestheticizing is a common approach to finished objects and processes and was, when applied as a technique of rehabilitation, a cheap solution. But it only works when a cycle has been completed, when a process has come to an end. Then one can showcase objects that tell you there was once economic activity on this site, there was industrial production here, and add a degree of aesthetic glamour. This is something that, at its highpoint in the 1980s and 1990s, and maybe still at the beginning of the third millennium, captured the imagination of many people, among them planners and designers. However, this does not work anymore. And this excitement was never universally shared. During the 1990s, I spent a lot of time in industrial wastelands in order to follow the processes and designs, and from time to time I was joined by colleagues and friends. Afterwards, however, the group of people I was with were often quite eager to spend some recreational time in a "real park" or a baroque garden. Above all, they were eager to spend time in some sort of regulated environment that did not so clearly exhibit the fact that it had slipped away from cultivation and care. What is disturbing about a *Brache* is that it has fallen out of control. It is associated with waste and ruin. Since no one uses the space, and sometimes nobody even knows how to use the space, there is no criterion for behaviour in relation to a *Brache*. This is unsettling because, apart from fences, there is no boundary, and nothing to civilize or cultivate the site. You have to cherish this aspect of *Brachen* if you want to cultivate an aesthetics for spaces of this kind.

Matthew Gandy What are your thoughts on urban ecology?

Susanne Hauser I think urban ecology became a fascinating academic discipline because there were these uncultivated zones to discover during the 1970s. These zones were, of course, very interesting. In a meticulously planned world such areas are extremely attractive. Studying them with the methods available to scientists at the time was really pioneering work. And these discoveries have, in the long run, become highly relevant for urban planning and design.

Matthew Gandy What does the idea of an urban landscape mean to you?

Susanne Hauser To see something as a landscape means to make use of a specific technology of vision: it means to take a specific point of view and to approach your surroundings as a continuous space stretching as far as your eyes can see. The contrast between city and countryside is not the relevant distinction here, although traditionally landscapes are associated with the countryside. The countryside implies an agrarian zone, or an agriculturally-oriented zone. This can include forests, rivers, and lakes. Even fish would belong in such a zone. The countryside can be very varied, but this does not turn it into a landscape. It only becomes a landscape when you look at it in this specific way. As such, we can certainly direct this technology of vision that has been practiced in relation to an agrarian idyll towards the city in order to see how urban space appears when viewed as a landscape. This approach has a long tradition too: ever since the eighteenth century there have been descriptions of the city as a landscape. We can find wonderful examples in literary texts, and these are often closely linked to the visual arts. These are effectively descriptions of a pictorial view of the city.

Matthew Gandy Would it be possible to view a *Brache* as a landscape?

Susanne Hauser To me, and to the pictorial and literary tradition in visual culture, a landscape is somewhat large-scale. Many *Brachen* in cities are not that large. In a classical view of the landscape, when landscape painting emerged, you look through a window, a frame onto a landscape, and the only boundary is the more or less obscured horizon. I think you would have to include this as a convention when considering *Brachen* as landscapes. However, we are also familiar with miniature landscapes. This is how one might describe a fallow piece of urban land, as a model of a landscape, a small version of a wider space.

Matthew Gandy Sometimes, a *Brache* can be an important public space, especially in the centre of the city.

Susanne Hauser *Brachen* are passionately appropriated, especially where there is little space. An important premise is that *Brachen* are secured. Also, they have to be opened up by those who administer, account for, or own them. These are very important premises if a quiet appropriation is to take place. I used to see this a bit differently. I thought pioneers would enter and open it up. However, for every city there comes a point when a site turns into a public space, and then these other steps become very important. Sometimes designing a park becomes superfluous. To secure and protect spaces that are already appropriated is a very important objective. I would like cities to be very courageous and support such things. There is one aspect of *Brachen* that we have not yet discussed: when they were discovered, these zones became a field for pioneers. They hold the promise of happiness, an "exotic landscape" in an otherwise strictly organized space: an "exoticism" inspired by the accidental discovery of fallow land. Spaces of this kind also promise a kind of utopia. No wonder that these empty sites enable people to pursue alternative lifestyles. This includes ecological gardens and different forms of collective life and work that have to be learned through experimentation—these things can happen on *Brachen*. Many alternative projects have flourished in abandoned zones. Sometimes they had the bad luck to contribute to upgrading these spaces so successfully that they caught the attention of speculative financial interests. We are not dealing with a simple dynamic.

Matthew Gandy I have a question about urban biodiversity since many botanists and other scientists talk about rare and endangered species in cities. How important are these arguments for *Brachen* and other types of marginal urban spaces?

Susanne Hauser The question of rare species is very important because on *Brachen* we can find plants that we can't find in urban gardens and parks or in the countryside. *Brachen* are refuges, and if you find such a refuge this is a very good argument for protecting it, and thus protecting these rare plants or assemblages of plants. This is an argument for nature conservation: the moment conservation develops an interest in a specific site, it is worthwhile to discuss species diversity on *Brachen*. The question of what is implemented in cities also depends on the intensity of demands for urban space: whether it will be staged as a protected zone for nature or whether nature conservation will have to give way to all sorts of different arguments. These processes of negotiation are held over every square metre in densely populated urban areas. Naturally, I would love to see a *Brache* with high biodiversity win once in a while. I'd like to see it stay as it is, or even continue to evolve as a site of cultural and ecological interest. However, as we are talking about plants here, we should not forget that they will continue to grow, and there is the process of ecological succession. The growth of certain plants can kill off other rare plants that existed before. You run into the classic challenges and problems of nature conservation with the question: What should we care for? Which stage of development do we want to maintain? What is the reason for not building a playground with a swing or a house but instead protecting these plants? These questions bring the *Brache* into discussions that can apply to any piece of land.

Matthew Gandy I have a question regarding the difficult relationship between nature and romanticism, namely the history of plant sociology. What is your take on the history of plant sociology?

Susanne Hauser We are dealing with an ideologically imprinted terrain marked by the identification of plants that are welcome and people who are welcome. We are also dealing with the opposite: the identification of plants that are not welcome and people who are not welcome. These distinctions really do occur. There are simple yet persistent metaphors, and it is a very difficult field. The word "neophyte" for non-native plants is supposed to be a neutral term but I much prefer the earlier expression "adventive plants." This term was coined in the 1920s by the predecessors of today's urban ecologists, and simply means plants that arrive from elsewhere. It's not so ideologically charged.

Sandra Jasper What are the most interesting or important questions for the future of *Brachen*?

Susanne Hauser Berlin is experiencing an increase in population density, especially within the S-Bahnring that demarcates the inner part of the city. So the issue is how even a small *Brache* can survive this trend. Very forceful policies will be needed to protect these spaces and to allow at least some of them to survive, possibly as an element of public parks. Whether they can be retained as *Brachen* remains to be seen. Because protecting these spaces in their current form will be difficult. It is important what will happen with the former Tempelhof airfield. I hope that very few further uses of this site will be allowed, and that Berlin can afford the luxury of keeping an open space in the midst of densely built-up areas. And then it is key to work against social disparities in the different districts. This is, of course, a fervent hope, since we currently have intensifying segregation processes that have never been so acute in Berlin. This is a political challenge that we have to confront. If we have residential areas with pleasant green courtyards and beautiful green squares on the one hand, and on the other hand we have densely crowded districts in which green spaces are built on, we will have arrived at a situation we could have avoided. The preservation of open spaces across all districts as far as possible and the prevention of segregation are very critical issues.

Sandra Jasper You experienced the time when the political party Alternative Liste was founded in West Berlin and the subject of nature was discussed in the environmental movement. Could you tell us a bit about different conceptions of nature at the time?

Susanne Hauser Since the late 1970s the public ecological debate has been of significance not only in Berlin but all over Germany. It has changed many things. I mentioned the associations with waste that can be provoked by *Brachen*. Those same ecological discussions contributed not only to an appreciation of the aesthetics of "wild growth" but also to thinking about contamination and pollution in industrial wastelands. It simultaneously generated and dismantled a certain aversion to industrial areas as more information became publicly available. The discussion was centred on environmentalism, and on the damage wrought by toxins such as polluted air and soil. These issues were discussed first in relation to nuclear energy. The question of what kind of idea of nature we should urgently develop to save the world was still in its very early stages. The idea of nature being oppressed and the idea of a subject-object relationship in which nature loses out was largely agreed upon in the early 1970s and 1980s. But surely it is not as simple as that. By now, the concept of nature has been hugely differentiated. I am thinking in particular of some of Donna Haraway's ideas that have been of great importance: firstly, they strongly relativized the nature-culture division; and, secondly, they suggested that humans are not solely cultural beings from head to toe, a point that has at times been lost sight of in this subject-object narrative. Today we are no longer talking about "nature" in this emphatic and "othering" way anymore. Today, humanity tends to be seen as a small and aggressive part of a "general ecology"; we talk, for example, about conviviality and the protection of the earth as a precondition, and not just for human survival. It is remarkable how much the public discourse has changed.

Acoustic botany: listening to nature in a former airfield

Sandra Jasper

A later skylark takes the sky,
A wiser world lies under;
And still we put our wisdom by
And give the bird our wonder.
Ralph Hodgson, "The skylark"[1]

Walking south from the Platz der Luftbrücke in Berlin on an early summer weekday, we hear the rhythmic, almost lulling swoosh of traffic from the four-lane Tempelhofer Damm where commuters are heading to the motorway. If we turn left and take a few steps, the traffic noise gradually blends into the rushing of wind and the distant sounds of barking dogs and human voices. Wandering deeper into a vast open space, we become encapsulated by the versatile song of hundreds of skylarks (*Alauda arvensis*), converting the atmosphere into a musical instrument. Looking up, we can see the small birds seemingly standing still in the sky over the *Wiesenmeer*, a "sea of meadows," that flourishes between the runways of the former Tempelhof airfield.

Since the airport's closure in 2008, the far-reaching roar of airplanes landing and departing over the tenements of Neukölln has given way to the sounds of wind, weather, animals, and people. Today, the former airfield, widely known as Tempelhofer Feld, is the largest *Stadtbrache* (urban wasteland) and space of spontaneous nature in Berlin. Located in the district of Tempelhof-Schöneberg, this 300-hectare field is marked by decades of infrastructural use with tarmac covered by lichens and ruderal plants growing in the cracks and interstices of former service roads. Its botany is characterized by a mix of different kinds of meadows that, by the end of the summer, will have grown waist-high. Flourishing between the landing strips, this expansive vegetation provides ecological niches for buzzing bees, chirping crickets, spiders scuttling through the grass, and many other species; even a sand lizard (*Lacerta agilis*) has been captured on camera.[2] For an area in the city centre, the site holds an incredible number of species that are usually common

Environmental monitoring map of the Berlin Tempelhof airfield, 2017. The map shows the 201 territories of the skylark spread across the airfield. Cartographic design: SWUP GmbH. Copyright: Grün Berlin.

in open and extensively used agricultural landscapes. At the latest count, the airfield has 241 species of bees and wasps,[3] 25 species of breeding birds,[4] over 20 orthopteran and butterfly species, and various biotopes with specific assemblages of plants.[5] Many plants and animals are considered rare or endangered, yet it is one particular bird, the skylark, whose presence this brief essay follows, as it has shaped ecological debates, management regimes, design interventions, and political discussions over the future of this vast urban site.

The skylark is a marker of landscape change. Originally associated with steppes and dry grasslands in Europe and Asia, it has been a common feature of agricultural landscapes for centuries. The bird has a drab appearance, with streaky brown feathers, a buff-white belly, and a small crest on its head, which provides excellent camouflage among crops and earth, and yet it has a dramatic flight and distinctive song. Between spring and late summer, the birds nest on the ground, preferably in arable fields with mosaic-like vegetation heights. The skylark is not a typical urban bird. It tends to avoid areas close to buildings, trees, hedges, and other vertical structures. But urban meadows can provide a refuge for the skylark. These urban habitats become increasingly important in light of the absence of skylarks from rural landscapes.

Voted "bird of the year" by a German conservation group for the second time in 2019, the skylark has become a so-called flagship species. Flagship species are "animals serving as symbols and rallying points for various conservation goals."[6] The skylark represents the rapid decline of many farmland bird populations across Europe and is utilized by conservationists as a symbol for an environmental politics directed against the "catastrophic agricultural policies of Berlin and Brussels."[7] Since the 1970s, skylark numbers have plummeted dramatically in northern and western Europe. The main causes of this decline are intensified farming and trends towards monocultures, with the merging of agricultural holdings. Reduced crop diversity with homogenous sward that is often unsuitable as nesting ground, fertilizer use that accelerates plant growth and disrupts seasonal breeding rhythms, and pesticides that destroy the weeds and invertebrates that serve as food all further accelerate the disappearance of the skylark.[8] After German reunification, arable land surrounding Berlin initially recovered from decades of intense soil exploitation by the agricultural cooperatives of the GDR. As portrayed in Volker Koepp's documentary film *Landstück* (2016), a brief window of time during which family-run organic farms and nature conservation areas took hold and provided habitats for birds is now being closed at an increasing pace. Global financial interests are now reaching beyond the city of Berlin, as far as the Uckermark in Brandenburg, where the state is selling land to foreign investors who push for monocultures and industrialized types of meat production.[9]

Unlike other flagship animals like the panda or tiger, the skylark's "non-human charisma" does not derive from its size, cuteness, exotic appeal, or other visual features stylized in emblems, but from its distinctive song or "acoustic charisma."[10] With the disappearance of the skylark from the acoustic landscape, a particular sense of loss is invoked, as has been recently expressed with reference to rural England by the writer Richard Mabey and the geographer Bill Adams.[11] This sense of loss and anxiety caused by the absence of birdsong has a longer cultural history, exemplified by the title of Rachel Carson's influential book *Silent Spring* (1962). It has been featured prominently as part of a wider environmental critique of modernity in the field of sound ecology since the late 1960s. Contemporary debates in sound ecology that link with discussions on the Anthropocene still see processes of urbanization as a major cause of the changing global soundscape, and predict that the world is turning increasingly silent and discordant.[12] However, they neglect the role cities can play as refuges for birds and other species that become part of urban acoustic ecologies, beyond an idealized rural or natural sonic realm.

If we listen closely to the city and train our "ornithological ear," we learn something about time and seasonality, topography and landscape. Hearing a skylark sing on a Berlin summer day, we will most likely find ourselves in an open space with the horizon in sight: a meadow sprouting in an abandoned plot of land; a former Hobrechtian *Rieselfeld* (sewage field) on the edge of the city; an airfield in the city centre. Airports in and around cities have become important refuges for skylarks and other ground-breeding birds. Unlike larger birds whose presence is deterred with lasers, with predators, or sonically, with flare guns and recorded bird

Skylark (*Alauda arvensis*) on the Tempelhof airfield in Berlin, July 2019. Photo: Sandra Jasper.

calls, skylarks do not interfere with human air traffic and are colonizing airfields in Munich, Frankfurt am Main, and Berlin-Tegel, amongst many other airports globally. The first in-depth study of avifauna on the Tempelhof airfield was conducted in 2005, when the airport was still in operation. Several endangered bird species were found on the site, including wheatear, tawny pipit, meadow pipit, whinchat, and skylark, whose 95 territories made up 20 percent of its overall population in Berlin.[13] Of the currently 25 species of breeding birds colonizing the airfield, several are listed in one of the Berlin, federal, or EU nature protection schemes, such as barn swallow, corn bunting, red-backed shrike, and common buzzard spotted on the edges of the site. With the public opening of the Tempelhof airfield in May 2010, birds that are less tolerant of human presence, like tawny pipit and meadow pipit, have disappeared and are still absent. Skylark numbers initially dropped as well, but have recently skyrocketed with a new record high of 221 territories in 2018, 40 percent of Berlin's overall population.[14] In other parts of the city, however, skylarks are becoming much rarer because of increasing construction and urban densification that has resulted in the loss of open spaces, wastelands, and other vacant land.[15]

Unlike other anomalous spaces in Berlin that remained hidden or inaccessible and were left to the independent dynamics of spontaneous nature for decades, the Tempelhof airfield was quickly appropriated by local residents, and drew the interest of scientists, conservationists, and planners alike. Prior to opening the site to the public, a management plan introduced measures to protect skylarks and other birds from human disturbances. Initial provisions to care for the ground-breeding birds included the installation of wooden poles around the meadows with "please do not disturb" signs during the breeding season from April to July, later further enforced with barrier tape, fencing off a specific zone in the south-eastern part of the airfield, closing the site to humans at night, annual mosaic-like mowing of the meadows in late August, and, from 2017, temporal and spatial restrictions on kite-sports as a compromise between protecting nature and allowing human leisure activities. All other spaces were left unrestricted, and a diverse range of human activities and grassroots initiatives developed over the years: we can find park-like areas with barbecue spots, a beer garden, community gardening projects with raised beds, and groups of lime trees and poplars providing shade.[16]

The Tempelhof airfield is one of the most contested spaces in Berlin. With the disappearance of air traffic, numerous debates, including a public referendum, emerged over the future use of the site and the changes in its adjacent neighbourhoods. In parallel to the manifold human and non-human activities unfolding on the former airfield, lingering plans to build on the site grew more substantive after its public opening in 2010.[17] In 2012, the Berlin Senate commissioned a scientific study on the environmental impact of building on the Tempelhof airfield. The Senate's master plan, which included a central park area and four new urban quarters on the edges of the site, would have impacted a range of protected and endangered species, but it legally violated nature conservation law only in the case of the skylark. Developing the airfield according to the Senate's plans would have destroyed over 50 percent of the skylarks' breeding sites, and would have dramatically impacted local populations. To continue with the development plans, an exceptional permission in terms of species-protection law and compensation sites elsewhere in Berlin for 89 pairs of birds were needed.[18] Anticipating that it would be able to successfully realize its planning proposal, the Senate closed costly long-term contracts with the Stadtgüter GmbH, a company managing land formerly belonging to Berlin's municipal infrastructures, to create so-called *Lerchenfenster* (lark windows) as compensation spaces in agricultural fields in Brandenburg, away from the city.[19]

Following the successful public referendum in May 2014, in which the majority of Berliners voted in favour of keeping the Tempelhof airfield unchanged as proposed by the grassroots citizen's initiative "100% Tempelhofer Feld," and also overwhelmingly voted against the Senate's competing proposal, building plans were put on hold. In recent months, however, these plans are resurfacing in anticipation of the municipal election to be held in 2021. The SPD (Social Democratic Party) is proposing to build on the edges of the field, including holding a second referendum after the current coalition agreement that rules out building on the site has ceased. In spring 2019, the Berlin Senate issued a master plan to identify allotment gardens across the city suitable for development. The dominant political discourse pits social against ecological futures, while the real tensions in Berlin lie with capitalist urbanization and speculative development. With the loss of *Brachen* and the closure of many gaps in the city's surface, the search for land suitable for building continues.

The skylark is a recurring symbol of European romanticism. It has captured the imagination of poets, composers, and landscape painters, who included the bird in various pastoral scenes. In *The Lark Ascending* (1914–1920), a composition by Vaughan Williams, the pentatonic lark figure is inspired by the bird's musicality. While the English poet's Ralph Hodgson's poem *The Skylark* (1910) idealizes the bird's song as part of a rural scene in response to the negative effects of industrialization, Williams's "modernist pastoral" has been read as a more nuanced and sympathetic view on industrialism, technology, and modernity.[20] The skylark's presence between the runways of a decommissioned airport reveals a slight twist to the idea of the urban pastoral introduced by the art historian Julian Stallabrass, and later adopted by cultural geographers working on art, gentrification, and urban change.[21] Stallabrass's neo-Marxian critique highlights how the trope of the pastoral (alongside its flattening of social hierarchies and histories), formerly rooted in representations of idealized rural landscapes, has been transferred to the city, in the artistic depiction of degraded urban landscapes and their working-class inhabitants. If we consider the Tempelhof airfield and its spontaneous nature, we can trace the visual and acoustic appearance of rural elements, the rural pastoral, in a post-infrastructural urban site: farmland animals, meadows, seasonal mowing cycles, birdsong, and grasslands rustling in the wind. The socio-economic critique inherent in the idea of the urban pastoral also holds for the Tempelhof airfield. In the course of its transition from noise-polluted airport to a public space of spontaneous nature, neighbourhoods surrounding the Tempelhof airfield, such as the Schillerkiez, are experiencing a rapid revaluation due to their new pristine quiet park location. Similar developments can be observed near the Gleisdreieck Park or at other locations within the inner part of the city close to green or waterside spaces. However, all of them are subject to dramatic rises in rents and real estate speculation. In that sense, the creation of quiet spaces within the inner urban area is accelerating what we might call "acoustic gentrification," a phenomenon that can be observed in many cities across the world, and that is closely associated with the "paradoxical effects" of urban greening projects.[22]

Botanical features of the urban landscape provide so-called ecosystem services and other utilitarian dimensions to urban greening, but they also fundamentally shape the multi-sensory experience of urban space. Plants provide shade and cooling in increasingly hot cities. Their canopies protect us from pouring rain. Their leaves rustle in the wind and deflect the cacophony of the city. The botanical realm, whether spontaneous or intentionally-designed, serves as a refuge for birds, insects, and other organisms. Listening to the skylark on a former airfield, we are reminded of how processes of rural and urban change are intrinsically linked through land speculation and migrating birds. In its current state, the Tempelhof airfield represents the possibility of accommodating both social and ecological futures. Wastelands have sparked multiple and alternative visions of the city in the past, a window into the history of Berlin that will be further closed by building on the airfield.

1 Excerpt from the poem, "The Skylark," originally published in 1910. Ralph Hodgson, *The skylark and other poems* (New York: St Martin's Press, 1959) pp. 1–3.

2 SWUP GmbH Landschaftsarchitektur, Stadtplanung und Mediation, *Berlin Tempelhofer Feld: Naturschutzfachliches Monitoring, Ergebnisse 2017.*

3 Christoph Saure, "Bienen und Wespen des ehemaligen Berliner Flughafens Tempelhof im Bezirk Tempelhof-Schöneberg (Hymenoptera)," *Märkische Entomologische Nachrichten* 13 (1) (2011) pp. 1–21.

4 Rainer Altenkamp, *Monitoring der Avifauna des Tempelhofer Feldes in Berlin im Jahr 2018 und Vergleich mit den Brutvogelerfassungen 2005 und 2010 bis 2017*, Assessment commissioned by Grün Berlin GmbH, 2018.

5 SWUP GmbH, *Berlin Tempelhofer Feld.*

6 Maan Barua, "Lively commodities and encounter value," in *Environment and Planning D: Society and Space* 34 (4) (2016) p. 732.

7 Naturschutzbund Deutschland e.V. (NABU), "Typischer Agrarvogel im Sinkflug: Die Feldlerche ist 'Vogel des Jahres 2019'" (last accessed 7 August 2019: https://www.nabu.de/tiere-und-pflanzen/aktionen-und-projekte/vogel-des-jahres/feldlerche/index.html).

8 The European Commission, "Skylark *Alauda arvensis* factsheet," EU Wildlife and Sustainable Farming project 2009 (last accessed 7 August 2019: https://ec.europa.eu/environment/nature/natura2000/management/docs/Alauda%20arvensis%20factsheet%20-%20SWIFI.pdf).

9 See the documentary film *Landstück*, directed by Volker Koepp (Germany, 2016, 122 mins).

10 See Jamie Lorimer, "Nonhuman charisma," in *Environment and Planning D: Society and Space* 25 (5) (2007) pp. 911–932.

11 See Bill Adams, 2019, "Listening and loss" (last accessed 7 August 2019: https://thinkinglikeahuman.com), and Richard Mabey, 2005, *Nature cure* (London: Chatto & Windus).

12 See, for example, Bernie Krause, *Voices of the wild: animal songs, human din, and the call to save natural soundscape* (New Haven: Yale University Press, 2015); and Andrew Whitehouse, "Listening to birds in the Anthropocene: the anxious semiotics of sound in a human-dominated world," *Environmental Humanities* 6 (2015) pp. 53–71.

13 Rainer Altenkamp, *Die Brutvögel auf dem Flughafen Tempelhof im Jahr 2005*. Assessment commissioned by Seebauer, Wefers und Partner GbR, Berlin, 2005.

14 See Altenkamp, *Monitoring der Avifauna des Tempelhofer Feldes in Berlin im Jahr 2018.*

15 See Winfried Otto and Klaus Witt, *Verbreitung und Bestand Berliner Brutvögel* (Berlin: Berliner Ornithologische Arbeitsgemeinschaft, 2002).

16 See Altenkamp, *Monitoring der Avifauna des Tempelhofer Feldes in Berlin im Jahr 2018.*

17 On the history and politics of participatory planning on the Tempelhof airfield, see Hanna Hilbrandt, "Insurgent participation: consensus and contestation in planning the redevelopment of Berlin-Tempelhof airport," in *Urban Geography* (38) 4 (2017) pp. 537–556.

18 The Senate's plans would violate the legal prohibition to disturb or destroy resting and breeding sites as regulated by the Federal Nature Conservation; see the report commissioned by the Berlin Senate: Gruppe F Landschaftsarchitekten, 2012, *Tempelhofer Freiheit Artenschutzrechtliche Folgenabschätzung und Konzeption zur Schaffung von Ersatzhabitaten für die Feldlerche*.

19 *Der Tagesspiegel*, "Das teure Tier von Tempelhof und Tegel," 10 July 2014 (last accessed 7 August 2019: https://www.tagesspiegel.de/berlin/ausgleichsflaechen-fuer-die-berliner-feldlerche-das-teure-tier-von-tempelhof-und-tegel/10182018.html).

20 George Revill, "The lark ascending: monument to a radical pastoral," *Landscape Research* 16 (2) (1991) pp. 25–30.

21 See Julian Stallabrass, *High art lite: the rise and fall of young British art* (London: Verso, 1999). For urban and geographical work on the urban pastoral, see Ben Campkin, *Remaking London: decline and regeneration in urban culture* (London: I.B. Tauris, 2013) pp. 146–148; and Andrew Harris, "Art and gentrification: pursuing the urban pastoral in Hoxton, London," *Transactions of the Institute of British Geographers* 37 (2) (2012) pp. 226–241.

22 See, for example, Joanna Kusiak, "Acoustic gentrification: the silence of Warsaw's sonic warfare," in Matthew Gandy and BJ Nilsen, eds., *The acoustic city* (Berlin: JOVIS, 2014) pp. 206–211; D. Asher Ghertner, "Nuisance talk: constructing eco-civility in world-class Delhi," in Anne Rademacher and K. Sivaramakrishnan, eds., *Ecologies of urbanism in South Asia* (Hong Kong: Hong Kong University Press, 2013) pp. 198–219. On the idea of "green gentrification" that emerged in a North American context, see, for example, Melissa Checker, "Wiped out by the 'greenwave': environmental gentrification and the paradoxical politics of urban sustainability," in *City and Society* 23 (2011) pp. 210–229; Sarah Dooling, "Ecological gentrification: a research agenda exploring justice in the city," in *International Journal of Urban and Regional Research* 33 (2009) pp. 621–639; and Jennifer Wolch, Jason Byrne, and Joshua P. Newell, "Urban green space, public health, and environmental justice: the challenge of making cities 'just green enough,'" in *Landscape and Urban Planning* 125 (2014) pp. 234–244.

There's life in dead wood: tracing a more-than-human urbanity in the spontaneous nature of Gothenburg

Mathilda Rosengren

On a hill in central Gothenburg lies a small, wooded area. With a magnificent view over the rooftops of the centre of the city, the wood is frequented by local residents, their children, and their other-than-human animal companions. It is a public space, but still informal enough to be one of those increasingly rare places in the city where humans and other-than-humans who find themselves on the margins of urban life are allowed to linger for a bit longer. Squeezed between some *funkis*-style residential housing blocks, a small public park, and some of the city's university grounds, the wood thus presents itself as a quasi-liminal zone of transition between different articulations of contemporary Gothenburgian life. In Sweden's second city, where the lack of housing and calls for urban densification are increasing by the year, this transitional space has also become prime land for both municipal and commercial developers. And yet, by and large, construction on the site has never really taken off. The wood has, as an urban planner at the municipal planning office put it, "somehow fallen between the cracks" during the past century's urban expansion.[1] Since the late 1920s, in lieu of a planned infrastructure, permanent housing, or an ordered park, what has crystallized here is an urban wood of nondescript, unassuming design, which emerged out of an intermingling of minimal municipal intervention (at times intentional, at other times unintentional) and informal, everyday socio-cultural and ecological practices.

What seems to have primarily encouraged this development is the area's slippery nature, in terms of topography, shape, and name. Firstly, the slanting sides of the hill make for relatively demanding and costly building processes, and the inevitable levelling of the mountain, forces each developer to face the irreversibility of, and the local scepticism to, their proposed constructions. Secondly, the wood has few, if any, defined borders and boundaries. On its northern side, a residential dead-end cuts it off from the park below, yet the beginning of the park mirrors the shrubs and trees of the wood to such an extent that it is still hard to sense where the one

"Liv i död ved," one of several signs put up by the municipality of Gothenburg in order to inform local residents of the ecological potentiality of "dead" wood (2017). Photo: Mathilda Rosengren.

begins and the other ends. To the south and to the west, the greenery stretches further into the residential areas, ignoring the occasional fence put up a long time ago and the few asphalted pathways now rippled by the force of the roots of neighbouring trees. Thirdly, the name of the wood too is in flux: today, its official denomination is *Högåsberget*, although in the past, and in local parlance, *Trollspisberget* has been the most commonly used.[2] And, to confuse matters further, locals use the geotag *Johannebergsparken* (which in fact is another nearby park up on the hill) to locate the area online.

The indefinability that such multifaceted slipperiness brings with it has rendered the wood close to invisible to an official urban imaginary. Throughout the past century, in planning proposals as well as newspaper articles, the area has predominantly been approached as an add-on, a margin, or a side-product, particularly of the public park in the north; very rarely is it dealt with directly, if at all. In a sense, it has become an unintentional, long-term experiment in non-design: allowing for moderately undecided urban becomings through a municipal "letting things be," but without completely subsuming to a more disorderly "letting things go."[3] And yet this "becoming of the unplanned" rather than the "being of the planned," also highlights a state of precariousness that may arise from the lack of a defined, human-made design. In the winter of 2016, when walking around the area together with one of the employees of the municipal Park and Nature Department (*Park och Naturförvaltningen*, PONF), the employee emphasized the predicament the wood's borderlessness and namelessness put it in: "If we don't put an [official] name on it [the wood], it is very easy to come and nibble on it here. You see this [happening elsewhere], nature areas and parks without names have no identity and they are very easy to appropriate during a densification process."[4] And it is true that, when the wood has surfaced to the consciousness of official municipal

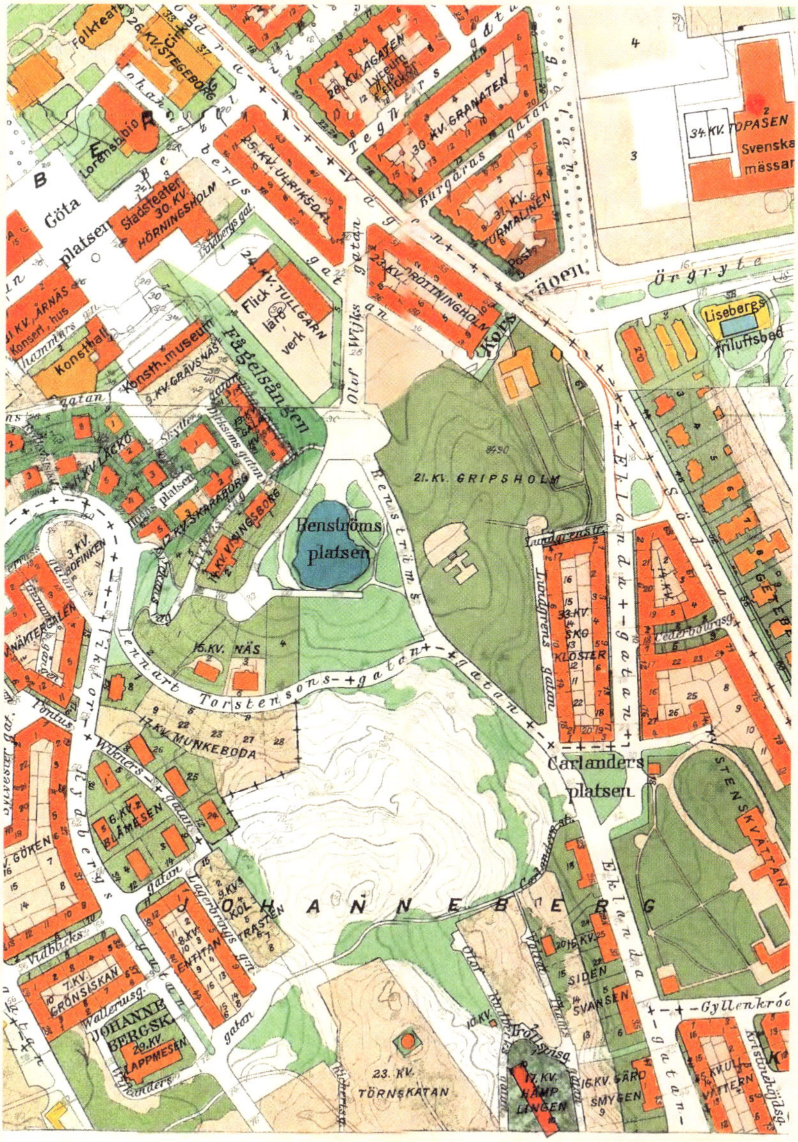

The map shows the state of the wood in 1923 at the time of the Jubilee Exhibition that year. Its steep topography and sparse vegetation is displayed in white. The green-shaded southwesterly slopes and dells indicate the considerably more wooded condition at the edges of the area. Copyright: Göteborgs Stad.

bodies or the general public, it is seemingly always in correlation with an emerging threat to its distinct non-design. If you dig a little in the city archives you will come across several proposals to build on the site. For instance, as an expansion of residential villas in the 1920s[5] or to accommodate new buildings for the Faculty of Philosophy in the 1970s.[6] Most recently, in the late 2000s to early 2010s, the wood was in danger of being almost completely consumed by yet another large-scale university redevelopment. In the end, after both protests from citizen initiatives and discontent voiced from within the municipal planning bodies themselves, the redevelopment was revised to only impact the stretch closest to the university campus.[7]

For each of these botched attempts to build on the grounds, there have been intricate, multifarious lines of (human-related) arguments for or against it—local politics blending with current national and international interests; individual needs mixing with larger socio-cultural trends, and so forth. Nevertheless, one argument for the retention of the wood throughout the past century has, simply put, been "wood" itself: wood as in *the wood*, an other-than-human constellation of urban life, gaining its spatial definition from trees, lichens, grasses, wildflowers, shrubs, brambles and other berry bushes. This is a spontaneous yet situated fusion of urban nature that one of the activists of a local citizen initiative referred to as "typical Gothenburgian nature."[8] However, it also means wood as in *the trees*, the lively beings stretching their branches over, and anchoring their roots in, the hilltop. They function as the ever-evolving core and structure of the hill's non-design, thus making *the wood* as an ecological constellation possible. And, finally, wood as in *dead wood*, where dying or dead trees pave the way for different expressions of living and foster new life for the future. Consequently, we see a world of versatile, interrelated "woods" unfolding here, making for the intriguing argument that this unplanned nature is inherently linked not just to the emergence of other-than-human life in the city, but also to the encouraging of specific eco-cultural practices in urban life itself. Today, the wood is of a predominately deciduous character, with a spontaneous mixture of oak, beech, ash, and common pioneer species, such as birch, aspen, and alder.[9] On the higher points of the hill, you can also find the occasional sessile oak tree in its local, coastal incarnation (the so-called *krattek*[10]). A recent zoning plan notes that the self-grown generation in the area is well-developed, with shrubs consisting mostly of hazel, honeysuckle, and young deciduous trees, with diverse soil conditions that allow for the flowering of wood anemone in the spring and the ripening of blueberry bushes in the late summer.[11]

When tracing the history of this specific urban ecological constellation, it makes sense to start in the 1920s, as this was arguably the last time when the area was heavily interfered with by humans in an official capacity. In 1923, the eastern section of the hill formed part of Gothenburg's extravagant, international Jubilee Exhibition celebrating the city's 300th anniversary. Previously, the area had been part of the edgeland between the rapidly expanding city and the farmed countryside around it. Now, it was included as a last outpost of the southern side of the exhibition area, and, in a sense, of the city itself. Conceived as a lookout point, a temporary lighthouse was built on the top of the hill, with a funicular to transport visitors up from and down to the freshly constructed public park below. Photographs from the time display a sparse vegetation on the slopes around the funicular railway, the smooth surface of the underlying stone of the hill being left clearly visible with only low bushes and very young trees growing in its crevices. This state, however, cannot be assigned to the construction of the exhibition alone. The reason why no greater wood had been able to establish itself in the area was most likely due to the fact that the poorer demographics of city dwellers used the hilltop vegetation as a source of firewood for their homes.[12] In the 1920s, the welfare reforms that would radically improve the general Swedish standards of living were still several years away, and the wood thus accommodated a way of life where making ends meet remained a daily struggle. This final major interference with the wooded area points to a different, now defunct, way of Swedish socio-cultural and economic (urban) life—one that would drastically change over the next decades, with the considerable strengthening of workers' rights and the ultimate establishing of the modern welfare state. Here, as social housing, central heating, and electric stoves (among many other things) came to signify the progress brought on by the implementation of the *Svenska Folkhemmet*—the social-democratic vision of a society with complete socio-economic equality—the previous reliance on urban wood dwindled.[13]

For the remainder of the twentieth century, with urban wood losing its value as a (human) necessity for living (at least for the poor), the utilizations of the woodland have circled around its recreational capacities and aesthetic qualities. As early as 1936, a newspaper article celebrating the scrapping of the plans to build the planned villas on the hill makes grandiose reference to the wood as *den vackra naturparken*, "the beautiful nature park," which together with the public park forms an aesthetically "unrivalled" and "rare" park landscape.[14] This valuing of spontaneous nature aligns well with the particular Swedish notion of *friluftsliv*, which promotes the virtues of an outdoor recreational lifestyle that actively encourages a "physical experience of nature."[15] The concept of "nature-based outdoor recreation," which started to seep through all levels of society in tandem with the introduction of the universal Annual Leave Act, continues to define the general Swedish conception and utilization of nature to this day.[16] However, though it does encourage some recreational aspects closely related to this notion, the wood in central Gothenburg does not fit neatly into this approach to nature. While the passage of time has allowed the trees to grow older and taller and has also allowed the vegetation around them to thicken, a human visitor cannot lose herself in the wood in that complete and idealistic manner. The wood is small and the built urban is, literally, always just around the corner. Simultaneously, as mentioned above, the spontaneous wood also gently queries the urban form itself: it queries how human urban dwellers occupy and make use of it, and its inherent relation to the other-than-human. As the spatial structure does not follow a human-made pattern, the urban dweller's engagement with the space becomes an interaction of an explicitly more-than-human kind. In a sense, an everyday, eco-cultural engagement emerges where modifications of the space are entwined with the temporalities and life cycles of *the wood* itself. Oftentimes, when the worst of winter is past and the grounds are bare again, children build cubbyholes out of old, dead branches. In the bright summer evenings, when the long days make up for the lack of street lights, couples and smaller groups gather on the cliffs of the hilltop–the wood in full bloom giving each glade a natural shielding from the outside world. One chilly autumn, someone had built a sauna on the highest point of the hill, using materials locally available and a live birch tree as support for the whole construction. Leaving very little trace behind, these are all temporary, informal additions to the wood, adapting to its physical and temporal rhythms rather than aiming to permanently shift the spatiality of the place. As such, they enable an utterly different experience of the everyday urban, void of the planned urban surfaces' dictates of interaction. And this, in turn, allows for another kind of (human) urban citizen to emerge, testing and perhaps altering her socio-cultural practices through her engagement with, rather than her controlling of, the other-than-human. Maybe what best describes this daily eco-cultural engagement, is the impassioned statement of a local resident opposing the redevelopments in the late 2000s: "The nature around Näckrosdammen [the pond in the middle of the public park] is wonderful all year round. On the slope above Näckrosdammen, ... we dam up brooks during the periods of rain. In the winter, we skate on the pond. We trace signs of spring. We delight in the magpies above Humanisten [the university]."[17]

Thus, the spontaneously growing trees continue to 'protect' the area from exploitation, partially by enabling the general cultural cherishing of the ideal of 'wild' nature, but also through making it possible for ordinary, everyday interspecies relations to play out in the unplanned environment.

Finally, it is not only in their "live" manifestation that the trees assume a protective role. In fact, today, it is as *dead wood* that they are particularly valuable for those who wish to appropriately manage green spaces in the centre of the city, like PONF, or save them from the most intense densification pushes, like the local citizen initiatives. After all, letting old trees "be" and allowing them to live and die of their own accord has granted the area the somewhat protective status of a "bird biotope."[18] Red-listed bird species, such as the lesser spotted woodpecker (*Dendrocopos minor*), frequent the area in their foraging for bugs and larvae—insects that are known to proliferate in just the branches and dead trunks of older deciduous trees.[19] Here a third and most current shift in human relations with the urban wood may be detected, a shift that brings to the fore an articulated importance of biodiversity in the city. This comes at a time when the scientific claims of the potential urban green spaces in terms of fostering new, eclectic clusters of biodiversity—a capacity rapidly decreasing in the farmed, monocultural landscape outside of cities—have begun to trickle down to also inform municipal bodies in Gothenburg.[20] The spontaneous urban wood is thus projected as an important space not only for recreational activities, as an aesthetic backdrop, or as alternative cultural expressions of urban living, but rather as an essential platform for life itself. In a recent public scheme to highlight the ecological importance of dead or dying trees in Gothenburg's green areas, PONF has started to put up informative signs on trees in various states of demise.[21] On the outskirts of the wood, there are several trees carrying such signs, stating: "Life in dead wood. Here, tree trunks have been left to benefit the biodiversity. Many insects, fungi, mosses, and lichens depend on old dying or dead trees for their survival."[22] According to the PONF employee, after local residents have read the signs, they become much more willing to accept an urban landscape displaying a certain degree of disorder—that is, a certain degree of non-design.[23] Then, as notions of biodiversity and narratives of ecologically threatened, yet thriving, areas are gaining in strength among the public and municipality alike, they have started to intermingle with the above mentioned socio-cultural concepts of nature.[24] And the wooded area, unassuming at first glance, is a good example of how such entwining may look in reality. Its right to existence being continuously under renegotiation, it offers a reflection of how a spontaneous, more-than-human non-design may query both the passages of time and being in an urban context: where spatial appropriations are in a constant flux, where temporality can be cyclical rather than linear, and where death does not signify the ultimate end but instead the continuous relational becoming of urban lifecycles. And this, in turn, provides a starting point to examining everyday, though rarely documented, social and cultural expressions of a more-than-human urbanity.

1 Interview with an urban planner, City Planning Office, Gothenburg, Sweden, December 2015.

2 Participant observations at urban planning meetings, Radar (architecture office), Gothenburg, Sweden, December 2016; interview with a landscape architect, Park and Nature Department, Gothenburg, Sweden, December 2016; interviews with activists/laypersons, citizen initiatives, Gothenburg, Sweden, January–February 2017.

3 The wood is still managed by the municipal Park and Nature Department; however, due to limitations in staff numbers, economical means, and so on, there is little interference in the area, Interview with a landscape architect, Park and Nature Department, Gothenburg, Sweden, December 2016.

4 "Om vi inte sätter namn på det så är det väldigt lätt att komma in och knapra lite på det här. Ser man ju, naturområden och parker som inte har namn, dom har ingen identitet och dom är väldigt lätta att ta i anspråk när man förtätar." Interview with a landscape architect, Park and Nature Department, Gothenburg, Sweden, December 2016 (author's translation)

5 Einar Hansson, et al., *Carlandersplatsen. Renströmsparken. Kulturmiljöunderlag* (Gothenburg: Melica, 2012) pp. 7–11.

6 M. Hirsch, "Grävskopornas nya arbetsplats: NÄCKROSDAMMEN!," *Expressen*, (17 February 1973) p. 9.

7 Conversation with an urban planner, City Planning Office, Gothenburg, Sweden, December 2016; interview with a landscape architect, Park and Nature Department, Gothenburg, Sweden, December 2016; interviews with activists/laypersons, citizen initiatives, Gothenburg, Sweden, January–February 2017.

8 Interview with an activist/layperson, citizen initiative, Gothenburg, Sweden, February 2017.

9 Stadsbyggnadskontoret, *Detaljplan för bostäder och verksamheter vid Carlandersplatsen och Renströmsparken inom stadsdelen Lorensberg, Johanneberg i Göteborg* (Gothenburg: Stadsbyggnadskontoret, Göteborgs Stad, 2012) p. 6.

10 Perfectly accommodated to an environment of strong winds and little shelter, the krattek (*Quercus petraea*) is a relatively small oak tree that grows in a bush-like manner,

with a bent and twisted stem and branches spreading horizontally and sparsely outwards.

11 Stadsbyggnadskontoret, *Detaljplan för bostäder och verksamheter vid Carlandersplatsen och Renströmsparken inom stadsdelen Lorensberg, Johanneberg i Göteborg* (Gothenburg: Stadsbyggnadskontoret, Göteborgs Stad, 2012) p. 6.

12 Conversation with a landscape architect, Radar (Architecture office), Gothenburg, Sweden, December 2016; conversation with a landscape architect, Liljewall (architecture office), Gothenburg, Sweden, June 2017.

13 Interestingly, the correlation between urban wood and simple heat would not resurface until the 2000s (albeit in a somewhat reversed scenario). Today, in the arguable era of the Anthropocene, scientists are touting the urban wood—in its live and breathing "tree" form—as a potentially vital actor in the cooling down of "heat islands" within the inner area of the city. See, for example, Sten Gillner et al., "Role of street trees in mitigating effects of heat and drought at highly sealed urban sites," *Landscape and Urban Planning* 143 (2015), pp. 33–42; and Janina Konarska, et al., "Transpiration of urban trees and its cooling effect in a high latitude city," *International Journal of Biometeorology* 60 (1) (2015), pp.159–172.

14 Morgontidningen, "Näckrosdammen med omgivning förblir park: Ändring av stadsplanen föreslås," *Morgontidningen*, 9 September 1936.

15 Thomas Beery, "Nordic in nature." *Environmental Education Research* 19 (1) (2013) p. 96.

16 Thomas Beery, "Nordic in nature," pp. 96, 100.

17 "Naturen runt Näckrosdammen är underbar året runt. I branten ovanför Näckrosdammen ... dämmer vi bäckar under regnperioder. På vintern åker vi skridskor på dammen. Vi följer vårtecken. Vi gläds åt skatorna ovanför Humanisten." Stadsbyggnadskontoret, *Samrådsredogörelse—Program för bebyggelse vid Renströmsparken och Carlandersplatsen, inom stadsdelen Lorensberg i Göteborg* (Gothenburg: Stadsbyggnadskontoret, Göteborgs Stad, 2009) p. 9 (author's translation).

18 Interview with a landscape architect, Park and Nature Department, Gothenburg, Sweden, December 2016.

19 Naturcentrum AB, *Inventering av biotoper för mindre hackspett kring Guldhedsdalen, Göteborgs kommun 2011. Underlag för detaljplan* (Gothenburg Stadsbyggnadskontoret, Göteborgs Stad, 2012) pp. 6–8.

20 Park-och naturförvaltningen, *Göteborg: Grönstrategi för tät och grön stad* (Gothenburg: Park-och naturnämnden, Göteborgs Stad, 2014).

21 The department strive to leave the trees as they are or, if they may pose a danger to humans walking by on the outer edges of the wood, they are cut down to an appropriate level and then parts are left at "safe" places in the wooded area. (*Grova träd. Råd och riktlinjer för hantering av grova träd och almved i Göteborgs kommun* (2011) Rapport 2011: 2. Park- och naturförvaltningen. Göteborg Stad).

22 "Liv i död ved. Här har stockar lämnats för att gynna den biologiska mångfalden. Många insekter, svampar, mossor och lavar är beroende av gamla döende eller döda träd för sin överlevnad" (author's translation).

23 Interview with a landscape architect, Park and Nature Department, Gothenburg, Sweden, December 2016.

24 There are even recent studies emerging (where the sampling of data in form of surveys were conducted just in Gothenburg) that argue for a connection between a human individual's increased aesthetic and aural appreciation of a green space and such space's levels of biodiversity; see Bengt Gunnarsson et al., "Effects of biodiversity and environment-related attitude on perception of urban green space," *Urban Ecosystems* 20 (2017) pp. 37–49.

From undead commodities to lively labourers: (re)valuing vegetal life, reclaiming the power to design-with plants

Marion Ernwein

Concepts of "gestion différenciée," "gestion harmonique," and "zéro phyto"[1] are ubiquitous in Francophone urban green space management. Sparked by changes in legislation, innovations in landscape architecture, and the diversification and intensification of park usages, all insist on the need to let go of dominant "horticultural" approaches to urban parks, and instead experiment with "rural," "wasteland," or "wild" aesthetics and forms of "ecological" management.[2] They involve new ways both of *designing* vegetal landscapes and of engaging with the spatialities and temporalities of plant life in everyday *maintenance* work. In this essay, I draw on research conducted in Geneva (Switzerland) to examine the forms of enrolment of plant life that respectively undergird the horticultural and ecological traditions of urban greening. I argue that they constitute two singularly distinct modes of valuation of plant life, the former predicated upon displaying *undead* vegetal commodities, the latter upon putting to work plants that are *lively* and capable. I discuss how value is ascribed to plant life and who has the power to do so, and, using two examples, argue that ecological *convivial experiments* should be conceived as a reclamation of the *power to design-with* plants, contrary to the horticultural industry's hold on the variety, forms, and modalities of vegetal life in cities.

Within the horticultural paradigm, urban greenery is predominantly designed as a *still life,*[3] with annual and biannual flowers among its most important features. Purchased from horticultural firms by green space services at various stages of their life (from seedling to adult plant), these are watered, fed, repotted, re-repotted, and trimmed, until they reach their adult stage. At that point, referred to as "finished" or "completed" plants, they can be transferred outside of the polytunnel, and into their final destination is a flowerbed. Gardeners leave enough room around each individual plant for a final spur of growth, after which the design is considered complete. Henceforth, flowers are expected to stay in the same stable state the whole season through, before being uprooted, composted, and replaced with new, and just as still, flowers, at the start of the next season. A green space manager details the design principles of such flowerbeds: "We would create grids, so we would make lines, and plant 1-2-3-4-5-6, 1-2-3-4-5-6, 1-2-3-4-5-6, then the next line we plant 3-4-5-6, 3-4-5-6, 3-4-5-6, and so on, so we would get a bed with structure, with volumes and depths." These horticultural compositions evidently leave little room for agency, spontaneity, or dynamism. Instead, they draw on a conception of plants as strokes of colour in a pictorial composition. This approach to greening relies equally on a dichotomy between these desired, stable, horticultural commodities and the less-desirable, proliferating "weeds." Producing these compositions as stable requires intensive (human) labour, to keep plants alive (watering and feeding them) and remove dead ones as well as all undesirable organisms ("weeds" and parasites).

"Ecological" approaches, on the other hand, are predicated upon nurturing the lively character and capacities of plants in order to diversify the species composition and aesthetic quality of urban green spaces. Within such approaches, wildflower and grassy meadows, live hedges, and beds of perennial flowers abound, most of which require little to no watering, less mowing/trimming, and fewer interventions overall. Detailing this approach, a member of the direction of Geneva's green space service explains: "time has come to stop using flabby plants." Increasingly, as he suggests, the heretofore highly appreciated horticultural plants are seen as lacking vitality. Their stability, and the human and environmental resources required to produce it, are not fit for purpose at a time of legal restrictions over the use of chemical phytosanitary products and decrease of public resources and workforce. Instead, grassy, perennial, and spontaneous plants, seen as more lively, are being newly valued.

Perennial plants, gardeners explain, have the capacity to survive the passing of seasons. They display more liveliness, and they expand, in sometimes surprising ways. New design and maintenance practices engage with these characters: "We used to plant flowers in lines, with specific distances," a gardener explains, but "now lines are over: we had to change our mental program." In flowerbeds, evolving plant structures increasingly replace the rigid lines and compositions of horticultural design. They rely on associating the varied modalities of growth of different types of plants—e.g. perennials, grasses, and annuals—and the complementarities of their behaviours, and observing, understanding, and nurturing their interactions. When "it happen[s] that a plant take[s] over another one, that some plants di[e] asphyxiated," gardeners "let them do, and ... wait to see what happens."

As for weeds, "if we call them spontaneous plants, we can rethink how we live with them," a gardener tells me; and a large-scale convivial experiment in Geneva's cemeteries forcefully illustrates this. In 2010, the City of Geneva's 25 hectares of cemeteries, whose grounds were heretofore mostly covered with gravel, were transferred from the funerals to the parks service. The latter decided to green them, so that more park-like maintenance could be adopted. A botanical survey

Spontaneous plants and lawn escapees reclaiming a path. Cimetière de Saint-Georges, Geneva, July 2016. Photo: Marion Ernwein.

undertaken as part of the planning process revealed that an endangered variety of lichen—*Placidium squamulosum*—was thriving in one of the cemeteries. The report recommended that the greening be made compatible with the preservation of lichen life, and in particular that no soil be added or gravel removed. Greening in the gravel and without threatening lichen life: what a challenge for a horticultural profession which associates greening with sowing lawns, equates *good* soils with *rich* soils, and categorizes moss and lichens as unpleasant at best. Forced to respond creatively, the service studied the spontaneous flora that was growing in the more remote, and less maintained, areas of cemeteries. Based on these observations, it designed a mix of species deemed able to green the cemetery while respecting lichen life. The mix included many of the species thus far deemed undesirable—among them *Achillea millefolium*, *Leontodon hispidus*, and *Plantago media*. In lieu, therefore, of established approaches to greening, which require removing the gravel, adding top soil, and sowing a lawn, the protection of a somewhat uncharismatic organism—a lichen—opened the way to working with the very "weeds" which had been fought against through decades of maintenance. The total cost of sowing hectares of such a mix, however, proved too high, and this provocative project was dropped. Instead, some areas were indeed seeded with an equivalent mix, while in most others maintenance of the gravel was put to an end; instead of being sown, the desired spontaneous grasses and flowers were allowed to reclaim surfaces—at their own pace. In areas which were seeded, the mix includes "fast-growing, ground-covering perennials" and "some lawn for social acceptability," which will occupy space while dormant seeds sprout and spontaneous plants slowly spread. The service is now observing how these two processes are unfolding throughout the cemetery and comparing their outcomes.

The key idea that I want to advance in the remainder of this essay is that ecological approaches of this kind are not merely convivial, open-ended experiments, but have introduced a singularly distinct mode of valuing plant life within the urban political economy of horticulture. While horticultural approaches had been predicated upon displaying *undead* plant commodities, ecological management is putting to work plants that are *lively* and capable. This change is predicated not only upon rethinking which modalities of plant life are desirable, but also what their life is *for*. Purchased by green space departments in their thousands, horticultural flowers must promise to stay alive throughout the whole season within the confined space of the flowerbed. They are *undead* commodities: while, like other lively commodities, their value is derived from their "remaining alive for the duration of their inclusion in the commodity circuit,"[4] it in fact resides in their ability to stay alive *without showing too much liveliness*. Their staying alive, furthermore, requires intensive resources, both human and technical. In contrast, the animate, interactive, ground-covering, spontaneous, and perennial plants used in ecological approaches are seen as capable *lively beings*, who can use their vital force, their interactive capacities, and their spatial skills to perform tasks, some of which are explicitly aimed at sparing the very resources demanded by horticultural plants. And indeed, during a press conference in the summer 2016, the direction of the green space department was clear: "On the one hand, we are optimizing resources and materials. On the other hand, we are now giving more room to vegetal intelligence ... This contributes to the reduction of our maintenance tasks."[5] The link made between new approaches to plant life, and the reduction of maintenance tasks suggests that, by controlling each other in flowerbeds, or by spreading and transforming the surface cover of cemeteries, urban plants are increasingly valorized for their maintenance-sparing *potential*.

I would suggest that such *potential* is in fact another name for plants' *labour power*—"the aggregate of those [intentional] and physical capabilities existing in a [plant] being, which [they] exercis[e] whenever [they] produc[e] a use-value of any description."[6] Without delving too much into the conceptual debates around the notion of non-human labour,[7] I take inspiration from anthropologist Tim Ingold's contention that animals can be enrolled in work situations in different ways, on a continuum from instrument to labourer,[8] in order to discuss how such a reading can help us to (re)think the question of agency in urban design. While many would object that *work* entails an intersubjective, collaborative experience, ill-fitted to the reality of plant life,[9] I want to suggest that feminist studies of work, with their insistence on modalities of work and labour that do not entail a conscious, reflexive self-definition as labourer, can inspire an experiment in thinking work beyond consciousness altogether.

In this final section, I want to examine the ethical and political implications of the two modes of valuation of plant life we have identified—*undead commodities* and *lively labourers*—for the distribution of agency in urban landscape design. While carefully designed, with their static lines and grids, the flowerbeds and arrangements of horticultural approaches are decidedly shaped by the mode of existence of plants as commodities: by horticultural firms, on which municipal green space services rely for the production and reproduction, each season, of new annuals, and who edict norms pertaining to the minimum number of flowers and colours to be included in a purchase. Floral variety, therefore, is strongly shaped by the increasingly internationalized, oligopolistic, horticultural market and its catalogue. A flower production manager explains: "The quantities we have to purchase now! Horticultural companies set norms, for instance if I want a total of 1,000 begonias, in 3 colours, so 300 in each colour, they won't let me. I have to purchase a minimum of 1,000 flowers in each colour, and the total purchase has to be at least 2,000 flowers." Municipalities that are reorienting their approach towards ecological management put a greater emphasis on their own ability to choose, grow, and nurture the plants they want to work with. This is no light decision: while the need to be constantly purchasing plants is lessened, having the capacity to design, nurture, and monitor lively plants requires good production infrastructures and design-oriented posts. In the years during which it was setting up this new approach, Geneva's green space department invested in a new horticultural production centre, and hired an unprecedented number of landscape architects.

This is because more, rather than less, design is required in order to *produce plants as labourers* within convivial experiments. When working with horticultural, generally exotic, taxa, flowerbeds are rarely designed according to plants' needs and their ecological relations (beyond perhaps the need for shade or sun). Given the short duration of time they are kept for, and the insistence on the visual quality of flower compositions (rather than on the ecological quality of their relations, for instance), few parameters are needed to achieve the balance. With the open-ended designs, and longer time-frames, of modes of ecological management, designers' attention is refocused on producing the right environmental interventions for plants. Spontaneity is carefully curated: plants needs to be put in the best conditions to express their potential, and for as long as they can. This, evidently, requires careful work. This work, and this agency to design non-design, are reclaimed from a political economy of undead commodities.

On the maintenance end, in spite of official discourses advocating using vegetal intelligence to decrease maintenance tasks, work is most definitely not merely *transferred* from humans to plants. Instead, the nature of human work changes to accompany the transformation of plants from undead commodities to lively labourers. Within horticultural modes of managing vegetal life, gardeners were working within the limits of a pre-set temporal agencement of tasks. Flowerbeds could be uprooted every 31st of May and 30th of October, and the grass cut every other week. Within the framework of ecological maintenance, increased attunement to plant life and, therefore, observational work is required. If flower meadows are to re-sow themselves, there is a short window of time during which they can be cut, and this can't be planned according to human schedules. Too soon or too late, and the plants will not have produced seeds, or these will be too mature, and the meadow won't be able to do its work. However, when compared to more active modes of intervention (such as weeding out), such labour is hardly visible—precisely because plant labour is invisible itself, due to the specific temporalities of plant life. Fears of being seen as passive by an urban public to whom they feel accountable are at the core of oppositional attitudes of workers towards this new approach to plant life in cities. For a renewed, reclaimed urban political economy of plant life to be emancipatory, the implications of the redistribution of labour beyond the human work collective need to be acknowledged. My hope is that acknowledging explicitly the more-than-human dimension of labour could inspire modes of bargaining and collective action that both celebrate decommodified urban ecologies and politicize the ways that not only plant life, but different types of labour, are valued.

1 Translatable as "differentiated management," "harmonious management," and "zero phyto."

2 On these concepts, see Gaëlle Aggeri, *La nature sauvage et champêtre dans les villes: origine et construction de la gestion différenciée des espaces verts publics et urbains; le cas de la ville de Montpellier*, PhD dissertation (ENGREF, 2004); Françoise Dubost, "Les paysagistes sous la bannière de l'écologie urbaine," *Ethnologie française*, 40 (4) (2010) pp. 629–638; Marine Legrand, 2015, *La mise en ordre écologique des parcs urbains: savoirs, pratiques et paysages: exemple d'un grand parc francilien*, PhD dissertation (Paris: Museum National d'Histoire Naturelle, 2015); Bernadette Lizet, "Du terrain vague à la friche paysagée. Le square Juliette-Dodu, Paris X[e]." *Ethnologie française*, 40 (4) (2010), pp. 597–608.

3 As suggested by Isabelle Arpin, Coralie Mounet, and David Geoffroy, "Inventaires naturalistes et rééducation de l'attention: Le cas des jardiniers de Grenoble," *Études rurales* 191 (5) (2015) pp. 89–108.

4 Claire Collard and Jessica Dempsey, "Life for sale? The politics of lively commodities," *Environment and Planning A: Economy and Space* 45 (11) (2013) p. 2684.

5 Cited in J. de Weck, "Ôter du béton pour verdir Genève au-delà de ses parcs," *Tribune de Genève* (30 August 2016).

6 From Karl Marx, 1867, *Capital*. Vol. 1.

7 For this, see Maan Barua, "Nonhuman labour, encounter value, spectacular accumulation: the geographies of a lively commodity," *Transactions of the Institute of British Geographers* 42 (2) (2017) 274–288; Alyssa Battistoni, "Bringing in the work of nature: from natural capital to hybrid labor," *Political Theory* 45 (1) (2017) pp. 5–31; Sarah Besky and Alex Blanchette, eds., *How nature works: rethinking labor on a troubled planet* (PLACE: School for Advanced Research/University of New Mexico Press, 2019); Marion Ernwein, *Les natures de la ville néolibérale: une écologie politique du végétal urbain* (Grenoble: UGA Editions, 2019).

8 See Tim Ingold, "The architect and the bee: reflections on the work of animals and men," *Man* 18 (1) (1983) pp. 1–20.

9 See, for instance, Jocelyne Porcher, "Animal work," in Linda Kalof, ed., *The Oxford handbook of animal studies* (Oxford: Oxford University Press, 2017) pp. 302–318.

Tracing the urban pastoral in Tallinn: Leo Marx, Karl Marx, and urban political aesthetics

Maroš Krivý

In the summer of 2013, 80 bulky bags filled with soil and plants transplanted from abandoned gardens were installed in the courtyard of the Contemporary Art Museum KUMU in Tallinn, Estonia. Spread along the courtyard's broad stairway, the installation *Pineapple or Artichoke?* was on display as part of the exhibition *Afterlives of Gardens*, named after a similarly titled book by English landscape historian John Dixon Hunt.[1] Unlike Hunt, who explores how gardens have been used rather than how they have been designed, the Tallinn exhibit addressed disused gardens as a form of unintentional design. As the titular reference to tropical plants implied (since Tallinn's climate of cool summers and cold winters is not suited to either pineapples or artichokes), there was a fantastic aspect to experiencing gardens as abandoned.[2]

What does *Pineapple or Artichoke?*, an aesthetically rendered horticultural cross-section of Tallinn, reveal about the ambiguities of urban nature in the post-socialist Baltic region? If the post-industrial trope of renaturalized and rewilded cities has become ubiquitous, then what about renaturalizing cultivated urban nature?[3] What forms of urban politics and economy does the botanical imagination centred on abandoned gardens contest and subtend?

In his classic interpretation of "an inchoate longing for a more 'natural' environment" expressed in the nineteenth-century North American literature, historian Leo Marx highlighted the contrast between the "garden" and the "machine."[4] Technological proress, he argued, was represented in that literature as both a prerequisite and a threat to pastoralism. Marx drew attention to an episode recounted by novelist Nathaniel Hawthorne: a rural setting filled with the sounds of birds, moving leaves, and a village clock is suddenly interrupted by the shriek of a locomotive whistle. Extrapolating the argument to the contemporary 1960s, Marx saw pastoralism as a driving force of the "current 'flight from the city,'" a reading of suburbanization that is in accord with the interpretations of highway building programmes as both enabling and threatening the suburban idyll.[5] Today, Marx's

Katrin Koov, Maria Pukk, and Ivar Lubjak, *Pineapple or Artichoke?* Photo: Maroš Krivý.

thesis needs to be updated for the age of the "back to the city movement by capital," in which wastelands and other overgrown urban landscapes have been acknowledged as the last vestiges of urban nature and reappropriated as the frontier of the "urban pastoral."[6]

At the same time, we need to consider what the "garden" means in different political and geographical contexts. In post-Soviet Estonia, there is a deep-seated ethno-national sense to experiencing nature, with geography having been introduced in the early twentieth century as a variant of *Heimatkunde,* or "local history."[7] Postwar history is largely portrayed as one in which the Estonian cultural landscape (the "garden") was colonized by Soviet industrialism (the "machine"). The defining experience of post-socialism as a form of post-colonialism, and the corresponding rejection of socialism as itself a colonial apparatus (rather than an element of anti-colonial struggle), form a backdrop to the odd marriage of neoliberalism and ethno-nationalism which took the political centre stage in the 1990s.[8]

The Soviet Union's collapse and the restoration of national sovereignty led to a sweeping wave of privatization and the ethnic segregation of Russian-speaking citizens.[9] In this context, the name "Marx" signified the proverbial ash heap of socialist history, while the metaphoric "garden" was the market that needed to be brought into being and safeguarded from interventions.[10] Mart Laar, the first Estonian prime minister (and later a recipient of the Cato Institute's Milton Friedman Prize), whose government was responsible for the bulk of privatization legislation passed in the 1990s, complained, for instance, that "Karl Marx is honoured and the invisible hand of the market is blamed for all failures, [which] is not fair."[11] In that sense, so to speak, the presence of another Marx in the garden poses the question: how does the specifically Baltic undoing of Marxism reflect and find itself reflected by the aesthetics of urban pastoralism in Tallinn?

In the 1990s, the introduction of foreign mortgage capital to former state socialist economies of the Baltics triggered expansive suburbanization. Single-family homes mushroomed in Tallinn, taking the suburbs in the US and Finland (the closest "Western" neighbour) as a model. This change, however, had distinctive cultural dynamics.[12] For many, the process of suburbanization was not experienced as a flight from the city, but rather as a process of resettling from one type of "suburb"—comprised of socialist mass housing estates—to another. The kernel of suburban detachment was the lawn, ranging from vast lawns that gradually blended in with the natural surroundings to miniscule lawns bounded by blind walls, but in any case conspicuously non-productive.

Suburban lawns contrasted with allotment gardens introduced in the post-war years to alleviate food shortage.[13] Introduced under Stalin's rule and promoted under Khrushchev, allotments provided food and, later, recreation, and represented a kind of "mass garden" supplement to mass housing. One example is Mähe, a farmland annexed by the Tallinn municipality in 1945 and developed in the 1950s on the scale of 50 hectares and about a thousand plots. Construction was limited to standardized sheds, with no water supply or sanitation and a ban on overnight stays. Despite the ban, sheds were soon turned into summer houses (so-called *dachas*), and, more recently, refurbished and upgraded into regular homes, creating an idiosyncratic urban fabric that Estonian geographers call "summurbia."[14] Today, there is an unconventional feel to Mähe, with its potpourri of self-rebuilt huts, bungalows and mansions cramped within a dense and narrow street layout; with areas up to 800 square metres, however, plots in Mähe were luxurious compared to allotments that mushroomed in the last Soviet decade.[15]

In the 1980s, Soviet machinery manufacturer Dvigatel distributed a stretch of marshland near the Tallinn airport to its employees. The place was colloquially known as Soodevahe ("surrounded by bogs"). Before long, a haphazardly subdivided colony, filled with shacks, greenhouses, raised garden beds, compost bins, and flowers, encircled the airport.[16] Soodevahe boomed in the 1990s, when the post-socialist rise in unemployment and poverty added to the value of home-grown produce, engendering a resilient informal economy and a vast infrastructure of open-air markets. When Dvigatel went bankrupt in 2004, however, the land of Soodevahe was acquired by the airport for expansion, effectively turning the allotment community into illegal squatters.[17] Adding ethnic insult to economic injury, a journalist writing in the same year characterized the colony as a "wasteland" and a "slum for the down and outs," who practiced "gardening in the Russian style."[18] In 2011, during the government's press conference, the then prime minister Andrus Ansip—infamous for his controversial, ethno-nationally charged decision in 2007 to remove a Soviet World War II memorial from Tallinn's city centre which sparked the so-called Bronze Night riots by members of the Russian-speaking minority—stated

sarcastically: "It is sad that when you land in Tallinn, you see this 'splendid' summer cottage area from the air. But soon that *dacha* area will disappear".[19]
In 2011, artist Timo Toots defied this sarcasm by organizing a summer-long festival in Soodevahe. In a colony that was already in the process of being deserted, he adapted derelict structures into makeshift hotels, bars, museums and observation decks, thus acknowledging Soodevahe as if it were a real city, and the now-illegal occupants its citizens.[20] In the spirit of relational aesthetics, he also organized a competition for the most beautiful garden. After the festival had ended, Soodevahe's fabric, complete with the layers of Toots's intervention, continued to decay until 2015, when bulldozers razed the sheds and greenhouses, leaving behind a trail of destruction resembling the aftermath of a tornado. As of 2018, the fragments of makeshift structures and sprouting garden flowers are still discernible amidst the rubble.
Even as the festival challenged the verbal and physical onslaught on Soodevahe by those in power, it brought to the fore the tensions between aesthetics and

Soodevahe in 2011. Photo: Annika Haas.

economy. Historian Daniela Sandler observed a similar phenomenon in post-unification Berlin, centred around the capacity of the relatively privileged social groups to "symbolically dissociate decay from misery in a way that others—ethnic minorities, recent migrants, or the very poor—cannot."[21] Toots's intervention failed to save Soodevahe but precipitated the rise of cultural interest in unkempt gardens and other forms of ostensibly spontaneous urban nature.

Thus, the popularization of decay as a form of design is the political and aesthetical context to the KUMU exhibit on disused gardens. *Pineapple or Artichoke?* (by architects Katrin Koov, Maria Pukk, and Ivar Lubjak) was inspired by and came on the heels of the publicity that Soodevahe received in Tallinn's cultural circles, but it also borrowed from influential precedents such as atelier le balto's *Le Jardin Sauvage* (Palais de Tokyo, 2002) as well as Piet Oudolf's installations *Giardino delle Vergini* (Venice Biennale, 2010), and *Hortus Conclusus* (Serpentine Gallery, 2011). Work on the exhibition started with a student workshop in spring 2013, and the first task was to map disused gardens across Tallinn. Using the same visual cues that were the object of aesthetic curiosity, such as the evident lack of maintenance and decay, student volunteers identified eleven such "hotspots," and singled out 80 gardens for plant collection. Plants (including bulbs and roots) were dug out, stacked in crates, and brought to the museum, where they were replanted into bulky bags pre-filled with soil. Installed in spring, *Pineapple or Artichoke?* was a slow-paced performance of sorts, as the foliage and bloom sprouted up. On display were numerous common garden cultivars, ferns and herbs (dill, mint), but also vegetables such as horseradish and pattypan squash, wildflowers ranging from dense-flowered mullein (*Verbascum densiflorum*) to common sorel (*Rumex acetosa*), and oxeye daisy (*Leucanthemum vulgare*), and invasive species that included Japanese knotweed (*Fallopia japonica*) and Canada goldenrod (*Solidago canadensis*).

As one of the authors explained to me, the exhibit was centred around the idea that there is an afterlife to gardens but not to nature.[22] In the exhibition catalogue, she wrote that abandoned gardens have been "designed by natural processes," but also described them as vacuoles for "contemplation, silence, absence and slowness" and "holes" that have "some sort of potential."[23] In a joint statement, the three authors similarly portrayed abandoned gardens both as "a little model of nature" and as "charged with possibilities."[24] They highlighted their "potential in strengthening the social cohesion" and, more generally, "the role and the potential of empty plots in the cities."[25] The curator of *Afterlives* commented in similar terms that, "in cities, wastelands are seen as the last remaining freedom, places ruled by sun, wind and untouched nature."[26]

These remarks reflect (to paraphrase Leo Marx) an inchoate longing not exactly for nature but for urban nature. The premise of *Pineapple or Artichoke?* seems to be threefold: nature is resilient, this resilience is best manifested in urban nature, and urban nature is the locus of urbanism to come. Tallinn's disused gardens have triggered interest in the resilience of plants in an urban setting. As places of respite and emptiness that are the "other" of cities, they also functioned as a kind of "pastoral" foil for projecting visions for a way of life that would be both urban

Pineapple or Artichoke? Working map with pinned hotspots of disused gardens. Soodevahe is in the bottom right corner, south of the airport. The Northern Tallinn peninsula is in the upper left corner. Photo: Katrin Koov.

and "natural." With wastelands having been increasingly acknowledged as the last vestiges of authentically urban experience, there is a sense in which the contemporary referent to Marx's metaphorical "garden" is renatured culture rather than cultivated nature—or, more specifically, renaturalized cultivated nature. Nevertheless, there is a tension between representing abandoned gardens as a form of urban nature that is "empty," and recasting emptiness as a potential.

While some plants were gathered in Soodevahe (whose forthcoming demolition gave the event an air of botanical rescue), the bulk was collected in the Northern Tallinn neighbourhoods of Kalamaja, Kopli, and Paljassaare. This is significant in yet another way. Since the late nineteenth century, Tallinn's industrialization was centred on Northern Tallinn, a peninsula that combined the advantage of a relatively central location with a sense of manufacturing and labour being isolated from the city. Primitive rental housing for workers is epitomized in the vernacural so-called Tallinn house typology (*Tallinna maja*), a two- to three-storey wooden apartment building consisting of single-room rental units, and a backyard garden. Surviving decades of decline and demolition plans, Northern Tallinn has recently experienced a surge of cultural interest and real estate investment. Since the financial crisis of 2008, the district has been consolidated as the city's principal frontier of gentrification, living off the cultural appreciation of the neighbourhood's vernacular atmosphere, which is reminiscent of an idealized past.[27]

There is an ambiguous sense to "potentials" of disused gardens, wastelands, and other ostensibly empty spaces that is repeatedly emphasized by the authors of *Pineapple or Artichoke?*: are these "potentials" aesthetic, economic, or political? The actual gathering of plants took place, ironically, in conjunction with the so-called World Cleanup Day, an annual get-together during which volunteers collect rubbish and other waste, first initiated in Estonia in 2008 and today held in more than 150 countries. The event's peremptory slogan of "Let's do it together!" (*Teeme ära!*), suggests a form of community activism that eludes questions such as how and by whom waste is recognized as waste in the first place, and how cleaning might be imbued with ethnic and class connotations.[28] We might ask whether the museum functions as a medium of appreciating or of cleaning the wastelands of Northern Tallinn. What was being appreciated, and what was being cleaned away while producing the botanical non-site in KUMU?

The removal of plants from Northern Tallinn's disused gardens to the museum, under the communal guise of "Let's do it together!," echoes uneasily the ongoing displacement of predominantly Russian-speaking and working-class inhabitants from that district. It may be that to dissociate the aesthetic value of disused or apparently disused gardens from the capacity to appreciate them aesthetically adds not only to segregation but also to homophily—that is, the idea that segregation is natural because similarity in status and shared cultural values breeds connection and fellowship.[29] The urban pastoralism that is put on display in *Pineapple or Artichoke?* cannot be easily separated from the neo-communitarian politics of place forged at the expense of those who are economically, culturally, and ethnically "other."

According to Leo Marx, "the machine's sudden entrance into the garden presents a problem that ultimately belongs not to art but to politics."[30] The aesthetics of pastoralism, in other words, conveys but cannot resolve the variety of contradictions arising from urbanization in particular moments of history. In contemporary Tallinn, disused gardens evoke pastoral feelings in ways that blur boundaries between the garden and the wasteland. The Baltic variant of urban pastoralism has been animated by the symbolic rejection of socialist mass housing, as well as of post-socialist urban sprawl.

The metaphoric "machine," in the story recounted above, is suburbanization—socialist and post-socialist. If, according to Leo Marx, urbanization and pastoralism were strangely coincidental, then urban pastoralism similarly coincides with gentrification. The aesthetic appreciation of gardens' afterlives is part and parcel of the emerging sensibility for the overgrown and unkempt, most likely to be found today in the formerly working class inner cities. We need, nevertheless, to recognize the limits to that sensibility, insofar as it remains inattentive to its own implications in uneven urban development.

So, can we extend the thoughts of Karl and Leo Marx together by rethinking the questions of property relations and the speculative dynamics of urban value in the light of the aesthetic operations of pastoralism and ever-shifting notions of urban nature? This prospective programme—let's call it urban political aesthetics—would examine how different forms of appreciation are mutually conditioned.[31] It would aim to develop a more nuanced understanding of aesthetic frameworks through which disused gardens, wastelands and other forms of urban natures are categorized, experienced, and judged, and how these frameworks mirror and add to new forms of urban injustice. That programme would not foreclose politics and aesthetics as two standalone realms, but elaborate possibilities for appreciating urban nature differently.

1 John Dixon Hunt, *The afterlife of gardens* (Philadelphia: University of Pennsylvania Press, 2004); Eha Komissarov, ed., *The afterlives of gardens* (Tallinn: KUMU, 2013). *The Afterlives of Gardens* was curated by Eha Komissarov.

2 The exhibit was titled after a 1996 guide on exotic produce: Leopold Meensalu and Gundo Roosve, *Ananass või artišokk: vähetuntud ning eksootilisi puu- ja köögivilju* (Tallinn: Maalehe Raamat, 1996). According to one of the authors, the exhibit's title was agreed prior to its concept and format. Katrin Koov, interview with the author, 16 October 2018.

3 Marcus Owens and Jennifer Wolch, "Rewilding cities," in Nathalie Pettorelli, Sarah M. Durant, and Johan T. du Toit, eds., *Ecological reviews: rewilding* (Cambridge: Cambridge University Press, 2018) pp. 280–302; Ross Exo Adams, "Natura urbans, natura urbanata: ecological urbanism, circulation, and the immunization of nature," *Environment and Planning D: Society and Space* 32 (1) (2014) pp. 12–29.

4 Leo Marx, *The machine in the garden: technology and the pastoral ideal in America* (Oxford: Oxford University Press, 2000 [1964]).

5 Marx, *The machine in the garden*, p. 5. See also Robert A. Beauregard, *When America became suburban* (Minneapolis: University of Minnesota Press, 2006).

6 Neil Smith, "Toward a theory of gentrification: a back to the city movement by capital, not people," *Journal of the American Planning Association* 45, 4 (1979) pp. 538–548. As an example of recent popularization of the aesthetics of the overgrown, see Julian Raxworthy, *Overgrown: practices between landscape architecture and gardening* (Cambridge: MIT Press, 2018). On the politics and aesthetics of wastelands, see Matthew Gandy, "Marginalia: aesthetics, ecology, and urban wastelands," *Annals of the Association of American Geographers* 103, 6 (2013) pp. 1301–1316; Nate Millington, "Nature, representation and ruin in Detroit," *International Journal of Urban and Regional Research* 37, 1 (2013) pp. 279–296. On urban pastoral see Julian Stallabrass, *High Art Lite* (London: Verso, 1999) p. 241, who described the shift, in the British art of the 1990s, of "the site of pastoral from the countryside to the inner city," and Andrew Harris, "Art and gentrification: pursuing the urban pastoral in Hoxton, London," *Transactions of the Institute of British Geographers* 37, 2 (2012) pp. 226–241.

7 Matthew R. Auer, "Environmentalism and Estonia's independence movement," *Nationalities Papers* 26, 4 (1998) pp. 659–676; Jussi Jauhiainen, "Edgar Kant and the rise of modern urban geography," *Geografiska Annaler. Series B, Human Geography* 87, 3 (2005) pp. 193–203.

8 Piret Peiker, "Estonian nationalism through the postcolonial lens," *Journal of Baltic Studies* 47 (1) (2015) pp. 113–132.

9 Merje Feldman, "Urban waterfront regeneration and local governance in Tallinn," *Europe-Asia Studies* 52 (5) (2000) pp. 829–850; Gregory Feldman, "The trap of abstract space: recomposing Russian-speaking immigrants in post-Soviet Estonia," *Anthropological Quarterly* 81 (2) (2008) pp. 311–342.

10 Consider a remark by the neoliberal economist Friedrich Hayek that governments should not limit but "cultivate a growth ... as the gardener does this for his plants." Friedrich A. Hayek, "The pretence of knowledge," *The Swedish Journal of Economics* 77 (4) (1975) pp. 433–442, p. 442.

11 Mart Laar, "Commentary: Europe and recovery," *European View* 8 (2009) pp. 105–106, p. 105.

12 Kadri Leetmaa et al. "Suburbanization in the Tallinn metropolitan area," in Kiril Stanilov and Luděk Sýkora, eds., *Confronting suburbanization: urban decentralization in postsocialist Central and Eastern Europe* (Chichester: Wiley, 2014) pp. 192–224.

13 Susan Noori et al., "Urban allotment garden. A case for place-making," in Simon Bell et al., eds., *Urban allotment gardens in Europe* (Abingdon: Routledge, 2016) pp. 291–320.

14 Kadri Leetmaa et al., "Socialist summer-home settlements in post-Socialist suburbanisation," *Urban Studies* 49 (1) (2012) pp. 3–21.

15 On the change in Mähe, see Lea Ouardi, *Selbstbestimmte Bau- und Wohnkultur in Mähe, Tallinn: Zur Transformation einer sowjetischen Sommerhauskolonie in ein postsowjetisches Wohngebiet,* (MSc dissertation, HafenCity University of Hamburg, 2016).

16 Sander Tint, *Re-framing Soodevahe, re-framing urban agriculture,* MA dissertation, Estonian Academy of Arts (2013); Sander Tint, "The prologue to Soodevahe or how to find a solution, on Brezhnev orders, to the problem of keeping the people fed," in Komissarov, ed., *The afterlives of gardens*, pp. 138–149.

17 A writer described Soodevahe as "squatting done by the elderly." Anna Iltnere, "Lifting the urban environment," *Arterritory*, 15 July 2011 (online at http://www.arterritory.com/en/lifestyle/architecture/185-lifting_the_urban_environment).

18 Valner Valme, "Aiandus vene moodi," *Postimees*, 15 May 2004.

19 Ansip, cited in Anon, "Valitsuse pressikonverentsi stenogramm," *The Government of the Republic of Estonia*, 12 May 2011, https://www.valitsus.ee/et/uudised/valitsuse-pressikonverentsi-stenogramm-12-mai-2011. On the Bronze Night, see Andres Kurg, "The monument of the Bronze Soldier and its publics," in Andreas Trossek, ed., *Kristiina Norman: after-war* (Tallinn: Centre for Contemporary Art, 2009) pp. 49–65.

20 Timo Toots, "Soodevahe," in Komissarov, ed., *The afterlives of gardens*, pp. 132–137; Giusy Checola, "Soodevahe: From the hotbeds to the clouds!," *Institute for Public Art*, 2011 (online at https://www.instituteforpublicart.org/case-studies/soodevahe/).

21 Daniela Sandler, *Counterpreservation: architectural decay in Berlin since 1989* (Ithaca: Cornell University Press, 2016) p. 22.

22 Katrin Koov, interview with the author.

23 Katrin Koov, "Garden Lives," in Komissarov, ed., *The afterlives of gardens*, pp. 120–131, 122 and 128.

24 Katrin Koov, Maria Pukk, and Ivar Lubjak, "Aedade järelelu," 8 May 2013 (online at http://oaasarhitektid.blogspot.com.ee/2013/05/aedade-jarelelu.html).

25 Koov, Pukk, and Lubjak, "Aedade järelelu."

26 Eha Komissarov, "Afterlives of gardens 2," in Komissarov, ed., *The afterlives of gardens*, pp. 10–81, p. 11.

27 Ingmar Pastak and Anneli Kährik, "The impacts of culture-led flagship projects on local communities in the context of post-Socialist Tallinn," *Czech Sociological Review* 52, 6 (2016) pp. 963–990. In 2013, Estonian architectural magazine MAJA coined the term "Kalamajafication," a form of gentrification by preservation termed after a subdistrict of Northern Tallinn, but the debate has eluded other than lifestyle aspects to the process. On preserving idealized urban atmospheres in Tallinn, see Kadri Semm, "Towards the experiential meaning of milieu for neighbourhood regeneration: discussions on the institutional designation of milieu-valued areas in Tallinn, Estonia," *Journal of Housing and the Built Environment* 28 (3) (2013), pp. 489–504.

28 According to the website, during the first Estonian event "people united together to clean up the entire country in just five hours" (https://www.letsdoitworld.org/about/overview/). On the conceptualization of waste in *Teeme ära!*, see Tarmo Pikner and Jussi Jauhiainen, "Dis/appearing waste and afterwards," *Geoforum* 54 (2014) pp. 39–48. On struggles centring on the designation waste, see Jesse Goldstein, "Terra economica: waste and the production of enclosed nature," *Antipode* 45 (2) (2013) pp. 357–375.

29 Homophily is a biological concept adopted in sociology, human ecology, and, recently, in media studies. Paul Lazarsfeld and Robert Merton "Friendship as a social process: a

substantive and methodological analysis," in Morroe Berger, ed., *Freedom and control in modern society* (New York: Van Nostrand, 1954) pp. 18–66; Miller McPherson et al., "Birds of a feather: homophily in social networks," *Annual Review of Sociology* 27 (1) (2001) pp. 415–444. For a critique, see Wendy Chun and Martina Leeker, "Intervening in habits and homophily: make a difference! An interview with Wendy Hui Kyong Chun by Martina Leeker," in Howard Caygill et al., eds., *Interventions in digital cultures: technology, the political, methods* (Lüneburg: Meson Press, 2017) pp. 75–86.

30 Marx, *The machine in the garden*, p. 365.

31 Such a project would build upon a tradition of critical landscape studies, such as Dennis Cosgrove, *Social formation and symbolic landscape* (Madison: University of Wisconsin Press, 1998); Kenneth Olwig, *Landscape, nature, and the body politic* (Madison: University of Wisconsin Press, 2002). See also Ed Wall and Tim Waterman, eds., *Landscape and agency: critical essays* (Abingdon: Routledge, 2017). On the concept of appreciation, see Michel Feher, *Rated agency: investee politics in a speculative age* (New York: Zone Books, 2018).

Tokyo ecology: the Akabane Nature Observation Park

Kumiko Kiuchi

The starting point for this essay emerged from an attempt to find a park in Tokyo similar to Berlin's Natur-Park Südgelände, which opened in the year 2000 on the site of former railway yards. The management of vegetation at Südgelände is carefully calibrated to allow different types of ecological succession to either flourish or be held in a state of suspended animation on a mix of aesthetic and scientific grounds.[1] The search for an equivalent in Tokyo initially seemed feasible. There are a number of large areas of unused vacant land in the reclaimed spaces around Tokyo Bay which have been left abandoned for years. Nature should have reclaimed some of them. In addition, cherishing wild plants appears to resonate with Japanese aesthetics. It still survives in the world of *haiku* and in the customs on the Japanese calendar: they are connected to wild plants (for example, the day of *nanakusa* when people eat rice porridge with seven wild plants). However, it proved to be more difficult to find an equivalent for the most radical features of Südgelände Park. As it turned out, the alien plants are often treated as "extra" in the sense that they are not usually considered as part of "potential natural vegetation": the concept that outlines how vegetation can exist without human intervention. Urban parks in Japan do not generally welcome the spontaneous presence of non-native species, as their expansion is believed to endanger native species. In this respect, the interest in spontaneous vegetation that has developed in Berlin, with links to ideas of "cosmopolitan ecology," is unlike ecological discourse in Japan.

The image of "weeds" or *zasso*, whose literal meaning is a mixture (雑*zatsu*) of plants (草*sou*) in Japanese, is not necessarily negative. Usage in Japanese literature suggests that *zasso* means not just a weed that prevents the growth of target plants but more broadly unnamed or insignificant plants growing wild, which contrasts with "wild plants" (*yasou*), the term people use when they try to "identify" the name of the plants.[2] In this sense, *zasso* or a place characterized by *zasso* can be considered an environment rather than a group of specific plants. *Zasso* is inextricably entwined with Japanese urban space, or rather with *akichi*, a plot of vacant land left unused for a certain period of time, or an open grass field or *harappa*, usually found on the edge of urban space along rivers or on reclaimed lands. Urban nostalgia for *akichi* and *harappa* is a recurring theme in Japanese literature. The image is prominent in the writing of those who were brought up in and around urban areas, not to mention in *Doraemon*, one of the best known manga/animations, in which *akichi* serve as hideaways for children. The Japanese architect Jun Aoki explains that the attraction of *akichi* is characterized by "a pile of earthen pipes and gravel ... where land lacks its original purpose"; it is an oasis that secures children freedom to choose and invent their new games.[3] Although Aoki does not touch on the presence of *zasso* in *akichi*, it is hard to find examples of *akichi* that are not illustrated with *zasso*.

On the other hand, the Japanese literary critic Takeo Okuno further explores the association of vacant land with childhood, concluding that it evokes the indelible landscape of childhood for those who are from urban areas and can never feel part of the authentic and natural landscape of the countryside. He also points out the ambivalent nature of a vacant plot: it is land whose empty appearance invites "intruders," yet it gives them the sense of "being monitored" at the same time because the assumption is that its owner does exist and is absent only temporarily. The sense that "you are not supposed to step in" is also associated with *chirei* or *genius loci*, connecting with "the spirits residing in the ground."[4] In Japan, even in urban areas, the belief still survives that every parcel of land is protected by a god. A ritual called *jichinsai* is still practiced around the country, in which the shinto priest prays to gods for permission to use a building site before any construction work begins. When tourists spot a shrine among skyscrapers, they are mostly fox shrines which are known for occasioning divine punishment when they are moved. Thus, vacant land evokes a strange combination of feelings of nostalgia, freedom, the allure of place and fear of violation, a feeling for and connections with the spiritual realm. I was hoping in the name of urban nostalgia to find a patch of land reclaimed from the rubble leftover from war-time destruction, nurturing the natural succession of the vegetation of weeds.

A reply from one of the city councils in Tokyo, which houses a number of early reclaimed sites constructed between the seventeeth century and the pre-war period in Tokyo Bay, was very brief. They had no vacant land, no record of monitoring weeds; they see parks as something planned and managed, not left untouched.[5] It did not take long to find out that the science of vegetation in Japan does not usually recognize a history of vegetation on reclaimed lands.[6] Yoshinobu Hoshino, professor at Tokyo University of Agriculture and Technology, the leading specialist on vegetation science and board member of the committee responsible for planning the Akabane Nature Observation Park, explains to me how to track down the original vegetation of land in urban areas, which, as a result of constant human interventions, do not usually retain their original vegetation. "We survey relatively untouched land in its vicinity, usually the grove of temples or shrines." He explains they are considered sacred and left relatively undisturbed. To my question about the possibility of a reclaimed site acquiring its own history of vegetation, his reply

was twofold. As for the Central Break Water Inner Landfill Site, one of the newest reclaimed islands in Tokyo Bay, he says that it "is located in the sea. There is no nature to consult around the vicinity. In such a case, a common practice is to plant a typical coastal vegetation in the area." On the other hand, he points to the case of the Hama-Rikyu Gardens, which were built on reclaimed land from the Edo Period, and acknowledges the possibility of identifying its potential natural vegetation.[7]
And yet sites reclaimed in the twentieth century may not be granted the same significance: they contain too many random substances, owing to a mix of gravel, rubble, and garbage, and they were not brought in from within Tokyo but also from outside, which makes it extremely difficult to understand the nature of the soil. This is because sites of this type are more likely to lack any historical continuity in soils in the first place. Reclaimed land is constructed nature: its origin is not natural. For that reason, there is no way of making assumptions about either its original or potential natural vegetation. Grass has grown on the site for the past hundred years, and yet this process cannot constitute the earlier history of vegetation. At this point, reclaimed land sites have to be taken off the list of my search for Südgelände Park in Tokyo.
Limiting my search to the "minimum management" of a park has caused me to discover the park which is the focus of this essay: the Akabane Nature Observation Park. The park is located in Kita City in the northeast of Tokyo's 23 Districts. It was the first nature observation park or "urban ecology park" to be constructed in an urban area in Japan.[8] It is unique in being secured as a "nature conservation

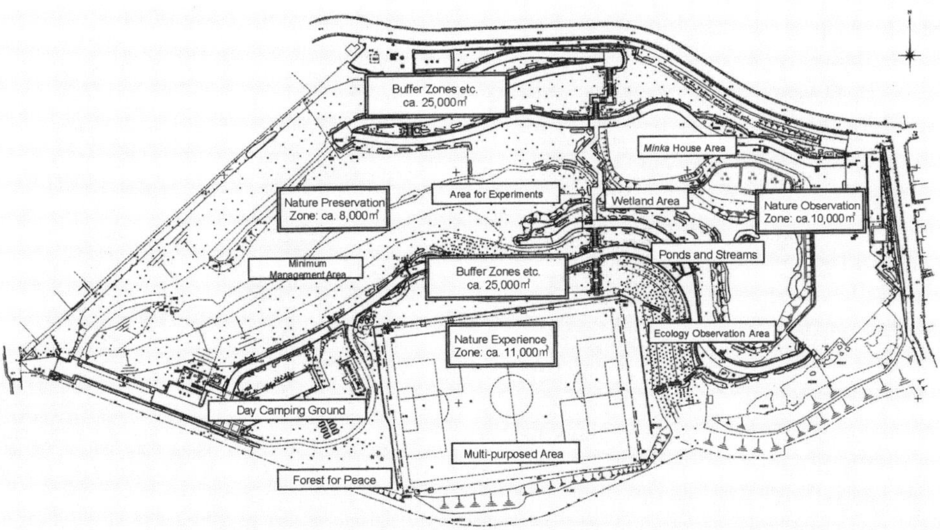

"The Zoning Plan" of Akabane Nature Observation Park. Source: *Akabane Nature Observation Park Volunteer Group, Akabane Nature Observation Park 10th Anniversary Booklet* (Tokyo: Akabane Nature Observation Park Volunteer Group, 2010).

zone" where wild plants grow with minimum human intervention. The intention is to observe the natural succession of plants, while allowing vegetation to display autonomous forms of change and resilience.[9] This park would not have been possible without the contributions and passion of Hiroyuki Kamei. Kamei, as a student at Tokyo University of Agriculture and Technology, was part of the laboratory of Professor Kiyoshi Okutomi, one of the foremost scholars in the field of vegetation science in Japan. After his graduation, Kamei began working for the Roads and Park Section of Kita City Council, managing local parks and public green spaces. As a life-long scholar in the field, he was critical of a post-war national afforestation policy that resulted in 40 percent of the existing forest (10 million hectares) across the country being turned into plantations, leading not only to the loss of biodiversity but also to huge maintenance costs.[10] Aided in his research by stalwart collaboration from his friends and colleagues, he conceived of the "nature conservation zone" as an experimental site for observing plants' autonomous recovery and how it creates a new environment. At the same time, gaining the support of the local council and residents was key to the materialization of the park. From a very early stage, the park project involved a number of local volunteers, who discussed ideas about the park and worked to materialize them. The deep commitment of the local residents also appears to be tied to the history of the land.

The site of Akabane Nature Observation Park (5-2 Akabane West, Kita City, Tokyo), which opened in March 1999, is located at the north-eastern edge of Musashino Plateau, one of the largest diluvial tablelands in Japan, covering 846 square kilometres of the Tokyo metropolitan area. Musashino Plateau houses a number of archaeological sites that date back to the Jōmon Period (14000–400 BCE).[11] The Plateau's geological formations are often characterized by the red-brown loam stratum (called Kantō Loam) consisting of the volcanic ashes of surrounding mountains between 50,000 and 10,000 BCE. The place name "Akabane" incorporates *aka* meaning the colour red because of the loam; *aka* appears in a number of other place names on the plateau.[12]

Kamei saw the potential of the land, with its valley-shaped structure located at the cliff line, and the water springing from the loam, which offered a good environment for the vegetation.[13] He found traces of pollen on the site dating back to 1000–2000 years ago, and other traces on a hill downstream from 5000–6000 years ago. By analyzing the pollen from the Jōmon period with reference to a map of the ancient vegetation, Kamei concluded that the ultimate community of the local vegetation should be a combination of evergreen and deciduous forest zones.[14] As there was no existing record of the natural succession of the zone, let alone the site, it was impossible to get site data for the places where natural vegetation hardly remained because of long-term military use and development of the land. He consulted a general model of the natural succession on the Kanto Plain[15] and surveyed local vegetation characterized mainly by ruderal species such as *Setaria viridis*, *Conyza sumatrensis*, and *Taraxacum officinale*, as well as native species including *Castanopsis sieboldii*, *Aphananthe aspera*, *Celtis sinensis* in the forests, and *Phragmites australis* and *Schoenoplectus triqueter* growing beside the water.[16]

However, the land on which the park was to be built was being employed to store used caterpillar vehicles, rail tracks, a chemical storage unit, and other waste materials underground, together with war rubble, some of which still remains on the site today.[17] Although Kamei mentions very little about its past history, its association with the military was long-standing. By 1927, the site had been incorporated into the Japanese Imperial Army ordnance depot, where weapons were stored, repaired, exchanged, distributed, and disposed of.[18] After World War II, the U.S. Army occupied the site to use it as Division 2 of the Tokyo Ordnance Depot (TOD), where a tank practice ground existed. When the site was returned to Japanese control in 1958, it was reallocated to the Japanese Self-Defense Army, who continued to be stationed there until the early 1990s. In 1988, it became a candidate site for the release of land on the government list.[19] This coincided with the publication of the *Environment White Paper* in 1987, which promotes the installation of "urban ecology parks." The term is defined in 5.1(3) of the paper as signifying "nature observation park where people can make contact with small animals such as wild birds."[20] The Ministry of Construction initially planned to build new accommodation for officials on the site.[21] After a protracted negotiation with the government, the land was paid off to the City Council for 13.3 billion yen, and the park was to be maintained as an "urban ecology park."[22] Considering the fact that it took eleven years from the inception to the opening of the park, it is assumed that the idea to include the "nature preservation zone" in the park must have been present from a very early stage in order to negotiate the terms and conditions.[23]

Strictly speaking, the land was paid off, not released, and the development of the site is intertwined with the history of Kita City. The release of the military land had been a long-term aspiration for the council and its residents since the end of World War II. Over 10 percent of the Council area was occupied by the military base and its related business corporations toward the end of the war. Kita City became a repeated target of aerial bombardment in 1945, with devastating consequences. In the aftermath, the municipality lacked housing, green spaces, and public facilities. Petitions demanding the release of the military base began immediately after the war, and portions of the land were gradually returned to the council. The San Francisco Treaty stipulated that occupied land was to be returned to Japan within 90 days, but Article 6 granted exceptions to the U.S. Army, which were applied to the TOD sites.[24] The parliament of the city council continued to pass unanimous resolutions demanding that the land be released on the grounds that they needed more space to secure green space and public welfare for residents (in 1963, 1972, and 1987).[25] During the Vietnam War in 1968, a number of activists organized a series of huge protests, both against the construction of a "field hospital" and against the relocation of Johnson Hospital to U.S. Camp Ōji, fearing increased noise from military convoys and potential epidemics spread by returning soldiers from Vietnam. Over 220,000 people (at a rough estimate, more than half the entire population) signed the petition to demand the return of the land to the Council in 1971. A portion of the ex-TOD land was returned to build a park and facilities for people with disabilities.[26] In the early 1990s, public opinion was geared toward the acceptance of the Self-Defense Army, exemplified by legislation enabling their peacekeeping operation in the Gulf. No resolution has been passed by the Kita City Council since 1987. The acquisition may have been a last straw in order to secure the land for public use.

The 5.5 hectares of the park today are divided into four zones: a Nature Protection Zone (Zone A with 8,000 square metres), a Nature Observation Zone (Zone B with 10,000 square metres), a Nature Experience Zone (Zone C with 11,000 square metres), and a buffer Zone (Zone D with 25,000 square metres).[27] The original valley structure was restored, and height differences were used to separate Zone A from Zone C. Zone A was allocated as the valley to make the most of the spring water from the ground. The water flows from Zone A to Zone B, allowing children to touch water and interact with aquatic animals such as crayfish. Footpaths were installed in the middle of the hill between Zones A and C to go down to Zone B so that visitors can have a view of Zone A, which is completely fenced off at the ground. Zone C is on top of the hill, minimizing interference with Zone A. This zoning system was an adaptation of the 1974 UNESCO Biosphere Reserve model, cited by Kamei in his 2015 lecture.[28] The 1974 UNESCO model quoted by Kamei locates the core area in the centre which is used for research and educational purposes; the surrounding buffer zone consists of facilities that restore the land's traditional usage, research facilities, and the land for the recovery of local vegetation; and the outer transitional area can also be used for residential purposes.[29] In the model of Akabane Nature Observation Park, Kamei roughly adopts this zoning, but modifies the definition of the core zone exclusively for the recovery of plants.

Based on this ground design, local volunteers were gathered and soon divided into smaller groups to discuss the details of each zone. Despite an unusual proposal of having a nature protection zone in a public park, locals responded fairly positively to the plan at the beginning. They did not see it as the protection of "weeds"; they liked the vision of a barren stretch of land devastated by military use regaining its original nature. The local magazine *Machi-kara* wrote that the park would fulfill the wishes of the residents in Kita City who wanted *harappa* rather than a park with recreational facilities, and received plenty of support.[30] One local saw it as a "symbol of peace" after long-term military use.[31] Another expressed the will to restore the original forest of Musashino Plateau; and another saw in it an association with the "forest of Totoro," based on the 1988 influential film by Hayao Miyazaki featuring the natural world reminiscent of the Musashino Plateau in the Jōmon period, where nature was untamed before irrigation began in Yayoi period.[32]

However, the initial excitement deflated as discussions on Zone C became antagonistic over the definition of "recreational purposes." One group favoured using the site for sports, whereas the other wished to use it for nature-oriented activities.[33] Some petitions were submitted to the council in order to put pressure on the course of the discussions.[34] The council was inclined to avoid any conflict with the locals because the project received the accreditation "urban ecology park" from the Ministry of Construction. Articles in *Machi-kara* reported a sulky atmosphere at the meetings, and published critical viewpoints asking why a park should be

The source of the spring water located in the Nature Preservation Zone flows downstream to the Nature Observation Zone to form a natural stream, 2019. Photo: Kumiko Kiuchi.

constructed for such an enormous budget and then keep residents out with fencing. It also questions the significance of Zone A by wrongly describing it as the equivalent of a small botanical garden, with doubts over its comparison with larger existing gardens in Tokyo.[35] There were a series of misunderstandings, confrontations, and disappointments along the way.

To resolve the conflict, the municipal authorities decided to secure a multi-purposed space for sports which was to become Zone C. Meanwhile, the discussion on the definition of "nature" did not easily resolve, and quite a few volunteers left the process, while another dedicated group remained.[36] During construction, the ground was entirely dug up to remove military waste and most of the plants. Kamei, as the manager of vegetation, made sure that the existing green spaces relevant to the recovery of natural vegetation were left untouched. Water plants were kept and replanted, and the original soil was sprinkled on the new ground so as to increase the probability that the same plants would return. Soil was mostly kept on site so as to retain the integrity of the ground.[37] In a couple of years a field of perennial plants grew where there had been completely barren land, while some young plants of *Cornus controversa* began to emerge.[38]

However, it took time for the locals to understand Kamei's approach. Some neighbours complained about "weeds" growing not only in Zone A, but in other Zones in the park[39] and that there were no trees growing on site.[40] Even the volunteers who were assigned to manage the plants which would impede a healthy transition of the natural succession mistakenly removed entire ivy plants instead of just cutting the stems as instructed. Kamei observes that both parties loathe the sight of untamed weeds, underlining the importance of gaining their understanding for the concept of the nature conservation zone.[41] Fortunately, by 2005, trees began to grow and a wider varieties of plants and animals came to be observed.[42] They picked up the seeds of *Quercus acutissima* and *Quercus serrata* and planted them in the park to help restore the Jōmon forest. The park as a symbol of peace (the idea once rejected by the Kita Council on the grounds that the park should not serve a political purpose) partly materialized with the planting of a tree which grew out of the seed taken from a persimmon tree exposed to the atomic bomb in Nagasaki on August 9 1945.[43] In closing this 2010 volume of Akabane Volunteers, Kamei evaluates very positively the recovery of vegetation on the site and suggests the possibility of further introducing aquatic animals while considering the vision of biodiversity that the park should aim for in the future.[44]

Kamei's essay "What I want to pass on to children in the 21st century: messages from the conservation of vegetation" elaborates on his theoretical position behind the idea for the park. What we should note here is his proposal concerning "semi-natural vegetation," which results from human interventions and plants'

Children searching for small aquatic animals in the stream, 2019. Photo: Kumiko Kiuchi.

natural succession. He proposes to clearly distinguish the semi-natural vegetation managed by humans from what happens when plants' natural succession is left to take place. The latter is often measured by the criteria of the former and is thus consistently underestimated despite its potential to empower the autonomous recovery of vegetation. It is often considered sparse vegetation, on account of an insufficient quantity of plants and deflected forms of succession.[45] Kamei's claim is that interventions into the semi-natural vegetation are not necessarily effective from a conservation point of view because they can often turn the clock of the natural succession back to the beginning, so that "unsound" vegetation merely re-emerges. Vegetation can change from artificial to semi-artificial, then ultimately toward a natural state when human interventions are kept to a minimum to assist with vegetation's autonomous recovery.[46] "An urban environment is not natural for vegetation, which means that it needs some maintenance. But in principle, vegetation should be left untouched. It can evolve autonomously."[47] Kamei believes that the management with minimum interventions will reduce running costs and lead to new ways to approach the problems of "dilapidated" semi-natural vegetation.

Akabane Nature Observation Park challenges vegetation scientists and urban designers who mistrust semi-natural vegetation and its autonomous recovery. Some experts welcome this experiment. The ecologist Yoshiyuki Hioki praises the park by writing the concept of "autonomous recovery" as "an exceptional attempt" taken up by an urban park.[48] Hoshino's assessment is that the park has provided data on the possibilities and limits for restoring nature in an urban environment, which is useful for future projects. What will be the future of Akabane Nature Observation Park? Kamei is no longer here to answer the question. Hoshino, who has been monitoring the site for 20 years, trusts that the Nature Conservation Zone will remain closed, and that the monitoring will continue to witness the natural succession of the vegetation. His unpublished research has so far verified that the proportion of local species has increased compared to the zones where vegetation is not protected. An anonymous spokesperson of the Park and Road Section of Kita City Council agrees with the importance of conservation but hopes that in the long run the zone can be opened up (even temporarily) to the residents, since, after all, the park is supposed to serve their interests.[49] Dr Shinichi Katada of Tokyo Kasei University, who also monitors the site on a regular basis, shares Takahashi's view, writing that a public park should in principle be open to the public.[50]

Akabane Nature Observation Park is an embodiment of the ecological characteristics of the Jōmon soil, the people's assiduous desire for the release of the military base for public use, and their strong aspiration for green space and public facilities, not to mention Kamei's passion for the autonomous recovery of vegetation. The process of the park's creation reveals the actual perception of "weeds" in Japanese culture, and an emphasis on a tamed wilderness, regarding it as "natural" and casually managing nature without considering its alterity. This is attested by the attitudes of some management-oriented vegetation scientists, as well as neighbours' complaints and volunteers' initial misunderstanding of the concept of the maintenance of the Nature Conservation Zone in the park. The park illustrates the process by which people come to learn the alterity of spontaneous urban vegetation. However, in comparison with Südgelände Park, Akabane may reveal the desire to return to the "origin" of the land; many volunteers shared the image of Jōmon forest as a blueprint for the park. The other side of the coin is that most signs of the military history of the site have been erased. One might see this operation as a selective restoration or repainting of the image of the land. Where has its history gone? Only the trees that were left and the soil that was sprinkled onto the site still bear its traces.

So, where does the concept of Südgelände Park take us in Tokyo? It seems to overlap (at least to my eyes) with the view expressed by the writer Yuichiro Ishikawa, who surveyed the soil of reclaimed lands in Tokyo Bay in the 1980s. Ishikawa took pleasure in digging the soil of reclaimed lands. He witnessed a chaos, with all sorts of vegetables growing from house waste and animals running wild on the newly reclaimed rich soil, consisting solely of human waste: "We should segregate this bare land for a very long time and keep it as a scientific site for biodiversity."[51] Now, the Central Breakwater is completed, and the Sea Forest Park is under construction. The plants and trees are selected from native varieties of the Kanto region to be in harmony with local species.[52] And yet the nature preservation site that was in the original plan of 2005 has made its way to the Water Stadium for the 2020 Olympics.[53] It may take a century or centuries for the reclaimed lands to be released from the spell of "no history," to be surveyed and recognized as a stratum of the Anthropocene. Until then, the potential of this comparison will remain unknown.

1 See Matthew Gandy's documentary *Natura Urbana: The Brachen of Berlin* (2017). I would like to thank Professor Yoshinobu Hoshino and the anonymous spokesperson of the Road and Park Section of Kita Council for providing important information and various materials on the park. Without their assistance, this report would not have been possible.

2 National Institute for Japanese Language and Linguistics, *Kotonoha Shonagon Japanese Corpus* (last accessed 3 May 2018: http://www.kotonoha.gr.jp/shonagon/). The title and the content of all Japanese sources are my translation. The list of references in Japanese is available on https://drive.google.com/drive/folders/1XK5iRytM7SW0DKglSZxVkZUrTVyAYNfZ.

3 Jun Aoki, "'Open field' and 'Amusement park,'" *Open field and amusement park* (Tokyo: Lixil Publishing, 2004) pp.11–12.

4 Takeo Okuno, *Indelible landscape in literature revised edition* (Tokyo: Shūeisha, 1989) pp. 77–83

5 Section of Water and Green, Chuo City, Tokyo, personal interview, 15 March 2019.

6 Yoshinobu Hoshino, personal interview, 6 April 2019; Anonymous, Bureau of Port and Harbor of Tokyo Metropolitan Government, personal interview, 23 April 2019 (hereafter abbreviated as BPH Tokyo).

7 Ref. Hiroshi Nakajima, "Planting, maintenance and future challenges of cultural heritage gardens: focusing on Kyu-Hamarikyu Gardens," *Journal of the Academic Society of Japanese Gardens* 32 (2018) pp. 35–40.

8 Kita City Council Construction Committee, "6 July Heisei 7," *Proceedings in Heisei 7* (Tokyo: Kita City Council, 1995) p.11.

9 There are a number of *ryokuchi* or open green spaces, along the River Arakawa in Tokyo. Arakawa Todabashi Green Space has a biological and ecological garden (newly

opened in March 2018) with no human interventions, see http://www.city.itabashi.tokyo.jp/c_kurashi/091/091499.html. Itabashi City Council, which manages the site, has never undertaken on-site monitoring and has no plan to do so at the moment.

10 Hiroyuki Kamei, "What I would like to pass on to children in 21st century: message from vegetation science," *Vegetation Science News* 19 (2015a) p. 73. This afforestation policy also results in a notorious pollen allergy problem occasioned by artificially planted pine trees in the country, which now account for 18 percent of the entire forest in Japan. See the link of the Ministry of Agriculture, Forestry and Fisheries of Japan: http://www.rinya.maff.go.jp/j/sin_riyou/kafun/qanda.html (last accessed 24 August 2019).

11 Naoto Suzuki, "Archaeology of Kita City in view of the recent excavation," *Society for the History of Kita City Bulletin* 40 (1996) pp. 4–5. There is a view that regards Jōmon as the origin of Japanese culture in its unique craftwork, its animism, its hunter-gatherer livelihood and/or its untouched nature before the introduction of irrigation systems. See the following websites: Tokyo National Museum, special exhibition "Jōmon: 10,000 years of prehistoric art in Japan," http://jomon-kodo.jp/ (last accessed 3 May 2019); Wakasa Mikata Jōmon Museum, https://www.town.fukui-wakasa.lg.jp/jomon/ (last accessed 3 May 2019).

12 Kiyomi Tsunoda, "Deciphering Musashino Plateau with a geographer," *Musashino Jurin* 1 (2018) p. 19.

13 Hiroyuki Kamei and Motoo Okazawa, "Construction project of Akabane Nature Observation Park: part 1," *Public Parks* 146 (1999) p. 34.

14 Hiroyuki Kamei, "What Akabane Nature Observation aims to achieve," public lecture, Fureai Hall, Akabane Tree Park for Sports, 15 September 2015, slide 21 (hereafter cited as 2015c).

15 The succession is described from the annual plants such as *Chenopodium album* and *Amaranthus blitum* to perennial plants including *Erigeron annuus* and *Oenothera biennis*. This is followed by the emergence of low shrubs of *Rosa multiflora* between four and six years; from the tenth year onwards low height trees such as *Rhus javanica* are observed; from the thirtieth year onwards *Quercus serrata*, *Cornus controversa* and *Padus grayana*; over 150 years *Castanopsis sieboldii* and *Machilus thunbergii* (ibid. slide 13)

16 Ibid., slides 7–8.

17 Akabane Nature Observation Park Volunteer Group, *Akabane Nature Observation Park Year Book Vol. 2.* January 1998–March 1999, (Tokyo: Akabane Park Volunteer Group, 2000) p. iii; Hoshino.

18 Shinichi Negishi, *Survey Report of Kita City Local Museum* 1 (1983) pp. 3, 8–9.

19 Akabane Nature Observation Park Volunteer Group (2000) p. 3

20 Department of the Environment, *Environment White Paper 1987*, (last accessed 5 May 2019: https://www.env.go.jp/policy/hakusyo/s62/6589.html). The term is redefined in the *Environmental Policy Outline* published by the Ministry of Construction in 1994 as the "nature observation park (urban ecology park), which provides small animals such as wild birds with a habitat and promotes the conservation of high-quality green environment involving species representative of the area, allowing contacts between humans and other creatures" (II.5⑦). (See: http://www.mlit.go.jp/sogoseisaku/envi/epomoc.htm#t2_5). Most of the "urban ecopark" focuses on small creatures and the recovery of their habitat so as to maximize the potential for the enhancement of biodiversity. In that Akabane features vegetation that prepares ground for such biodiversity, it is quite original as an urban ecology park project, see Tohru Morioka, et al., "Analysis and evaluation of spatial linkage of biotopes in and around urban ecology park," *Environmental Systems Research* 25 (1997) pp. 51–58.

21 National Diet Library, *National Diet Proceedings Search System*, "112th Session of the First Division of the Committee on Budge in *The Proceedings of the House of Representatives*," (1988) p. 30 (last accessed 27 April 2019: http://kokkai.ndl.go.jp/SENTAKU/syugiin/112/0384/11203090384001.pdf).

22 Kamei and Okazawa, "Construction project of Akabane Nature Observation Park: part 1," p. 34.
23 Hoshino, personal interview.
24 Research Committee of the History of Kita City, *History of Kita City: chronology modern history* (Tokyo: Kita City, 1996) pp. 500–507.
25 Kita City Council, *Proceedings of Kita City Council: Showa 47 Fourth Session No. 14–17* (1972) pp. 351–354; *Proceedings of Kita City Council: Showa 48 Third Session No. 10–12* (1973) pp. 213–216; *Proceedings of Kita City Council: Showa 62 First Session No. 1–4* (1987) pp. 375–380. In 1975, a majority of the councillors supported a resolution, see: *Proceedings of Kita City Council: Showa 50 Fourth Session No. 2–7* (1975) pp. 522–526.
26 Research Committee of the History of Kita City, *History of Kita City*, pp. 639–644.
27 Kamei and Okazawa, "Construction project of Akabane Nature Observation Park: part 1," p. 35; Akabane Nature Observation Park, "Park Map," (last accessed 28 March 2019:https://www.city.kita.tokyo.jp/d-douro/bunka/koenichiran/documents/attachment_1_2.pdf).
28 UNESCO's "Man and the Biosphere Programme" was launched in 1976. The model Kamei refers to may be a work-in-progress version, although it does not much differ from the current UNESCO model, see UNESCO, "Zoning Schemes," (last accessed 3 May 2019: http://www.unesco.org/new/en/natural-sciences/environment/ecological-sciences/biosphere-reserves/main-haracteristics/zoning-schemes/).
29 Kamei, "What Akabane Nature Observation aims to achieve," slide 24.
30 Toshihiko Toyoda, "A desirable park," *Machi-kara* 22 (1996) p. 6.
31 Yasuko Hashimoto, "Romantic dream project: Akabane Nature Observation Park," *Machi-kara* 22 (1996) p. 5.
32 Akabane Nature Observation Park Volunteer Group (2000) pp. 3–16.
33 Ibid., pp. 3–13.
34 Kita City Council. *Proceedings of Kita City Council No. 8* (1992) p. 175; *Proceedings of Kita City Council No.10* (1995) pp. 185–186.
35 Takehiko Honma, "What is a multi-purposed space!!," *Machi-kara* 10 (1997) pp. 6–8.
36 Akabane Nature Observation Park Volunteer Group, *Akabane Nature Observation Park 10th anniversary booklet* (Tokyo: Akabane Nature Observation Park Volunteer Group, 2010) pp. 41–42.
37 Hiroyuki Kamei, "Construction project of Akabane Nature Observation Park: part 2," *Public Parks* 148 (2000) pp. 16–17.
38 Hiroyuki Kamei, "How the activities of volunteers influence the natural recovery of vegetation in Akabane Nature Observation Park," *JILA Technical Reports of Landscape Architecture* 1 (2001) p. 134.
39 Ibid., p. 133.
40 Akabane Nature Observation Park Volunteer Group, 2010, p. 1.
41 Kamei, "How the activities of volunteers influence the natural recovery of vegetation in Akabane Nature Observation Park," pp. 133–134.
42 Akabane Nature Observation Park Volunteer Group, 2010, p. 1. Looking back, Kamei summarise that from fifth year onwards *Mallotus japonicus* began to grow among the local species such as *Clerodendrum trichotomum, Phragmites australis, Miscanthus sinensis,* and the persistent *Solidago canadensis var. scabra* which are often considered as to be a notoriously invasive species here. This vegetation has gradually been replaced by trees that the volunteers planted as well as *Cornus controversa, Aphananthe aspera, Magnolia kobus,* and *Carpinus tschonoskii* (Kamei, "What Akabane Nature Observation aims to achieve," slide 37).
43 Kita City Council Construction Committee, *Construction Committee of Kita City Council Proceedings of Heisei 7* (1995): 10 verso. ref. "Revive time: Kaki Tree Project" (last accessed 28 May 2019: https://kakitreeproject.com/).
44 Akabane Nature Observation Park Volunteer Group, 2010, p. 54.
45 Kamei, "What I would like to pass on to children in 21st century: message from vegetation science," pp. 64–65, p. 71.
46 Ibid., p. 72.

47 Kamei, "What Akabane Nature Observation aims to achieve," p. 76.
48 Yoshiyuki Hioki, "Mitigation in urban space," *Shintoshi* 56 (11) (2002) pp. 19–20.
49 Road and Park Section of Kita City Council, Tokyo, private interview, 16 April 2019.
50 Shinichi Katada, "Re: Concerning Akabane Nature Observation Park in Kita City," 23 April 2019, email.
51 Yūichirō Ishikawa, *Wandering in reclaimed land* (Tokyo: Rural Culture Association Japan, 1991) p. 226.
52 PBH Tokyo, personal interview.
53 Jyunichi, Watanabe, "Construction of 'Sea Forest' in the central breakwater inner landfill site," *Public Parks* 180 (2008) p. 29; Bureau of Port and Harbor, "Sea Forest," (last accessed 16 April 2019: https://www.kouwan.metro.tokyo.lg.jp/kanko/uminomorileaflet2018en.pdf).

Red leaves

Suili Xiao

In the field of critical urban studies, Beijing is perhaps best known for its vast expansion in recent years, plus the dramatic and often brutal reconstruction of old neighbourhoods and the high levels of air pollution that threatened the viability of the 2008 Olympics. Less widely recognized, however, is the emerging discussion about the value of urban nature and the significance of undeveloped land for aesthetic appreciation and public recreation. Over the last ten years, urban environmental discourse in China has been characterized by increasing interest in facets of urban design such as "eco-city construction," "ecological infrastructure," and other international dimensions to what might be termed "urban greening."

For visitors to Beijing in the autumn, one of the most striking landscapes that they might encounter is the Xishan hills located in the west of the metropolitan area. As the weather cools in late October, and the first frosts are experienced, the entire landscape erupts into a fiery vista of "red leaves" that has been a source of inspiration for artists, poets, and increasingly for the wider population.

The scene is captured in the work of the artist Keran Li in his painting *Wan Shan Hong Bain* (万山红遍) which roughly translates as "Thousands of hills in a crimsoned view." Keran Li's depiction of the autumn colours of Xishan was painted in the early 1960s, but it is rendered in the classical tradition of Chinese landscape painting known as Shanshui (山水画) which evolved many centuries earlier.[1] Li's work is an explicit homage to Mao Zedong, who described "a thousand hills crimsoned" in a nationalist paean which enlisted the natural world into his larger political project. "Under a frosty sky," wrote Mao, "all creatures strive for freedom."[2] As if the trees themselves, through bursting into colour, were lending support for a wider programme of societal transformation. It is important to recognize, however, that in the early 1950s the Xishan hills were a destroyed landscape: almost all of the original forest has been cleared away, often in desperation as a source of fuel for cooking and heating. All that survived were a few scattered trees amidst the debris of war, as well as the impact of mining, quarrying, and other industrial activities. What Keran Li presents in his painting is not a "natural landscape" in any sense, or even a space with a high degree of ecological continuity, but a landscape undergoing a large-scale process of reconstruction and afforestation. In the newly created communist state, forestry was to play a key role in "green space

Thousands of Hills in a Crimsoned View （万山红遍，Wan Shan Hong Bian) (1964). Courtesy of 中国画库 (Chinese Painting Gallery).

construction" and regional development.[3] The afforestation plans for the Xishan hills were undertaken with the slogan of "greening first, beautifying followed" as part of a wider state instituted transformation of the existing landscape. While it once languished in relative obscurity, the art of Keran Li is now back in vogue, and the steeply rising prices for his work reflect the emerging tastes of wealthy collectors, with an interest in "authentic" types of Chinese landscapes.The large-scale afforestation "campaign" for the Xishan hills was carried out in the late 1950s using some 600,000 labourers, drawn mainly from the People's Liberation Army. The "conquering of nature" through this vast public works project resulted in the planting of nearly 3,500 hectares of forest. This was followed by the introduction of "scientific forest management" by the Xishan Forest Farm created in 1962 as part of a wider impetus towards the maintenance of large-scale landscapes for scenery and recreation. The underlying principles of forestry through mass mobilization persist today and, reflected in events such as the annual Arbor Day that encourages public participation in the care and maintenance of forest trees.

The hills and mountains in the western part of Beijing cover approximately one-sixth of the metropolitan area (as defined by the urban municipality). Long before the destruction and reconstruction of this landscape, the area had served for many centuries as a place of refuge or religious worship for city dwellers. This area had always been an intricate patchwork of different cultures of nature, including temples and imperial gardens as well as more "natural" fragments of the original forest at the edge of the city. The growing popularity of the Xishan hills is thus woven into a much longer history of urban interactions with nature. Every autumn there is now a "red leaves festival" that attracts hundreds of thousands of visitors. Increasing public use has forced environmental managers to adopt more sophisticated measures to protect environmentally sensitive areas, including the recent creation of "ecological conservation zones." As a recognition of the complex balancing act between social and environmental objectives, the area has now been designated as the Xishan National Forest Park with intense and on-going levels of governmental intervention.

By the 1990s, after 40 years of large-scale tree planting efforts, the Xishan hills had achieved a forest cover of over 90 percent through a combination of both human endeavour and natural succession. Interest in "forest tourism" had also grown steadily, with over three million annual visits by the mid-2000s and a diversification between various forms of "mass tourism" and independent visitors or backpackers referred to as *lvyou* (驴友) or "donkey friends," who seek out more "wild" types of nature with fewer types of management intervention or commercial types of recreational facilities. Concern about public health, especially in the wake of the SARS outbreak in Beijing in 2003, has also contributed to the urban popularity of hiking, trekking, and greater contact with nature on the urban fringe.

Forest management practices for the Xishan hills also became more internationalized in the 1990s, with approval from the state forestry administration of PRC signalling a greater openness to international developments in environmental thought, including new techniques in ecological management. The traditional Chinese

Red leaves landscape on Xishan Hills (西山红叶，Xi Shan Hong Ye) (2007). Courtesy of 西山林场 (Xishan Forest Farm).

emphasis on trying to give artificial landscapes the semblance of "natural" or "unadorned" spaces was supplemented by a new interest in applying ecological insights into vegetation dynamics, such as the "close-to-nature" forestry developed in Germany and "scenic beauty estimation" in the United States.[4] This change in forestry practice reflects a new kind of synthesis between science and aesthetics enabled by a more techno-managerialist ethos including novel approaches to the handling of environmental data. An initial focus of interest was how better to care for native tree species such as the Chinese red pine (*Pinus tabuliformis*) as part of a wider drive to produce "optimum landscapes" that could combine aesthetic, ecological, and social principles.[5] This shift in emphasis is also illustrated by the application of "scenic beauty estimation" techniques to determine ideal colour ratios for autumn foliage. (This is a clear sign of American influence. American newspapers even publish "fall colour maps" to indicate the shifting contours of the "peak" experience.)

The creation of the ideal autumn landscape, with the most vibrant colours, raises tensions between variants of aesthetic and ecological authenticity. The popular autumn display of the Xishan hills is actually derived from a mix of about ten species. While most of these species are native such as the smoke tree (*Cotinus coggygria*), there has been intense debate concerning the inclusion of the non-native torch tree (*Rhus typhina*). The torch tree, originating from North America, had been specifically selected as suitable for planting by the Institute of Botany of the Chinese Academy of Sciences in 1959, owing to its aesthetic and horticultural properties.[6] As recently as the early 2000s, *Rhus typhina* has been considered a standard choice for afforestation projects in the Beijing metropolitan area. However, at the time of preparation for the 2008 Beijing Olympics, a change in the landscape design discourse occurred, leading to a greater emphasis on the planting of native species. Subsequently, some ecologists began to characterize *Rhus typhina* as an invasive species that should be targeted for elimination.[7] The ecologist Guangmei Wang in particular applied the North American and Australian screening systems to predict the invasive potential of *Rhus typhina*. "From a biological point of view," claims Wang, "*R.typhina* is a plant invader in Beijing" and "we therefore suggest [that] the government should remove the name of *R. typhina* from the main tree species list in afforesting Beijing."[8] Others disagreed, however, and defended the continuing presence of *Rhus typhina* in the forest landscape on the grounds that it does no ecological harm. The attempt to optimize autumn colours had become a field of contention: the aesthetic question had shifted towards the underlying botanical composition of the colour scheme.

The case of the Xishan hills shows that the question of what might be considered "natural" is never settled, and that the meaning of cultural authenticity reflects prevailing ideas. The intense international focus on Beijing during and after the 2008 Olympics had a ripple effect through urban environmental discourse. However, even if ecologists disagree about what plant species should be present in the mountain forests of western Beijing, these spaces are more vital than ever for the city's wider population.

Walking along the narrow clay road, I can hear birdsong emanating from the dense stands of Chinese red pine (*Pinus tabulaeformis*) and false acacia (*Robinia pseudoacacia*) as grasshoppers leap out of the grass in all directions. It doesn't matter to me that the Xishan hills are a largely contrived type of "natural landscape." After all, what is nature but a way of seeing the world around us? As an urbanite, I am simply happy to find some respite from the city below.

1 See, for example, Li Xiaoying, Hu Yong, and Duan An-an, "On Red Leaves culture," *Journal of Beijing Forestry University (Social science)* 5 (2) (2006) pp. 20–23. For a critical assessment of Chinese landscape traditions see Chang Tan, "Landscape without nature: ecological reflections in contemporary Chinese art," *Journal of Contemporary Chinese Art* 3 (3) (2016) pp. 223–241.

2 The lines are taken from Mao Zedong, "The spring refreshing the garden, Changsha," which was written during the 1920s. An alternative translation with a useful commentary is provided by Chunhou Zhang and C. Edwin Vaughan, eds., *Mao Zedong as poet and revolutionary leader: social and historical perspectives* (Oxford: Lexington Books [1925]) p. 33.

3 Chundi Chen, *Planning urban nature: urban green space planning in post-1949 China: Beijing as a representative case study* (Lincoln University, unpublished PhD thesis, 2013).

4 See, for example, Jin Kuining et al., "Assessment on close-to-nature transformation of *Pinus tabulaeformis* plantations in Xishan Region, Beijing," *Journal of Northeast Forestry University* 37 (7) (2009) pp. 42–44.

5 See Xiaofei Hao et al., "The proactive design approach of forest landscapes in Britain," *World Forestry Research* 20 (2) (2007) pp. 73–78; Liming Jia et al., "Principle of tending techniques on recreational forest of *Pinus tabulaeformis* in Beijing Mountainous Area by SBE Method," *Scientia Silvae Sinicae* 43 (9) (2007) pp. 144–149.

6 R. H. Uva, J. C. Neal, and J.M. Ditomaso, *Weeds of the Northeast* (London: Comstock Publishing Associates, 1997).

7 See, for example, Zhanjiang Zhang et al., "Ecophysiological evaluation of the potential invasiveness of *Rhus typhina* in its non-native habitats," *Tree Physiology* 29 (2009) pp. 1307–1316; Huafeng Wang et al., "Biological invasions in rapidly urbanizing areas: a case study of Beijing, China," *Biodiversity and Conservation* 20 (11) (2011) pp. 2483–2509; Yifu Yuan et al., "Competitive interaction between the exotic plant *Rhus typhina* L. and the native tree *Quercus acutissima* Carr. in Northern China under different soil N:P ratios," *Plant and Soil* 372 (1–2): (2013) pp. 389–400; and Yuping Hou et al., "Effects of exotic plant *Rhus typhina* invasion on soil properties in different forest types," *Acta Ecologica Sinica* 35 (16) (2015) pp. 5324–5330.

8 Guangmei Wang et al., "Invasion possibility and potential effects of *Rhus typhina* on Beijing municipality," *Journal of Integrative Plant Biology* 50 (5) (2008) pp. 522–530.

Cartographic imaginations

Part 5

Urban plants: a window on how ecology becomes evolution

Peter Del Tredici

The plants that grow spontaneously in abandoned or unmanaged urban landscapes deserve to be admired for their ability to grow under extremely harsh conditions. In general, such plants need to be *adaptable* (i.e. non-specialized) in all aspects of their life history, from germination through to seed production and dispersal; *opportunistic* in their ability to take advantage of locally abundant resources (water, light, and nutrients) that may be available for only a short period of time; and *tolerant* of the adverse growing conditions (heat and drought) created by covering the soil with pavement.[1]

Through a quirk of evolutionary fate, many of these species have evolved life-history traits in their native habitats that "pre-adapt" them to flourish in cities. Indeed, numerous studies have pointed out that many urban plants are native to exposed limestone cliffs and rocky outcrops, or to grasslands with sandy, alkaline soils.[2] The authors argue—by analogy—that the tall brick or granite-faced buildings and concrete foundations of cities are geologically equivalent to the mountainous environments where these species originated. In a similar vein, they suggest that the increased use of de-icing salts along walkways and highways has produced high pH microhabitats which are also colonized by limestone-loving species, including many from coastal habitats.

Many pre-adapted urban plants also originated in natural habitats that experience high levels of disturbance, including riverbanks (seasonal flooding), grasslands and prairies (burning and grazing), eroded slopes (unstable soil), and coastal or arid zones (salty soils).[3] Pre-adaptation is a powerful idea for understanding urban plant ecology for two reasons: firstly, it helps to answer questions about why some species are common in cities whereas others are not, and, secondly, it replaces a static, "native" definition of nature based on history and geography with a dynamic, "cosmopolitan" definition based on fitness and flux.

Relative to adjacent non-urban areas, cities are characterized by 1) increased levels of atmospheric nitrogen deposition and carbon dioxide; 2) increased growing season length and temperature; 3) shorter, warmer winters; 4) increased levels of

Princess tree, *Paulownia tomentosa*, colonizing an abandoned brick building in New London, Connecticut. Photo: Peter Del Tredici.

impervious surface and storm water runoff; 5) increased soil compaction and reduced moisture retention; and 6) increased road salt applications and elevated soil pHs.[4] Recent research across gradients of both space and time has determined that up to 40 percent of the plants that grow in large urban areas in Europe are non-native to the area, and that urbanization favours the growth of species that are tolerant of soils that are relatively *fertile, dry, sunny,* and *alkaline*.[5] In light of their unique environmental conditions and the cosmopolitan nature of their flora, cities clearly fit the definition of a "novel ecosystem" that has been irrevocably altered by human activity.[6]

In the remainder of this article, I will describe nine different urban environmental conditions that wild plants are pre-adapted to, along with examples of species that flourish under these conditions. While these examples are based primarily on personal observations of spontaneous vegetation in the cities of northeastern North America, the underlying ecological principles are applicable to urban areas across the globe.[7]

Prostrate knotweed, *Polygonum aviculare*, is well adapted to being stepped on. Photo: Peter Del Tredici.

Urbanization favours species that grow well in soils that are relatively fertile, dry, sunny, and alkaline. Photo: Peter Del Tredici.

The seeds of tufted lovegrass, *Eragrostis pectinacea*, only germinate in the gaps between the short sides of the bricks because they are slightly wider than those between the long sides. Photo: Peter Del Tredici.

Firstly, drought-tolerant, tap-rooted annuals with a prostrate growth habit are adapted to growing in sunny, sandy, or gravelly soils as well as limestone or granite cliffs and rock outcrops. These plants are pre-adapted to growing in sidewalk cracks with compacted soil and to being trampled by people. While pavement cracks appear to be stressful habitats, they typically support an abundance of plant life by virtue of the fact that they readily accumulate water and nutrients that flow in from surrounding impervious surfaces. The cosmopolitan array of tap-rooted, crack-inhabiting annuals in north temperate cities provide a striking example of what might be called *convergent pre-adaptation*: carpetweed (*Mollugo verticillata*) from Central America, purslane (*Portulaca oleracea*) which probably comes from India, spotted spurge (*Euphorbia maculata*) from eastern North America, and prostrate knotweed (*Polygonum aviculare*) from Europe. A number of fibrous-rooted grasses and rushes also grow in sidewalk cracks and are tolerant of trampling, including smooth crabgrass (*Digitaria ischaemum*), tufted lovegrass (*Eragrostis pectinacea*), and path rush (*Juncus tenuis*). Larger pavement openings, such as those that surround street trees, typically support a greater diversity of taller, drought-adapted, trampling-resistant plants than pavement cracks.[8]

Secondly, weathering associated with the widespread use of de-icing salts along walkways and roadways often results in the development of alkaline microhabitats along their edges that are typically colonized by species (mainly European) that come from grasslands with limestone-rich soils. Examples include mugwort (*Artemesia vulgaris*), spotted knapweed (*Centaurea biebersteinii*), oxeye daisy (*Leucanthemum vulgare*), broadleaf plantain (*Plantago major*), curly dock (*Rumex crispus*), and dandelion (*Taraxacum officinale*). Along highways where salt applications are particularly heavy and maintenance is minimal, woody species like tree of heaven (*Ailanthus altissima*) and black locust (*Robinia pseudoacacia*) often dominate unmown slopes. In addition, nitrogen deposition associated with precipitation—acid rain—also contributes to the deterioration of concrete and creates localized pockets of alkalinity where drought-tolerant, calciphilic species like chicory (*Cichorium intybus*) and dandelion (*Taraxacum officinale*) grow.

Thirdly, atmospheric deposition of nitrogen in urban areas is roughly twice that of rural areas—in order of 8.7 kilograms per hectare per year. Deposition rates are highest in the spring, and are closely correlated with vehicle emissions.[9] Atmospheric nitrogen deposition, mostly in the form of ammonium, has a profound

The chain-link fence provides a safe-site for this "bonsaied" American elm, *Ulmus americana*, in Hartford, Connecticut. Photo: Peter Del Tredici.

impact on soil biogeochemistry and can promote more robust growth in plants, including nitrophilic summer annuals like lambsquarters (*Chenopodium album*), common mallow (*Malva neglecta*), amaranths (*Amaranthus* spp.), purslane (*Portulaca oleracea*), and barnyard grass (*Echinochloa crus-galli*) as well as perennials like nettles (*Urtica* spp.) and docks (*Rumex* spp.). It is perhaps no coincidence that many common urban plants are members of families that do not typically form symbiotic relationships with mycorrhizal fungi—including the Amaranthaceae, Brassicacaee, Caryophyllaceae, and Polygonaceae. Species belonging to these families tend to require higher levels of soil nitrogen for their growth than plants belonging to families that form mycorrhizal partnerships.

Fourthly, early-successional trees that typically grow on eroded slopes, disturbed forest edges, or river floodplains typically show a strong capacity for vegetative regeneration from basal sprouts, rhizomes, or root suckers.[10] In urban environments, species that can sprout vigorously from the base or from roots are selectively favoured by the activities of maintenance crews who hack plants back in an effort to eliminate them. Examples of resilient trees include box elder (*Acer negundo*) silver maple (*Acer saccharinum*), tree of heaven (*Ailanthus altissima*), northern catalpa (*Catalpa speciosa*), Chinese mulberry (*Morus alba*), princess tree (*Paulownia tomentosa*), black locust (*Robinia pseudoacacia*), and various elms (*Ulmus* spp.).

Fifthly, river corridors and floodplains provide an abundance of high-light and high-disturbance edge habitats. They are characterized by fluctuating water levels and heavy soils, and the trees that grow naturally under such conditions are pre-adapted to grow on urban streets where the soil is often compacted and low in oxygen. Examples of tough bottomland species native to northeastern North America and perform well as street trees include: silver maple (*Acer saccharinum*), river birch (*Betula nigra*), green ash (*Fraxinus pensylvanica*), honey locust (*Gleditsia triacanthos*), sweetgum (*Liquidambar styraciflua*), pin oak (*Quercus palustris*), and the once ubiquitous American elm (*Ulmus americana*).

Sixthly, the term "urban heat-island" describes the fact that urban areas trap and store more heat during the daytime than adjacent non-urban areas with less paving and fewer buildings. This stored heat is released at night, typically keeping cities significantly warmer than the surrounding countryside. Examples of spontaneous trees that respond positively to warmer and drier urban microclimates include tree of heaven (*Ailanthus altissima*), silk tree (*Albizia julibrissin*), northern catalpa (*Catalpa speciosa*), and princess tree (*Paulownia tomentosa*).

Among herbaceous plants, those that utilize the C_4 photosynthesis pathway—which are more productive and efficient in water-use in hot, dry environments than C_3 plants—are significantly more abundant and diverse than they are in non-urban areas.[11] The authors attribute this distribution pattern to the fact that C_4 plants are selectively favoured under urban heat island conditions. Examples of common urban C_4 plants include: purslane (*Portulaca oleracea*), spotted spurge (*Euphorbia maculata*), carpetweed (*Mollugo veticiallata*), various pigweeds (*Amaranthus* spp.), and most notably the so-called "warm season grasses" in the genera *Cynodon*, *Digitaria*, *Echinochloa*, *Eragrostis*, *Panicum*, and *Setaria*.

Seventhly, disturbance-adapted winter annuals that germinate in fall and flower in spring are common in the urban landscape. They are disproportionally of European as opposed to North American or Asian origin, and seem to be increasing in abundance under the combined influences of climate change and urbanization. In cities, the mild fall weather extends for a longer period of time than it does in the surrounding countryside, which allows the rosette stage of the plant to grow much larger. With warmer, shorter winters, the rosettes typically start growing earlier in spring, and this promotes increased flower and seed production. Examples of urban winter annuals include garlic mustard (*Alliaria petiolata*), yellow rocket (*Barbarea vulgaris*), shepherd's purse (*Capsella bursa-pastoris*), hairy bittercress (*Cardamine hirsuta*), and Virginia pepperweed (*Lepidium virginicum*). All of these species are members of the Brassicaceae, or mustard family.

Eighthly, in urban environments, chain link fences provide unique opportunities for the establishment and growth of vines. Not only do they provide climbing plants with the opportunity to get above the competition, but they also provide them with protection from maintenance crews. Woody vines (lianas) that grow well on chain link fences include: porcelain berry (*Ampelopsis glandulosa* var. *brevipedunculata*), bittersweet (*Celastrus orbiculatus*), and Japanese honeysuckle (*Lonicera japonica*); herbaceous perennial vines include hedge bindweed (*Calystegia sepium*), black swallow-wort (*Vintoxicum nigrum*), and the semi-woody bittersweet nightshade (*Solanum dulcmara*). In addition to supporting the growth of vines, chain link fences can act as "safe sites" for the establishment and persistence of tree saplings by protecting them from the ravages of mowers and weed whackers. Trees with the capacity to sprout from the base are almost impossible to get rid of once they become enmeshed within a chain link fence.

Ninthly, opportunistic woody plants that come into leaf as soon as temperatures warm up in the spring or retain their leaves until a hard frost kills them in late fall are able to take advantage of the increase in growing season length that is a result of the combined impacts of climate change and the urban heat-island effect. For these species, the timing of bud break in the spring and/or leaf drop in the fall are more strongly influenced by temperature than by photoperiod. For whatever reason, many of the Asian and European shrubs that have naturalized in the understories of the forests of eastern North America come into leaf earlier and retain their leaves longer than the native species growing in the same area.[12] Examples of early leaf-producing species include Japanese barberry (*Berberis thunbergii*), privets (*Ligustrum* spp.), honeysuckles (*Lonicera* spp.), crab apples (*Malus* spp.), and multiflora rose (*Rosa multiflora*); late leaf-retaining species include glossy buckthorn (*Frangula alnus*), common buckthorn (*Rhamnus cathartica*), and black alder (*Alnus glutinosa*).

As important as pre-adaptation is in illuminating the story of urban vegetation, it is really just the introductory chapter to the longer book of evolution. Modern molecular research has shown that many of our urban plants (and animals) have undergone measurable changes in their genes (genetic) or in the expression of their genes (epigenetic) after migrating into cities or other drastically disturbed landscapes.[13]

It has also been shown that many of the species that flourish in these habitats are hybrids that emerged after their once-isolated parents were brought together by globe-trotting humans. Reports of hybridization among disturbance-adapted plants have become increasingly common as modern transportation technologies have accelerated the breakdown of geographical barriers that once kept species separate.[14] In general, hybrids seem to be better suited to colonizing disturbed habitats than either of their parents and are disproportionally common in landscapes that have been transformed by human activities.[15]

The history of urban vegetation can be summarized as moving from pre-adaptation based on evolutionary history to epigenetic or genetic change through natural selection, and finally to genomic transformation through hybridization. To the surprise of many scientists, cities now present unique opportunities to study how quickly ecology is transformed into evolution.

1 See Herbert G. Baker, "The evolution of weeds," *Annual Review of Ecology and Systematics* 5 (1974) pp. 1–24; Peter Del Tredici, *Wild urban plants of the northeast: a field guide* (Ithaca: Cornell University Press, 2010); and Sonja Knapp, Ingolf Kühn, Jens Stolle, and Stefan Klotz, "Changes in the functional composition of a central European flora over three centuries," *Perspectives in Ecology, Evolution and Systematics* 12 (2010) pp. 235–244.

2 Oliver L. Gilbert, *The ecology of urban habitats* (London: Chapman and Hall, 1989); Rüdiger Wittig, "The origin and development of the urban flora of central Europe," *Urban Ecosystems* 7 (2004) pp. 323–339; Douglas Larson, Uta Matthes, Peter E. Kelly, Jeremy Lundholm, and John Garrath, *The urban cliff revolution* (Markham, Ontario: Fitzhenry and Whiteside, 2004); and Jeremy T. Lundholm and A. Marlin, "Habitat origins and microhabitat preferences of urban plant species," *Urban Ecosystems* 9 (2006) pp. 139–159.

3 Herbert Sukopp, "Human-caused impact on preserved vegetation," *Landscape and Urban Planning* 68 (2004) pp. 347–355; Rüdiger Wittig, "The origin and development of the urban flora of central Europe"; Jeremy T. Lundholm and Paul J. Richardson, "Habitat analogues for reconciliation ecology in urban and industrial environments," *Journal of Applied Ecology* 47 (2010) pp. 966–975; and Rüdiger Wittig and Ute Becker, "The spontaneous flora around street trees in cities—A striking example for the worldwide homogenization of the flora of urban habitats," *Flora* 205 (2010) pp. 704–709.

4 Herbert Sukopp, "Human-caused impact on preserved vegetation"; Monika E. Sieghardt, Erich Mursch-Radlgruber, Elena Paoletti, Els Couenberg, Alexandros Dimitrakopoulus, Francisco Rego, Athanassios Hatzistathis, and Thomas Barfoed Randrup, "The abiotic urban environment: impact of urban growing conditions on urban vegetation" in C. C. Konijnendijk, K. Nilsson, T. Randrup, and J. Schipperijn, eds., *Urban forests and trees* (Berlin: Springer-Verlag, 2005) pp. 281–323; and K. George, Lewis Hans Ziska, James A. Bunce, and Bruno Quebedeaux, "Elevated atmospheric CO_2 concentration and temperature across an urban-rural transect," *Atmospheric Environment* 41 (2007) pp. 7654–7665; S. T. A Pickett, M. L. Cadenasso, J. M. Grove, C. G. Boone, P. M. Groffman, E. Irwin, S. S. Kaushal, V. Marshall, B. P. McGrath, C. H. Nilon, R.V. Pouyat, K. Szlavecz, A. Troy, and P. Warren, "Urban ecological systems: scientific foundations and a decade of progress," *Journal of Environmental Management* 92 (2011) pp. 331–362; and S. M. Decina, P. H. Templer, L. R. Hutyra, C. K. Gately, and P. Rao, "Variability, drivers, and effects of atmospheric nitrogen inputs across an urban area: emerging patterns among human activities, the atmosphere, and soils," *Science of the Total Environment* 609 (2017) pp. 1524–1534.

5 Petr Pyšek, "Alien and native species in Central European urban floras: a quantitative comparison," *Journal of Biogeography* 25 (1998) pp. 155–163; Sandrine Godefroid,

Dennis Monbaliu, and Nico Koedam, "The role of soil and microclimatic variables in the distribution patterns of urban wasteland flora in Brussels, Belgium," *Landscape and Urban Planning* 80 (2007) pp. 45–55; Audrey Muratet, Nathalie Machon, Frederic Jiguet, Jacques Moret, and Emmanuelle Porcher, "The role of urban structures in the distribution of wasteland flora in the greater Paris area, France," *Ecosystems* 10 (2007) pp. 661–671; and Sonja Knapp, Ingolf Kühn, Jens Stolle, and Stefan Klotz "Changes in the functional composition of a central European flora over three centuries," *Perspectives in Ecology, Evolution and Systematics* 12 (2010) pp. 235–244.

6 Ingo Kowarik, "Novel urban ecosystems, biodiversity, and conservation," *Environmental Pollution* 159 (2011) pp. 1974–1983; Steward T. A. Pickett et al., "Urban ecological systems: scientific foundations and a decade of progress," *Journal of Environmental Management* 92 (2011) pp. 331–362.

7 Peter Del Tredici, *Wild urban plants of the northeast*; Peter Del Tredici, "Spontaneous urban vegetation: reflections of change in a globalized world," *Nature and Culture* 5 (3) (2010) pp. 299–315.

8 Rüdiger Wittig and Ute Becker, "The spontaneous flora around street trees in cities."

9 S. M. Decina, S. M., P. H. Templer, L. R. Hutyra, C. K. Gately, and P. Rao, "Variability, drivers, and effects of atmospheric nitrogen inputs across an urban area: emerging patterns among human activities, the atmosphere, and soils," *Science of the Total Environment* 609 (2017) pp. 1524–1534.

10 Peter Del Tredici, "Sprouting in temperate trees: a morphological and ecological review," *Botanical Review* 67 (2) (2001) pp. 121–140.

11 Grant A. Duffy and Stephen L. Chown, "Urban warming favors C4 plants in temperate European cities," *Journal of Ecology* 104 (2016) pp. 1618–1616.

12 Jason D. Fridley, "Extended leaf phenology and the autumn niche in deciduous forest invasions," *Nature* 485 (17 May 2012) pp. 359–362.

13 Pierre Meerts, T. Baya, and C. Lefèbvre, "Allozyme variation in the annual weed species complex, *Polygonum aviculare* (Polygonaceae) in relation to ploidy level and colonizing ability," *Plant Systematics and Evolution* 211 (1998) pp. 239–256; P.-O. Cheptou, O. Carrue, S. Rouifed, and A. Cantarel, "Rapid evolution of seed dispersal in an urban environment in the weed *Crepis sancta*," *PNAS* 105 (10) (2008) pp. 3796–3799; C. M. Donihue, C. M. and M. R. Lambert, "Adaptive evolution in urban ecosystems." *Ambio* 44 (3) (2014) pp 194–203; M. Alberti, C. C. Correa, J. M. Marzluff, A. P. Hendry, E. P. Palkovacs, K. M. Gotanda, V. M. Hunta, T. M. Apgar, and Y. Zhou, "Global urban signatures of phenotypic change in animal and plant populations," P.N.A.S 114 (34) (2017) pp. 8951–8956; Marc T. J. Johnson, Cindy. M. Prashad, Melanie Lavoignat, and Hargurdeep S. Saini, "Contrasting the effects of natural selection, genetic drift and gene flow on urban evolution in white clover (*Trifolium repens*)," *Proceedings of the Royal Society*, Part B 285 (1883) (2018); and Menno Schilthuizen, *Darwin comes to town*. (New York: Picador, 2018).

14 Julio E. Perez, Mauro Nirchio, Carmen Alfonsi, and Carlos Muñoz, "The biology of invasions: the genetic paradox," *Biological Invasions* 8 (2006) pp. 1115–1121; Kristina A. Schierenbeck and Normn C.Ellstrand, "Hybridization and the evolution of invasiveness in plants and other organisms," *Biological Invasions* 11 (2009) pp. 1093–1105; and M. T. Johnson and Jason Munshi-South, "Evolution of life in urban environments," *Science* 358 (2017) eaam8327.

15 Edgar Anderson, *Introgressive hybridization* (New York: John Wiley & Sons, 1949).

Discovering and mapping urban plants

Mark Spencer

For many, the phrase "Garden of England" encapsulates an idealized embodiment of "Englishness." Thatched cottages embraced by clematis and rose. Dense hedges full of birds, flowery fields full of animals. Orchards and small holdings producing an abundance of food and flowers. Today, the county of Kent can lay claim to being "England's garden." This was not always so. For centuries, the now lost historic county of Middlesex nurtured the beating commercial, cultural, and political heart of England, London. Much of what is now modern-day Greater London covers the former county of Middlesex. The county had its origins as a territory of the Middle Saxons, and it is mentioned in the Doomsday Book. Roughly speaking, its boundaries were formed by the rivers Lea to the east, the Thames to the south, and the Colne and its distributaries to the west. The northern edge was largely marked by the southern boundary of modern day Hertfordshire. By the start of the sixteenth century, much of the county was given over to providing fresh fruit, vegetables, dairy, and meat produce for the growing city of London. In 1889, Middlesex lost its urbanized southeast to the newly created County of London. Much of the County of London constitutes what is now considered Inner London. Following the massive expansion of London, largely due to the rapidly expanding underground network, the County of London was abolished, and modern Greater London came into being in 1965; most of Middlesex was engulfed by Greater London, and the remaining fraction was passed to Surrey. From a botanical perspective, these shifts in administrative boundaries are, in themselves, not significant. However, they do reflect the more significant change in character of Middlesex: once a rural landscape, by the mid-twentieth century the former county is almost entirely urban.

The steady process of urbanization meant that some areas of Middlesex given over to gardens and the horticulture trade were soon absorbed within the metropolis. During the late seventeenth and eighteenth centuries, the area immediately to the north of Shoreditch in what is now (in part) Hoxton and Haggerston within the modern borough of Hackney, was at one time an important area for the cultivation of exotic plants being brought to England from the North American colonies. From further afield, especially South Africa, plants arrived via the Dutch East Indies Company and the then famous botanic gardens at Leiden and Amsterdam. Among others, many of whose names are now lost, the horticulturist Thomas Fairchild tended challenging and rare plants that were sold to the well-educated and rich of London's expanding suburbs. Fairchild and his competitors were among the first to grow aloes and geraniums from South Africa and agaves from the Americas. He stands out from the crowd because he was one of the few of these working-class people to attend the Botany Club at the Temple Coffee House alongside luminaries like Sir Hans Sloane and Leonard Plukenet, who was appointed superintendent of the royal gardens at Hampton Court under the patronage of Queen Mary. Fairchild is also recorded in the proceedings of the Royal Society as the first (known) European to purposefully hybridize a plant. The plant, known as Fairchild's Mule was the progeny of a carnation (*Dianthus caryophyllus*) and a sweet William (*Dianthus barbatus*).[1] By the mid-nineteenth century, much of an area was given over to housing and industry and the gardeners had moved northwards and eastwards. Today, horticulture is largely restricted to the upper reaches of the River Lee and southern Hertfordshire. However, the plants that were being grown by these early horticulturists have now become parkland mainstays, especially London plane (*Platanus* × *hispanica*). Many plants introduced during this period from the soon-to-be-relinquished North American colonies now grow wild along our railways and canals. Among them, pale-blue and off-white Michaelmas daisies (*Symphyotrichum* spp.), known to Georgian gardeners as starworts, compete with native plants and another colonial introduction, golden-rod (*Solidago* spp.).

Not only was London and the surrounding area an early place of innovation and experimentation in English horticulture, it was also one of the first places in Britain where the modern science of botany started to unfurl. Even before the founding in 1673 of the Chelsea Physic Garden, which was England's second-oldest botanic garden after the one in Oxford (founded in 1621), the lands around London were being explored by botanists. Today, the act of looking for wild plants (or "botanizing" as it is often known), is an established element of the pantheon of natural history activities alongside twitching, birding, and pan-species lists. In earlier centuries, the act of looking for wild plants was often described as "simpling," "herborizing," or "excursioning." In the summer of 1629, the botanist Thomas Johnson participated in expeditions to explore the plant life of Kent and Hampstead Heath. He was part of a "society" or "fellowship" of ten men who first set out to travel through north Kent to the Isle of Thanet. His account, published in 1629, is not the earliest example of botanizing in this country, but it is the earliest to be published independently from the wider discourse on our plant life.[2] The account of the plants of Hampstead Heath is brief (only three pages) but it does provide an insight into the havering that still plagues botanists today. Three of the "fellowship"(Buggs, Weale, and Wallis), failed to attend, the weather was poor, and the "lowering sky" threatened rain. Johnson and his friends "thought it a shame that we who had faced greater hazards should shirk from such a trifle." They passed through Kentish Town (itself a place that regularly features in many of the early wild plant observations of Middlesex due to its proximity to the Heath) and were obliged to take shelter in Highgate when the skies opened. They then made for the wood (probably

Kenwood, which in earlier times was often named Caen Wood). It is evident from their records that the wood at that time was more open than the dense and, at times, tangled wood of today. How do we know this? Several of the plants recorded back then are no longer to be found, as they require fairly open, sunny, and nutrient-poor habitats with only moderate shade. Plants such as Johnson's Serratula flo[s]. pur[purea] & albis (saw-wort, *Serratula tinctoria*), Astragalus Sylvaticus Thalii (bitter vetch, *Lathyrus linifolius*), and Morsus Diaboli (devil's-bit scabious, *Succisa pratensis*) are now regionally extinct over much of today's Greater London. The loss of grazing animals such as sheep and rabbits and the influx of nitrogen-rich pollutants from cars and dogs have seen them off. Others, mainly trees such as the hornbeam (*Carpinus betulus*), known to Johnson as either Betulus or Carpinus, continue to persist or even thrive in the expanded woodland. Today's Hampstead Heath bears little resemblance to the landscape that Londoners once knew. The Heath was akin to some of the wilder, more open landscapes that persist in modern London such as Richmond Park. It was also home to many of the plants that we currently think of as defining heathland, namely heathers (*Calluna vulgaris* and *Erica* spp.) and gorse (*Ulex* spp.). Johnson and his fellowship recorded about 30 plant species from the Heath. Most of these, such as stag's-horn clubmoss (*Lycopodium clavatum*) and bilberry (*Vaccinium myrtillus*) are long extinct, while others such as heath speedwell (*Veronica officinalis*) persist, although no doubt in greatly diminished numbers. The open parts of the modern Hampstead Heath now largely consist of grassland that is often botanically indiscernible from the average school sports pitch. The wooded areas have fared better, and Kenwood is still an important refuge for London's fungi.

The ecological distinctiveness of cities largely lies in their insularity. They are not like the surrounding environments. Cities tend to be hotter, drier, and windier than the surrounding landscape. In the context of most evolutionary processes and time, cities are very young habitats. And yet there is already evidence that there is active evolution in urban biota. I don't know of any examples from London, but I have no doubt that if we looked we'd find them. However, in the French city of Montpelier, populations of recent colonist *Crepis sancta* (a member of the daisy family) are evolving differing seed-dispersal strategies to populations of the same species in rural areas. In the portion of London north of the Thames (which bisects the city), I have noticed that wall lettuce (*Mycelis muralis*), another member of the daisy family, appears to be most abundant in the Inner London boroughs. These areas are largely made up of Georgian and Victorian buildings, which were built using lime mortar. In natural and semi-natural habitats, wall lettuce favours rocky soils overlying chalk and limestone. The aged lime mortar of Georgian and Victorian buildings is a very acceptable proxy, unlike the cement construction of the more recent buildings that predominate in the outer boroughs. This observation does not hold true to the south of the Thames, where the underlying chalk rises close to the surface in several of the outer boroughs.

The native plant life of London is facing an extinction crisis. Many species that were once common have now become exceedingly scarce and continue to decline. I am

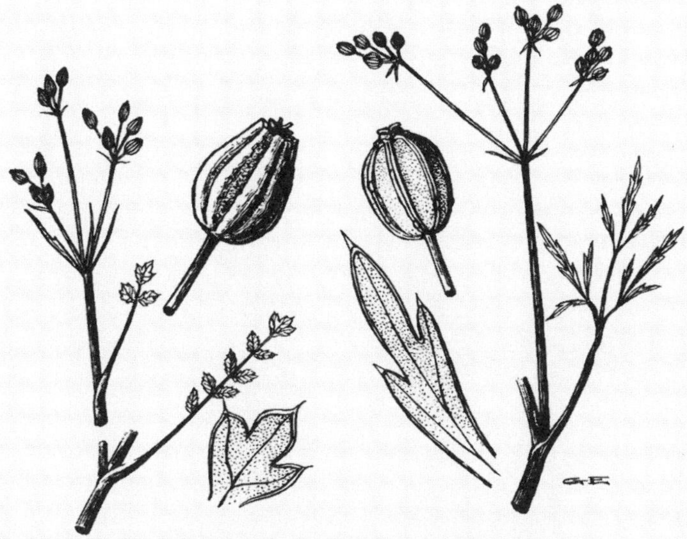

The atlas of London's flora published in 1983 also served as an identification guide for some of the rarer species by combining maps with illustrations. In this case *Petroselinum segetum* (left) is pictured alongside the locally frequent *Sison amomum* in the hope of its rediscovery in London. Drawings by Graham Easy.

aware that this is quite a stark statement, and it is one that some may gainsay. Aside from the obvious loss of plant habitat through urbanization, how can it be demonstrated that the green parks, canal sides, and woodlands of London are in any way depauperate compared to past centuries? The answer lies with the botanizing efforts of past and present Londoners. Botanists have been observing and recording the wild plants of London since the time of Johnson and his predecessors (such as the herbalist John Gerard and the Flemish physician Matthias de l'Obel, who both recorded the wild and cultivated plants of London). The continuity of observing and documenting wild plants is probably one of the longest in the world, and covers almost five centuries. Not surprisingly, information for the earlier centuries is often sparse and requires careful examination before being compared with more recent observations. Often, changes in place names can render the search for a historic location almost impossible, or a historic plant name may be misleading to the modern reader. Today, thanks to Carl Linnaeus, the eighteenth-century Swedish scientist who founded modern taxonomy, the scientific name *Leucojum* is unequivocally used for plants known in English as "snowflakes" that are related to that plant of the deep-midwinter, the snowdrop (*Galanthus*). Prior to Linnaeus, *Leucojum* was usually applied to white-flowered relatives of cabbage (*Brassica*)—very different plants. Thus, shifts in language, both scientific and vernacular, can lead to major errors when interpreting the past domiciles of wild plants.

The early modern history of London's wild plants has largely been uncovered by the work of Victorian and twentieth-century botanists. This has mainly been achieved by referring to unpublished manuscripts, correspondence and the published works of the sixteenth-to-eighteenth century botanists of London or those visiting the city and its environs. There remains one extensive resource that is still to be fully documented. In the botany collections of our national museums, there are still herbarium collections dating from this period that remain largely unstudied. Herbariums (or *hortus siccus*—dried gardens, as they were once known) are collections of dried plants. They represent a unique record of the world's plants, and they may offer a unique insight into London's past and now lost botanical riches. In the Sloane Herbarium in London's Natural History Museum, there is a superb collection of British and Irish plants made by Rev. Adam Buddle. During his life, his abilities were so renowned that he was affectionately known as "chief amongst the moss croppers." Buddle appears to have been botanically active for a rather a short period (it would appear that his herbarium was compiled between 1692 and 1707), but in that time, he made many significant observations on our plant life.

Today, Hounslow Heath in west London is a relatively undistinguished area of open grassland and scrub with a small area of restored heathland. The observations by Buddle and his compatriots show that prior to the heath being taken over as a military parade ground it was an extraordinarily rich place teeming with rare plants such as starfruit (*Damasonium alisma*), which now teeters on the brink of extinction across much of western Europe, and branched horsetail (*Equisetum ramossimum*), recorded by Buddle from the heath in 1705. This last is by far the oldest record of this rare plant in Britain, and its recent recognition radically rewrites the history of this plant here. Today, very little remains of the heath, as much of it is now under housing or within the boundaries of Heathrow Airport. Sadly, the work of Buddle is largely unknown today, mainly because his manuscript remains unpublished in the British Library. Now, he is best known for being the man after whom the garden shrub *Buddleja* is named after; not the invasive non-native *B. davidii* that is currently engulfing much of lowland Britain, but its relative *B. americana*. The latter plant was the only one known to Linnaeus when he created the generic name in the eighteenth century. *B. davidii* did not arrive on these shores until the late nineteenth century, and only became established in the wild following World War I.

The Victorian era heralded a rapid expansion in the public appeal of natural history and botany. Local, often church-led, natural history clubs and wild flower societies were founded across the country. Many of these organizations have now faded away, but some remain. Nationally, the Botanical Society of Britain and Ireland (BSBI) can trace its origins back to 1836 and the erstwhile Botanical Society of London. There is also the Wildflower Society which was "founded in 1886 by Edith Vere Annesley, to teach her youngest sister, Alice, to find and name wild flowers on their afternoon walks." Across what is now modern-day London, numerous societies were formed, most of which are no longer extant. The London Natural History Society (LNHS) originated from the founding of the Haggerstone Entomological Society in June 1858. Its first meeting place was the Carpenter's Arms, which lies between Shoreditch and Dalston. The following year and for the next 30 years, the Society met in a room above the Brownlow Arms, Brownlow Street.

Today, pubs never feature as meeting venues, but they often serve as places to adjourn to after meetings or particularly cold walks! The LNHS continues to hold indoor meetings, lectures, and outdoor walks exploring the capital's plants, fungi, invertebrates, birds, reptiles, amphibians, and mammals.

One of the more curious and enduring legacies of Victorian natural history was the establishment of the Watsonian vice-county system. The system was devised by Hewett Cottrell Watson, a brilliant man who studied phrenology (which he later disavowed), statistics, brain function, and what later became known as evolutionary theory. He was a regular and important correspondent of Charles Darwin's. He was also interested in biogeography and was an authority on the distribution of British wild plants. This led him to publish the vice-county system in the third volume of *Cybele Britannica* published in 1852.[3] Watson took his cue from the county boundaries of Victorian England. He then modified these or created subdivisions if he considered the area too large. Under the Watsonian system, Cornwall was divided into West Cornwall (vc 1) and East Cornwall (vc 2) and England's largest county, Yorkshire, was divided into five vice-counties. The vice-county system is a fixed geographic system of dividing Britain and Ireland into subdivisions. This is in marked contrast to the various forms of administrative boundary that are subject to change. Today's administrative Derbyshire has different boundaries to what the county had in the nineteenth century. The totally fixed nature of the vice-county boundaries is a relatively recent innovation. In 1947, spurred on by disagreements over vice-county boundaries, the botanist J. E. Dandy produced a series of base maps for the Watsonian vice-counties. These are held by the Natural History Museum, and were digitized in 2002 by the National Biodiversity Network (NHN) trust to celebrate the 150th anniversary of the vice-county system. The administratively redundant county of Middlesex now only persists as vice-county 21. For London's botanists, Middlesex and the adjoining vice-counties that London partially encompasses are more important than the current GLA and London borough boundaries for recording the city. The vice-county system may seem "quaint," but the standardization of boundaries means that botanists do not duplicate recording efforts by inadvertently crossing boundaries. It also means that records can more easily be compared over time, something that is very hard to do with mutable boundaries. The system has become so successful that vice-counties have been adopted by other specialties such as bryology (the study of mosses and their relatives), Lepidoptera (the study of butterflies and moths) and ornithology (the study of birds). Each vice-county now has one or sometimes two vice-county recorders whose role is to collate botany records for that vice-county. I am the vice-county recorder for Middlesex, a voluntary post I was nominated into by my predecessor Rodney Burton who himself succeeded Douglas "Dougie" H. Kent.

The LNHS started collecting and managing plant distribution records in 1917 and commenced publishing lists of these records in 1928. Despite the long-standing enthusiasm for consistently documenting the presence of London's wild plants, it was not until 1964 that the society considered embarking upon a project to map the distribution of the native and non-native plants found growing wild in London

Rodney M. Burton's *Flora of the London Area* was published by the London Natural History and covered the period from 1965 to 1976.

and the surrounding area. This undertaking was inspired by the BSBI's (then known as the Botanical Society of the British Isles) recently published (1962) *Atlas of the British Flora*. The *Atlas* consisted of dot-maps based upon a ten-kilometre grid aligned to the UK National Grid. Prior to this, most mapping exercises, such as Robert Lloyd Praeger's *The Botanist in Ireland* (1934) used various forms of shading (and no grid-lines) to denote plant distributions. Incidentally, Praeger introduced the vice-county system to Ireland (there, the vice-counties are also numbered consecutively but are prefixed with the letter 'H' for Hibernia). The LNHS project commenced on 1 January 1965 and was to cover an area known as the "LNHS polygon." The polygon is based upon the society's recording scope, which covers a 20-mile radius centred upon St Paul's Cathedral and encompasses the whole of the Middlesex vice-county as well as the parts of West Kent (vc 16), Surrey (vc 17, South and North Essex (vcs 18 & 19), Hertfordshire (vc 20) and the easternmost tip of Buckinghamshire (vc 24) that either border Greater London or have been engulfed by its twentieth-century expansion. The project involved the cumulated efforts of hundreds of volunteers and collecting data from 856 tetrads (a 2 × 2 km square) between 1965 and the early 1980s. These efforts resulted in the publication by Rodney Burton of the *Flora of the London Area* in 1983.

Recording and documenting the plant life of a given area is very time-consuming. Most county floras, as they are known, take at least 20 years to complete. In 2006 I succeeded Rodney Burton as the BSBI vice-county recorder for Middlesex and the equivalent LNHS role as "vascular plant recorder." Shortly afterward, I proposed to the LNHS botany committee that we should undertake a new mapping project. This project operates under the working title of The London Flora Project. It operates in a very similar way to that used by the earlier LNHS scheme, but with some differences. Probably the most significant of these is that we are attempting to record at the monad (a 1 × 1 km square). This has increased the number of squares to "bash," as it is known, from 856 tetrads to 3,424 monads (there being four monads in each tetrad). Also, since the publication of the last London flora, we have entered the era of the computer. Records may still be collected on recording cards with tick boxes or jotted down in note books, but online platforms for recording are increasingly being utilized.

Extensive datasets are being compiled on spreadsheets and the data stored by our local biological recording centre, Greenspace Information for Greater London (GIGL). The advent of organizations like GIGL with the capacity and the resources to store offers significant benefits as well as challenges. Shortly after starting the current project, I asked about the whereabouts of the recording cards for the earlier London flora project, only to learn that they had been disposed of by relatives of the woman who had been caring for them after she had passed away. We had lost much of the original data from that scheme, and we were obliged to use the dot maps in Burton's flora and optical character recognition software to extract the data. While much of the data was rescued, a huge amount of information was lost forever. Even though the digital environment has its drawbacks, the ability to store data in multiple locations should reduce the risk of future losses. I now have my Middlesex data backed up in GIGL, the BSBI's own database, as well as on the National Biodiversity Network's (NBN) system. On the downside, the current project has faced an enormous task in terms of transferring records collected over the last 200 years into digital format. Herbariums, publications, journals, and old county floras have been scoured to retrieve data that otherwise would be unavailable for comparison with the current recording effort. There is also the added complication that the LNHS polygon overlays the pre-existing BSBI vice-county system and the modern GLA and London boundaries. This requires a lot of collaboration. Records collected by volunteers need to be checked for accuracy and transformed into a standardized format prior to transferring to GIGL and ultimately the BSBI and NBN. The modern botanizer undertakes their square bashing exercise in much the same way as predecessors like Johnson, Buddle, Kent did. We don suitable clothing and, with notebook and pen in hand, we head out. If we are organized, in our bags there will be a hand lens, a copy of the botanist's preferred guide. In my case, this is the fourth edition of Clive Stace's *New flora of the British Isles*. Unlike our Victorian and early twentieth-century forebears, we don't carry a vasculum; instead, it is likely to be a rather more prosaic plastic bag. Vasculums are no longer used by botanists; essentially, they are metal cases used to store plant specimens in for later identification or preparation as herbarium specimens. Unfortunately, they are rather cumbersome, and have been usurped by the carrier bag. I am lucky enough to own two, one of which was passed down to me by my predecessor Rodney Burton, who received it from Dougie Kent, who was given it by the great Job Edward "Ted" Lousley. The vasculum still has his name and address on the inside.

Recording in cities like London is very different to recording in the wider environment. The major difference is that land ownership is much more fractioned. It can be very hard to find the owner of a piece of land in order to request permission to gain entry and record. In many cases, entry is not possible. Railways are usually off-limits, and this is very frustrating, as London's railways are rich and diverse refugia for our native and non-native plants. I have been known to resort to binoculars (as have others). Cities are also very crowded, and it becomes necessary to develop a thick skin when botanizing, as crawling on your hands and knees in a central London park is not going to go unnoticed. In one case, a LNHS volunteer was severely reprimanded for conducting a nose-to-ground examination of the turf outside Buckingham Palace! The botanist in the guise of a security risk. Much of our interesting plant life grows on cracks in pavements, and recording these requires care in avoiding death by Post Office van as well as the latrines of the local dogs. One of the prevailing debates that we have is "what to record?" Sometimes, it can be very hard to determine whether a plant is truly wild or whether it is a planted. This may seem trivial, but recording all the planted trees and shrubs in parks would massively increase the recording burden and skew the maps. While we all haver at times, the answer is generally "can you identify whether the plant is reproducing and persisting in that location?" If the answer is yes, then we record. Even so, this apparently simple guidance can lead to small huddles of LNHS botanists standing on pavements looking at somebody's front garden, musing on the status of a plant by the garden gate.

So, why go to all this effort? Cities as focal points of human activity are very valuable environments for understanding how the natural world is responding to the pressures of the Anthropocene. London has different climatic conditions to the surrounding landscape, and as such it offers a viable model for how our wild plants will respond to environmental change. London is also one of the most important focal points for the introduction of non-native invasive species. Plants like buddleia and tree of heaven (*Ailanthus altissima*) are well-established here, and are probably actively evolving. It is also evident that many of our native urban plants are declining and are heading towards regional extinction. As things stand, I now know of only one green-winged orchid (*Anacamptis morio*) plant in Greater London. Conversely, many non-native species are on the increase, and plants like Guernsey fleabane (*Erigeron sumatrensis*) are now dominant in many parts of London.

Despite increased public awareness of the importance of the environment, much of London's green space is increasingly hemmed in and tidied. Large swathes of the city were bombed in World War II, and for many years these sites were important habitats for our plants and other wildlife. Following London's property market boom, most of these sites no longer remain. The resurgence in the popularity of our canals and waterways has resulted in a major increase in the numbers of people visiting these spaces. In many cases, this has resulted in towpaths being mown and wild thickets trimmed or replaced with appealing municipal plantings. This effect has been particularly severe in the area around the King's Cross development, where nearly all of the semi-natural urban vegetation has been eradicated and replaced with prairie-style horticultural plantings. We are eradicating our urban natural heritage, much of which either survived the initial stage of urbanization or colonized and adapted. The Oxford ragwort (*Senecio squalidus*), a non-native plant that hails from Mount Etna in Sicily and travelled to London from Oxford via the burgeoning Victorian rail network, appears to be declining in inner London. The rough walls and cracked paving of our bomb sites and canals that emulate its mountain home are being tidied away, and so is this fascinating plant. Luckily, railways remain an important home for Oxford ragwort and other plants.

One native species has very recently made the railways its preferred London home. Twenty years ago I thought, along with other London botanists, that rue-leaved saxifrage (*Saxifraga tridactylites*) was heading towards extinction in London. There were probably less than 100 individuals of this small, early spring-flowering annual remaining here. Then, about a decade ago, it went through a rapid resurgence and started to be seen in many locations across London. It now appears to have become well-established on railway clinker beds near several major train stations; on occasion, it turns up in cracks in pavements. To be honest, I have no idea what caused the change, but I suspect the plant may have developed resistance to weedkillers. Worldwide, there is increasing evidence of resistance to herbicides in agricultural systems. Evidence from the built environment is limited, but it is very likely to be present. One widespread non-native London plant, Guernsey fleabane (*Erigeron sumatrensis*) is known to have developed resistance to glyphosate within its native range of South America. In north and west Parana state in Brazil, *E. sumatrensis* plants in fields used to grow glyphosate resistant soybean (*Glycine max*) have developed resistance to the chemical. In many urban areas, glyphosate is the most popular means of controlling vegetation on paths, a habitat which *E. sumatrensis* abounds in. It is possible that urban areas are largely overlooked sources of herbicide resistance in plants.

From a plant-distribution and mapping perspective, urban botany differs greatly from environments. The presence of roads, buildings, railways, and canals leads to a patchwork of microhabitats that a plant species can occupy. As a consequence, using one kilometre dot mapping results in a mapped distribution that may appear random. The habitats that many urban plants occupy are often so small that traditional mapping struggles to reflect why plants grow where they do. Nevertheless, the significant difference in the composition of urban plant life compared to the adjoining landscapes means that recording is valuable. Documenting how recent arrivals such as membranous nettle (*Urtica membranacea*) colonize our cities and towns is an important part of the process of understanding biological responses to human induced change in the Anthropocene.

The work of the LNHS is entirely voluntary, the organization receives no support or aid for this work from regional or national authorities. The data that the society (and many others across the country) generates is of regional and national value. Plant distribution data and maps are used by planning authorities and government agencies to make important decisions about the management of our environment in a very wide range of fields. Sadly, many amateur natural historians are increasingly frustrated with a system that benefits from their expertise and data but largely excludes them from the decision-making process and fails to recognize the value of the community's contribution. It will be several more years before the current London Flora Project is complete. As well as mapping the distributions of approximately 2000 species, I and others will have to write summary accounts describing the most interesting changes in London's flora since the publication of Rodney Burton's Flora of the London Area in 1983. We will all have to wait a while longer before we can fully understand the current status of many of London's plants. In the meantime, we continue heading out. This coming summer, I'm tackling the canals of west London, looking for pondweeds (*Potamogeton* spp.), grappling-hook in hand.

1 Thomas Fairchild, *The City Gardener, containing the most experienced method of cultivating ... such ever-greens ... shrubs ... exotick plants, etc. as will be ornamental, and thrive best in the London Gardens* (London, 1722).

2 Thomas Johnson, *Botanical journeys in Kent and Hampstead: a facsimile reprint with introduction and translation of his Iter plantarum 1629 and Descriptio itineris plantarum 1632* (Pittsburg, PA: The Hunt Botanical Library).

3 Hewett Cottrell Watson, *Cybele Britannica: or British plants and their geographical relations* (London: Longman & Co., 1852).

Mapping the urban flora of Berlin

Birgit Seitz

Thirty years ago, we had the idea of making an atlas of Berlin's flora. We started fieldwork in 1988 in the western part of the city, as the Berlin wall still existed. From spring until autumn every second Saturday, a group of botanists came together to search for all wild growing plants in a particular area. The excursions were organized by the Botanical Society of Berlin and Brandenburg. Not only trained botanists but also other interested people such as students or ordinary members of the public came to learn more about wild plants in the city. The mapping of urban flora was a pioneer project of citizen science in Berlin.

Over 25 years, we visited nearly every type of place in the city. We explored urban areas like railway sites, backyards, cemeteries, and wastelands, and suburban areas like forests, meadows, and fields to determine and map every wild-growing tree, shrub, and herb. In many cases, we visited sites we wouldn't have encountered without this project.

Over time, it was interesting to observe the changes in Berlin's flora. The fall of the Berlin wall just one year after the beginning of our project had significant implications for the study of the flora. After 1990, our investigation area extended into the eastern part of Berlin. The opening of the border led to a "botanical euphoria" across the city, because we could enter places that had not been not accessible for a long time.

In subsequent years, Berlin developed rapidly, becoming the capital of Germany and an important European metropolis. However, changes in urban planning like the new buildings in the government district also led to the loss of habitats for spontaneous urban vegetation. We could closely examine the way larger urban wastelands vanished within a very short time. And, in some cases, we could also observe the expansion of species that were mainly introduced by human activities.

To document the long-term dynamics of the Berlin flora, we decided to explore the existing historical data from herbaria and published sources. Thanks to a long tradition in the field of floristic investigation we could draw on a large database in Berlin. We realized that our mapping project was no more than the blink of an eye in terms of the longer botanical history of the city.

Current occurrence of *Dysphania botrys* in front of the Berlin Reichstag—a relic of former fallow land. Photo: Heiderose Häsler.

The first floristic data was published 1578 in an herbal book by Leonhard Thurneisser zum Thurn.[1] He collected plants in the former herb garden of the monastery Graues Kloster. The oldest localized floristic record was published in the *Flora Marchica* of Elssholz (1663), *Stipa pennata* in front of the Georgentor (now Alexanderplatz).[2] In the year 1787, Carl Ludwig Willdenow published the first flora of Berlin, *Florae Berolinensis Prodromus*, which featured 822 species of wild and cultivated plants.[3] With the founding of the Botanical Society of the province of Brandenburg (now the Botanical Society of Berlin and Brandenburg) in the year 1849, the floristic investigation of Berlin and Brandenburg gained new impetus. The results of floristic investigations were published in an annual journal which serves as a vital historical record. In 1859, Paul Ascherson, one of the key figures in the Botanical Society, published a systematic flora of Berlin.[4] It was an outstanding and detailed flora, summarizing the floristic investigations of Berlin up to this point in time. This flora and the Society's journal delivered most of the historical data for the atlas of Berlin's flora.[5] Even Ascherson wrote about the changes in Berlin's flora due to industrialization and the intensification of agriculture. In fact, Berlin's role as an industrial and trade centre led not only to the loss of habitats and species, but also to the introduction of several non-native species. Lists of introduced plants were summarized by Ascherson in 1854 and by Oskar Alexander Richard Büttner in 1884 in his *Flora Advena Marchica*.[6] Some now widespread species like *Galinsoga parviflora* or *Impatiens parviflora* were naturalized nineteenth-century escapes from Berlin's Botanical Garden.

This was the time when the systematic mapping of plants began in some regions of Germany. Two different concepts were pursued at the time: the mapping of the precise position of selected species, and the mapping of the whole flora within defined grid fields. The first call for the systematic grid mapping of all plants across the whole of Germany was initiated by Johannes Mattfeld at the Berlin Botanical Museum in 1922. The aim was the recording of all wildgrowing (including non-native) species within a grid pattern of 250 metres on the basis of topographical maps. Unfortunately, these cartographic data were destroyed during World War II. In post-1960 Germany, the grid mapping project started again as a part of the floristic mapping of Central Europe. It was initiated by Friedrich Ehrendorfer and Ulrich Hamann in 1964 on the basis of the topographical maps on a scale of 1:25,000. For the western part of Germany (the BRD), the data was collected at the University of Göttingen by Heinz Ellenberg, and later at the Universities of Bochum and Regensburg. The central office of floristic mapping in the eastern part of Germany (the GDR) was at the University of Halle. The role of the central offices was the coordination and data collection of several regional mapping projects.

In the mid-twentieth century, the floristic investigation of Berlin prospered again, with the emerging discipline of urban ecology led by Herbert Sukopp and others.[7] An outstanding example for the recent evolution of species was the increasing diversity of the evening primrose (*Oenothera*) after World War II. *Oenothera coronifera* originated in Berlin through hybridization, and nineteen taxa have thus far been recorded.

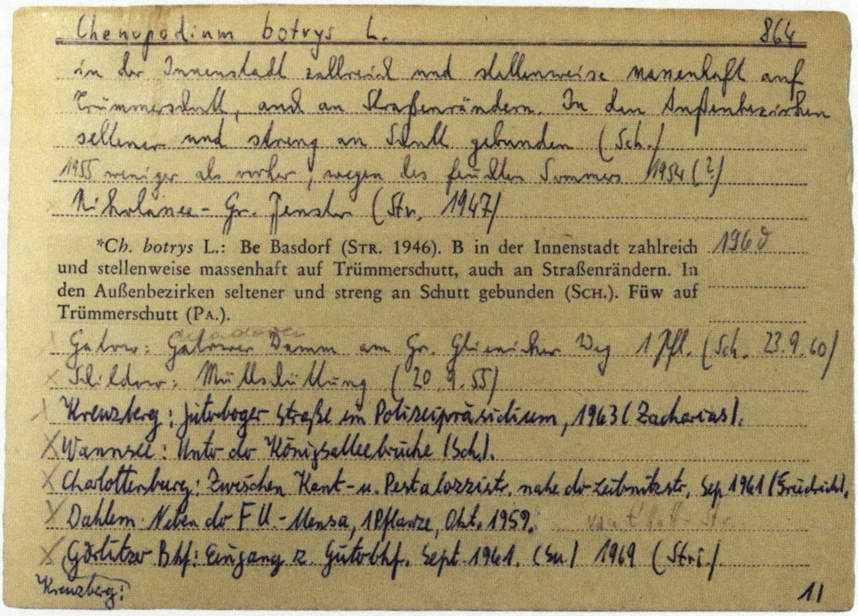

Chenopodium botrys L. 864

*Ch. botrys L.: Be Basdorf (STR. 1946). B in der Innenstadt zahlreich und stellenweise massenhaft auf Trümmerschutt, auch an Straßenrändern. In den Außenbezirken seltener und streng an Schutt gebunden (SCH.). Füw auf Trümmerschutt (PA.).

Historical traces of *Dysphania botrys* (former name *Chenopodium botrys*) in Berlin after World War II. Card index by Herbert Sukopp.

In 1962, Herbert Sukopp became the first to call for the mapping project "Flora of Berlin." His aim was to document the changes in the flora since the days of Ascherson, who had published his flora in 1859. Sukopp collected copious data in his card index system, especially for rare and neophytic species. Some years later, Berlin joined the German grid mapping project, based on the use of topographical maps. The aim was to contribute data for the German project, but also to prepare a separate flora for Berlin. The result was an atlas of Berlin's flora, which was published in the year 2012. After this, the collection of data has been continued especially for rare and endangered species with a conservation priority, and also for a new Red List of Berlin plants, which was released in 2018.[8]

For the Berlin atlas project, about 150 botanists and other citizen scientists, mostly members of the Botanical Society of Berlin and Brandenburg, collected data from 1988 to 2012. Berlin was divided into 153 grid fields, with each covering about seven square kilometres (2.5 to 2.5 kilometres). In each grid field, we mapped all the wild plants, making at least three inspections per year in spring, summer, and autumn to get data from all phenological phases. A point in the map indicates the occurrence of a species in this field, regardless of whether this species was growing in one or many populations, or if the populations are large or small. With this method, it was possible to show the geographical distribution of all the wild plants present in Berlin, with each species having its own map. To find a representative set of species in one grid field, we mapped different habitats like forests, parks, streets, meadows, and lawns. Of course, we could never be sure to find all the species, but with this method we could find a representative range of species with our available resources.

To show long-term changes in the flora of Berlin from the beginning of floristic investigation until now, we drew on a huge amount of data. Altogether, we collected about 180,000 records, a quarter of them derived from the time before the beginning of the fieldwork in 1988. The atlas shows 1,900 maps out of a total flora for Berlin of about 2,500 recorded taxa. About 1,500 species are currently established, meaning that they are growing in at least one spontaneous population for longer than 25 years, and that they have built up self-reproducing stocks over at least two generations.

Like that of most other cities, the flora of Berlin is characterized by a high number of non-native species. Until now, about 1,300 neophytes (about 300 established and 1,000 nonestablished species) and about 1,200 indigenous species have been found in Berlin.

Compared with the flora of other cities in Germany, the total number of species in Berlin is markedly high (Stuttgart has 1,820 recorded species, Hamburg 1,643, and Leipzig 2,165). This can be explained by the high number of introduced species, but also by the high diversity of semi-natural habitats, especially towards the edge of the city such as forests, lakes, and meadows in areas such as Köpenick. In addition, Berlin is one of the best-investigated cities, with a long historical tradition in floristic studies.

We found 27 species occurring in all grid fields across the metropolitan area; 24 of these were indigenous species and three were neophytes. Examples for the

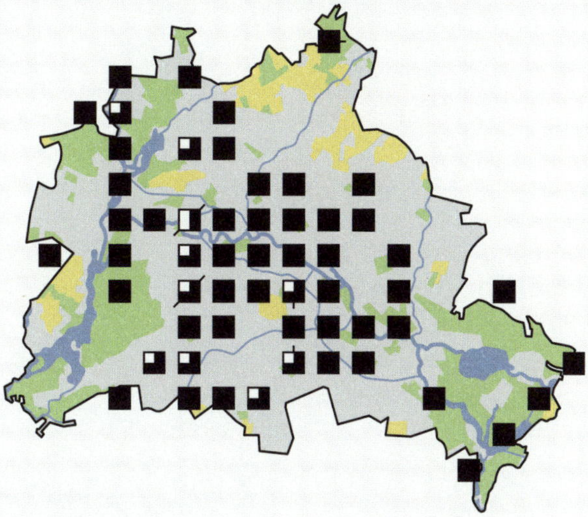

Distribution map of *Dysphania botrys* in the atlas of the flora of Berlin showing discovery places between 1950 and 1990 (half squares, three-quarter squares) and after 1990 (filled squares, from Seitz et al. 2012).

most frequent indigenous species include *Acer platanoides, Bromus sterilis, Calamagrostis epigeios, Dactylis glomerata, Plantago lanceolata,* and *Urtica dioica*. The three most frequent neophytes in the city were *Berteroa incana, Oenothera biennis* s. l., and *Solidago canadensis*.

Of the 1,527 established species, one in six are now extinct; that is, they could not be discovered for the last ten years. One-third of the currently occurring species are threatened. One-third of the extinct species were last reported before 1900, when Berlin expanded to a metropolis, and small villages like Schöneberg, Rixdorf, and Lietzenburg, with their rural landscape characterized by fields and meadows, vanished to make way for a dense block structure. With this intensifying phase of urbanization, many species associated with arable farming, or with marshes and wetlands in particular, were eradicated. The historic distribution of these species can now be studied in distribution maps. A few examples are mentioned in the following text and figures.

Arnoseris minima is a species associated with arable land that grows on sandy soils. Due to the intensification and fertilization of agriculture, it has become quite rare since the 1960s in the remaining fields. On the botanical map, one can also see the places where it was growing before 1990 (the empty dots), and where it has become extinct due to the loss of habitats.

Loss of habitats and the lowering of the groundwater table were also responsible for the extreme declines of nutrient-poor wetland species like *Orchis militaris*, which is also threatened at a national scale. It is fascinating to see the history of this species in the map: this is now a very rare species, even though it occurred in thirteen additional grid references before 1900.

Urbanization and industrialization also had positive effects on the occurrence of some species. The development of new transport routes brought new species (mostly non-native) to the city. Since 1993, *Senecio inaequidens* from South Africa has spread along railway and water infrastructure routes. *Agrostis castellana*, a grass from Southern Europe and West Asia, was first detected in 1964, and prefers growing in the western part of Berlin. *Sisymbrium volgense* originates from the Russian steppes, and was first detected in Berlin in 1885. Interestingly, it still grows predominantly in the eastern part of Berlin.

A typical species for the urban parts of Berlin is *Dysphania* (formerly *Chenopodium*) *botrys*, which grows on open, ruderal sites. It was much more frequent on rubble ground after World War II. *Buddleja davidii* is a thermophilic species from Asia, which grows only in the warmer inner part of the city. Other species avoid the urban parts of Berlin and grow only on the outskirts, like *Danthonia decumbens*, a typical forest species found on acidic, sandy soils.

The maps show the huge diversity of wild growing plants in a metropolis like Berlin. But any map is just a snapshot in time: the distribution of species reflects an on-going ecological dynamic. Some species have already vanished since the publication of the atlas in 2012, some have been rediscovered, and others have spread significantly. The indigenous *Equisetum pratense*, for example, was rediscovered in 2016 in the palace gardens of Charlottenburg where it was last recorded in 1977. The non-native grass *Eragrostis multicaulis* has spread so quickly since 2012 that it has now become established in Berlin. Although this work can never be completed, it provides motivation for an on-going study of the distribution of wild growing plants in Berlin, and the need to find new sites which have not been recorded in the maps thus far.

Large-scale mapping projects for such a range of different species are not possible without the support of many volunteers, as well as funding from scientific societies, conservation authorities, and other sources. The data provides a fundamental basis for nature conservation, for the threat assessments compiled for Red Lists, or as a basis for political decision making. Reliable data help to improve conservation efforts and to set political priorities. Scientific models developed by ecologists and conservation biologists also need reliable data in order to predict the effects of environmental changes like the impact of invasive species or climate change. Additionally, involving citizens in mapping projects encourages not only the development of identification skills, but also an engagement with wider biodiversity concerns.

1 Leonhard Thurneisser zum Thurn, *Historia, sive descriptio plantarum omnium, tum domesticarum quam exoticarum [...]* (Hentzske: Berlin, 1578).

2 J. S. Elssholtz, *Flora marchica, sive catalogus plantarum, quae partim in hortis electoralibus Marchiae Brandenburgicae [...] partim sua sponte passim proveniunt* (Reichel: Berlin, 1663).

3 Carl Ludwig von Willdenow, *Florae Berolinensis Prodromus* (Wilhelm Vieweg, Berlin, 1787).

4 Paul Ascherson, *Verzeichnis der Phanerogamen und Gefäßkryptogamen, welche im Umkreise von sieben Meilen um Berlin vorkommen: Flora der Provinz Brandenburg, der Altmark und des Herzogthums Magdeburg; Zweite Abtheilung* (Hirschwald: Berlin, 1859).

5 Birgit Seitz, Michael Ristow, Rüdiger Prasse, Bernd Machatzi, Gunther Klemm, Reinhard Böcker, and Herbert Sukopp, "Der Berliner Florenatlas." *Verh. Bot. Ver. Berlin Brandenburg,* Rangsdorf: Natur+Text, Beiheft 7 (2012).

6 Paul Ascherson, "Die verwilderten Pflanzen in der Mark Brandenburg," *Zeitschr. ges. Naturw.* 3 (1854) pp. 435–463; Richard Büttner, "Flora advena marchica," *Verh. Bot. Ver. Prov. Brandenburg* 25 (1884) pp. 1–59.

7 Herbert Sukopp, ed., *Stadtökologie: Das Beispiel Berlin* (Reimer: Berlin, 1990).

8 Birgit Seitz, Michael Ristow, Justus Meißner, Bernd Machatzi, and Herbert Sukopp, "Rote Liste und Gesamtartenliste der etablierten Farn- und Blütenpflanzen von Berlin," in Der Landesbeauftragte für Naturschutz und Landschaftspflege/Senatsverwaltung für Umwelt, Klima und Verkehr, ed., (Berlin, 2018).

Nature is for everyone: investigating attitudes to urban biodiversity

Leonie Fischer

While working on this essay, I am staying in Rome, one of Europe's largest cities. There is a conference dedicated to the place of people in environmental studies, and we are talking about how people engage with "green infrastructure" in cities. There are discussions about how urban green space can foster creativity, support people's well-being, and also contribute to public health. We talk about the benefits of street trees, the management of park meadows, and the pollinators, birds, and beetles within these green spaces. Still, many questions remain unanswered, although many insights have been gained in recent years. The meaning of "green space" for urbanites has become a key topic for researchers from various disciplines, and for practitioners and policy makers who are paying increased attention to the benefits of urban greenspace for both people and nature.

When not occupied with the conference, I find time to wander through one of the most densely built-up cities in Europe. Much of its so-called grey infrastructure evolved historically. Although there is empirical evidence of biodiversity, I can barely find any place where I can spend any time in green surroundings in order to gain some respite from the hot summer weather, and take a deep breath and relax.[1] Many of the green spots on the map belong to private land owners; some of them are old villas with historical gardens and parks. I admire the centuries-old olive trees, oaks, and pines. And I wonder how the people of this city relate to these old traces of garden design. Are these gardens still places for outdoor recreation? Back on the busy streets, there is another other type of green space that predominates: spontaneous vegetation working its way through cracks in old walls, climbing along wall tops and roofs, and surviving around the street trees, and in forgotten planting pots. It is this wild, spontaneous vegetation that makes me curious: How does it contribute to the daily life of the city's residents? Do they see it at all? How do they like it once they discover it? Do people appreciate, or even use this specific kind of *wild* urban nature?

We were looking at these questions from a scientific, systematic angle, to elucidate the intersection of cultural and biological diversity. Whether biodiversity within urban green spaces has positive or negative effects on humans, including the way people like and perceive species richness, remains critically neglected in studies.[2] Pioneer studies in the 1980s determined that people generally prefer green over grey settings.[3] Today, however, in the context of expanding urbanization, it is rarely so simple as green versus grey spaces. If green spaces do people some good, we need arguments to enhance quality of life in densified cities to keep the remaining green spaces and make the best of it, especially for those people who have little contact with nature.[4] Thus, in elucidating what people like or dislike within urban green space, it is important to design and plan sustainable cities that include urban nature that people can appreciate; this can help to better create spaces within cities that serve people for recreation, reduce stress, and even contribute to social cohesion. Thus, future urban planning will not only need to provide enough green spaces for urban populations but also to consider what types of nature might appeal to a broad public.

When we consider contemporary cities, how do questions of biodiversity and social diversity intersect? How might these underexplored questions be addressed? Urban green spaces are often key locales in which people from different socio-economic and ethnic groups mix, including diverse age groups. The question of public space and social interaction is also significant, because many contemporary cities are themselves becoming more diverse with heterogeneous communities.

Based on these considerations, we conducted a field survey in which we combined social and ecological science to study public preferences in relation to green space und their attitudes towards urban vegetation in five European cities: Bari, Berlin, Edinburgh, Ljubljana, and Malmö.[5] Nearly 4000 people took part in the survey, giving us the chance to statistically analyze an enormous database on social differences and attitudes towards biodiversity and green space. In a smaller companion study, we applied ethnobotanical methods to interviewing people who dedicate themselves to urban foraging, that is, people who gather wild edible plants in cities for consumption.[6] In both studies, we analyzed the intersections between socio-cultural diversity and attitudes towards biodiversity, including urban vegetation.

Our field surveys revealed a range of findings that help us to better understand the interface between people and biodiversity within cities. The research findings clearly show that nature is important to almost everyone. The first part of our survey suggested three views in particular: people like high levels of plant diversity in urban surroundings; people agree that high levels of plant diversity improve the liveability of cities; and this broad support for urban biodiversity is largely independent from the socio-cultural background of respondents. Within urban meadows in parks, wasteland sites, and tree pits along streets, people favoured botanical assemblages with the highest levels of biodiversity and disliked, for example, tree pits without any vegetation at all. When people were asked to value different types of vegetation according to their contribution to creating liveable cities, they consistently preferred the highest biodiversity levels in all three forms of urban green space.

The socio-cultural characteristics of respondents that were most strongly related to people's preferences were those that described their affinity to nature, such as respondents' nature orientation, the frequency with which they used green spaces, and the role that they attribute to nature itself. Interestingly, people with a professional "green" background attributed higher liveability to all wasteland sites than non-professionals. More traditional variables that explain respondents' socio-cultural backgrounds such as age, gender, or education were hardly related to the valuation of urban biodiversity. These insights suggest that if people are often outdoors, or have other ties to nature (for example, through gardening), this direct contact with nature makes them value urban biodiversity even more. Nevertheless, our field survey also showed that people of all walks of life value urban green spaces rich in plant species, a statement which is true for both formal green spaces such as parks, as well as for informal elements such as plants that grow in tree pits or the wilder vegetation to be found in urban wastelands.

The second part of our study determined that more than 90 percent of the interviewees across the five European cities regularly go to urban parks, and that they go there mainly for recreational uses. Their favourite park uses can be described as physical activity, including walking. Social activities such as meeting friends or relatives were reported by 25 percent of our respondents, and about 15 percent of people visit parks mostly for nature-related activities. While some outdoor activities were favoured by specific socio-cultural groups, other types of interactions were enjoyed by all social groups. The type of activities respondents enjoy could be related to the respondent's occupation, current work, and education, and it also mattered whether someone worked in an environmental job conducting physical and social activities in parks, but this was not the case for nature-related park uses. In general, differences between social groups were lower for nature-related activities. Our results suggest that urban green spaces enable a wide variety of people to experience nature on a regular basis, and in a variety of ways.

The uses that people reported related both to their socio-cultural backgrounds and to geographical context (i.e. which city they lived in). These were especially relevant for the physical use of parks, with various differences between cities emerging in relation to age, occupation, or education. One nature-related activity that was reported surprisingly often (by an average of 5 percent of respondents across all the cities, going up to 12 percent in Malmö) was people collecting nature products, with this representing their major outdoor activity in urban parks. In this regard, the companion study on urban foraging (for Berlin only) showed that the cultural context of people matters. The practice of regularly collecting wild edible plants in urban surroundings was traced back to traditions in the forager's families and people who were exposed to foraging experiences during childhood often continued the practice later on in life. Also, some personal stories pointed to legacy effects from the post-war or communist eras in Berlin on the respondent's foraging practices.

These outcomes highlight the variety of green space uses, and demonstrate how cultural diversity and urban nature intertwine. In order to adjust the planning of species-rich urban green spaces to suit people's attitudes, the geographic and cultural context needs to be taken into consideration. This is revealed through the field survey for both the valuation and the uses of urban green, as both differed slightly in the different geographic regions that were studied. This implies that cities can plan for green spaces that include many different species, and that the management and maintenance of urban green space can be adapted to strategies that conserve and support biodiversity in accordance to local settings. Although most people were very positive about biodiversity in urban green spaces, the survey did reveal some variation across the different cities in terms of public expectations towards different types of green space. For park uses, demands are wide-ranging within the physical and social activities that people perform, but they are more similar between different social groups when it comes to nature-related activities. Across a range of cities, we found that urban green spaces can enable people to benefit from nature, that these spaces help people to relax and recuperate from the stresses of urban life, and that people enjoy the diversity of urban green space in all its different forms, ranging from large parks to tree pits.

While working on this essay, I am staying in a city that is a mosaic of historic streets and plazas, packed with houses, villas, and churches. I can see people enjoying the afternoon sun on little balconies, between white and pink Bougainvillea. Later, I discover wild rocket and common purslane growing by the roadside. Along the street leading to a world-famous viewpoint are a row of persimmon trees, the branches heavy with fruit. I am sure that someone will pick them once they are ripe.

1 Laura Celesti-Grapow, Petr Pysek, Votjech Jarosik, and Carlo Blasi, "Determinants of native and alien species richness in the urban flora of Rome," *Diversity and Distributions* 12 (2006) pp. 490–501.

2 Alexandra Botzat, Leonie K. Fischer, and Ingo Kowarik, "Unexploited opportunities in understanding liveable and biodiverse cities; a review on urban biodiversity perception and valuation," *Global Environmental Change* 39 (2016) pp. 220–233.

3 See Stephen Kaplan, Rachel Kaplan, and John S. Wendt, "Rated preference and complexity for natural and urban visual material," *Perception & Psychophysics* 12 (1972) pp. 354–356; and Roger S. Ulrich, "View through a window may influence recovery from surgery," *Science* 224 (1984) pp. 420–421.

4 Daniel T.C. Cox, Hannah L. Hudson, Danielle F. Shanahan, Richard A. Fuller, and Kevin J. Gaston, "The rarity of direct experiences of nature in an urban population," *Landscape and Urban Planning* 160 (2017) pp. 79–84.

5 For example, we showed people a set of different scenes that displayed typical urban nature: a park meadow, an urban forest, vegetation along streets, and an abandoned wasteland area with herbs, shrubs, and trees. We asked people how they liked these scenes, especially as each scene was shown with varying species richness, that is, we showed the same urban nature scene with many different species (high biodiversity), with some species variety (medium biodiversity), and with only little variety in the plant combination (low biodiversity). In the same questionnaire, we asked people to share information on what they usually use green spaces for: Do they go there for recreational activities like sun-bathing or for reading a book? Do they go for a walk—alone or with their dog? Do they meet their friends and families outside in a green space? See Leonie K. Fischer, Jasmin Honold, Alex Botzat, Daniel Brinkmeyer, Rozalija Cvejić,

Tim Delshammar, Birgit Elands, Dagmar Haase, Nadja Kabisch, Stefanie J. Karle, Raffaele Lafortezza, Mojca Nastran, Anders Busse Nielsen, Alexander P.N. van der Jagt, Kati Vierikko, and Ingo Kowarik, "Recreational ecosystem services in European cities: sociocultural and geographical contexts matter for park use," *Ecosystem Services* 31 (2018) pp. 455–467; and Leonie K. Fischer, Jasmin Honold, Rozalija Cvejić, Tim Delshammar, Sven Hilbert, Raffaele Lafortezza, Mojca Nastran, Anders Busse Nielsen, Marina Pintar, Alexander P.N. van der Jagt, and Ingo Kowarik, "Beyond green: broad support for biodiversity in multicultural European cities," *Global Environmental Change* 49 (2018) pp. 35–45.

6 Urban foraging is one way people interact with biodiversity in a very down-to-earth way. Within the last years, the practice has gained in popularity among many different people: besides using the collected plants for food or medicinal purposes, people report that they forage just for the enjoyment of the practice, or because they think it contributes to a healthy lifestyle. There are now even high-end restaurants that promote themselves as using not only regional or organic food but also as incorporating wild-growing flowers, herbs, and fungi in their menu. The practice of urban foraging largely relies on the local species pool, given by the plants that were planted for landscaping purposes in urban parks, leftovers of old gardens in abandoned lots, or wayside plants that grow spontaneously. In our study, we asked foragers in Berlin, Germany, to share information on their motivations for foraging, the species they collect, the places they go to forage, and their personal social and cultural backgrounds. See Jonah L. Landor-Yamagata, Ingo Kowarik, and Leonie K. Fischer, "Urban foraging in Berlin: people, plants and practices within the metropolitan green infrastructure," *Sustainability* (2018) 10, 1873. For further literature on foraging in cities, see also Christoph D. D. Rupprecht, "Informal urban green space: residents' perception, use, and management preferences across four major Japanese shrinking cities," *Land* (2017) 6 59; and Charlie M. Shackleton, Patrick T. Hurley, Annika C. Dahlberg, Marla R. Emery, and Harini Nagendra, "Urban foraging: a ubiquitous human practice overlooked by urban planners, policy, and research," *Sustainability* (2017) 9, 1884.

Urban cemeteries in Berlin and beyond: life in the grounds of the dead

Ingo Kowarik

It has long been known that urban cemeteries are also places of nature.[1] In 1948, for example, the ecologist Bouly de Lesdain reported some remarkable lichen species growing on the graves of the Montmartre cemetery in Paris.[2] Today, the importance of cemeteries for biodiversity and nature conservation is increasingly recognized in many cities around the globe.[3] However, the first systematic investigations into the flora of a large set of urban cemeteries were not carried out in Berlin until the 1980s,[4] along with other in-depth studies on urban land use types within the island city.[5]

Cities all over the world have one thing in common: they encompass numerous cemeteries, most of which were built outside the gates of the city after burial sites at churches had become scarce. Since many cities have grown rapidly, many cemeteries are now located in the middle of the city, as "green islands" set within the built environment. In districts where large green spaces are lacking, cemeteries have a critical role in offering people in their neighbourhood direct access to biodiverse spaces for recreation. The Père Lachaise cemetery, for example, with an area of 44 hectares, is the largest green area in the centre of Paris, with more than 4,000 trees.[6] As burial places, and as places of remembrance, cemeteries often enjoy a higher degree of protection from development than many other open spaces.

Old cemeteries are an important part of our cultural heritage. In addition to the culture of remembrance and the architecture of the graves, the history of garden design and the use of plants also plays an important role, as it reflects the garden styles of the cemetery's time of origin. Therefore, many cemeteries are also garden monuments, such as most of the nineteenth century cemeteries in the centre of Berlin.[7] Here, as in other Central European cemeteries, graves are mostly planted with ornamental plants, and occasionally with woody plants. Trees often line paths as allées, divide different cemetery quarters, and emphasize special places.

Campanula persicifolia (peach-leaved bellflower) as an escaped ornamental on the Jewish cemetery in Berlin-Weißensee. Photo: Birgit Seitz.

Walls as artificial rock complex provide habitats also for rare ar endangered fern species such as *Cystopteris fragilis* (left) and *Asplenium trichomanes* (right). (Both photos show the same situation). Photos: Birgit Seitz.

Today, there are 224 cemeteries in Berlin. The total area of 1105 hectares is more than five times the size of the city's central park, the Tiergarten, which covers 210 hectares. Most of Berlin's cemeteries date back to the nineteenth century, when the city of Berlin was in a rapid phase of expansion. In her pioneering work, the botanist Anne Graf examined 50 cemeteries in what was then West Berlin. She found 690 species of wild ferns and flowering plants on a total area of 297 hectares. That is equal to almost half of the total flora of West Berlin at the time, found in less than 1 percent of the land area of the city. A particular wealth of species were found in older cemeteries, and in those cemeteries that had differently maintained areas, including wilder spaces. Also in Paris, an analysis of almost 1,000 vegetation relevées scattered over the city area showed that almost half of all wild plant species could be documented in only 31 relevées from 15 cemeteries.[8]

Of the 690 plant species found by Graf in Berlin's cemeteries, 128 were on the Red List from 1982,[9] thus representing a high proportion of the endangered plant species known to occur in Berlin. Surprisingly, these species stem from very different habitats, such as fields in the case of *Aphanes arvensis*, forests for *Anemone nemorosa*, and dry grasslands for *Helichrysum arenarium*. There are also meadow plants including *Campanula patula*, various sedges and other wetland species, and also species adapted for rock surfaces such as mosses, ferns, and lichens. However, at least 14 of the rare Berlin cemetery plants are naturalized garden plants that were originally planted on the graves and are most probably genetically distinct from wild populations. Examples include columbine (*Aquilegia vulgaris*) and bugle (*Ajuga reptans*). Most of the rare species were also scarce in cemeteries, or only found in small populations. In this respect, we should not overestimate the contribution of cemeteries to botanical species protection.

However, urban cemeteries do offer city dwellers access to a kind of urban nature that is often more diverse than in other green areas. Compared to other open spaces, cemeteries are often "biodiversity hotspots" in densely built-up urban areas. In Graf's study, smaller cemeteries with an area of up to three hectares had more species than parks of the same size or plots of vacant land did in Berlin. The relatively high species-richness of small cemeteries is likely due to many escapees from cultivation that contribute significantly to cemetery floras.[10] In districts where there is little open space, cemeteries take on special significance as a kind of lush and tranquil public space, as found in a recent study in Norway.[11]

Why are cemeteries so species-rich? This is mainly due to the interaction of three factors. The first of these is the high diversity of environmental conditions in cemeteries, which translates into numerous types of ecological niches for plants (and also animal species) that would otherwise rely on habitats elsewhere, perhaps even outside the city altogether in different types of landscapes.

Tree plantations, groves, allées, and undergrowth create habitats for plant species of near-natural and plantation-type forests, forest edges and hedgerows. Moreover, senescent trees in cemeteries often show cavities and rotten wood in different stages of decay.[12] These are key habitats for birds and bats and for a wealth of

fungi and invertebrates, including highly endangered species such as the hoverfly *Pocota personata* in London's Abney Park cemetery.[13]
Grassland strips between graves and along paths can be populated by meadow plants. At Gamla Kyrkogården (the old cemetery in Malmö, Sweden), flowering meadow islands that are occasionally spared by mowing glow in early summer. On the drier sandy soils of Berlin cemeteries, even dry grassland plants like the beautiful dwarf everlast (*Helichrysum arenarium*) thrive. Well-kept graves and paths can be used by short-lived plants from disturbed locations. Studies in Turkey and other countries have revealed how cemeteries have become refuges for a range of orchid species.[14]
Another special feature of cemeteries is that they are, from an ecological point of view, intricate rock formations comprised of gravestones, walls, and mausoleums. Such artificial "rocks" are special locations for ferns, mosses, and lichens. Thus 119 moss species and 72 different lichen species were found at Berlin's Südwestfriedhof in Stahnsdorf.[15] At the Jewish cemetery in Berlin-Weißensee, besides the more common wall rue (*Asplenium ruta-muraria*), highly endangered fern species such as the common fragile fern (*Cystopteris fragilis*) and the highly endangered maidenhair spleenwort (*Asplenium trichomanes*) grow on walls.[16]
The second reason for the biodiversity of cemeteries is the history of plant use leaving its mark on the wild flora. A variety of ornamental plants, shrubs, and trees are planted on cemeteries, including some with symbolic meaning such as the evergreen (*Vinca minor*) as a symbol of eternal life or pendulous forms of trees to symbolize mourning. At the Jewish cemetery in Weißensee, for example, 113 different tree and shrub species can be found, including several forms of mourning ash (*Fraxinus excelsior* 'Pendula') that are up to 130 years old.[17] The variety of woody plants and herbaceous ornamental plants is also reflected in the wild flora of the cemetery. Forty-two species growing wild today in Weißensee are old ornamental plants. Some of the spring flowering plants are particularly striking, especially the Siberian squill (*Scilla siberica*), which has not only spread in large patches in Weißensee, but also plunges many other cemeteries into a magical blue. Snowdrops (*Galanthus nivalis*) and various *Gagea* species also occur among many other, former ornamental plant species.
The third reason for this species-richness in cemeteries is the coexistence of areas with different levels of maintenance, including the wilder parts. The latter reflect a changing cemetery culture. For some decades, the demand for burial areas has been declining, as more people are choosing cremation both in Germany and elsewhere. Some cemeteries have been completely or partially abandoned because there is no room for new burials. Thus, many cemeteries became wilderness islands in the middle of the city. Examples include the famous Highgate cemetery and other Victorian cemeteries in London,[18] along with further sites in Berlin and other cities.
The Jewish cemetery in Berlin-Weißensee is in large parts overgrown, whereas other parts are more or less maintained. This causes different species to be favoured, for example forest species versus grassland species.[19] The tree mapping

shows how quickly a cemetery can become a forest through natural processes: of the nearly 7,000 trees that are found in the cemetery today, over 2,000 were planted as avenue trees or on the grave areas, while the majority of the trees grew wild. The Norway maple (*Acer platanoides*) is by far the most common tree species in Weißensee. Its escape from plantings led to the emergence of a new type of forest that did not previously occur in the Berlin landscape, as other tree species such as oaks and pines dominated the predominantly nutrient-poor sandy soils. The new maple forests, on the other hand, benefit from the nutrient-rich soils of cemeteries and other urban locations. However, maples often form a dense and dark canopy under which few other species can thrive.

From an ecological perspective, the wild cemetery forest in Weißensee shows how, within a few decades, a kind of "novel wilderness" can develop in a thoroughly designed and maintained cemetery. As with the "ancient wilderness" of forest remnants, it is the natural processes in rewilded cemeteries that shape the development and decay of biocoenoses and ecosystem dynamics. However, with the burials, the structural elements, and the plethora of cultivated plants, cemeteries offer completely new opportunities for the development of nature, resulting in the emergence of a type of "novel wilderness" as in other urban settings.[20]

This novel wilderness probably fascinates all visitors of the cemetery. At the same time, however, it points to the terrible causes of its origin. With around 115,600 graves, the cemetery in Berlin-Weißensee, founded in 1880, is one of the largest Jewish cemeteries in Europe. Its grave architecture, and the use of ornamental plants and shrubs which are mostly absent from older Jewish cemeteries, indicate a rapprochement between the Jewish community and the design and maintenance of other cemeteries in Berlin.[21] And yet, today's wilderness in Weißensee is not only a result of urban nature dynamics. It is also a material reflection of the Holocaust and the absence of relatives who might have tended the graves. Reflecting on Matthew Gandy's concept of "forensic ecology," we can derive data from the hybrid mixtures of original plantings and the wild natural elements in order to collaboratively produce evidence for both biodiversity significance and processes of cultural and historical change.[22] To integrate wilderness into a future concept for the development of the cemetery is therefore an important contribution to the preservation of historical evidence of the past.

Cemeteries can be conceived as laboratories in which nature and the city find new and often unexpected combinations. They are often not only green islands within the urban matrix but also biodiversity hotspots "set within a maelstrom of intensifying development pressures."[23] The importance of cemeteries for urban green space systems and their biodiversity is increasingly recognized today, far beyond Berlin.[24]

Biodiversity can be promoted in all cemeteries through the spatial differentiation of maintenance and the conservation and promotion of natural elements. If old cemeteries are used much less or in some cases not at all for burials, then there is scope for new, wild natural features to flourish in the middle of the city. This brings new opportunities and new challenges. Old trees with rotting wood, for example, provide important habitats for many highly specialized fauna, but they must not endanger visitors with falling branches or trunks. The concept of the "cemetery forest," which was developed for the Jewish cemetery in Berlin Weißensee, shows how security and natural elements can be conceptually combined.[25] A basic idea here is the juxtaposition of areas with different levels of maintenance, even including wilder parts. Where trees cause danger, branches and parts of the crown are carefully cut back, but only as far as necessary to allow ageing processes to continue as long as possible.

On an old, no-longer-needed cemetery in Neukölln, another approach was adopted to integrate the area into Berlin's green infrastructure. The former cemetery had been transformed to an urban park. Through the integration of old cemetery shrubs and trees and spontaneous wild vegetation, and with some design interventions such as the inclusion of benches, a new type of public park is being created here by combining different elements of nature and culture. This is the newly created Anita Berber Park. As different as the handling of these two cemeteries may be, both examples illustrate a change in contemporary discourse about how to respond to wild urban nature within more formal types of green spaces. As different as challenges and approaches to solutions may be, cemeteries in the city are exciting interfaces between culture and nature, where new patterns of biodiversity emerge and where the dynamics of nature can be experienced directly by all visitors.

1 Oliver L. Gilbert, *The ecology of urban habitats* (London: Chapman & Hall, 1989).

2 M. Bouly de Lesdain, "Ecologie (phanérogames, mousses et lichens) de quelques sites de Paris," *Encyclopédie biogéographique et écologique* 4 (1948).

3 Viktor Löki, Balazs Deák, Andras Balazs Lukács, and Attila V. Molnár, "Biodiversity potential of burial places–a review on the flora and fauna of cemeteries and churchyards," *Global Ecology and Conservation* (2019) e00614.

4 Anne Graf, "Flora und Vegetation der Friedhöfe in Berlin (West)," *Verhandlungen des Berliner Botanischen Vereins* 5 (1986) pp. 1–211.

5 Herbert Sukopp, ed., *Stadtökologie: Das Beispiel Berlin* (Berlin: Reimer, 1990).

6 APUR, 2011, *Situation et perspectives de la place de la nature à Paris, 9e atelier—Les cimetières.* (last accessed 19 January 2020: https://www.apur.org/fr/file/46934/download?token=Xa8PXzpE).

7 Jörg Haspel and Klaus-Henning von Krosigk, eds., *Gartendenkmale in Berlin: Friedhöfe* (Petersberg: Michael Imhof Verlag, 2008).

8 APUR, see p. 6.

9 Herbert Sukopp et al., "Liste der wildwachsenden Farn- und Blütenpflanzen von Berlin (West) mit Angaben zur Gefährdung der Sippen und Angaben über den Zeitpunkt der Einwanderung in das Gebiet von Berlin (West)," *Landschaftsentwicklung und Umweltforschung* 11 (1982) pp. 19–58.

10 Graf "Flora und Vegetation der Friedhöfe in Berlin (West)," see p. 6.

11 Helena Nordh, Katinka H. Evensen, and Margrete Skår, "A peaceful place in the city—a qualitative study of restorative components of the cemetery," *Landscape and Urban Planning* 167 (2017) pp. 108–117.

12 Ryan A. Bovyn, Michael C. Lordon, Allison E Grecco, Abigail C. Leeper, and Jalene M. LaMontagne, "Tree cavity availability in urban cemeteries and city parks," *Journal of Urban Ecology* 5 (1) (2019), juy030.

13 Matthew Gandy, "The fly that tried to save the world: saproxylic geographies and other-than-human ecologies," *Transactions of the Institute of British Geographers* 44 (2019) pp. 392–406.

14 V. Löki, A. Molnár, K. Süveges, H. Heimeier, A. Takács, T. Nagy, R. Fekete, A. Lovas-Kiss, K.C.A.J. Kreutz, G. Sramkó, and J. Tökölyi, "Predictors of conservation value of Turkish cemeteries: a case study using orchids," *Landscape and Urban Planning* 186 (2019) pp. 36–44.

15 "DBU-Projekt Südwestfriedhof Stahnsdorf: Schlussbericht (last accessed 19 January 2020: http://friedhofsfinder.stiftung-historische-friedhoefe.de/friedhof/brandenb/st_dorf/DBUbericht.htm).

16 Ingo Kowarik, Sascha Buchholz, Moritz von der Lippe, and Birgit Seitz, "Biodiversity functions of urban cemeteries: evidence from one of the largest Jewish cemeteries in Europe," *Urban Forestry & Urban Greening* 19 (2016) pp. 68–78.

17 Birgit Seitz, Ingo Kowarik, Andreas Lemke, Moritz von der Lippe, Tobias Arera-Rütenik, Sascha Buchholz, Anne Hiller, Norbert Kühn, Volker Otte, Ellen Richter, Jens Scharon, and Tobias Teige, "Abschlussbericht des Forschungsvorhabens Integration von Naturschutzzielen bei der Bewahrung und Entwicklung des Jüdischen Friedhofs in Berlin-Weißensee, Berlin (2015)," see (last accessed 19 January 2020: https://www.dbu.de/OPAC/ab/DBU-Abschlussbericht-AZ-29773.pdf).

18 Gilbert, *The ecology of urban habitats,* p. 3; Matthew Gandy, "Queer ecology: nature, sexuality, and heterotopic alliances," *Environment and Planning D: Society and Space* 30 (4) (2012) pp. 727–747.

19 Kowarik et al., "Biodiversity functions of urban cemeteries," p. 14; Seitz et al., "Abschlussbericht des Forschungsvorhabens Integration von Naturschutzzielen," p. 17.

20 Ingo Kowarik, "Urban wilderness: Supply, demand, and access," *Urban Forestry & Urban Greening* 29 (2018) pp. 336–347.

21 Tobias Rütenik, Tobias Horn, Elgin von Gaisberg, and Isabelle Arnold, "115,628 Berliners: The Weissensee Jewish Cemetery—documentation of the comprehensive survey of the burial sites," *Beiträge zur Denkmalpflege in Berlin* 40 (2013) pp. 1–112.

22 See Gandy, "The fly that tried to save the world."

23 See Gandy, "The fly that tried to save the world," p. 5.

24 Helena Nordh and Grete Swensen, "Introduction to the special feature 'The role of cemeteries as green urban spaces,'" *Urban Forestry and Urban Greening* 33 (2018) pp. 56–57; Löki et al., "Predictors of conservation value of Turkish cemeteries," p. 5.

25 Seitz et al., 2015, "Abschlussbericht des Forschungsvorhabens Integration von Naturschutzzielen," p. 17.

Appendix

Contributors

Bergit Arends is a curator and researcher, creating and studying interdisciplinary curatorial and artistic processes, currently focusing on the environment and the visual arts. She was recently based in the Research Department at the Tate Gallery and is now a British Academy postdoctoral research fellow at the University of Bristol. Material from her PhD thesis entitled *Contemporary art, archives and environmental change in the age of the Anthropocene* (2017) was included in the award-winning publication *Chrystel Lebas—field studies: walking through landscapes and archives* (Amsterdam: Fw: Books, 2018). She has published in *Interdisciplinary Science Reviews, Botanical drift: protagonists of the invasive herbarium* (Sternberg Press, 2018), and on decolonising natural history museums. She has also curated several contemporary art projects for natural history museums in London and Berlin.

Lucilla Barchetta is an anthropologist who recently completed her PhD in Urban Studies at the Gran Sasso Science Institute (L'Aquila, Italy). Her work focuses on the intersection of political ecology with urban studies and is sustained by an in-depth ethnographic approach to everyday life in cities. She is currently a research fellow in the Department of Cultures, Politics, and Society at the University of Turin, where she participates in a broader project on the relationship between the construction of Italian whiteness and processes of urban environmental change. A book based on her thesis entitled *Riverbanks made by walking: understanding the temporalities of urban natures through atmospheres* will be published by Agenzia X in 2020.

Dorothee Brantz is professor of urban environmental history at the Technische Universität Berlin where she also directs the Center for Metropolitan Studies. She has published widely on topics ranging from the greening of cities, urban resilience, human-animal relations, and the environmental history of warfare. Currently she is working on a book project about the role of seasons in the city.

Livia Cahn studies urban anthropology at the University of Cambridge and the EHESS, Paris. She is currently based in Brussels, where she is a founding member of Ecologies de Bruxelles, a university-based collective that tackles a host of environmental questions and interrogates how to narrate them. She is co-author of *Terres des Villes* (éditions de l'éclat, 2017). Her work is based on an active engagement in the urban context and an enthusiasm for collaboration with researchers, architects, artists, and farmers, in an on-going enquiry into what ethnography can contribute to contemporary debates in matters relating to urban ecologies.

Mona Caron is a Swiss-born, San Francisco-based artist, who uses muralism, illustration, and photography in both her art and her wider environmental activism. Her focus is on community-informed and site-specific murals in public spaces. She has created large-scale murals in the North America, Europe, South America, and Asia, and has delved into stop-motion animation as part of her WEEDS project. She also co-creates visuals for street campaigns and outreach on behalf of social and environmental movements including 350.org, the Coalition of Immokalee Workers, Zero-Waste Detroit, the US Social forum, La Coordinadora por el Agua y la Vida, the Fundación Abril of Cochabamba Bolivia, and Acción Ecologica (Ecuador).

Nigel Clark is professor of social sustainability and human geography at Lancaster University. He is the author of *Inhuman nature: sociable life on a dynamic planet* (Sage, 2011) and co-editor (with Kathryn Yusoff) of a recent *Theory, Culture & Society* special issue on "Geosocial Formations and the Anthropocene" (2017). He is currently working on a book tentatively titled *Planetary social thought* (with Bronislaw Szerszynski).

Peter Del Tredici is a botanist specializing in the growth and development of trees. He retired from the Arnold Arboretum of Harvard University in 2014 after working there for 35 years. He taught in the Landscape Architecture Department at the Harvard Graduate School of Design from 1992 to 2016 and the Urban Planning Department at MIT from 2016 to 2019. His interests are wide ranging and include such subjects as the root systems of woody plants, the ecology of hemlock trees, and the natural and cultural history of the Ginkgo, which he has been studying since 1989. His recent work focuses on urban ecology and climate change and he is currently working on the second edition of *Wild urban plants of the Northeast: a field guide* (Cornell University Press, 2010).

T. J. Demos is a cultural critic and professor of visual culture at University of California, Santa Cruz, and director of its Center for Creative Ecologies. He writes about contemporary art, global politics, and ecology and is the author, most recently, of *Against the Anthropocene: visual culture and environment today* (Sternberg Press, 2017) and *Decolonizing nature: contemporary art and the politics of ecology* (Sternberg Press, 2016). He is currently working on a Mellon-funded research project, art exhibition, and book project dedicated to the questions "what comes after the end of the world?" and "how can we cultivate futures of social justice" within capitalist ruins?

Seth Denizen is a researcher and design practitioner trained in landscape architecture and evolutionary biology. He is currently completing a PhD in geography at the University of California, Berkeley, where his doctoral research investigates the vertical geopolitics of urban soil in Mexico City.

Sonja Dümpelmann is a landscape historian and is professor of landscape architecture in the Stuart Weitzman School of Design at the University of Pennsylvania. She is the author of *Seeing trees: a history of street trees in New York City and Berlin* (Yale University Press, 2019), *Flights of imagination: aviation, landscape, design* (UVA Press, 2014), and a book on the Italian landscape architect Maria Teresa Parpagliolo Shephard (VDG Weimar, 2004). Her edited volumes include *A cultural history of gardens in the age of empire* (Bloomsbury, 2013); *Women, modernity, and landscape architecture* (with John Beardsley; Routledge, 2015); *Airport landscape: urban ecologies in the aerial age* (with Charles Waldheim; GSD, 2016); and *Greening the city: urban landscapes in the twentieth century* (with Dorothee Brantz; UVA Press, 2011).

Henrik Ernstson is lecturer of geography at the University of Manchester. His publications include *Grounding urban natures: histories and futures of urban ecology* (The MIT Press, 2019; edited with Sverker Sörlin) and *Urban political ecology in the Anthropo-Obscene: interruptions and possibilities* (Routledge, 2019; edited with Erik Swyngedouw), along with articles in *Antipode, Landscape & Urban Planning, Urban Studies, and Theory Culture & Society.* He is currently researching the intersection between colonial and imperial remains of urban infrastructure in settler colonial societies, while developing the use of film as part of critical humanities research.

Marion Ernwein is a departmental lecturer in human geography at the University of Oxford and a junior research fellow at Mansfield College, Oxford. Her research interests are in plant politics, urban nature, and urban political ecology. Her publications include *Les natures de la ville néolibérale: Une écologie politique du végétal urbain* (UGA Editions, 2019), along with articles in *ACME, Geoforum* and *Environment and Planning A,* among other journals.

Leonie Fischer is professor of landscape planning and ecology at the University of Stuttgart. She is a trained gardener and landscape planner and received her PhD in the natural sciences. She worked previously in the Department of Ecosystem Science and Plant Ecology at the Institute of Ecology of the Technische Universität Berlin and the main themes of her work are ecological relationships in human influenced habitats, the human-nature intersection in cities, and approaches to urban restoration.

Matthew Gandy is professor of geography at the University of Cambridge. His publications include *Concrete and clay: reworking nature in New York City* (The MIT Press, 2002), *The fabric of space: water, modernity, and the urban imagination* (The MIT Press, 2014), and Moth (Reaktion, 2016), along with articles in *New Left Review, International Journal of Urban and Regional Research, Society and Space* and many other journals. He is currently researching the interface between cultural and scientific aspects to urban biodiversity.

Susanne Hauser is professor of history of art and cultural studies at the Universität der Künste Berlin. Her research focusses on urban and landscape studies (*Metamorphosen des Abfalls: Konzepte für aufgegebene Industrieareale*, Campus, 2001; *Ästhetik der Agglomeration*, Müller + Busmann, 2006) and the history and theory of architecture (co-editor of *Kulturtechnik Entwerfen*, transcript, 2009; of *Architekturwissen I+II*, transcript, 2011/13; and of *Architektur in transdisziplinärer Perspektive*, transcript, 2015). She is currently writing an essay on the concept of "knowledge" in recent discourses on architecture, urban design, and landscape architecture.

Sandra Jasper is junior professor of geography at the Humboldt-Universität zu Berlin. Her research interests are in urban nature, soundscapes, and feminist theory. Her research has been published in the *Annals of the American Association of Geographers, The Journal of Architecture*, and *Dialogues in Human Geography*, among other journals. She is currently completing her first monograph on the experimental spaces of West Berlin for which she received a Graham Foundation grant.

Kumiko Kiuchi is associate professor at the Institute for Liberal Arts at the Tokyo Institute of Technology. She has published extensively on modernism, especially on the Irish writer Samuel Beckett, and is a regular contributor to the UK-based literary and arts magazine *Snow lit rev*. She introduced Patrick Keiller's Robinson Trilogy to Japan. Her recent research interests include the analysis of geographical features in modern and contemporary literature and photography, and comparative research on urban space in photography and films between Tokyo and London.

Ingo Kowarik is professor of ecosystem science and plant ecology at the Technische Universität Berlin. His research interests cover the fields of urban ecology, biodiversity conservation, and invasion ecology, including people-nature intersections in cities. In his role as honorary state commissioner for nature conservation he has also supported the integration of urban biodiversity into many park and urban development projects in Berlin. He has published several books and more than 150 articles in scientific journals.

Maroš Krivý is a research associate in the Department of Geography, University of Cambridge, and director of the graduate programme in urban studies at the Faculty of Architecture, Estonian Academy of Arts. He is a writer and urbanist who works at the intersections of architectural history and urban geography, and has published in leading international journals such as *International Journal of Urban and Regional Research, Planning Theory, Political Geography, Architectural Histories, Journal of Architecture, Thresholds,* and *Avery Review.* He contributed to the edited collections *Neoliberalism: an architectural history* (K. Cupers, H. Mattsson and C. Gabrielsson, eds.), *Second world postmodernisms* (V. Kulić, ed.), and *East west central* (Á. Moravánszky, ed.).

Jens Lachmund is a sociologist and Lecturer in Science and Technology Studies at Maastricht University. His work has focused on the historical sociology of medicine and on the social study of science, urbanism, and the environment. His publications include *Greening Berlin* (The MIT Press, 2013), and the edited volumes *Science and the city* (with Sven Dierig and Andrew Mendelsohn, Osiris 18, 2003) and *Spatializing the history of ecology: sites, journeys, mappings* (with Raf de Bont, Routledge 2017).

Marcus Nyman is a human geographer in the Department of Geography at the University of Cambridge where he recently completed his PhD thesis on "urban foraging" practices and emerging cultural and ecological relationships between people and plants in cities. His academic interests include sustainable food systems, the politics of urban space and nature, and environmental governance. He has previously worked in the field of sustainability certification and sustainable urbanism and now works for the Royal Society for the Protection of Birds.

Uriel Orlow is a London and Lisbon-based artist whose methods are research-based, process-oriented, and multi-disciplinary, and include film, photography, drawing, and sound. His artwork is concerned with spatial manifestations of memory, blind spots of representation, and forms of haunting. Orlow's work has been shown in museums and galleries internationally, including at the Tate Modern in London, the Palais de Tokyo in Paris, the Kunsthaus Zürich, and the Centre d'Art Contemporain in Geneva, as well as in Berlin, Ramallah, Marseille, Cairo, Alexandria, Istanbul, Mexico City, New York, and elsewhere. Recent publications of his work and writing include *Theatrum Botanicum* (Sternberg Press, 2018) and *Soil Affinities* (Shelter Press, 2019).

Daniel Paiva is a researcher at the Center for Geographical Studies of the Institute of Geography and Spatial Planning of the University of Lisbon. He recently completed his doctoral thesis on listening and soundmaking practices in urban environments. His research has been published in journals such as *Geography Compass, Journal of Historical Geography, Geografiska Annaler: Series B, Human Geography, Tijdschrift voor Economische en Sociale Geografie,* and *Space and Culture.* Daniel is currently researching the design of nature experiences in urban environments.

Mara Polgovsky Ezcurra has been lecturer in history of art at Birkbeck College, University of London since 2018 after holding a junior research fellowship at Queens' College, Cambridge. Her research focuses on contemporary Latin American art and intellectual history, with an emphasis on the politics of aesthetics and the study of notions of life, embodiment, presence, interactivity, and agency in time-based media. Her publications include the monograph *Touched bodies: the performative turn in Latin American art* (Rutgers University Press, 2019), the essay collection *Marcos Kurtycz: corporeality unbound* (Fauna-Jumex, 2020), and the edited volume *Sabotage art: politics and iconoclasm in contemporary Latin America* (2016). She has curated a number of research-led exhibitions, including, most recently, *Reality machines: an art exhibition on post-truth* (CRASSH, Cambridge, 2018). In 2019, Polgovsky received the College Art Association *Art Journal*'s award.

Yan Wang Preston is a Chinese photographer who is now based in the UK. In 2019, she won first prize in the landscape category at the Sony World Photography awards. Her major publications include Forest (Hatje Cantz, 2010), which explores changing urban landscapes in Chinese cities, and *Mother River* (Hatje Cantz, 2018), which is based on a series of photographs taken along the entire course of Yangtze River as part of her interest in "deep mapping" and multi-sensory approaches to the visual representation of nature and landscape. Her forest project won the Syngenta Photography Award in 2017, and she has exhibited her work widely in both solo and group shows. In addition to her artistic practice, she teaches photography at Huddersfield University.

Bhavani Raman is associate professor of history at the University of Toronto. Her research pertains to histories of bureaucracy, law, and archives of India and the wider Tamil world. She is the author of *Document Raj: scribes and writing in early colonial South India* (University of Chicago Press, 2012) and articles on the bureaucratic structures, extraordinary law and land management of early colonial Madras. Her current research on ecological landscapes of the coastal city of Chennai has led to explore the history of the city's waterscapes. Her essays have appeared in *Comparative Studies in Society and History, Journal of Economic and Social History of the Orient*, and the Indian news portal, *The Wire*.

Nida Rehman is the Lucian and Rita Caste Assistant Professor in the School of Architecture, Carnegie Mellon University, and recently completed her PhD in the Department of Geography at the University of Cambridge. Her dissertation draws from critical urban geography, post-colonial studies, and medical anthropology to explore the landscapes and ecologies of epidemic mosquito-borne diseases, and the technologies and spatial practices to control them, in Lahore, Pakistan. She is a key organiser of the seminar series *Urban climates: power, development, and environment in South Asia* (2019) funded by the Urban Studies Foundation.

Mathilda Rosengren is a visual anthropologist and geographer with a particular interest in the relational structuring of urban nature. Until recently she was a doctoral student in geography at the University of Cambridge, researching the relation between notions of living with difference, "unplanned" urban nature, and official practices of urban planning in Berlin and Gothenburg. She is the co-author and editor of *Urban appropriation strategies: exploring space-making practices in contemporary European cityscapes* (transcript Verlag, 2018).

Birgit Seitz works on biodiversity analysis at the Institute of Ecology at the Technische Universität Berlin. She has been working with the flora of Berlin and Brandenburg for many years. Since 1990 she has been involved in the floristic mapping of Berlin and contributed significantly to the publication of the *Atlas of Berlin's Flora* and the *Red list of vascular plants of Berlin*. She was awarded the Berlin Nature Conservation Prize in 2018 for her commitment to researching the flora of Berlin.

Mark Spencer is a botanist who has been exploring London's wild plants for many years. He is particularly interested in non-native species and the impacts of environmental change and urbanization on our flora. He is leading the London Natural History Society's *London Flora Project* which aims to document the city's rapidly changing flora. He is also the honorary botany curator of Carl Linnaeus's herbarium at the Linnean Society of London, the Botanical Society of Britain and Ireland's Middlesex vice-county recorder, and a research associate at the Natural History Museum, London.

Bettina Stoetzer is a cultural anthropologist and associate professor of anthropology at MIT. Her research focuses on the intersections of ecology, migration, and urban social justice. Her forthcoming book *Ruderal city: ecologies of migration and urban life in Berlin* (Duke University Press) examines how human-environment relations become a key register through which urban citizenship is articulated in contemporary Europe. She is also the author of *InDifferenzen: Feministische Theorie in der Antirassistischen Kritik* (argument, 2004), *Shock and awe: war on words* together with Gonzalez/Eekelen/Tsing (New Pacific Press, 2004), along with articles on urban ecology, race, affect, and migration. She is currently working on a new project on wildlife mobility, climate change, and nationalism in the United States and Germany.

Herbert Sukopp is a botanist and ecologist. He is professor (emeritus) and former director of the Department of Ecosystem Science and Plant Ecology at the Institute of Ecology of the Technische Universität Berlin. His research interests include urban ecology, the integration of non-native species, nature conservation, vegetation science, and the history of geobotany. Amongst his many national and international advisory roles, he was state commissioner for nature conservation in Berlin. He has authored over 650 publications including numerous books and scientific journal articles.

Alexandra Toland is a Berlin-based visual artist and environmental planner with research interests in ecosystem services, urban ecology, soil, and culture, and the Anthropocene. She is junior professor for arts and research at the Bauhaus University Weimar, where she directs the PhD Programme in art and design. She has published on the topic of soil and art in books and journals, including most recently the co-edited book *Field to palette: dialogues on soil and art in the Anthropocene* (CRC Press 2018).

Moritz von der Lippe is a researcher and lecturer at the Institute for Ecology at the Technische Universität Berlin. He researches and publishes on urban ecology, invasion ecology, and nature conservation in urban landscapes. He is currently working on the influence of urban land use on the occurrence and persistence of rare species and on the transformation of semi-natural grasslands along urbanization gradients.

Lois Weinberger is an Austrian artist whose poetic and political work involves investigating marginal zones. In his artistic work, ruderal plants or "weeds" and the way they are involved in all areas of life serve as a starting point for notes, drawings, photographs, objects, texts, and films, as well as projects in public space. His work has contributed significantly to discussions on art and nature since the 1990s. Venues of recent exhibitions include the Tinguely Museum, Basel, the Watari-Um Museum of Contemporary Art, Tokyo, and documenta 14, Athens and Kassel. Recent publications on his work include *Debris field: Erkundungen im Abgelebten* (ed. Franziska Weinberger, documenta and Museum Friedericianum, 2017) and *Lois Weinberger* (ed. Philippe Van Cauteren, Hatje Cantz, 2013).

Suili Xiao is currently based at the Leibniz Institut für ökologische Raumentwicklung, Dresden, and was recipient of a German Chancellor fellowship from the Alexander von Humboldt Foundation. She holds a PhD in urban forestry from the Beijing Forestry University. In addition to her postdoctoral research on urban biodiversity and urban ecology she has also undertaken a range of environmental consultancy for nature reserves in Chinese cities.

Bo Zheng taught at the China Academy of Art from 2010 to 2013, and currently teaches in the School of Creative Media, City University of Hong Kong, where he leads the Wanwu Practice Group. His work is immersed in "multispecies vibrancy" and explores different forms of social and botanical marginalization. His projects include the creation of spontaneous gardens, the political history of urban plant use, and the exploration of queer ecologies through works such as *Pteridophilia* (2016 ongoing) and *Weed Commons* (2016). His work has been exhibited widely at events that include the Venice, Shanghai, and Taipei biennials, and has most recently been exhibited at Martin Gropius Bau, Berlin, where he is artist-in-residence.

Acknowledgments

This essay collection emerged from a European Research Council-funded project entitled *Rethinking Urban Nature* that explores different facets of nature—especially spontaneous forms of urban nature such as wastelands and other types of marginal spaces. The research for several of the essays (including those by Matthew Gandy, Sandra Jasper, Maroš Krivý, Marcus Nyman, Nida Rehman, and Mathilda Rosengren) were directly funded by the ERC project. We would also like to thank the Volkswagen Foundation for supporting an interdisciplinary workshop in Berlin entitled *Horror vacui: art, ecology, and urban wastelands*, co-organized with Stephen Barber and Susanne Hauser; this enabled many of the themes to be discussed in greater detail. Thanks also to Alison Kirkland for her assistance with copyediting the text and to Rosie Knowles for her editorial support in preparing the manuscript. At JOVIS in Berlin, we would especially like to thank Susanne Rösler, Theresa Hartherz, and Jutta Bornholdt-Cassetti.

erc
European Research Council
Established by the European Commission

rethinking urban nature

Imprint

Copyediting: Alison Kirkland, Ashford, Kent
Design and typesetting: Susanne Rösler, jovis, Berlin
Lithography: Bild1Druck, Berlin
Printed in the European Union

Bibliographic information published by the Deutsche Nationalbibliothek
The Deutsche Nationalbibliothek lists this publication in the Deutsche Nationalbibliografie; detailed bibliographic data are available on the Internet at http://dnb.d-nb.de

jovis Verlag GmbH
Lützowstraße 33
10785 Berlin

www.jovis.de

jovis books are available worldwide in select bookstores. Please contact your nearest bookseller or visit www.jovis.de for information concerning your local distribution.

ISBN 978-3-86859-519-2